The Guggenheim Museum and the Art of this Century

Art of This Century *The Guggenheim Museum and Its Collection*

©1993, The Solomon R. Guggenheim Foundation,
New York
All rights reserved
Published 1993, second impression 1994

The drawings by Frank Lloyd Wright reproduced in this
book are ©1955, 1957, 1962, 1986, 1987, 1988, 1989, and 1993
The Frank Lloyd Wright Foundation, Scottsdale, Arizona.
Used by permission. All rights reserved

ISBN 0-8109-6865-7 (hardcover)
ISBN 0-89207-073-0 (softcover)

Guggenheim Museum Publications
1071 Fifth Avenue
New York, New York 10128

Hardcover edition distributed by
Harry N. Abrams, Incorporated
100 Fifth Avenue
New York, New York 10011

Printed in Germany by Cantz

Art of This Century: The Guggenheim Museum and Its Collection
has been made possible through an endowment fund
established by the Andrew W. Mellon Foundation.

This publication has been sponsored in part through the
generosity of Sotheby's.

Frontispiece: Dan Flavin, *Untitled (to Tracy, to celebrate the
love of a lifetime)*, 1992, expanded version of *Untitled (to Ward
Jackson, an old friend and colleague who, during the fall of 1957
when I finally returned to New York from Washington and joined
him to work together in this museum, kindly communicated)*, 1971.
Fluorescent light, variable dimensions. Solomon R.
Guggenheim Museum, Partial gift of the artist in honor of
Ward Jackson 72.1985. Installed at the Solomon R.
Guggenheim Museum for the 1992 exhibition *Dan Flavin*.
Photo by David Heald.

Cover: The skylight in the main rotunda of the Solomon R.
Guggenheim Museum. Photo by David Heald.

1

Preface and Acknowledgments
Thomas Krens

7

The Genesis of a Museum
A History of the Guggenheim
Thomas Krens

43

Frank Lloyd Wright and the
Solomon R. Guggenheim Museum
Bruce Brooks Pfeiffer

85

Paintings of Modern Life and Modern Myths
Late-Nineteenth- and Early Twentieth-
Century Representations of Gender, Class,
and Race in the Thannhauser Collection
Andrea Feeser

109

1912
Lisa Dennison

149

Technology and the Spirit
The Invention of Non-Objective Art
Michael Govan

181

Peggy's Surreal Playground
Jennifer Blessing

221

Art of This Century and
the New York School
Diane Waldman

257

Against the Grain
A History of Contemporary Art
at the Guggenheim
Nancy Spector

291

The Institution as Frame
Installations at the Guggenheim
Clare Bell

314

Exhibition and Publication History

Preface and Acknowledgments

Thomas Krens

The Guggenheim Museum has a long and distinguished tradition of producing publications devoted to its holdings of Modern and contemporary art. The very first catalogue of the collection assembled by Solomon R. Guggenheim appeared in 1936, a full year before the foundation that bears his name was chartered, and three years before his museum opened. Under Thomas M. Messer, director of the museum from 1961 through 1988, the Guggenheim earned a reputation for meticulously researched books documenting its major masterworks; indeed, Angelica Zander Rudenstine's two-volume *The Guggenheim Museum Collection: Paintings 1880–1945* (1976) and her *Peggy Guggenheim Collection, Venice: The Solomon R. Guggenheim Foundation* (1985), as well as Vivian Endicott Barnett's *The Guggenheim Museum: Justin K. Thannhauser Collection* (1978) are not only used by scholars interested in the Guggenheim's collection, but are often cited as models of museum scholarship in general.

Recent publications have stressed the author's role in interpreting aspects of the museum's collection, which allows for the application of diverse art-historical methodologies in the writing of essays. Since the reopening of the Guggenheim in June 1992 after a two-year renovation and expansion project, several such publications have been produced, notably: *Guggenheim Museum: A to Z*, a concise, highly readable overview of the collection of the Solomon R. Guggenheim Museum in New York, with entries that situate specific works within their historical, social, and cultural climates; a revised, second volume devoted to the Thannhauser Collection, which includes updated scholarship and two new, major essays by art historians Paul Tucker and Fred Licht; and *Paul Klee at the Guggenheim Museum*, a book that captures the Guggenheim's rich holdings of works by this Modern master through new photography and a comprehensive essay by Klee scholar Andrew Kagan.

Art of This Century: The Guggenheim Museum and Its Collection is for many

reasons a significant addition to the literature on the Guggenheim. While calling on the fundamental research conducted by Rudenstine, Barnett, and other scholars who have worked at the museum over the past four decades, it has also provided several art historians with the opportunity to write thematically on the collection. The book begins with a historical overview of the Solomon R. Guggenheim Foundation, which was chartered in 1937 primarily to provide Guggenheim a means of exhibiting his collection of non-objective paintings and which has grown in the subsequent years to encompass the Solomon R. Guggenheim Museum and the Guggenheim Museum SoHo, both in New York City, and the Peggy Guggenheim Collection in Venice, Italy; in addition, the Guggenheim Museum Bilbao, in Spain's Basque Country, is scheduled to open in 1997. A major essay by Bruce Brooks Pfeiffer, director of the Frank Lloyd Wright Foundation in Scottsdale, Arizona, charts the fascinating architectural-design process that led to the erection of Wright's greatest masterpiece, a building that since its opening in 1959 has become synonymous with the Guggenheim. Seven scholarly—yet wholly engaging—essays by staff members of the Guggenheim follow, each examining some period encompassed by the holdings of the Solomon R. Guggenheim Foundation. The profusely illustrated essays, arranged chronologically, provide a diverse yet coherent portrait of Modern and contemporary art.

The title of this book is taken from Peggy Guggenheim's famous New York gallery of the 1940s, Art of This Century. In 1979, the Solomon R. Guggenheim Foundation took on full responsibility for her extraordinary collection of Surrealist and abstract art, which remains on view in her palazzo on Venice's Grand Canal. This volume is the first to draw on a broad selection of masterpieces from both the New York and Venice collections—as such, it truly provides a unique and vital overview of the art of our century.

Books such as this are increasingly more difficult to realize in today's economy. Yet the Guggenheim remains steadfastly committed to a publications program that continually promotes new research on its permanent collection. The museum has been joined in this goal by the Andrew W. Mellon Foundation, which for almost a decade has supported some of our most important endeavors in research and publishing. In 1984, the Mellon Foundation awarded the Guggenheim a generous gift in the form of a permanent endowment, its purpose being "to assist the museum in producing serious publications that require careful preparation, scholarly research, and professional evaluation." The Mellon Foundation has also encouraged the museum to use the gift to allow its curators "to advance their professional training and achievements." *Art of This Century: The Guggenheim Museum and Its Collection* fulfills the mandate of this visionary gift in a tangible way. The Guggenheim is very grateful for the opportunity created by the Mellon Foundation to continue to publish important and innovative books about the permanent collection.

We also express grateful acknowledgment to Sotheby's, which provided partial sponsorship for this publication.

The funding and encouragement described above were essential to the realization of this book, as were the talents and dedication of so many people on the staff of the Guggenheim Museum. The book was shaped over the course of several years, with its final contents defined by a group consisting of Michael Govan, Deputy Director; Lisa Dennison, Collections Curator; Nancy Spector, Associate Curator; and Anthony Calnek, Managing Editor. As the essays by Clare Bell, Assistant Curator; Jennifer Blessing, Assistant Curator; Lisa Dennison; Andrea Feeser, former Curatorial Assistant; Michael Govan; Nancy Spector; and Diane Waldman, Deputy Director and Senior Curator, demonstrate, when scholars are given the time, resources, encouragement, and freedom to write, they will often produce compelling,

original, and significant additions to the literature of art history. Cara Galowitz, Manager of Graphic Design Services, showed tremendous care in the layout of this beautiful book. David Heald, Manager of Photographic Services, reshot all of the Guggenheim's paintings and sculpture reproduced in this volume, and, with Cara Galowitz, went to extraordinary lengths to check the veracity of the color separations at every stage of production. They were aided by Pamela Myers, Administrator for Exhibitions and Programming. Anthony Calnek and the rest of the Publications Department staff—Laura Morris, Assistant Editor; Elizabeth Levy, Production Editor; and Jennifer Knox, Editorial Assistant—edited the book and brought it to completion with great enthusiasm, perseverance, and talent. Samar Qandil, Photography Coordinator, gathered photographs; Juliet Nations-Powell, Curatorial Assistant, conducted research that led to the color-plate captions; Simone Manwarring, intern in the Registrar's Department, aided in the compilation of the exhibition history; Jennifer Knox compiled the comprehensive bibliography, the first detailing the full scope of the Guggenheim's publishing activities; and, as with so many books, Ward Jackson, Archivist, and Sonja Bay, Librarian, provided invaluable assistance. While these individuals made readily identifiable contributions, *Art of This Century: The Guggenheim Museum and Its Collection* truly results from the efforts of the entire staff. It is to the staff as a whole, then, that I offer profound and collegial thanks.

—*November 1993*

Plate 1. Vasily Kandinsky, *Blue Mountain (Der blaue Berg),*
1908–09. Oil on canvas, 106 x 96.6 cm (41 ¼ x 38 inches).
Solomon R. Guggenheim Museum, Gift, Solomon R.
Guggenheim 41.505.

The Genesis of a Museum
A History of the Guggenheim

Thomas Krens

When the Solomon R. Guggenheim Museum inaugurated its famed Frank Lloyd Wright building in 1959, the museum itself was already twenty years old and the collection was more than thirty years in the making. What originated as a private accumulation of some of the finest examples of twentieth-century European avant-garde painting had emerged over the years as a professional institution devoted to the edification and education of an increasingly art-aware public. Unlike other museums founded in New York at roughly the same time—the Whitney Museum of American Art, distinguished by its national parameters, and the Museum of Modern Art, notable for its encyclopedic approach to the history of Modernist culture—the Guggenheim was initially committed to one specific aesthetic vision: non-objectivity in art. Articulated by its first director, Hilla Rebay, epitomized visually by the paintings of Vasily Kandinsky, and backed by Solomon R. Guggenheim, this collective vision of pure painterly abstraction served as the catalyst for a remarkable, though idiosyncratic, assemblage of canvases and works on paper.

The founder of the museum that bears his name, Solomon R. Guggenheim was born into a large, affluent family of Swiss origin, which amassed its fortune in American mining during the nineteenth century. In the manner of the educated, prosperous elite, Guggenheim and his wife Irene Rothschild were brought up in a tradition of philanthropy and connoisseurship, and became enthusiastic patrons of the arts, accumulating a collection of works by Old Masters, including Flemish panel paintings and French Barbizon canvases, American landscapes, Audubon prints, and oriental manuscript illuminations. Although fashioned after exemplary American art collections assembled by such entrepreneurs as Henry Clay Frick and J. P. Morgan, Guggenheim's decisions about acquisitions suffered from his lack of expertise, a rather undefined personal taste, and his relatively late entry into a highly competitive market. The tenor of Guggenheim's patronage shifted dramatically, however, in 1927, when he first encountered the young German baroness Hilla Rebay von Ehrenwiesen, who introduced him to experimental trends in contemporary European painting.

The daughter of a Prussian military officer (who was also a gifted woodworker and painter), Rebay studied art and music at an early age. Though extremely talented as a portrait painter, Rebay eventually gravitated toward the most radical tendencies in European art. The Dada artist Jean Arp, Rebay's suitor from 1915 until 1917, initiated her into the avant-garde art world: he presented her with a copy of Kandinsky's treatise *On the Spiritual in Art* (*Über das Geistige in der Kunst*, 1912) for Christmas of 1916 and during that year introduced her to Herwarth Walden, owner of the Berlin gallery Der Sturm, where she exhibited her paintings in 1917. Impressed by the artists with whom she exhibited at Der Sturm, including Robert Delaunay, Albert Gleizes, Kandinsky, and the man who would become her longtime confidant and lover—Rudolf Bauer—Rebay embraced the idea of non-objectivity in art as both a style and an aesthetic philosophy. Differentiating between abstraction as an aesthetic derivation of forms found in the empirical world and non-objectivity as pure artistic invention, Rebay devoted herself to the latter, believing it was infused with a mystical essence. Her own studies, at the age of fourteen, with Rudolf Steiner in the esoteric religion of theosophy laid the foundation for her lifelong pursuit of the spiritual in art.

The word "non-objective" is Rebay's translation of the German term *gegenstandslos*, which means, literally, "without object." Used in Kandinsky's theoretical writings and in Bauer's correspondence with Rebay, the term came to signify for her a unity of the highest aesthetic and spiritual principles. "Never before in the history of the world," wrote Rebay years after she first formulated her artistic mission, "has there been a greater step forward from the materialistic to the spiritual

Top: Fig. 3. Solomon R. Guggenheim.

Bottom: Fig. 4. Hilla Rebay, with one of her collages, ca. 1929–30. Courtesy The Hilla von Rebay Foundation.

Top: Fig. 5. The Museum of Non-Objective Painting on East Fifty-fourth Street, New York.

Bottom: Fig. 6. Installation view of *In Memory of Vasily Kandinsky*, presented in 1945 at the Museum of Non-Objective Painting on East Fifty-fourth Street. At right are *Painting with White Border* (May 1913) and *Improvisation 28* (1912).

than from objectivity to non-objectivity in painting. Because it is our destiny to be creative and our fate to become spiritual, humanity will come to develop and enjoy greater intuitive power through creations of great art, the glorious masterpieces of non-objectivity."[1]

Upon moving to America in 1927, Rebay began a personal crusade to promote the art in which she so profoundly believed. Guggenheim commissioned her to paint his portrait that same year. Impressed by Rebay's impassioned commitment and lured, perhaps, by the thought of pioneering a relatively untouched area of collecting, Guggenheim began in 1929 to systematically purchase works by non-objective artists.

During the spring of 1929, the Guggenheims accompanied Rebay on a European tour. Introduced to Kandinsky in the artist's studio in Dessau, Germany, Guggenheim purchased an important oil painting, *Composition 8* (1923, plate 2), the first of more than 150 works by the artist to enter the collection throughout the years. Even though Bauer held a privileged position in Rebay's vision of non-objective art—she arranged for Guggenheim to entirely subsidize Bauer's production, providing a monthly income in return for paintings—it was the presence of Kandinsky's work that ultimately defined the tenor of the collection.

Russian-born Kandinsky is associated with the earliest formulation of pure nonmimetic painting. The artist's color-infused canvases of dynamically converging and contrasting forms demonstrate his philosophy of abstraction, which is defined in his most widely read theoretical writings: *On the Spiritual in Art* and *Point and Line to Plane* (*Punkt und Linie zu Fläche*, 1926). Inspired by the theosophical teachings of Steiner (as was Rebay), Symbolism and its Romantic antecedents, the intense and direct new visions of the French Fauves and German Expressionists, as well as by the atonal music of Arnold Schönberg, Kandinsky developed a painting technique that, he professed, resonated with spiritual

harmony. Comparing colors to musical tones and shapes to specific emotional states, he devised a formal vocabulary expressive of what he termed the artist's "inner necessity." While it has since been proven by scholars that Kandinsky's seemingly nonmimetic forms were actually abstracted from models drawn from literature or biological phenomena, his written proclamations and evocative canvases convinced Rebay that his work exemplified her own goals as a painter and curator devoted to non-objectivity.

In addition to the work of Kandinsky and Bauer, early acquisitions included paintings by Marc Chagall, Delaunay, Gleizes, Fernand Léger, Amedeo Modigliani, and László Moholy-Nagy. Soon the walls of Guggenheim's suite at the Plaza Hotel were covered to capacity with the new collection. Inevitably, his thoughts turned toward the possibility of publicly exhibiting the work, and in 1937 he established the Solomon R. Guggenheim Foundation for the "promotion and encouragement and education in art and the enlightenment of the public."[2] With the foundation incorporated, Guggenheim envisioned the construction of a museum designed to house the ever-increasing collection. Seizing upon his intentions, Rebay immediately began to plan how best to realize their dream. Her correspondence from the 1930s is filled with proposals to erect a "museum-temple" of non-objective art. Schemes included an exhibition hall at Rockefeller Center to be designed by Frederick Kiesler and Edmund Körner; a relocation to Charleston, South Carolina, where Guggenheim owned an estate; and a debut at the 1939 New York World's Fair in a specially fabricated circular pavilion. Finally, in 1939, Guggenheim rented a former automobile showroom in Manhattan on East Fifty-fourth Street, which Rebay transformed, with the assistance of architect William Muschenheim, into a functioning, temporary exhibition space called the Museum of Non-Objective Painting. Only the purest examples of non-objective art were shown in the new museum; abstract or representational

Plate 2. Vasily Kandinsky, *Composition 8*, July 1923.
Oil on canvas, 140 x 201 cm (55 ⅛ x 79 ⅛ inches).
Solomon R. Guggenheim Museum, Gift, Solomon R.
Guggenheim 37.262.

Top: Fig. 7. The dining room in Solomon Guggenheim's suite at the Plaza Hotel in New York, with Marc Chagall's *Paris through the Window* (1913) to the right.

Bottom: Fig. 8. Solomon Guggenheim's suite at the Plaza Hotel, with three paintings by Rudolf Bauer. Courtesy The Hilla von Rebay Foundation.

works by artists considered precursors—also included in the collection by this time—remained at Guggenheim's Plaza suite. Rebay, assuming the position of the museum's first director, decorated the gallery walls with pleated gray velour and covered the floors with thick gray carpeting. The plush velvet-upholstered seats, subtle indirect lighting, recorded music by Bach and Beethoven, and the odor of incense wafting through the rooms created an atmosphere designed to spiritually enlighten as well as aesthetically entertain. The museum was a great success, attracting many young American abstract painters, whom Rebay welcomed and supported and whose work she eventually exhibited.

A woman of formidable energy and determination, Rebay instituted a series of traveling loan exhibitions devoted to Guggenheim's collection, while simultaneously organizing shows in the East Fifty-fourth Street space. For each of the loan exhibitions, held at the Gibbes Memorial Art Gallery, Charleston (March 1–April 12, 1936); the Philadelphia Art Alliance (February 8–28, 1937); and the Baltimore Museum of Art (January 6–29, 1939), an illustrated catalogue was published with didactic essays by Rebay on the principles and goals of non-objectivity. Her texts reveal an obsession with the metaphysical and an implicit belief in the teleological progression of history and culture. Although Rebay's proclamations may sound naïve today, her reflections on this particular strain of Modernist thought remain a remarkable document of the period.

In 1943, to meet the demands of the by-then flourishing Museum of Non-Objective Painting, Rebay initiated her campaign to build a permanent structure to accommodate the Guggenheim collection and the activities of the foundation. It took little time for her (apparently with the assistance of Irene Guggenheim) to select the renowned American architect Frank Lloyd Wright for the project. When she saw an exhibition of Wright's work in Berlin in 1910 and read his published writings, Rebay discovered a kindred spirit in matters of art and its presentation. Wright's description of organic architecture recalls the art for which Rebay proselytized—a regenerative art full of moral and utopian implications that seemed to materialize as a direct expression of its creators' souls:

Out of the ground into the light—yes! Not only must the building so proceed, but we cannot have an organic architecture unless we achieve an organic society! . . . We who love architecture and recognize it as the great sense of structure in whatever is—music, painting, sculpture, or life itself—we must somehow act as intermediaries—maybe missionaries.[3]

In 1946, when construction of the new building seemed imminent, an exterior and interior model was presented to members of the press. *Life* magazine published an article featuring photographs of Wright's model, which was complete with electrical wiring and a mock exhibition. Entitled "New Art Museum Will Be New York's Strangest Building," the article made the cylindrical structure famous—or perhaps infamous—well before it was built. Philip Johnson, director of the Department of Architecture and Design at the Museum of Modern Art and himself an architect, expressed interest in the museum to Wright in 1952, stating:

The Museum of Modern Art would like very much to formalize our greeting to your museum by giving a one-person show to your design. . . . It would be of greatest interest to the public, and it seems to us that it would also help the Guggenheim Foundation to a good publicity send-off.[4]

Though Wright agreed, the exhibition never took place; the public had to wait seven more years before construction was completed.

Several factors contributed to prolonging the project, including two alterations in the site itself. Wright made major revisions in the plans for the building, though the spiral form remained a constant. (For a full discussion of the design process that led to the finished building, see "Frank Lloyd Wright and the Solomon R. Guggenheim Museum," pages 43–80.) When Guggenheim—who intentionally delayed building because of postwar inflation—died in 1949, construction was further postponed until a new administration was in place at the museum. Encountering resistance from the museum's trustees to support the unprecedented and increasingly expensive building project, Wright astutely suggested it be reconceived as a memorial to Guggenheim. In 1952, the name of the institution was officially changed to the Solomon R. Guggenheim Museum.

The modification in name from the Museum of Non-Objective Painting, which indicated a strictly circumscribed aesthetic scope, to the more neutral, yet commemorative, Solomon R. Guggenheim Museum reflects certain institutional revisions that occurred around the time of its benefactor's death. In 1948, the museum purchased the entire estate of Karl Nierendorf, a New York art dealer who specialized in German painting. This acquisition enriched the collection by some 730 objects, including eighteen Kandinskys, 110 Paul Klees, six Chagalls, and twenty-four Lyonel Feiningers. Perhaps more importantly for the future of the institution, Nierendorf's holdings expanded the scope of the museum's focus by the inclusion of many major Expressionist and Surrealist works. Particularly notable among the former is Oskar Kokoschka's historic *Knight Errant* (1915).

During the early 1950s, the museum was widely criticized for the limited scope of its programming. Though Rebay had always been receptive to and supportive of young, emerging artists, her criterion of non-objectivity was construed by many as too biased and restrictive. Aline Louchheim (later Aline Saarinen), the art critic for the *New York Times*, questioned whether the museum was "justifying its tax-free status as an educational museum," and described the institution as "an esoteric, occult place in which a mystic language was spoken."[5] In response to such serious remonstrations, Harry F. Guggenheim, then president of the foundation, issued a statement announcing revised exhibition programming that would include "objective" examples of Modern art.[6] Realizing that no true shift in exhibition policy could occur with Rebay still in charge of the museum, the trustees requested her resignation, which they received in March 1952. Seven months later, it was announced that James Johnson Sweeney had accepted the position she had vacated. Formerly director of the Department of Painting and Sculpture at the Museum of Modern Art, Sweeney approached his new curatorial and directorial role with a broader sensibility than Rebay, augmenting the collection with works that encompassed more aspects of Modern art than the non-objective. Attempting to fill serious gaps in the collection—such as the almost complete absence of sculpture, which Rebay did not admit due to its "corporeality"—he instituted an aggressive acquisitions program. Before Sweeney resigned in 1960, eleven Constantin Brancusis, three Alexander Archipenkos, seven Alexander Calders, bronzes by Max Ernst and Alberto Giacometti, as well as other major works such as Paul Cézanne's *Man with Crossed Arms* (ca. 1899, plate 3) and seminal Abstract Expressionist paintings by Willem de Kooning, Franz Kline, and Jackson Pollock were acquired. In addition to Sweeney's purchases, the museum received a bequest from the estate of Katherine S. Dreier, who, along with Marcel Duchamp, had founded the Société Anonyme. Most important among the twenty-eight works of art donated by the Dreier estate in 1953 were Brancusi's *Little French Girl* (1914–18), an Archipenko bronze (1919), Piet Mondrian's *Composition* (1929), an untitled Juan Gris still life (1916), and three Schwitters collages dating from the early 1920s.

Sweeney's revision of acquisition policies was symptomatic of the dramatic institutional changes that he initiated upon assuming directorship of the museum. Ten members of Rebay's

Fig. 9. "Speaking of Pictures . . . New Art Museum Will Be New York's Strangest Building," *Life*, October 8, 1945.

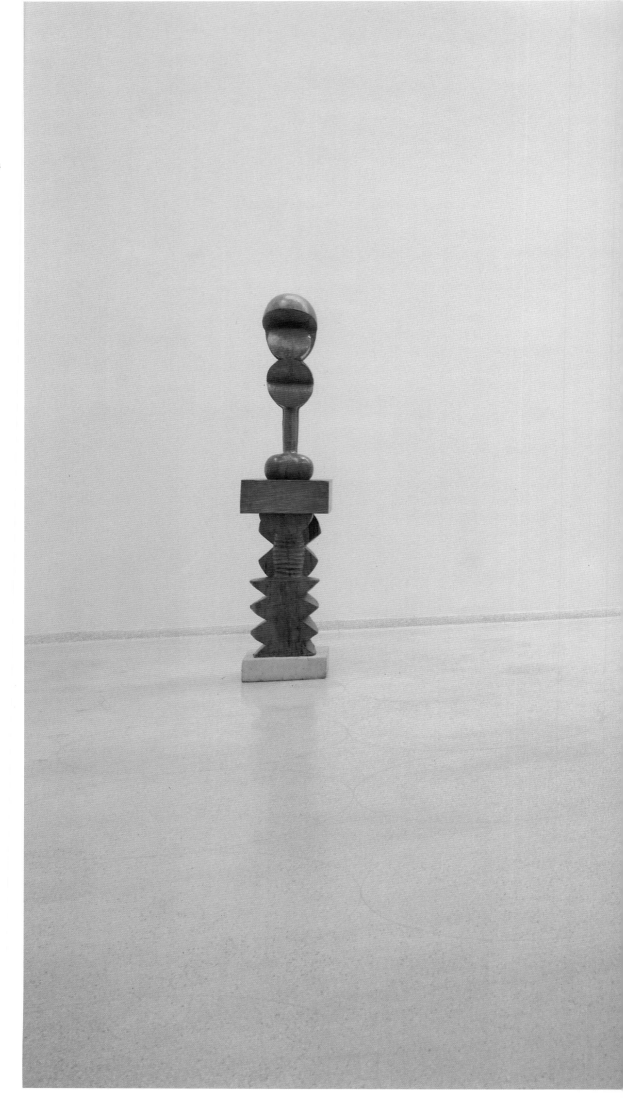

Fig. 10. Temporary installation (summer 1993), in the Solomon R. Guggenheim Museum's High Gallery, of works by Constantin Brancusi in the museum's collection. Left to right:
Adam and Eve, 1916–24. Eve: oak, 118.1 cm (46 ¼ inches) high; Adam: chestnut, 88.6 cm (34 ⅞ inches) high; on limestone base. 53.1329.a–d.
The Sorceress, 1916–24. Wood, 100 cm (39 ⅛ inches) high, on limestone base. 56.1448. Shown on *Oak Base*, 1920. Oak, 97.5 cm (38 ⅛ inches) high. 58.1516.
King of Kings, early 1930s. Oak, 300 cm (118 ⅛ inches) high. 56.1449.
The Seal (Miracle), 1924–36. Marble, 108.6 x 114 x 33 cm (42 ¼ x 44 ⅞ x 13 inches), on limestone base. 56.1450.
Photo by Lee Ewing.

Top: Fig. 11. Frank Lloyd Wright, Solomon R. Guggenheim Museum, interior perspective, 1958. Pencil on tracing paper, 85.4 x 98.1 cm (33 ⅝ x 38 ⅝ inches). The Frank Lloyd Wright Archives, The Frank Lloyd Wright Foundation 4305.011.

Center: Fig. 12. Frank Lloyd Wright, Solomon R. Guggenheim Museum, interior perspective, 1958. Pencil on tracing paper, 86.4 x 101.6 cm (34 x 40 inches). Private collection 4305.012.

Bottom: Fig. 13. Frank Lloyd Wright, Solomon R. Guggenheim Museum, interior perspective, 1958. Pencil and colored pencil on tracing paper, 87 x 97.2 cm (34 ¼ x 38 ¼ inches). The Frank Lloyd Wright Archives, The Frank Lloyd Wright Foundation 4305.010.

staff were terminated on his first day of work.[7] In the spirit of professionalism, Sweeney hired a registrar, initiated a conservation program, established a photography department, and expanded the library. Redecorating the exhibition spaces in the townhouse at 1071 Fifth Avenue, where the museum had been relocated in 1947, he dispensed with the plush, curtained walls in favor of clean, white surfaces and displayed the paintings without their customary heavy gold or ornate wood frames. Sweeney also rescued the many "objective" masterworks languishing in storage or hidden away in Guggenheim's Plaza suite, highlighting them in a series of *Selections* exhibitions during his early tenure. Interspersed with the collection-oriented exhibitions were critically acclaimed loan shows assembled at the museum by Sweeney, such as the first large-scale American exhibition of Delaunay's oeuvre, the first retrospective of Brancusi's sculpture, and the first comprehensive museum analysis of Giacometti's work, all held in 1955. Sweeney also instituted a program of exhibitions of important but not excessively valuable works, which were lent for periods of six to nine months to various small American museums and university galleries that lacked resources in Modern art; this practice was elaborated upon and fully realized during the 1980s through the Guggenheim's Collection Sharing Program.

When asked by the *New York Times* how he equated his revised policies with Solomon R. Guggenheim's innovative but narrowly focused vision, Sweeney replied that he found "non-objective a linguistic confusion." "More importantly," stated the *Times* article, "he believes the significance of the great works in the collection lies in their fundamental aesthetic values, not in the fact they fit into a verbal category."[8]

Sweeney's installation technique corresponded to his emphasis on formal and, hence, visual correlations among works of art, as opposed to thematic or conceptual subdivisions. He did not, for instance, employ didactic wall labels, believing that aesthetic objects are self-explanatory, experiential entities.

"When you install pictures so that visual and not intellectual focal points are contrasted, thinking of space relationships and tensions between objects," he once explained, "these relationships and contrasts bring out criticism, which is more important than chronological or historical data."[9]

It was in the area of installation design that Sweeney disagreed most profoundly with Wright's plans for the new museum building. Initially, Sweeney's pragmatic attitude toward the museum environment ran counter to Wright's conception of the institution as a haven for contemplation, relaxation, and artistic experimentation. Their correspondence records often bitter conflicts over specific architectural details, as well as each man's thoughts concerning the role of the museum. Fortunately for Wright, he found advocates in Harry Guggenheim and his wife Alicia, who remained committed to Solomon Guggenheim's and Rebay's vision for the new structure even though they supported critical policy changes. When Sweeney repeatedly demanded more space for administrative offices as well as areas for conservation, preparation, and photography—all requisite for the modern, professional art institution—Wright attempted to accommodate his requests. But he would not condone the director's rejection of his designs for natural lighting, gently sloping display walls, and color scheme. Convinced that Sweeney would not abide by his plans for the interior of the museum, Wright prepared a series of perspective drawings illustrating sample exhibitions (figs. 11–13); these drawings offered a graphic tour through the museum's interior as Wright envisioned it. The architect distributed copies of this series, along with an essay called "The Solomon R. Guggenheim Museum: An Experiment in the Third Dimension," to the trustees and to various architecture journals as testimony to his intentions. Wright favored natural light, which, according to his design, would flow in from above through the glass dome and from behind the paintings through a narrow glass band running along the exterior

Plate 3. Paul Cézanne, *Man with Crossed Arms (Homme aux bras croisés)*, ca. 1899. Oil on canvas, 92 x 72.7 cm (36¼ x 28⅝ inches). Solomon R. Guggenheim Museum 54.1387.

Plate 4. Joan Miró, *The Tilled Field* (*La Terre labourée*), 1923–24. Oil on canvas, 66 x 92.7 cm (26 x 36 ½ inches). Solomon R. Guggenheim Museum 72.2020.

wall of the spiral. Artificial illumination would be available in the event of poor weather and for evening viewing. Defending his lighting scheme in a 1955 letter to Sweeney, Wright wrote in his usual flamboyant manner:

The strength of the Guggenheim, as you know, is as a space in which to view the painter's creation truthfully, that is to say honestly, *in the varying light as seen by the painter himself and in which it was born to be seen. . . . A humanist must believe that any picture in a fixed light is only a "fixed" picture! If this fixation be ideal, then see death as the ideal state for man. The morgue!*[10]

Wright's plan for the installation of paintings along the spiral ramp is evident in his perspective drawings: the canvases, supported by the slanted base of the gently sloping rear walls, were intended to tilt slightly backward, as if on easels. Wright believed that their proximity to the viewer would sustain the human scale he was attempting to secure in the building. Sweeney and the trustees thought this design would subjugate the paintings to the architectural scheme and wanted, instead, to "float" the canvases perpendicular to the ground by means of support rods projecting from the walls. In an attempt once again to justify his intentions, Wright explained to Harry Guggenheim that he conceived of "the building and the painting as an uninterrupted, beautiful symphony such as never existed in the world of Art before."[11] The theoretical battle with Sweeney and the administration continued over the choice of color for the interior. Though Wright envisioned the walls painted in soft ivory tones, Sweeney favored bright white, much to the architect's dismay. Employing his persuasive, dramatic writing style, Wright pronounced his thoughts on the subject:

White, itself the loudest color of all, is the sum of all colors. If activated by strong light it is to color like a corpse. To use it as a forcing-ground for a delicate painting would be like taking high C in music as a background for orchestral tonality. Easy to *see this as ruinous in music—if one is not deaf. If not color blind, whitewashed environment is just as ruinous to the sensitive color-sense of painting. Background becomes foreground! Therefore in violation of the balance of the values of almost any color-composition the corpse takes over. But soft ivory . . . is luminous-receptive: sympathetically self-effacing instead of competitive.*[12]

Such disputes continued, with Wright formulating increasingly eloquent explications of design and theory, virtually until his death in April 1959, six months before the museum opened to the public.

When Wright's building opened on October 21, 1959, enormous crowds of people lined up to experience the architecture and to see the impressive inaugural exhibition of highlights from the collection. Newspaper accounts at the time reported an attendance on opening day of some three thousand people. Although generally favorable, opinions on the structure were restrained. While extolling the building as a sculptural masterpiece, art critics voiced concern for the integrity of the art object within such an overwhelming architectural environment. On one extreme, Emily Genauer pronounced that the museum "has turned out to be the most beautiful building in America . . . never for a minute dominating the pictures being shown." On the other, Ada Louise Huxtable wrote that the structure is "less a museum than it is a monument to Frank Lloyd Wright."[13] The fact that Wright began referring to the building during the last few years of design as the "Archeseum," an appellation that caused considerable alarm among the trustees, only justified the critics' apprehension. Over the years, however, artists and curators have found the distinctive space a welcome challenge. As Wright intended, the self-enclosed structure composed of pure, curving lines has offered new possibilities for installations, exhibitions, and the contemplation of art.

Shortly after the museum opened, Sweeney resigned as director. H. H.

Plate 5. Fernand Léger, *The Great Parade* (definitive state)
(*La Grande Parade* [état définitif]), 1954. Oil on canvas,
299 x 400 cm (117 ¾ x 157 ½ inches). Solomon R.
Guggenheim Museum 62.1619.

Arnason, who had been director of the Walker Art Center in Minneapolis, was enlisted to serve as a trustee and the Vice President for Art Administration. He was asked to oversee the general development of the museum until a new administration was established. While at the Guggenheim, Arnason organized a number of important exhibitions, including a retrospective of Philip Guston's work and the first survey of Abstract Expressionism in a New York museum.

In 1961, Thomas M. Messer assumed the directorship of the Guggenheim. He enlarged upon Sweeney's efforts to modernize and professionalize the museum's staff and administrative structure. During his twenty-seven-year tenure, Messer initiated an ambitious publications program focused not only on temporary exhibitions but also on the growing collection, which required in-depth cataloguing of works, as well as the institution of scholarly research projects. Masterworks from the collection are meticulously documented, for instance, in Angelica Zander Rudenstine's two-volume work *The Guggenheim Museum Collection: Paintings 1880–1945* (1976) and Vivian Endicott Barnett's *The Guggenheim Museum: Justin K. Thannhauser Collection* (1978).

Three years after the Wright building opened to the public, Messer reinstated some of the architect's original installation techniques, which Sweeney had abolished. A letter from Lawrence Alloway, curator at the Guggenheim at the time, to the painter Francis Bacon records Messer's intervention:

In the early days of the museum, when it was painted white, the paintings were projected off the wall by bars. This is no longer done, so that the paintings rest back on the wall in the accustomed manner. In addition, the museum is no longer painted dead white. Thus the effect of glare which people used to experience here is no longer felt. Not only that, but the pictures are now hung in line with the slope of the ramp, and not, as used to be the case, at an absolute horizontal. The effect of this is of complete stability of the painting in the visual field.[14]

Under Messer, the curatorial and technical staff was enlarged in proportion to the increased exhibition and publishing activities that were taking place. Acquisitions followed the same comprehensive trend established by Sweeney: Léger's late painting *The Great Parade* (1954, plate 5), Egon Schiele's *Portrait of Johann Harms* (1916), František Kupka's *Planes by Colors, Large Nude* (1909–10), Brancusi's marble *Muse* (1912), as well as numerous works by Joan Miró, Calder, Klee, and Giacometti, entered the collection as critical examples of Modern art. In the more contemporary category, Messer was responsible for the acquisitions of Bacon's large triptych *Three Studies for a Crucifixion* (1962), several paintings by Jean Dubuffet (a favorite of his), Anselm Kiefer's monumental canvas *Seraphim* (1983–84), Robert Rauschenberg's *Red Painting* (1953), and David Smith's stainless-steel sculpture *Cubi XXVII* (1965, plate 114). A keen proponent of the international avant-garde, Messer also acquired works by Latin American and Eastern European artists throughout his tenure. Exhibitions organized by Messer and his curatorial staff were equally wide-ranging, covering the early Modern period with a major Kandinsky retrospective in 1963; a trilogy of scholarly shows devoted to discrete stylistic periods in Kandinsky's development, held between 1982 and 1985; a 1965 show representing the contributions of Gustav Klimt and Schiele; a Klee retrospective in 1967; a Mondrian centennial tribute in 1971; and a survey in 1973 of works by Miró related to poetry, to cite only a few examples. Exhibitions of contemporary art included shows devoted to Roy Lichtenstein (1969), Carl Andre (1970), John Chamberlain (1971), Eva Hesse (1972), Joseph Beuys (1979), and Enzo Cucchi (1986).

The collection was dramatically enriched in 1963, when the foundation received a portion of Justin K. Thannhauser's prized collection of Impressionist, Post-Impressionist, and Modern French masterpieces as a permanent loan. These paintings and sculptures formally entered the

Plate 6. Pablo Picasso, *Woman with Yellow Hair*
(*Femme aux cheveux jaunes*), December 1931. Oil on canvas,
100 x 81 cm (39 ⅜ x 31 ⅞ inches). Solomon R. Guggenheim
Museum, Thannhauser Collection, Gift, Justin K.
Thannhauser 78.2514 T59.

museum's collection in 1978, two years after Thannhauser's death. The Thannhauser bequest provided an important historical survey of the period directly antedating that represented by the Guggenheim's original holdings and enhanced its concentrations of works by Pablo Picasso (with, for example, *Woman with Yellow Hair*, 1931, plate 6) and School of Paris artists. In 1981, Hilde Thannhauser, Justin's widow, augmented the gift with three additional paintings, by Georges Braque, Picasso, and Vincent van Gogh. Upon Hilde's death in 1991, the museum received her bequest of ten important works: five by Picasso, one each by Cézanne, Klee, Edouard Manet, and Jules Pascin, and the museum's first painting by Claude Monet. The 1963 procurement of the Thannhauser paintings and sculptures, including major Cézannes, Paul Gauguins, and Picassos, necessitated an expansion of the museum's exhibition space in order to display them adequately. The Justin K. Thannhauser Wing was created on the second floor of the Monitor building in 1965 (the Monitor was renamed for the Thannhausers in 1989).

The creation of galleries in the Monitor required the relocation of administrative offices, the library, and storage space. In response to the now-acute need for additional work areas, the foundation commissioned Taliesin Associated Architects, the heirs to Wright's practice, to design an adjoining structure on the site behind the museum that had been reserved for an annex building originally envisioned by Wright. Designed by William Wesley Peters, Wright's son-in-law, and completed in 1968, the new annex helped to alleviate the most immediate functional needs. For example, the relocation of the conservation department, housed on the seventh ramp of the rotunda, to the annex allowed the museum to open the entire spiral for public viewing for the first time. Although planned as a six-story structure, the annex was actually provided with only four floors due to unforeseen budgetary constraints. Nevertheless, because the administration recognized that future

expansion would be inevitable, the foundation was designed and constructed to carry a ten-story building.

To the list of visionary collectors who have contributed to the exemplary holdings of the museum, the name of Peggy Guggenheim must be added. Though an autonomous entity and geographically separate, the Peggy Guggenheim Collection in Venice has been an integral part of the Solomon R. Guggenheim Foundation since 1976, when Peggy bequeathed her art and the palazzo that houses it to the New York–based institution. Peggy Guggenheim's sensitivity to stylistic currents overlooked by her uncle Solomon—namely Surrealism and early postwar American gestural painting—resulted in a collection of more than three hundred objects, rich in genres that are absent from the New York museum's holdings. When considered in concert, these two collections form a bicontinental entity that begins to trace the complex and multivalent history of twentieth-century art.

Peggy Guggenheim was always considered something of a renegade, escaping to Europe when her family had emigrated from there a generation earlier. Wealthy, high-spirited, and rebellious, she sought adventure and excitement while the majority of the Guggenheims were investing money and building empires. At the age of forty, Guggenheim discovered a vocation for which she was well suited: art patronage. In January 1938, she opened the Guggenheim Jeune gallery in London with the intellectual and artistic support of her friends and colleagues Duchamp and Samuel Beckett. Her opening exhibition featured the work of Jean Cocteau; subsequent shows included presentations devoted to Kandinsky and the Surrealist painter Yves Tanguy.

In June 1939, Guggenheim decided to abandon her ownership of the gallery in order to found a museum of Modern art. She asked the art historian and critic Herbert Read to be its director, and together they drew up a list of the painters and sculptors whose

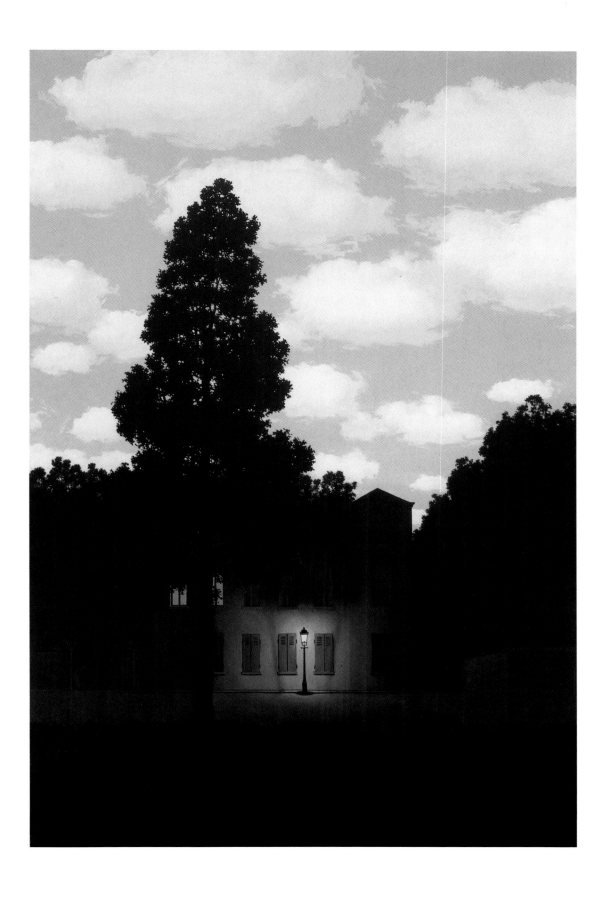

Plate 7. René Magritte, *Empire of Light (L'Empire des lumières),* 1953–54. Oil on canvas, 195.4 x 131.2 cm (76 ¹⁵⁄₁₆ x 51 ⅝ inches). Peggy Guggenheim Collection 76.2553 PG102.

representation would create an accurate portrait of twentieth-century art. Using this list, which was revised by Duchamp and Nellie van Doesburg, Guggenheim formed the core of her personal collection. While eventually relinquishing plans for a museum because of the impending war, lack of physical quarters, and a diminishment of interest on her part, she continued to purchase paintings and sculptures in France until she was forced to flee Europe as Hitler's troops approached Paris. Her motto at that time was "buy a picture a day," and, according to her autobiography *Out of This Century*, she lived up to it, adding Brancusi's *Maiastra* (1912?) and *Bird in Space* (1932–40, plate 87), Giacometti's *Woman with Her Throat Cut* (1932, plate 90), and works by Victor Brauner, Salvador Dalí, Jean Hélion, Léger, René Magritte (including his *Empire of Light*, 1953–54, plate 7), and Man Ray to her collection before leaving France.

Upon her return to the United States during the war, Peggy Guggenheim opened a museum/gallery devoted exclusively to Modern art, on Fifty-seventh Street in New York City. The gallery, Art of This Century, was designed by Kiesler in the most experimental manner. Preceding her uncle Solomon by one year, Peggy commissioned a museum environment that became known as a work of art itself. "Kiesler had really created a wonderful gallery—very theatrical and extremely original," she wrote in her autobiography. "Nothing like it had ever existed before. If the pictures suffered from the fact that their setting was too spectacular and took away people's attention from them, it was at least a marvelous décor and created a terrific stir."[15] Guggenheim's description of the gallery interior vividly recalls this phenomenal environment:

The Surrealist Gallery had curved walls made of gum wood. The unframed paintings, mounted on baseball bats, which could be tilted, at any angle, protruded about a foot from the walls. Each one had its own spotlight. The lights went on and off every three seconds . . . first lighting one half of the gallery and then the other. . . . In the

Abstract and Cubist Gallery . . . two walls consisted of an ultramarine curtain which curved around the room with a wonderful sweep and resembled a circus tent. The paintings hung at right angles to it from strings. In the center of the room the paintings were clustered in triangles, hanging on strings as if they were floating in space. Little triangular wooden platforms holding sculptures were also suspended in this manner.[16]

On the opening night of the gallery, October 20, 1942, Guggenheim wore one earring made by Tanguy and another by Calder to prove her impartiality between Surrealism and abstraction. In addition to providing her New York audience with the finest examples of European Modern art—as did Pierre Matisse and Julien Levy at this time—Guggenheim exhibited works by then little-known American painters whose automatic, expressionist style had been inspired by Surrealism: William Baziotes, Robert Motherwell, Mark Rothko, and Clyfford Still. Pollock, a "discovery" of hers, was given his first solo exhibition in late 1943 at Art of This Century. In 1950, she organized the first Pollock show held in Europe in the Sala Napoleonica of Venice's Museo Correr. About the exhibition, Guggenheim explained:

It was always lit at night, and I remember the extreme joy I had sitting in the Piazza San Marco beholding the Pollocks glowing through the open windows of the Museum. . . . It seemed to place Pollock historically where he belonged, as one of the greatest painters of our time.[17]

In 1947, after the war and the breakup of her marriage to Ernst, Guggenheim returned to Europe, where her personal collection was exhibited at the 1948 Venice Biennale and subsequently at the Strozzina in Florence and the Palazzo Reale in Milan. Deeply attracted to Venice, Guggenheim purchased the Palazzo Venier dei Leoni, an uncompleted, one-story, eighteenth-century palace designed by Lorenzo Boschetti to be the widest structure on the Grand Canal. In 1949, she opened her collection,

Following six pages:
Fig. 15. The Palazzo Venier dei Leoni in Venice, formerly Peggy Guggenheim's residence and now home to the Peggy Guggenheim Collection. Photo by David Heald.

Fig. 16. Frank O. Gehry and Associates' model for the Guggenheim Museum Bilbao, Spain. Photo by Joshua White.

Fig. 17. Hans Hollein's model for the Guggenheim Museum Salzburg, Austria. Photo by Edith Jekel.

installed throughout the palazzo, to the public, presiding over this private museum until her death in 1979.

Several exhibitions since then have united examples of non-objective, Cubist, Surrealist, and Abstract Expressionist art from the Peggy Guggenheim Collection and the Solomon R. Guggenheim Museum. These shows have attested to the remarkable comprehensiveness of the combined collections, while demonstrating the truly international profile of the Solomon R. Guggenheim Foundation, under whose auspices both institutions operate.

The acquisition in early 1990 of the Panza di Biumo Collection of American Minimalist and Conceptual art (including Bruce Nauman's *Green Light Corridor*, 1970–71, plate 8) confirmed the Guggenheim's position as one of the leading museums in the world for art of the *entire* twentieth century. As one of the great private collections defining the aesthetic identity of the Guggenheim, the Panza Collection gives the museum the postwar depth and quality to match the strength of its prewar holdings.

The scope of the Guggenheim's collection was further enlarged in December 1992, when the Robert Mapplethorpe Foundation gave the museum a two-part gift that will form the basis of a collection of twentieth-century photography (an area that had been virtually ignored by the Guggenheim in the past): the gift includes two hundred of Mapplethorpe's finest photographs (including a series of self-portraits, among them fig. 18) and unique objects. The agreement between the Guggenheim and the Mapplethorpe foundations provides for the designation of a Robert Mapplethorpe Gallery within the museum's Fifth Avenue building and for the initiation of a program of exhibitions devoted to photography.

As the end of the twentieth century approaches, art museums and cultural institutions throughout the world are facing a crisis of definition. The Guggenheim Museum, like many other museums in the United States and Europe, will face critical decisions about its future. It must assess its capacity to continue to collect and its capacity to fulfill the principal functions of stewardship and preservation that are central to its mission. Indications of the direction that this institution will take in the coming years are found in the events of its recent past.

By the early 1980s, the repeated annexing of offices in the Wright building for gallery space, the consequent physical restraints placed on the staff, and accelerated institutional development required immediate action and an ambitious solution. In 1982, the foundation contracted Gwathmey Siegel and Associates Architects to furnish a design that would provide new galleries and reduce insufficiencies in operating space without disrupting the Frank Lloyd Wright structure. Before Thomas Messer retired in 1988, he had initiated plans for the construction of a tower based on Wright's original design for an eleven-story annex, which would act as a backdrop to the dominant sculptural form of the spiral museum. The addition, now completed, provides more administrative spaces, thus allowing public access to previously restricted portions of the original structure. Four new rectilinear galleries open onto the rotunda's spiral, providing an uninterrupted circulation pattern very much in the spirit of Wright's design. By permitting a sequential and spatial integration of all portions of the existing complex for the first time, the design enables the public to experience the entire interior of both parts of the original building.

The Wright building has also undergone a major restoration. Guided by the administration's desire to return all elements of the museum's architecture to their original state, the restoration process was as committed to historical accuracy as to preservation. As an institution, the Guggenheim has finally come to terms with Frank Lloyd Wright's design. The top-floor ramps, the skylighted bays, the smaller rotunda in the Thannhauser Building, the roof terrace, and the original restaurant space are now completely integrated into the public presence of the Guggenheim

Fig. 18. Robert Mapplethorpe, *Self-Portrait*, 1988.
Gelatin-silver print, edition of ten, 61 x 50.8 cm (24 x
20 inches). Collection The Robert Mapplethorpe
Foundation. © 1988 The Estate of Robert Mapplethorpe.

Museum. The restoration of the Wright
building to its pre-original condition
has redeemed a troublesome history and
resolved a basic dilemma—the
antagonism between the architecture
and the art that it was meant to
house—that has bedeviled the museum
from its inception.

Perhaps the most significant
development in recent years affecting
the future course of the Guggenheim
Foundation has been the steady
transformation of the Peggy
Guggenheim Collection from a purely
private collection housed in an
unfinished Venetian palazzo to a
modern art museum operating in
accordance with the most advanced
professional standards of museum
operation. Under the direction of
Messer, the Peggy Guggenheim
Collection and its home, the Palazzo
Venier dei Leoni, were stabilized and
reoriented through the introduction of
sophisticated systems of inventory,
research, and climate control. As
physical improvements were realized in
the palazzo, a professional museum staff
was developed and a yearlong program
of exhibitions was introduced. These
changes helped turn the Peggy
Guggenheim Collection into one of
Venice's most important cultural
attractions, drawing more than 175,000
visitors a year to its relatively modest
display spaces.

It was with these changes in scope
and program in Venice that the
Guggenheim Foundation was able to
recognize more clearly, by the end of the
1980s, the potential of a fully integrated
international institution with one
collection situated in two locations.
Even as the two branches of the
Guggenheim were developing their
individual programs during the 1980s,
it became increasingly apparent that
neither could realize its institutional
objectives in isolation from the other.
Two separate institutions under one
director and board of trustees made
little practical sense. The respective
curatorial and administrative staffs often
overlapped as the collections came
increasingly to complement one
another, and exchanges, loans, and
exhibitions interconnected to a

significant degree. Despite the progress
at forging a closer working relationship
between the two institutions, it became
clear, however, that the fundamental
barrier to realizing the potential of one
museum on two continents was the lack
of sufficient space in Venice. With
approximately one-tenth the space of
the Solomon R. Guggenheim Museum,
the Peggy Guggenheim Collection was
not in a position to function as a full
partner to the museum in New York,
and thereby generate the economies of
operation and the benefits of collections
utilization that could result from a
single curatorial group, a joint
administration, and a common program
and collection. Venice was simply not
large enough to take on parts of the
collection based in New York or host
any of the exhibitions that were
designed for larger-scale spaces. The
logical course, therefore, was to plan an
expansion in Venice that would enable
it to participate more successfully in the
overall Guggenheim Foundation
program. One particular location—the
old customs house at the end of the
Grand Canal, the Dogana—was the
natural site.

With changes in the museum
administration in 1988 (the year in
which I succeeded Thomas Messer as
director), the board of trustees began to
discern that the objectives and
requirements of the Peggy Guggenheim
Collection were beginning to merge
with those of the Guggenheim Museum
in New York. Construction for the
expansion and renovation of the Wright
building began that year. The
controversial program was completed in
June 1992. But because of various
reductions in programming to
accommodate political and financial
realities in New York City, it had
become clear that the expansion still
would not satisfy the programmatic
requirements of the collection that were
so carefully articulated when the
planning process was begun almost a
decade ago—the foundation's mission
to collect, conserve, present, and
educate with respect to twentieth-
century and contemporary art would
still be constrained. With the space
requirements for large-scale

contemporary art in mind, and the desire to reach a new audience in New York, a lease was negotiated for four floors of a loft building in the historic cast-iron district in SoHo. The celebrated Japanese architect Arata Isozaki was commissioned to design the two interior floors that would be devoted to public space. The Guggenheim Museum SoHo, which also opened to the public in June 1992, features approximately 30,000 square feet of new exhibition space. With the addition of the SoHo site and the new uptown tower, the museum's exhibition space in New York is greatly increased, enabling the Guggenheim to expand its overall programming and to display a larger percentage of its prized permanent collection.

While the New York expansion was underway, several developments in Europe indicated that the goal of creating a truly international institution would move closer to becoming a practical reality. As the complex process of discussion, presentation, and negotiation for an additional site in Venice began, a new opportunity in Europe surfaced for the Guggenheim in July 1988. Peter Lawson-Johnston, the grandson of Solomon R. Guggenheim and now president of the foundation, was approached by private citizens from Salzburg about the possibility of establishing a Guggenheim Museum in their city. At first, the notion of another site for the Guggenheim seemed unrealistic. Salzburg's size, its relative proximity to Venice, and its strong identity as a center of music, not to mention the city's distinctly baroque architectural character, all seemed to argue against this proposal, despite the general inclination of the Guggenheim Foundation to consider international development. In the year that followed, despite steady and increasing attention from the Austrians, the Guggenheim resisted seriously considering the Salzburg proposal. The catalytic event that changed that thinking, however, was the extraordinary proposal of Austrian architect Hans Hollein for a museum to be built *within* the rock of the Mönchsberg mountain. Originally conceived as a project for the Museum Carolino Augustium, Hollein's proposal was the winner of an international competition sponsored by the city.

The extraordinary appeal of Hollein's project rested with his challenge to traditional thinking about contemporary architecture and museums of Modern and contemporary art. Parallels to the Frank Lloyd Wright building, not necessarily in aspects of design, but in the fundamental radicality of the approach to museum architecture, became immediately apparent. The brilliance of the Hollein proposal for an underground museum is found first of all in its absolute compatibility with the existing architecture of Salzburg. What could be more perfectly Postmodern than a building with no façade, an exterior completely at one with its environment in its virtual invisibility, and yet at the same time a wonderfully exuberant though essentially conservative exhibition space? Perhaps the most subtle and fundamental aspect of this project, the feature that separates it most from the usual exercise in contemporary museum architecture, is Hollein's segregation of the two principal and often contradictory functions of museum architecture. On the one hand, the museum building must attract and impress a public audience with the quality of its conceptual design; on the other, it must subordinate the architecture to the art, to fulfill the original function as a space for the display of art. In this project, Hollein accomplishes a unique and difficult duality—one that has proved elusive to most modern museum commissions. Specifically, he takes advantage of the special circumstances and composition of the Mönchsberg by scooping out of the heart of the rock a towering and dramatic central atrium and placing over it, at ground level from the top of the plateau, a vast skylight. The result may well turn out to be one of the most spectacular interior spaces ever created. Yet the galleries hollowed from the rock and adjacent to the atrium suggest a certain austerity that may be entirely appropriate and hospitable to the display of works of art within.

As a commentary on architecture, the Hollein project is simultaneously both the opposite and the complement of the Frank Lloyd Wright building in New York. As difficult as the Wright building reputedly has been for the art that has been displayed within it, the building, nevertheless, is far more than the aggressive strength of its architecture, and is remarkably hospitable to certain experiences of the artistic object. Sculpture in particular has been shown to considerable advantage in the "post-neutral space" environment of the Guggenheim, to which the Beuys, Richard Long, and Mario Merz exhibitions of the past decade have so elegantly testified. As a discourse on twentieth-century values—which are so closely linked to the art and culture of the period—the Wright building itself is an extraordinary work of art. Architectural quality and architectural adventure are attributes that have been associated with the Guggenheim since its inception. These qualities are also found in Hollein's proposal for a museum in the rock. A feasibility study for the Guggenheim Museum Salzburg was formally presented to members of the Austrian government in 1990. The federal government (Bund) then indicated that it would provide a majority share of the capital costs, provided that the regional state government (Land Salzburg) and the municipal government (Stadt Salzburg) provided a percentage of the funding. The project has been much debated in the Austrian press since then, with attention focused on issues ranging from the environmental impact of the building to the need for a contemporary and Modern visual-arts museum in a city that prides itself on a classical-music culture.

The synergy created by these European projects yielded an unexpected, yet astonishing, opportunity for the Guggenheim in 1990. Late that year, representatives of the Basque government approached the Guggenheim Foundation with a proposal: would the Guggenheim consent to lend its name and expertise to a new museum to be located in the Basque capital of Bilbao and funded entirely by the Basque government? Bilbao, on the northern coast of Spain, is that country's fourth-largest city. Originally a steel town, the prosperous city has recently undertaken an aggressive redevelopment program and is positioning itself to become a major financial and cultural center in the new Europe. The proposed Guggenheim Museum Bilbao would be a cornerstone of that program. In April 1991, accompanied by Carmen Giménez, the Guggenheim's Madrid-based Curator of Twentieth-Century Art, I toured Bilbao and met with several representatives of the Basque administration. As a result of this visit, the Guggenheim suggested several prerequisites for serious discussions on the project, among them being a commitment to build a structure of sufficient importance and stature that it would make the new museum a significant architectural statement in its own right; a parallel commitment to the development of an indigenous collection for a Bilbao museum with acquisitions funds provided by the Basque administration; and consultation with the Guggenheim Foundation at every planning stage. With these points agreed to—and with a dramatic location chosen on the banks of the Nervión River—an architectural competition and a feasibility study were conducted. On December 13 of that year, an agreement was signed to create a new Guggenheim Museum in Bilbao, currently slated to open in 1997.

The winning entry in the architectural competition was submitted by an American architect, Frank O. Gehry. Perhaps that architect's greatest achievement to date, it is of equal distinction to Hollein's Salzburg project. Gehry's sculptural structure, to be made of sandblasted stainless steel and limestone (materials that are locally available), is emblematic of its locale and as important and unique in its own right as the Frank Lloyd Wright–designed Guggenheim. It promises to be one of the world's foremost museums of Modern and contemporary art, distinguished not only by its architecture, but also by its collection and special-exhibitions programming.

The Guggenheim was attracted to Bilbao by the site, the scope of the city's redevelopment plan, and its commitment to developing an institution that would enable the foundation to fulfill its mission to collect and present twentieth-century art of the highest possible quality to the widest possible audience. The success of the projects in Bilbao and Salzburg, as well as the plans to expand in Venice, will depend in large part on the degree of public enthusiasm in Spain, Austria, and Italy for an alliance with a private cultural foundation from the United States, for architectural adventure, and for the art of this century. The Guggenheim's commitment to these projects reflects its history, its traditions, the breadth of its collection, and its dedication to cultural excellence.

Notes

1. Hilla Rebay, "Definition of Non-Objective Painting," in *Catalogue of the Solomon R. Guggenheim Collection of Non-Objective Paintings*, exh. cat. (Charleston, S.C.: Carolina Art Association, 1936), p. 12.

2. Charter of the Solomon R. Guggenheim Foundation, June 25, 1937.

3. "An Organic Architecture: The Architecture of Democracy," The Sir George Watson Lectures of the Sulgrave Manor Board for 1939. The text of four lectures delivered by Wright at the Royal Institute of British Architects in May 1939. Excerpted in *Frank Lloyd Wright: Writings and Buildings*, selected by Edgar Kaufmann and Ben Raeburn (New York: E. P. Dutton, 1974), p. 278.

4. Letter dated April 3, 1952, in *Frank Lloyd Wright: Letters to Architects*, selected by Bruce Brooks Pfeiffer (Fresno: The Press at California State University, 1984), p. 152.

5. Quotations are from Aline B. Saarinen, "Lively Gallery for Living Art," *The New York Times Magazine*, May 30, 1954, p. 16. The initial critical article, "Museum in a Query," appeared in *The New York Times*, April 22, 1951. Saarinen's criticism of the museum is documented in Toni Ramona Beauchamp, "James Johnson Sweeney and the Museum of Fine Arts, Houston: 1961–1967," Master's thesis, University of Texas at Austin, 1983.

6. "Museum Changing Exhibition Policy," *The New York Times*, August 5, 1951.

7. Beauchamp, p. 62.

8. Aline B. Louchheim, "A Museum Takes on a New Life," *The New York Times*, March 1, 1953.

9. Quoted in Dore Ashton, "Museum Prospect: Director of Guggenheim Discusses His Plans," *The New York Times*, November 18, 1956. This approach is relatively uncommon today among art-historically oriented curators, who respond to the call for social contextualization while avoiding formal analysis. In 1989, however, Germano Celant, the Guggenheim's Curator of Contemporary Art, installed the retrospective *Mario Merz* in a completely nonlinear fashion, accentuating visual contrasts and complements rather than defining chronological development, a practice suggested by the implicitly synchronic quality of Merz's production.

10. Letter dated October 5, 1955, in *Frank Lloyd Wright: The Guggenheim Correspondence*, selected by Bruce Brooks Pfeiffer (Fresno: The Press at California State University; Carbondale: Southern Illinois University Press, 1986), pp. 214–15.

11. Letter dated July 15, 1958, in *Frank Lloyd Wright: The Guggenheim Correspondence*, p. 270.

12. Quoted in *Frank Lloyd Wright: The Guggenheim Correspondence*, p. 248.

13. Emily Genauer, quoted by Peter Blake in "The Guggenheim: Museum or Monument?", *Architectural Forum*, December 1959; Ada Louise Huxtable, "That Museum: Wright or Wrong?", *The New York Times*, October 25, 1959. Both cited in Beauchamp, p. 68.

14. Letter dated May 16, 1963, in the Solomon R. Guggenheim Museum Archives.

15. Peggy Guggenheim, *Out of This Century: Confessions of an Art Addict*, rev. ed. (New York: Universe Books, 1987), p. 274.

16. Ibid., pp. 274–75.

17. Quoted in John H. Davis, *The Guggenheims (1848–1988): An American Epic* (New York: Shapolsky Publishers, 1988), pp. 370–71.

Following two pages: Fig. 19. Frank Lloyd Wright,
Solomon R. Guggenheim Museum, perspective
(night rendering), ca. 1950–51. Tempera and black ink on
composition board, 66 x 94 cm (26 x 37 inches). Collection
Peter Lawson-Johnston, New York.

Frank Lloyd Wright and the Solomon R. Guggenheim Museum

Bruce Brooks Pfeiffer

1943–49

On a summer's morning in Wisconsin, early in June 1943, Frank Lloyd Wright found among his morning mail a handwritten letter on small blue stationery, dated June 1 and signed "Hilla Rebay." The letter was a request—almost a plea—for Wright to design a new museum for Solomon R. Guggenheim's collection of non-objective paintings. In describing the works of art and the sort of building she envisioned for them, Baroness Rebay approached the affair with zealous enthusiasm, writing, "I feel that each of these great masterpieces should be organized into space and only you so it seems to me would test the possibilities to do so. . . . I need a fighter, a lover of space, an originator, a tester and a wise man. . . . I want a temple of spirit, a monument!" She ended the letter, "May this wish be blessed."[1]

"I appreciate your appreciation," Wright replied. "I would like to do something such as you suggest for your worthy foundation."[2]

Thus was initiated an intense era of work, of struggle—a saga—that would occupy Wright for the next sixteen years. No other commission in his long career consumed him as did this challenge to design and build the Solomon R. Guggenheim Museum. Toward the end of his life, when the building was under construction, Wright—who was noted for his fine health—admitted, "I have not been too well, as you probably have heard and part of my distress is due to the struggle over the Museum."[3] A month later, he wrote, "Since some fifteen years ago, I have fought steadily through thick and thin—through every sort of adverse circumstances and at great expense to myself to preserve the integrity of all this affair of building this new idea in museums according to the bequest."[4]

He endured the struggle, the adverse circumstances, and the fight simply to get a museum built unlike any other in the annals of architecture. When Wright and Guggenheim first met in 1943, long before any sketches or drawings existed for the project, Guggenheim made his objectives clear: "I do not want to found another museum such as now exists in New York. . . . No such building as is now customary for museums could be appropriate for this one."[5] A contract was signed by Wright and Guggenheim on June 29, 1943, but it would be nine months before a definitive site for the museum was selected and purchased. During that time, ideas were coming to the architect, but without a specific site he believed he could not create a specific design. He expressed this anxiety to Rebay when he wrote, "I hope we can get a plot before [late January] as I am so full of ideas for our museum that I am likely to blow up or commit suicide unless I can let them out on paper."[6]

Within days of this letter, dated December 18, 1943, he had decided to start designing, site or no site. Wright's letter to Rebay of January 20, 1944, written while he was starting work on the Guggenheim design, puts on record a rare and detailed account of what was being, as he phrased it, "let out on paper":

I've been busy at the boards—putting down some of the thoughts concerning a museum that were in my mind while looking for a site. . . . If non-objective painting is to have any great future it must be related to environment in due proportion as it pretty much is already, not to the high ceiling. . . . A museum should have above all a clear atmosphere of light and sympathetic surface. Frames were always an expedient that segregated and masked the paintings off from environment to its own loss of relationship and proportion, etc., etc.

A museum should be one extended expansive well proportioned floor space from bottom to top—a wheel chair going around and up and down, throughout. No stops anywhere and such screened divisions of the space gloriously lit within from above as would deal appropriately with every group of paintings or individual paintings as you might want them classified.

The atmosphere of the whole should be luminous from bright to dark—anywhere desired: a great calm and breadth pervading the whole place, etc. . . . Well, I've just had to get it out of my system and it is taking definite shape not as language but as a building adaptable to the New York plot. . . . When I've satisfied myself with the

Left: Fig. 20. Frank Lloyd Wright at the construction site of the Solomon R. Guggenheim Museum, ca. 1957. Photo by William H. Short.

preliminary exploration I'll bring it down to New York before going West and we can have anguish and fun over it.

The whole thing will either throw you off your guard entirely or be just about what you have been dreaming about.[7]

Wright's allusion to a "well proportioned floor space from bottom to top—a wheel chair going around and up and down" gives the strong hint of a spiral plan. What was actually down on paper at that point has not survived. But what is clearly known about Wright's method of design he himself revealed to his apprentices of the Taliesin Fellowship when he said, some years later, "I never sit down to a drawing board—and this has been a lifelong practice of mine—until I have the whole thing in my mind. I may alter it substantially, I may throw it all away, I may find I'm up a blind alley; but unless I have the idea of the thing pretty well in shape, you won't see me at a drawing board with it."[8]

Wright's idea of using the spiral in a building predates his Guggenheim Museum design by nearly twenty years. In 1924, Wright designed for Gordon Strong a tourist facility on Sugar Loaf Mountain in Maryland in which three spiral ramps circumnavigated the exterior. Five years later, Wright wrote to Strong, asking him to return the drawings of the unbuilt project: "It seems something of the kind is contemplated on the other side, in France, only in that case, it is a *museum*. Some interest has arisen in this idea as I have worked it out for you and I have been asked many times to see it."[9] There is nothing before this rather enigmatic letter on record to give a clue as to the nature of the commission, and nothing follows. But it is quite clear that in 1929 Wright was considering the use of the spiral for an art museum.

Wright firmly believed that what he was designing for Guggenheim would make the viewing and enjoyment of art a far richer and more meaningful experience than the traditional museum plan. In 1958, he wrote:

Walls slant gently outward forming a giant spiral for a well-defined purpose: a new unity between beholder, painting and architecture. As planned, in the easy downward drift of the viewer on the giant spiral, pictures are not to be seen bolt-upright as though painted on the wall behind them. Gently inclined, faced slightly upward to the viewer and to the light in accord with the upward sweep of the spiral, the paintings themselves are emphasized in themselves and are not hung "square" but gracefully yield to movement as set up by these slightly curving massive-walls.[10]

Early sketches reveal that Wright was not only considering the ramp for exhibition purposes and the sloped wall on which to place the paintings, but he was also concerned with the scale and the lighting of the interior. The ceilings were planned to be relatively low, in comparison with other museums, so that the public could view the art in a more intimate environment.

Placing the works of art in a setting of more human scale grew quite naturally out of his own experience with and preference about the display of art. At Taliesin (figs. 21–22), his home in Spring Green, Wisconsin, which he had begun in 1911, Wright displayed his own Asian art collection—Japanese folding screens, prints, and *kakemono* (hanging scrolls), Chinese landscape paintings, and wood, bronze, iron, and stone sculptures from both Japan and China—as an integrated feature of the interior. The screens were set flat against the walls and bordered merely by a strip of cypress to match the other cypress woodwork throughout the residence. *Kakemono* were similarly hung flat against the walls or stone piers. Japanese prints were matted in soft, tan paper and placed on specially designed freestanding easels. The wood sculptures were carefully placed on shelves and decks around the interior, while bronze, iron, and stone sculptures were placed outdoors in the gardens and courts. Everywhere, these works of art appeared in harmony with the architecture and extremely sympathetic to the overall environment.

Lighting played an important role in Wright's earliest drawings for the new museum. Besides the large dome over the central open court, another light source—a narrow, continuously running skylight—was planned over the sloped walls, in addition to fixtures for incandescent light installed in the same location. Wright explained to Rebay and Guggenheim that the inspiration for the direct lighting from wall and skylight also came from his own work space at Taliesin.[11]

With the ramp idea firmly fixed in his thinking (save for one flat-floor scheme), Wright proceeded to make several designs in order to study the one he finally wished to develop. Variations as to placement of the ramp and the color of material, for example, were carefully rendered as part of the initial set of preliminary drawings in 1944.

One of the earliest studies made by Wright (fig. 24) shows the elevation of the exhibition spaces with low ceilings in addition to several sectional drawings depicting the various ways of lighting the galleries to the left. This was followed by a hexagonal plan (fig. 26) for the gallery to the right and "the Monitor"—or office, staff, and residence space—to the left. The elevation (fig. 25) and view (fig. 23) that correspond to this plan show copper and glass tubes along with poured concrete. Immediately after he made this scheme, Wright changed the level floors to a sloping ramp, a concept that first appears as a "footnote" on the hexagonal plan, where he wrote "constant ramp." Wright drew another interior elevation (fig. 27) entitled "Various Allotments of Exhibition Space," denoting the ramp, and dated it September 1943. In the plan (fig. 28), a circular spiral ramp is placed to the right, the Monitor to the left. Each band of the ramp diminishes in size as it rises, permitting a continuous skylight to run along the outer, upper edge of the ramp (fig. 29). From this sketch elevation drawn by Wright, the study elevation (fig. 30) was developed by his apprentices. The final perspective (fig. 31) renders the building in rose marble. At the same time, Wright was considering a ramp that would expand as it rises, as the rather unusual sketch combining section and elevation shows (fig. 32). Here, Wright drew a cut-line down the central portion of the elevation so as to present

a glimpse of the interior. To the right, he made a small "thumbnail" view of the museum. In the next four drawings he made (figs. 33–36), Wright developed the scheme shown in the sectional elevation sketch, with the ramp on the right-hand side of the site. Then Wright moved the ramp to the left side, as three drawings—a sketch plan (fig. 37), a section (fig. 38), and a final perspective (fig. 39)—show. It was the final perspective drawing that Wright signed and placed on the cover of the group of sketches, which he then presented to Guggenheim and Rebay.

These early schemes were lavishly drawn up in watercolor, showing a choice of white, deep rose, or beige marble. The building was conceived as a poured-concrete structure, with the marble applied over it in thin sheets, like a membrane. The drawings themselves are unique in the collection: by this time in his career Wright was using graphite pencil and colored pencils for his renderings. (Occasionally, he would use a sepia or black ink, and sometimes he made what was called a "night rendering"—a drawing made on black illustration board with tempera and colored inks; see, for example, fig. 19.) But the set he made and then took to New York to show Guggenheim and Rebay was painted more than drawn, perhaps in keeping with the commission for a building to house paintings. "When [Guggenheim] saw the first sketches I made and that I took to him in New Hampshire at his request," Wright recollected, "he went over them several times without saying a word or looking up. Finally when he did look up there were tears in his eyes, 'Mr. Wright,' he said, 'I knew you would do it. This is it.'"[12]

Several plans and sections were incorporated into the set, and some elevations show the manner of hanging pictures. The interior elevations with paintings on the walls have a distinctively different feature about them: their frames, or more specifically, their lack of frames. In Wright's drawings, paintings are displayed with no more than a narrow, almost imperceptible band around them.

An interesting event happened in

Top: Fig. 21. Taliesin, Frank Lloyd Wright's house in Spring Green, Wisconsin.

Bottom: Fig. 22. Taliesin, interior view.

23

24

25

26

27

28

Fig. 23. Perspective, 1943. Watercolor on paper, 50.8 x 61 cm (20 x 24 inches). The Frank Lloyd Wright Archives, The Frank Lloyd Wright Foundation 4305.748.

Fig. 24. Sections (left), interior elevation (above right), and plan (below right), 1943. Pencil on tracing paper, 67 x 91.4 cm (26 ⅜ x 36 inches). The Frank Lloyd Wright Archives, The Frank Lloyd Wright Foundation 4305.078.

Fig. 25. Elevation, 1943. Colored pencil on paper, 50.8 x 62.2 cm (20 x 24 ½ inches). The Frank Lloyd Wright Archives, The Frank Lloyd Wright Foundation 4305.006.

Fig. 26. Plan, 1943. Pencil on tracing paper, 47 x 93.7 cm (18 ½ x 36 ⅞ inches). The Frank Lloyd Wright Archives, The Frank Lloyd Wright Foundation 4305.091.

Fig. 27. Interior elevations and plans, September 1943. Pencil and colored pencil on paper, 50.8 x 61.6 cm (20 x 24 ¼ inches). The Frank Lloyd Wright Archives, The Frank Lloyd Wright Foundation 4305.002.

Fig. 28. Ground-floor plan, 1944. Pencil on tracing paper, 45.8 x 68.6 cm (18 x 27 inches). The Frank Lloyd Wright Archives, The Frank Lloyd Wright Foundation 4305.063.

29

30

31

Fig. 29. Schematic elevation, 1944. Pencil and colored pencil on tracing paper, 62.2 x 88.9 cm (24½ x 35 inches). The Frank Lloyd Wright Archives, The Frank Lloyd Wright Foundation 4305.076.

Fig. 30. Study elevation, 1944. Colored pencil on paper, 50.8 x 61.9 cm (20 x 24⅜ inches). The Frank Lloyd Wright Archives, The Frank Lloyd Wright Foundation 4305.007.

Fig. 31. Perspective, 1944. Watercolor on paper, 50.8 x 61 cm (20 x 24 inches). Collection of Erving and Joyce Wolf. 4305.747.

Fig. 32. Sectional elevation, 1943. Pencil and colored pencil on tracing paper, 66.7 x 77.2 cm (26¼ x 30⅜ inches). The Frank Lloyd Wright Archives, The Frank Lloyd Wright Foundation 4305.014.

Fig. 33. Perspective, 1944. Watercolor and ink on paper, 51.1 x 61.3 cm (20⅛ x 24⅛ inches). The Frank Lloyd Wright Archives, The Frank Lloyd Wright Foundation 4305.745.

Fig. 34. Perspective, 1944. Watercolor and ink on paper, 50.8 x 61.6 cm (20 x 24¼ inches). The Frank Lloyd Wright Archives, The Frank Lloyd Wright Foundation 4305.746.

32

33

34

35

36

37

38

39

Fig. 35. Perspective, 1944. Watercolor on paper, 50.8 x 61 cm (20 x 24 inches). Collection of Erving and Joyce Wolf. 4305.749.

Fig. 36. Elevation, 1944. Pencil and colored pencil on paper, 60 x 61.6 cm (23 ⅛ x 24 ¼ inches). The Frank Lloyd Wright Archives, The Frank Lloyd Wright Foundation 4305.025.

Fig. 37. Ground-floor plan, 1944. Pencil on tracing paper, 51.8 x 57.8 cm (20 ⅛ x 22 ¾ inches). The Frank Lloyd Wright Archives, The Frank Lloyd Wright Foundation 4305.068.

Fig. 38. Section, 1944. Pencil on tracing paper, 74.9 x 88.6 cm (29 ½ x 34 ⅞ inches). The Frank Lloyd Wright Archives, The Frank Lloyd Wright Foundation 4305.041.

Fig. 39. Perspective, 1944. Watercolor and ink on paper, 69.8 x 97.2 cm (27 ½ x 38 ¼ inches). The Frank Lloyd Wright Archives, The Frank Lloyd Wright Foundation 4305.008.

Fig. 40. Georgia O'Keeffe, *Pelvis with Shadows and the Moon*, 1943. Oil on canvas, 101.6 x 123.8 cm (40 x 48 ¼ inches). Private collection.

Wright's life at just about this time. His friend Georgia O'Keeffe had decided to give him her painting *Pelvis with Shadows and the Moon* (1943, fig. 40) some time before, but sent it to him only after her husband, Alfred Stieglitz, died.[13] Wright had seen it and other works at Stieglitz's New York art gallery, An American Place, and was especially taken by the method of framing. Wright noted this in his acknowledgment of the gift: "The masterpiece arrived properly framed! That is to say *none* showing."[14] The painting was framed in thin metal bands, ⅛-inch wide by 2 inches deep.

The site that was finally purchased for the museum, on the southeast corner of Fifth Avenue and Eighty-ninth streets, turned out to be only 25 feet less in breadth than the preliminary sketches had shown, which was "made up for by the additional depth," Wright wrote. "The area is nearly *almost exactly the same*—the Gods are kind."[15] Now the preparation of plans could go ahead in earnest. Guggenheim placed Rebay in charge of the project, and asked only that letters to Rebay be copied for him. During the ensuing months, Rebay's once-zealous enthusiasm gave way to doubts about the direction the new gallery was taking. In fact, the bulk of Wright's correspondence to her centered on trying to placate her fears and relieve her anxieties. It seemed that she still thought of a museum as a tall, square room. And to that end, a special "Grand Gallery" was designed (the present-day High Gallery) where larger, more imposing works could be exhibited. Wright describes his conception of the Grand Gallery:

The Holy of Holies should be on the main floor, not on the ground floor . . . The ground floor is never quiet. That will be impressively open above to the sky and on two sides to the park and be a general rendezvous—tea service from the kitchen, etc., etc.[16]

In July 1944, Guggenheim wrote to Wright assuring him that the preliminary sketches were entirely satisfactory and authorized him to go ahead with the next phase of the project, the production of the working

drawings that would be used to construct the building. The first set—twenty-nine sheets of architectural drawings and thirteen of structural drawings—was signed by Wright on September 7, 1945. It reveals a structure quite different from what stands now. The character of the first set of drawings—seven other complete sets would eventually be made—is more in keeping with Rebay's initial idea of a temple to non-objective paintings.

In referring to the building and to public access within the museum, Wright often used the phrase "the downward drift." Clearly, it was his intention that visitors would enter the building, take the elevator to the top level, and begin their descent. From any place on the grand ramp visitors could see where they had been and where they were going. Wishing to bypass a section of the exhibition, they needed only to get back on the elevator and get off at the desired level. The Grand Gallery would be near the end of the tour, and finally on the ground floor visitors would end at the front door, adjacent to a small café and tea garden.

Other aspects of the building, evident in the section drawings, reveal features not commonly associated with museum design. An observatory housed in a glass sphere was planned for the very top, off to the side of the rotunda (fig. 46), above the elevator machinery. In the auditorium beneath the ground floor of the main rotunda, seating was arranged so that the audience could recline, as in a planetarium, to view slides of paintings projected on the ceiling above (fig. 47). It was Rebay's desire that this viewing be accompanied by a string quartet playing Bach and Mozart! In the Monitor, adjacent but connected to the main exhibition ramp, was another, smaller theater, called the Ocular Chamber. Here the seats, as in the auditorium, reclined for viewing images cast up from a sunken central projector, but the surface for the images was a half dome (fig. 48). The Monitor held museum offices and apartments for Guggenheim and Rebay. Later, Guggenheim felt it prudent to remove living quarters from the museum. He reasoned that Rebay, in practicing her own work as a painter, would be free from curatorial distractions if she had an independent studio away from museum activities, while he himself already had a residence at the nearby Plaza Hotel. Consequently, a revision was called for; the section that had previously housed private apartments was turned over entirely to offices and staff workrooms. When Wright brought the drawings east and Guggenheim countersigned them with his initials, it seemed from that point on the building was ready to go into construction. World War II was over and building materials were now freed up from the war effort. But Guggenheim was of the firm belief that building costs, which were beginning to surge, would eventually go down. Thus, the construction of the museum was postponed.

Both Guggenheim and Rebay were convinced that a model of the museum was absolutely essential to explain the workings of its unique form both to themselves and others. Wright concurred with their wish and prepared a set of special drawings for the sake of making the model. By the end of August 1945, the model was completed and sent to New York. The first model (figs. 44–45) sent to New York in 1945 was made at Taliesin by Wright's apprentices, members of the Taliesin Fellowship. Constructed of Plexiglas, sections were heated so that they could be curved, then they were assembled and painted a cream color to represent the poured concrete of the final structure. Plexiglas scored with lines represented the glass tubing of the main dome, other glass areas, and the continuous skylight that wrapped around the exterior of the ramp. Glass tubes were first used by Wright in the skylights and partitions of the Johnson Wax administration building ten years earlier; he had found the crystalline light that emanated from the tubes most desirable. After being displayed in New York, the model was sent back to Taliesin, but it was irreparably damaged during shipment. In 1947, to reflect plans for an annex to the museum, another model had to be made (figs. 41–43).[17]

With the working drawings signed

and approved by both architect and client, Guggenheim and Rebay once again began to express certain fears that the building would dominate the paintings and that the toplighted wall would provide inadequate lighting. Wright tried to assuage their fears in a letter to Guggenheim:

Now, to understand the situation as it exists in the scheme for the Guggenheim Memorial all you have to do is to imagine clean beautiful surface throughout the building all beautifully proportioned to human scale. These surfaces are all lighted from above with any degree of daylight (or artificial light from the same source) that the curator or the artist himself may happen to desire. The atmosphere of great harmonious simplicity wherein human proportions are maintained in relation to the picture is characteristic of your building.[18]

But the constant concerns, mainly on the part of Rebay, about the building dominating the paintings and about the lighting system continued to hound Wright year after year. He began to wonder, and asked in his letters to Rebay, why she had selected him as her architect in the first place. Although the model had been received enthusiastically, Wright increasingly began to doubt if Rebay really understood the building and its purpose. Guggenheim's faith in Wright, however, remained steadfast.

In 1946, two years after the initial property on Fifth Avenue was purchased, a narrow townhouse on the Eighty-eighth Street side was also acquired, which the museum planned to use as its temporary quarters. Wright advised against investing large sums of money for a building that would eventually be torn down. He suggested, instead, that another structure, to be called the annex, be built to serve as a temporary gallery and office facility, but which eventually could be connected with the main structure. Guggenheim agreed to this, and Wright made the working drawings at great speed and sent them to New York.[19] At the same time, Wright made another perspective to show the addition of the annex at the rear of the museum (fig. 49). But

Top: Fig. 41. Frank Lloyd Wright's 1947 model of the museum, view of Fifth Avenue façade.

Center: Fig. 42. Wright's 1947 model of the museum, view of 88th Street entrance.

Bottom: Fig. 43. Wright's 1947 model of the museum, view from the corner of 88th Street and Fifth Avenue.

Following four pages:
Fig. 44. Frank Lloyd Wright, Hilla Rebay, and Solomon R. Guggenheim with Wright's 1945 model of the museum.

Fig. 45. Wright's 1945 model of the museum.

46

47

48

Fig. 46. Section (detail showing observatory), 1944.
Pencil and colored pencil on tracing paper, 66 x 88.6 cm
(26 x 34 ⅞ inches). The Frank Lloyd Wright Archives,
The Frank Lloyd Wright Foundation 4305.035A.

Fig. 47. Section (detail showing auditorium), 1944.
Pencil and colored pencil on tracing paper, 66 x 88.6 cm
(26 x 34 ⅞ inches). The Frank Lloyd Wright Archives,
The Frank Lloyd Wright Foundation 4305.035B.

Fig. 48. Section (detail showing the Ocular Chamber), 1944.
Pencil and colored pencil on tracing paper, 66 x 88.6 cm
(26 x 34 ⅞ inches). The Frank Lloyd Wright Archives,
The Frank Lloyd Wright Foundation 4305.035C.

again, Guggenheim, no doubt impaired by his failing health, procrastinated. Further revisions were made on the main building to try to lower construction costs, which were rapidly rising, especially in New York City. The architect finally promised Guggenheim that he would build his museum for the appropriated $2 million if he himself could make the necessary changes. Wright realized that Guggenheim's health was failing and wanted him to see the museum built. The architect revised the plans, proposing the removal of 380,000 cubic feet so that it would come closer to the appropriated sum. But Guggenheim refused to look at the plans when brought to him, saying, "No, Mr. Wright. I like it as it is. If we have prosperity what does a million more or less mean to me."[20] Filled with hope by Guggenheim's response, Wright wrote to Rebay in June 1949, "You say we might have started long ago. Tell me when. Meantime Life doesn't. The Cosmos sweeps onward and upward while we crawl on the surface like flies on a transparent window-pane."[21] Five months later, Guggenheim was dead. It seemed that hopes for building his memorial had died with him.

1950–59

In 1950, Harry S. Guggenheim, Solomon's nephew, was made president of the Solomon R. Guggenheim Foundation. Wright immediately wrote to him:

Never for a moment have I lost the feeling that here was the only American multimillionaire, who, when he died, instead of placing his means at the disposal of what passed for respectability in conventional art-museums—though laughed at by his friends—intended to face the future. He backed up his feelings as well as his faith by the liberal bequest to represent to the future a distinguished quality. *Other millionaires cuddled up to the Past for their memorial when they died. Not so Solomon R. Guggenheim. No. He died facing the way he had lived— forward.*[22]

Although he pressed for Harry

Guggenheim's support in order to get the museum built, construction was again postponed.

In 1951, the remaining parcel of land was acquired. The full front on Fifth Avenue, from Eighty-eighth to Eighty-ninth streets, made a far more desirable building site than the one previously available. Wright went back to work to revise the plans accordingly. The large spiral ramp had been shifted from the south to the north side several times. Wright's earliest schemes, made before a site was purchased, show the large ramp to the right side of the site (on the south end). When the Eighty-ninth Street corner parcel was bought in 1944, the ramp was relocated to the north, as in the drawings and models of 1945 and 1947. When the corner at Eighty-eighth Street was acquired in 1951, the spiral ramp was shifted back to the south. For each of these changes, a new set of working drawings was required. After this last shift was made, Wright, in response to the changing administrative requirements of the museum, suggested the construction of a tall building behind the museum for a historical gallery, staff offices, workrooms, and storage (figs. 52–53). Rising behind the museum would be an eleven-story structure containing private studio apartments that could be rented out as a supplementary source of revenue. It was this 1951 design by Wright that served as a precedent for the 1992 addition of a "backdrop" building behind the museum.

In 1952, Rebay resigned as director. The museum was now moving in a new direction, expanding its collection, being rearranged along broader lines. With the appointment of James Johnson Sweeney to succeed Rebay, these programs demanded another set of changes in the architectural plans as well.

However tedious and time-consuming all these changes were, Wright was constantly improving the scheme to simplify the final result, which would come after another two sets of working drawings, in 1954 and 1956. All the while, the burden of making the building's cost commensurate with Guggenheim's bequest weighed heavily

49

50

51

52

53

Fig. 49. Perspective from 88th Street, 1947. Ink, pencil, and colored pencil on tracing paper, 50.2 x 73 cm (19 ¼ x 28 ¾ inches). The Frank Lloyd Wright Archives, The Frank Lloyd Wright Foundation 4727.013.

Fig. 50. Perspective, 1948. Ink and pencil on tracing paper, 50.8 x 75.6 cm (20 x 29 ¾ inches). The Frank Lloyd Wright Archives, The Frank Lloyd Wright Foundation 4305.015.

Fig. 51. Perspective, 1948. Pencil on tracing paper, 40.3 x 89.5 cm (15 ⅞ x 35 ¼ inches). The Frank Lloyd Wright Archives, The Frank Lloyd Wright Foundation 4305.016.

Fig. 52. Perspective, 1951. Ink, pencil, and colored pencil on tracing paper, 66 x 100.3 cm (26 x 39 ½ inches). The Frank Lloyd Wright Archives, The Frank Lloyd Wright Foundation 4305.017.

Fig. 53. Perspective, 1953. Tempera on board, 68.6 x 101.6 cm (27 x 40 inches). The Frank Lloyd Wright Archives, The Frank Lloyd Wright Foundation 4305.062.

54

55

Fig. 54. Perspective, 1952. Ink on mylar, 77.8 x 110.5 cm (30 ⅛ x 43 ½ inches). The Frank Lloyd Wright Archives, The Frank Lloyd Wright Foundation 4305.306.

Fig. 55. Perspective, 1957. Pencil on tracing paper, 83.8 x 127 cm (33 x 50 inches). The Frank Lloyd Wright Archives, The Frank Lloyd Wright Foundation 4305.009.

on Wright's ingenuity. Many details had to be sacrificed in order to stay within budget, but this was something at which Wright was a master. Over and over again he remarked that "limitations are an artist's best friend." No building in Wright's career illustrated this maxim better than the Guggenheim.

By 1952, the whole building had taken on a more unified, solemn appearance (fig. 54). Throughout the project's development, Wright was troubled by the vertical, unrestful nature of the spiral, although he knew it was essential to the purpose and design of the building. The first sketches show a horizontal form engaging the spiral and tying it to the Monitor; but by 1951 the horizontal band reaches across the entire Fifth Avenue elevation, both spiral and Monitor rising out of it. Yet again, in 1957, he further accentuated this horizontal band by having it protrude out, just before it reached Eighty-eighth Street, and then continue back to engage the mass that houses the Grand Gallery (fig. 55). The space created by this extension was called the "Architecture Archive."[23] (In 1978, architect Richard Meier created the Aye Simon Reading Room in this space, connecting it to the main gallery via a keyhole-shaped doorway.) All of these design factors, intended to economize, strengthened the integrity of the design.

There was a brief span of time before the Guggenheim Museum was built when another Frank Lloyd Wright building stood on Fifth Avenue between Eighty-eighth and Eighty-ninth streets. This was a temporary pavilion that was designed to house a world-touring exhibition of Wright's work entitled *Sixty Years of Living Architecture* (figs. 56–57). The exhibition, which opened in January of 1951 in Philadelphia and was sponsored by Gimbel's department store, consisted of original drawings, architectural models, mural-sized photographs of executed buildings, and furniture and decorative objects. In 1953, it was installed in a pavilion that Wright designed for the exhibition on Fifth Avenue. Adjacent to the pavilion was a model home—a Usonian house—

also designed by Wright specifically for the exhibition. Entrance for the public was through the old townhouse at 1071 Fifth Avenue, which was serving at that time as a temporary gallery for the Guggenheim collection pending construction of the museum. An archway in the north wall on the ground level led into the pavilion, which was roofed in glass and Masonite panels supported by a framework of pipe columns. When the exhibition ended, the pavilion was demolished.

As construction of the museum became imminent, consultations were necessary with Sweeney, Harry Guggenheim, and city officials over the building permit and construction details. For these sorts of discussions, Wright was usually able to assign his apprentices to represent him. His son-in-law William Wesley Peters was well trained, as both an engineer and architect, to handle the more complex jobs such as the Johnson Wax building. Other apprentices at Taliesin could manage the homes being built around the country. But the Solomon R. Guggenheim Museum was a job that Wright felt needed his constant personal supervision. In order to facilitate this, he decided to establish a New York office.

Although Wright was a great exponent of decentralization and a firm believer that cities were, essentially, evil, he could not conceal his love for New York. His favorite place to stay when in town was at the Plaza Hotel, which became the logical choice for an office. A two-room apartment with vestibule, kitchen, and bath was rented and refurbished according to his design (fig. 58). A sitting room served partly as reception area and office, while a bedroom could be screened off during the daytime and used for another office/drafting room. Sleek, black lacquer tables, easels, and hassocks were made by Wright's apprentices at Taliesin; the fabrics and carpets were lush and elegant—deep plum velvet draperies and golden-peach wool carpet. The walls were covered in rice paper with gold-leaf speckles. Into this environment he brought some of his favorite works of oriental art from

Top: Fig. 56. Pavilion designed by Frank Lloyd Wright for the exhibition *Sixty Years of Living Architecture*, 1953. View from Fifth Avenue. Photo by Pedro E. Guerrero.

Bottom: Fig. 57. Interior view of pavilion for *Sixty Years of Living Architecture*, 1953. Photo by Pedro E. Guerrero.

Taliesin along with the O'Keeffe painting, arranging them on easels along with a complete set of Sweet's Catalog File (a set of reference books for architects). After Wright's death in 1959, among his papers was found a "press notice" he himself had penned on Plaza notepaper just after moving into his new apartment/office. It reads:

Frank Lloyd Wright at the Plaza

He has always worked where he ate and slept and is doing so now with the air of magnificence and expense one associates with the Plaza. He has done the rooms over in the vein of the original Plaza as conceived by Henry Hardenberg {sic}—and managed at the same time to get a practicable working office, showroom, and sleeping quarters out of it—all pretty harmonious with Plaza elegance—with certain additions that Mr. Wright thinks would have pleased Henry Hardenberg {sic}. Unfortunately the apartment as it existed before he began it was not photographed so what happened is anyone's guess.

FLLW.[24]

On August 14, 1956, ground was broken. The construction contract was given to George Cohen of Euclid Construction Company. Wright appointed architect William Short as the Clerk of the Works. Short was to remain on site each day of construction, make certain that the architect's plans were carefully carried out, and report to him on a weekly basis; he also documented the construction in a detailed series of photographs (for example, figs. 59–64). It must have seemed to Wright, standing in the excavated area where the grand ramp was soon to rise, that something of a miracle had taken place: thirteen years had passed almost to the month since the commission was given. Everything and everyone seemed to have tried to thwart its execution. Doubts and problems beset Wright at all stages. But now, during the summer of 1956, the building was finally rising, and continued to do so throughout 1957 and 1958.

A group of artists sent a letter to

Sweeney and the trustees voicing their concern that any space with sloped walls and a ramped floor would be totally unsuitable for the exhibition of paintings. When confronted with this letter, Wright responded to Harry Guggenheim, assuring him that the design of the building would better serve paintings precisely because of the slanted wall, the skylight above, and the ramp for easy circulation. At the same time, Wright realized that Sweeney had very strong, and very conventional, ideas about the exhibition of paintings. One thing that Sweeney definitely did not want was to place the pictures on the sloped wall, as had been intended from the very start of the project in 1943.

To demonstrate to the trustees and director the manner in which the art could be best exhibited, Wright prepared a group of interior perspectives in 1958 (figs. 11–13). On each drawing, he titled the placement of the exhibition area in relation to its "station" on the ramp and also gave the approximate sizes for pictures. Beginning at the top ramp was "The Watercolor Society," depicting paintings both on the sloped wall and on freestanding easels. Next came the "Average," meaning the general way of showing the oil paintings and freestanding sculpture, followed by the "Middle of the Road," halfway down the ramp, and finally "The Masterpiece," a large Kandinsky-like painting occupying one entire bay. The four interior perspectives made by Wright and his apprentices in 1958 also show his concern for the placement of hassocks and benches along the way. Sweeney chose not to follow these suggestions, and when the museum opened in October 1959 the paintings were mounted on pikes projecting from the wall, as if floating in a white void. Sweeney had insisted on an all-white interior, despite Wright's specification of a soft, off-white or cream color. The effect of seeing the vibrantly colored paintings, so unrelated to the architectural space and clashing with an unsympathetic dead white, was startling and disturbing. Right up until his death, Wright was involved in a bitter controversy with Sweeney over these matters.

When construction of the ramp had reached its top level by 1958, and the formwork had been stripped from the general ramp levels below, the public at large was able to get a glimpse of how the final opus would eventually appear upon completion. The building's exterior, nearly finished, caused even more of a furor than during the design phase. Artists continued to criticize the building as impractical for exhibition purposes, and the general public ridiculed its place on elegant Fifth Avenue. But the building was forged through to completion and opened to the public on October 21, 1959. By that time, Wright had been dead six months.

Two months before his death, Wright acknowledged the support of Harry Guggenheim when he wrote,

Dear Harry:

. . . I cannot tell you how much your reassurance means in this late day of the supreme effort involved in the museum. That you are prepared to stand by the philosophy that gave the building its present form. It is there in good shape and working against the odds you yourself have stood against and are experiencing—the transition from the carpenter and his square to the more liberal and universal atmosphere of Nature.

Affection, Frank Lloyd Wright.[25]

1960–92

Museums across the world seem besieged with the problem of space requirements as their collections and office spaces expand and the demand for more exhibition areas steadily increases. Added to these needs are the growing requirements for conservation and climate control. The Guggenheim Museum is no exception. Its expansion in both collections and programs has necessitated a series of physical changes to the building.

In some cases, the original intentions of the architect were either never fully carried out or they were drastically altered. The ground-floor space that Wright intended to be the café, for example, was used for conservation and framing departments. Justin K. Thannhauser gave the museum a portion of his collection of Impressionist and Post-Impressionist art in 1963 on permanent loan. Since this gift was not part of the changing collection, the museum decided to convert space on the second floor of the Monitor from library to galleries. These alterations were designed by William Wesley Peters of Taliesin Associated Architects.[26] An arched opening was cut through from the main ramp to connect with this new exhibition space. A portion of the fourth floor in the Monitor was converted to gallery space in 1980 in order to house an installation drawn from the permanent collection.

When the first change took place in the Monitor in 1963, Peters designed the annex, located on Eighty-ninth Street, to house the offices previously located in the Monitor. With the thought of further expansion in mind, the four-story annex was built, in 1968, on a foundation that could adequately support ten floors when needed. The requirement for a bookstore space and the relocation of a tearoom was satisfied by enclosing the original drive-through passage between the rotunda and the Monitor for those two functions. But the major change that has occurred in the last thirty-four years is without a doubt the tower on Eighty-ninth Street, rising six stories higher than the four-story Peters annex. This new addition, designed by Gwathmey Siegel and Associates Architects and completed in 1992, provides four floors of exhibition space, three of which are each two stories high, and two additional floors of office space. The tower engages the Frank Lloyd Wright rotunda behind the triangular stair tower at the second, fourth, fifth, and seventh floors, but does so in such a way that the drama and completeness of the main ramp is not impaired or disturbed. The lighting continues the sentiment that Wright employed in the rotunda: a general ambient toplighting with concealed focus lighting. The exterior limestone face of the new building resembles the original tall "backdrop" building designed by Wright in 1951. The café on

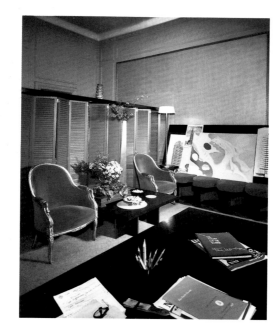

Fig. 58. Frank Lloyd Wright's suite at the Plaza Hotel, ca. 1956. Photo by Pedro E. Guerrero.

Figs. 59–64. Construction of the Solomon R. Guggenheim Museum, 1956–59. Photos by William H. Short.

Reinforcing rods have been laid at the ground level of the rotunda in order to pour the concrete floor slab.

The ramp rises from the ground-floor slab to the level of the first floor of the Thannhauser Building. In the foreground, the floor of the café has been poured, and formwork has been constructed for the floor of the Aye Simon Reading Room.

The floor slab has been poured to the third turn of the ramp, in the High Gallery, and at the third floor of the Thannhauser Building.

Construction on the fifth turn of the ramp has commenced. The main structure of the Thannhauser Building is complete.

Formwork has been erected in order to pour the structural members of the skylight.

The structure of the skylight, roof, and ramp has been completed.

the ground floor has been put in place as originally planned. The second, third, and fourth levels of the Monitor (rechristened the Thannhauser Building in 1989) now open onto the main gallery, providing three full floors for showing the permanent collection.

The restoration that was undertaken simultaneous to the expansion was greatly needed. New mechanical systems were installed, the continuous skylight cleaned and put back into operation, and countless details, after a period of more than thirty years, finally put to rights. The building emerges now more in keeping with Frank Lloyd Wright's design than when it opened in 1959.

Wright wrote "Ziggurat," the Mesopotamian word meaning "to build high," on some of the early studies for the Guggenheim Museum. Since the ramp of his building expanded as it rose, he referred to it as the "optimistic ziggurat." Certainly there have been other buildings employing the ramp as the main feature of access, dating back to as early as 2100 B.C. For example, Deir el Bahari, the funerary temple of Queen Hatshepsut in Egypt, employed processional ramps to connect the terraces of the temple from level to level. But in the Guggenheim Museum the ramp takes on an all-embracing role: it is not only the means of access, circulation, and exhibition, it constitutes the very form of the building itself. The ramp ends on one edge as a parapet overlooking the central court, and on the other as it slopes up to become the wall surface, both inside and out. It is both floor and ceiling. Wright's concept of open, flowing, interior space as the reality of the building reaches its zenith here. He often called his work, and the aim of his work, the "destruction of the box in architecture."

Most architecture is, basically, a box, trimmed and decorated in different manners, pierced with holes for windows and doors, the interior space a cluster of boxes within the larger box. The limitation of materials before the twentieth century had dictated that it be so (prominent exceptions being Gothic cathedrals and Islamic mosques).

At the end of the nineteenth century and the beginning of the twentieth, new materials and new ways of putting them together were applied to architectural practice. Concrete reinforced with steel, sheet metal, plate glass, steel in tension (think of the Brooklyn Bridge), plastics, and new methods of construction gave to both architect and engineer a vocabulary never before available. Architecture as well as engineering could now take a different direction, liberated from the concepts that had bound them for more than thirty centuries.

Wright was the first, and remained the most innovative, architect to take this vocabulary and build it into a new language of form. The Guggenheim Museum is the apotheosis of this architecture-engineering integrated into one entity. There is no way in which the form of the museum, its physical appearance, can be separated from its structure any more than the leaves and branches of a tree can be considered separate from its roots and trunk. It is a "plastic" building in that by the use of reinforced concrete it takes a form that is moldable. The building is the perfect symbol of democracy: no stratified layers, no fixed levels. Its form seems to move up as it moves down; there is nothing static or confining about it. Perhaps this is its greatest contribution to the history of architecture.

Designed in the first half of the twentieth century, the Guggenheim points the way to architecture of the twenty-first century. The old post-and-beam type of construction is no longer needed, or even economical, with the development of materials such as reinforced concrete, glass, and steel. The only limitation is human imagination. The Solomon R. Guggenheim Museum, in this respect, could serve as a valuable inspiration for future generations of architects if they would but grasp the idea, the principle, that gave life to the building in its role to serve humanity.

1. Letter to Frank Lloyd Wright, June 1, 1943. All letters quoted in this essay are in the Frank Lloyd Wright Archives, the Frank Lloyd Wright Foundation, Scottsdale, Arizona.

2. Letter to Rebay, June 10, 1943.

3. Letter to Harry S. Guggenheim, November 28, 1958.

4. Refers to the bequest by Solomon R. Guggenheim of funds to build the Wright design. Letter to Harry S. Guggenheim, December 27, 1958.

5. Letter from Wright to Harry S. Guggenheim, May 14, 1952.

6. Letter to Rebay, December 18, 1943.

7. Letter to Rebay, January 20, 1944.

8. From a lecture delivered on September 12, 1952.

9. Letter to Gordon Strong, July 10, 1929.

10. Manuscript, dated June 1958, in the Frank Lloyd Wright Archives.

11. Letter to Rebay, August 27, 1946.

12. Letter from Wright to Harry S. Guggenheim, May 14, 1952.

13. Letter from O'Keeffe to Wright, May 1942.

14. Letter to O'Keeffe, February 14, 1947.

15. Letter to Rebay, March 20, 1944.

16. Letter to Rebay, March 21, 1944.

17. This model is now in the Frank Lloyd Wright Archives; it was revised in 1950 to conform with the new shape of the ramp's exterior slope.

18. Letter to Guggenheim, August 14, 1946.

19. When the annex was designed in 1947, Wright did not have a New York architectural license. Accordingly, he sought the services of Arthur Holden, of Holden McLaughlin Associates, a New York firm. Holden was charged with obtaining the building permits for both the museum and the annex. The working drawings from this time bear the names of both Holden's firm and Wright.

20. Wright, quoting Guggenheim in a letter to Rebay, June 23, 1949.

21. Ibid.

22. Letter to Harry S. Guggenheim, May 14, 1952.

23. Drawing 4305.440, the Frank Lloyd Wright Archives, the Frank Lloyd Wright Foundation.

24. Item 0003.012, the Frank Lloyd Wright Archives, the Frank Lloyd Wright Foundation.

25. Letter to Harry S. Guggenheim, February 12, 1959.

26. The firm is a wholly owned subsidiary of the Frank Lloyd Wright Foundation.

Plate 9. Edouard Manet, *Before the Mirror (Devant la glace),*
1876. Oil on canvas, 92.1 x 71.4 cm (36 ¼ x 28 ⅛ inches).
Solomon R. Guggenheim Museum, Thannhauser
Collection, Gift, Justin K. Thannhauser 78.2514 T27.

Paintings of Modern Life and Modern Myths

Late-Nineteenth- and Early Twentieth-Century Representations of Gender, Class, and Race in the Thannhauser Collection

Andrea Feeser

Late-nineteenth- and early twentieth-century representations of work and leisure often reveal conflicting ideas about women of various classes and about people of color. The Thannhauser Collection at the Guggenheim Museum is rich in such paintings by Impressionist, Post-Impressionist, and early twentieth-century artists. Close readings of many works in the collection provide insights into why Edouard Manet, Paul Gauguin, Pablo Picasso, and other artists regularly depicted women and nonwhite people in restricted and subservient roles.

From the mid-nineteenth century, modernization—which saw the application of new technologies that altered living and work spaces, the continued aggressive colonization of foreign lands, and the burgeoning of capitalism with its expanding range of commodities—produced broad changes in French society and culture, which in turn affected artistic representation. Artists embraced or rejected these new conditions, and devised differing techniques and styles to give life to their artistic visions. Avant-garde artists explored sexuality, popular culture, and geographical areas thought to be "primitive," using these social and psychic realms to provide them with transgressive experiences that they could depict in their art. But although their work challenged artistic tradition and frequently confounded the morals of the majority, it nevertheless represented conventional beliefs about the roles played by men and women of different races and classes. There is nothing given or natural about these roles; indeed, they were largely determined by powerful men's needs, desires, and fears and the changing historical conditions that shaped these emotions.

The art criticism of the poet Charles Baudelaire, who collaborated with Manet and whose work influenced that of the Symbolists, eloquently expresses many of the assumptions and contradictions evident in nineteenth- and early twentieth-century art. In his 1863 essay "The Painter of Modern Life," Baudelaire argues that beauty and art are comprised of both the "eternal" and

the "modern," the latter of which he associates with the ephemeral. He maintains that the changing aspects of any given period are those elements that define an age and that point to man's shifting tastes in his quest for an ideal.

Sections of Baudelaire's essay devoted to women contain contrary and class-based images. The poet describes women as "the shimmer of all graces of nature, condensed into one being,"[1] but notes that "their beauty [is] enhanced by every kind of artifice, regardless of what social class they belong to."[2] In a description of women in amusement halls, he details a "shady type of beauty" who "either displays an alluring and barbaric form of elegance of her own invention, or she apes, more or less successfully, the simplicity current in higher circles. . . . She is a perfect image of savagery in the midst of civilization. . . . Her eyes are cast towards the horizon, like a beast of prey."[3]

Baudelaire's essay also contains sections that both celebrate and denigrate people of other races. In his appreciation of fashion and women's makeup, for example, he lauds the dress and adornment of "savages" as a "symptom of the taste for the ideal."[4] In his report on the French military presence in Turkey, he praises a picture of a Turkish general that captures "the noble aristocratic air that usually belongs to the master races."[5] However, in a discussion of Turkish prostitution in which he notes the oppression inherent in the institution, he refers to the Armenian, Greek, Hungarian, Jewish, Polish, and Wallachian prostitutes as "women of easy virtue (if one can speak in such terms, where the Levant is concerned)."[6] Baudelaire offers the following definition of a modern artist:

His gaze steady . . . exactly the same gaze he directed just now at the things about him . . . {the artist works quickly}, as though he was afraid the images might escape him. . . . All the materials, stored higgledy-piggledy by memory, are classified, ordered, harmonized, and undergo that deliberate idealization, which is the product of a childlike perceptiveness.[7]

For Baudelaire, the modern painter operates as a dandy, a man of privilege who has the power and resources to explore the wealth of his surroundings, and who anonymously observes and retains all the details of the world around him in an attempt to distill the eternal from the transitory. Although the poet argues that the modern painter captures the ultimate "truth" of experience, his description of that process points to the fact that the representation is formed *by* the artist and not merely impressed *upon* him. The "truth" that any creator expresses is no final determination, but an impression shaped by beliefs that materially or psychically uphold it.

For the privileged members of the upper-middle and upper classes who possess the resources to enjoy free time, "leisure, nature, beauty, femininity, and culture are loosely grouped together, in opposition to labor."[8] The subject matter and the techniques employed by Manet and the Impressionists[9] demonstrate their varied relationships to this bourgeois belief. Unlike officially sanctioned mid-nineteenth-century paintings, which regularly feature themes from myth or history, travels to exotic countries, and moralizing or allegorical genre scenes, Impressionist pictures contain *contemporary* scenes from urban, suburban, and occasionally rural life, which sometimes represent people at work but predominantly show them at leisure.[10]

Although the Impressionists had individual styles of painting that changed over the course of their careers, they are recognized for having captured episodes from contemporary French life through sketchlike brushstrokes, bright color, and unusual, often cropped vantage points, which evoke a scene caught at a rapid glance. Their paintings appeared to contemporary audiences to have constituted quick impressions rather than finished, laboriously constructed products.[11] The physical fragmentation in the construction of Impressionist pictures, which initially troubled viewers and which is perhaps most associated with the work of Claude Monet, came to signify for spectators effortless, inspired

genius, valued for its supposed access to natural, instinctive perception, and its denial of "mere 'work.'"[12]

Edgar Degas's *Dancers in Green and Yellow* (ca. 1903, plate 10) represents female urban entertainers at work. In this image, four ballet dancers are shown waiting in the wings. Today, ballet is a form of entertainment associated with the upper class, but in Degas's time it was largely an activity performed by lower-middle-class women for a middle- and upper-class audience. However, although most dancers had solid financial means, they were popularly thought to come from low parentage.[13] The dancers shown in this picture exhibit great physicality: they lean and crouch, with their bare arms and legs forcefully bending and thrusting into space. Degas's brilliant color and rich texture create an air of refinement and dazzle that is strangely at odds with the awkward, almost bestial treatment of the dancers' faces and bodies. These working women, whose job it is to provide a form of leisure for their audience, wear the magic garments characteristic of the ballet, but do not possess the ethereal deportment one expects of ballerinas. Indeed, their "rat"-like faces[14] and hunched, attentive positions liken these performers to animals. Although their bodies are freed by their costumes— unlike the restrictive everyday clothing they would normally wear—their outfits' low necklines, strapless bodices, and short skirts offer up their abundant flesh to male delectation. After performances, the theater wings (in which Degas stationed his dancers) were often filled with *abonnés*, bourgeois men with season tickets to the Opéra who admired dancers and who regularly pursued sexual liaisons with them.[15]

Pierre Auguste Renoir's *Woman with Parrot* (1871, plate 11) and Manet's *Woman in Evening Dress* (1877–80, plate 12) depict women of higher rank at leisure. In Renoir's picture, the artist represents his mistress wearing a pretty dress, standing in an elegant middle-class interior, and holding a parrot, a common pet at the time.[16] Although parrots have been associated with sexuality,[17] the reference here is discrete;

Plate 10. Edgar Degas, *Dancers in Green and Yellow*
(*Danseuses vertes et jaunes*), ca. 1903. Pastel on several pieces
of paper, mounted on board, 98.8 x 71.5 cm (38 ⅞ x
28 ⅛ inches). Solomon R. Guggenheim Museum,
Thannhauser Collection, Gift, Justin K. Thannhauser
78.2514 T12.

Left: Plate 11. Pierre Auguste Renoir, *Woman with Parrot*
(*La Femme à la perruche*), 1871. Oil on canvas, 92.1 x 65.1 cm
(36 ¼ x 25 ⅝ inches). Solomon R. Guggenheim Museum,
Thannhauser Collection, Gift, Justin K. Thannhauser
78.2514 T68.

Above: Plate 12. Edouard Manet, *Woman in Evening Dress*
(*Femme en robe de soirée*), 1877–80. Oil on canvas, 174.3 x
83.5 cm (68 ⅛ x 32 ⅞ inches). Solomon R. Guggenheim
Museum, Thannhauser Collection, Gift, Justin K.
Thannhauser 78.2514 T28.

feathery, richly textured brushwork adds to the painting's air of having captured a lovely young bourgeois woman passing some free time playing with her feathered companion.

However, the picture's emphasis on somber hues, the woman's ambivalent expression, and the somewhat claustrophobic space she occupies indicate that this work is not merely a glimpse at a frivolous pastime. The dark houseplants in the background and the spiky greens beneath the birdcage seem to close in on the artist's model, restricting her space like that of her bird. That the woman can be read as a caged bird is further suggested by her ruffled dress with its red "plumes" of ribbon, and by her contained, slightly bored or sorrowful inward regard.

Unlike Renoir's work, Manet's *Woman in Evening Dress* situates a female model within a warmly lit exterior environment. In this painting, the brushwork is much sketchier and evokes a shimmering play of sunlight on the woman's dress and through the trellis behind her. The juxtaposition of the model with a basket of flowers and her placement before a cluster of flowering vines metaphorically suggest her embodiment of "the flower of youth." Indeed, Manet's dispersal of sketchy strokes across the surface of the canvas serves to embed the woman partially within the garden around her, thus suggesting her conflation with "nature." Such an association has a long life within the history of representation, surviving in condensed and powerful form in the mythic Mother Earth.

Like Renoir's painting, however, *Woman in Evening Dress* contains elements that frustrate reading the picture as an instance of the purely pleasurable. The woman in Manet's painting is also situated in a claustrophobic space. The work contains little indication of depth; the model is placed almost immediately in the foreground, with space barely receding behind her. Her expression is equally flattened, and her pose is awkward: she holds her arms to her sides and slightly in front of her body, almost as if she were a doll with stiff limbs. The prominent black-and-white stripes on her elaborate dress firmly encase her upper body, conveying a sense of restraint. Therefore, although the painting equates the female body with nature, it also undermines the woman's naturalness. Indeed, in this painting, the "outdoor" space the woman inhabits is a man-made, domestic garden.

The contradictory messages conveyed in these three paintings point to very real contradictions in the lives of nineteenth-century French women. Proper ladies such as those represented in Renoir's and Manet's pictures were meant to embody the freedom, beauty, and grace associated with nature; however, their lived experience was completely manufactured. Their "womanly" curves were artificially and painfully enhanced through corsets and bustles, although physical features considered overly erotic were hidden: their legs were covered, and their hair was pinned up. Unlike men, they were unable to freely roam through Paris or its environs: they had to be chaperoned, and certainly did not venture into sexually charged spaces such as seedy cafés or brothels.[18] The only forms of physical work that bourgeois women engaged in were light domestic chores; they functioned in highly restricted spaces as decorative companions, household managers, and child producers for their bourgeois male counterparts.

Extreme physical labor fell to women of lower classes. Their work in the entertainment industry—as prostitutes, dancers, singers, waitresses, or barmaids—or labor in service professions—as seamstresses, milliners, laundresses, servants, or artists' models—enabled them to occupy a wider range of environments than bourgeois women. However, these spaces were often those in which men of privilege sought to possess them sexually. Since lower-class women were thought to be more sexual "creatures" than women from higher stations, representations of their bodies contain signs of eroticization while at the same time denigrating them for their lower status. Unlike their bourgeois female counterparts, who were supposed to embody nature's beauty and purity,

Plate 13. Henri de Toulouse-Lautrec, *Au salon*, 1893.
Pastel, gouache, and pencil on cardboard, 53 x 79.7 cm
(20 ⅞ x 31 ⅜ inches). Solomon R. Guggenheim Museum,
Thannhauser Collection, Gift, Justin K. Thannhauser
78.2514 T73.

lower-class women were seen to represent the "baser" side of nature—earthy, animal sexuality.

The Impressionists' relationship to nature—or man-made versions of it—is transformed in crucial ways in Post-Impressionist works.[19] Although they produced many scenes of leisure, Henri de Toulouse-Lautrec and Georges Seurat virtually banished the natural from their work, whereas the physical nuances and emotionally stirring aspects of landscape were important components of Paul Cézanne's, Vincent van Gogh's, and to a lesser extent, Gauguin's art. Like van Gogh, Gauguin fled his bourgeois urban lifestyle to the "country," first painting in Brittany, with its plethora of tourists seeking a "timeless" rural environment,[20] and finally to foreign lands, where he hoped to lead a harmonious "native" existence. Each of these artists had been associated with and informed by Impressionism prior to establishing his own style of painting.[21] The Impressionists' conception of nature as a field of enjoyment and personalized vision initially made their work attractive as "an ideal domain of freedom" for Post-Impressionist artists.[22] The Post-Impressionists, however, came to find the work of their Impressionist peers too focused on perceived sensations of outer phenomena. Despite the diversity of Post-Impressionist painterly concerns, the artists were each committed to picturing their experiences of the external world as "'essences' grasped in a tense intuition."[23]

A kind of visual condensation accompanies this emphasis on essences. Unlike the Impressionist sense of the momentary, evoked through slashing brushstrokes and the cropping of images, the Post-Impressionists constructed their canvases through points, patches, swaths, or flat areas of color meant to fix the visual array and its "inner" structure. This inner structure, although organized by the artist, was thought to represent either laws of perception or of the spirit. As with the work of the Impressionists, however, that of the Post-Impressionists does not transcend time and history, a

condition readily apparent in the artists' treatment of urban and rural work and leisure.

Toulouse-Lautrec focused on scenes from city life, and was especially drawn to its seedier aspects. His *Au salon* (1893, plate 13) represents a few prostitutes in their quarters. Like Degas, whose work he greatly admired, Toulouse-Lautrec depicts nonidealized figures, defining their forms and the space they occupy through rich, glowing colors and sinuous, flattened shapes informed by Japanese prints, contemporary posters, and the work of his peers Louis Anquetin, Émile Bernard, and van Gogh. As with Degas's *Dancers in Green and Yellow,* the female workers in Toulouse-Lautrec's pastel are waiting to provide leisure entertainment, and the lounging prostitute's arching, abandoned stretch evokes the highly physical and sexual nature of her work. This gesture, in conjunction with the woman's slightly feline face, suggests that the artist equates her with a cat. The stretch also points to the woman's fatigue and boredom, which are more evident in the prostitute in profile: her heavy-lidded and dark-circled eyes stare vacantly into space.

Although the stretching body of the far prostitute seems to open up to the viewer, the two prostitutes seated in the foreground are turned away from full view; indeed, the red-haired woman is seen only from behind. Unlike Degas's dancers, the women's bodies are closed off from delectation, and the difficulties of their labor are revealed in their tired, bored demeanors. However, as with Degas's performers, the messages conveyed about the women are contradictory: their bodies are sexual objects, but they are not inviting and luscious. They are awkward, somewhat self-contained, and in both pictures have bestial qualities.

Like Toulouse-Lautrec, Seurat consistently painted scenes from urban life. In his well-known *Three Models* (1886–88, in the Barnes Collection, Merion, Pennsylvania, fig. 73) he depicts three female models in varying stages of undress in front of a section of his painting *A Sunday on La Grande Jatte—1884* (1884–86, in the collection of the

Plate 14. Georges Seurat, *Farm Women at Work*
(*Paysannes au travail*), 1882–83. Oil on canvas, 38.5 x 46.2 cm
(15 ⅛ x 18 ¼ inches). Solomon R. Guggenheim Museum,
Gift, Solomon R. Guggenheim 41.713.

I heard Rodin had a beautiful head at the Salon.
I have been to the seaside for a week and very likely am going thither again soon. — Flat shore sands — fine figures there like Cimabue — straight stylish. Am working at a Sower:

the great field all violet the sky & sun very yellow. It is a hard subject to treat. Please remember me very kindly to Mrs Russell — and in thought I heartily shake hands.
Yours very truly
Vincent

My dear ~~Russell~~ for ever so long I have been wanting to write to you — but then the work has so taken me up. We have harvest time here at present and I am always in the fields.
And when I sit down to write I am so abstracted by recollections of what I have seen that I leave the letter. For instance at the present occasion I was writing to you and going to say something about Arles as it is — and as it was in the old days of Boccaccio. —
Well instead of continuing the letter I began to draw on the very paper the head of a dirty little girl I saw this afternoon whilst I was painting a view of the river with a greenish yellow sky.
This dirty 'mudlark' I thought yet had a vague florentine sort of figure like the heads in the 'Monticelli' pictures. and reasoning and drawing this wise I worked on the letter

I was writing to you & I enclose the slip of scribbling. that you may judge of my abstractions and forgive my not writing before as such.
Do not however imagine I am painting old florentine scenery — no I may dream of such — but I spend my time in painting and drawing landscapes or rather studies of colour.
The actual inhabitants of this country often remind me of the figures we see in Zola's work.
And Manet would like them as they are and the city as it is.
Bernard is still in Brittany and I believe he is working hard and doing well.
Gauguin is in Brittany too but has again suffered of an attack of his liver complaint. I wished I were in the same place with him or he here with me.
My brother has an exhibition of 10 new pictures by Claude Monet — his latest works. for instance a landscape with red sun set and a group of dark fir trees by the sea side

The red sun casts an orange or blood red reflection on the blue green trees and the ground. I wished I could see them.
How is your house in Brittany getting on — and have you been working in the country.
I believe my brother has also another picture by Gauguin which is as I heard say very fine two negro women talking. it is one of those he did at martinique.
Mc Knight told me he had seen at Marseilles a picture by monticelli a flowerpiece.
Very soon I intend sending over some studies to Paris and then you can, if you like, choose one for our exchange.
I must hurry off this letter for I feel some more abstractions coming on and if I did not quickly fill up my paper I would again set to drawing and you would not have your letter.

Plate 15. Vincent van Gogh, *Letter to John Peter Russell*, late June 1888. Ink on wove paper, 20.3 x 26 cm (8 x 10 ⅛ inches). Solomon R. Guggenheim Museum, Thannhauser Collection, Gift, Justin K. Thannhauser 78.2514 T189.

Art Institute of Chicago, fig. 72). Both works are Pointillist, executed through the application of contrasting dots of color. These dabs were meant to fuse in the eye of the viewer rather than on the canvas, thereby eliciting purportedly purer, more vibrant color, supposedly truer to the experience of things seen. Although not a mechanical process, Pointillism's laborious and repetitive elements recall mechanized work, a phenomenon that increasingly informed modern life. The figures in Seurat's paintings possess a mechanical aspect as well; although pronounced curves structure the women's bodies, their forms appear stiff and partially flattened, as in some of the popular, mass-produced posters Seurat admired.[24] The three models do not interact with one another—a circumstance that injects a feeling of alienation into the picture—and only the woman in the middle looks out, somewhat awkwardly meeting the viewer's gaze. The other models appear either bored or inattentive; the bow of their shoulders suggests fatigue, and like Seurat's tiny dots, points to the actual work involved in creating a painting, and perhaps specifically the labor that went into the construction of leisure pictured in *A Sunday on La Grande Jatte—1884.* The models' nakedness, marked with these signs of labor, thwarts overt eroticization of their bodies, although Seurat's decision to represent the unclothed female—these women were among many lower-class women paid to disrobe for artists' study—is a longstanding convention in European painting.

Seurat's *Farm Women at Work* (1882–83, plate 14), created before the artist devised his Pointillist technique, represents rural women. Instead of dots, the artist has produced a visual fabric of tight dashes of color, abbreviated marks that have a greater affinity with the sketchy, but more open, Impressionist brushstroke. Unlike the laborers in *Three Models*, who appear somewhat divorced from one another and their environment, the women working in Seurat's earlier picture partially fuse with the crop they tend. Bent close over the earth, with their arms virtually absorbed by vegetation, their bodies seem to meld smoothly with their surroundings. However, the abrupt treatment of the peasants' bodies and the almost agitated character of the brushstrokes in the painting suggest that the women are not installed within a "natural," harmonious order. The peasants' forms are virtually undifferentiated, as if they were variations of the same robot, and the deep bend of their bodies indicates that their labor—planting or gleaning—is backbreaking. The difficult, rote, and depersonalized nature of their work has a visual parallel in the almost crabbed, prickly dashes of color that structure the painting.

The sense of alienation and tiring, physical labor in Toulouse-Lautrec's and Seurat's pictures is missing from many of van Gogh's images of rural laborers. Although he was acutely aware of and portrayed suffering among the lower classes—as a young man he lived with impoverished workers, proselytizing Belgian miners to Christianity—he also romanticized peasants, and believed that his representations of some of them had spiritual qualities.[25] Van Gogh was also deeply moved by Japanese art, which, like most of his Impressionist and Post-Impressionist contemporaries, he appreciated and collected in the form of woodblock prints.[26] His ideas about the Japanese reveal the extent to which he romanticized much that was foreign to him and how much he longed for access to an unmediated experience of nature:

If we study Japanese art, we see a man who is undoubtedly wise, philosophic and intelligent, who spends his time . . . studying . . . a single blade of grass. But this blade of grass leads him to draw every plant and then the seasons, the wide aspects of the countryside, then animals, then the human figure. . . . Come now, isn't it almost a true religion which these simple Japanese teach us, who live in nature as though they themselves were flowers?[27]

In 1888, the year he wrote these lines to his brother, Theo, van Gogh left Paris for Arles, where he believed that he would have a "Japanese" experience of

Plate 16. Vincent van Gogh, *Head of a Girl,* late June 1888. Ink on wove paper, 18 x 19.5 cm (7⅛ x 7¹¹⁄₁₆ inches). Solomon R. Guggenheim Museum, Thannhauser Collection, Gift, Justin K. Thannhauser 78.2514 T20.

nature. Working directly from his surroundings, van Gogh transformed his sitters, the interiors he inhabited, and the countryside into thick, swirling masses of brilliant color, or into expressive dabs and dashes of ink. The intense physical quality of the artist's style was meant to communicate his passions and those of humanity, and palpably suggests the presence of the artist's hand and heart. Van Gogh's powerful stroke has been and is still read as a material sign of the artist's suffering, his pantheistic union with nature, and his "genius."

An illustrated letter from van Gogh to his artist friend John Peter Russell (1888, plate 15) features two pictures of people from the countryside: a man sowing and a portrait of a little girl. Van Gogh ends his letter with the drawing of a sower, a figure that interested him greatly and which he based on the work of his predecessor Jean-François Millet.[28] In this hurriedly executed, small drawing, a male peasant stands erect in the field, his arm thrown far to the side to fling seed over the earth. With a large sun blazing behind him, and with his bowed legs firmly planted in the ground, the anonymous peasant appears to function as the embodiment of growth and regeneration. Indeed, the potential fecundity of the earth appears linked to this figure: the active, slightly curved lines that structure the ground all converge onto his form.

The detailed drawing of a child (plate 16) that van Gogh included with the letter suggests that the artist had a more complicated relationship to the lower classes, which he admired and romanticized. The artist's scratchy, hatched strokes of ink seem to capture the specific mien of an unattractive, disheveled child with matted hair, wide-set eyes, and pug nose, who is incongruously attired in an exotic costume. In his letter, van Gogh identifies the little girl as a "dirty 'mudlark,'" with a "vague florentine sort of figure" like those in paintings by the artist Monticelli. This strange mixture of romanticism and disdain, whereby the child is associated with both picturesque figures and a grubby

animal, not only reinforces the artist's fascination with the exotic, but also points to a class-based contempt.[29] Van Gogh's drawing of the child reveals the extent to which the artist's relationship to the countryside and its inhabitants was not "natural," but was conditioned by cultural biases such as those that inform his writing on the Japanese.

Van Gogh was keenly interested in the ideas of Bernard and Gauguin, artists who formed a working relationship in 1888 at an artists' colony in Pont-Aven and with whom van Gogh corresponded. That same year Gauguin spent two months painting with van Gogh in Arles, where he convinced the Dutch painter to try working from memory rather than from life. Like Bernard and the Symbolist poets and critics whom he befriended, Gauguin privileged the imagination over natural phenomena, arguing that his "synthetist" use of color and shape captured the physical and emotional sensations associated with an object. Like van Gogh, Gauguin sought access to a simple, utopian existence by drawing on the art of foreign cultures and by living in communities that he considered "primitive."

Gauguin's *In the Vanilla Grove, Man and Horse* (1891, plate 17) was painted the year the artist first went to Tahiti and depicts a man with his horse standing in front of a bank of vegetation within which two women appear to be tending vanilla plants. The shapes of the females barely emerge from the growth that surrounds them; indeed, the body of the woman carrying a basket at the upper right is at first barely discernible. Though ostensibly laboring, the females seem to hover weightlessly amidst the rich green foliage, coalescing with it as if they were actual extensions of the plants. By contrast, the solid figure of the male, whose firm body possesses the same strength and graceful bearing of the horse, is a pronounced presence. Sensual curves define his trim form, and his flesh has a warm, rich luster. The pairing of the women with the plants and of the man with the horse suggests that Gauguin identified the Tahitian women with nature and its fecundity,

Above: Fig. 74. Detail of the West Frieze of the Parthenon. Reproduced in C. Yriarte, *Les Frises du Parthénon*, Paris, 1868.

Top left: Plate 17. Paul Gauguin, *In the Vanilla Grove, Man and Horse* (*Dans la vanillère, homme et cheval*), 1891. Oil on burlap, 73 x 92 cm (28 ¾ x 36 ¼ inches). Solomon R. Guggenheim Museum, Thannhauser Collection, Gift, Justin K. Thannhauser 78.2514 T15.

Bottom left: Plate 18. Paul Gauguin, *Haere Mai*, 1891. Oil on burlap, 72.4 x 91.4 cm (28 ½ x 36 inches). Solomon R. Guggenheim Museum, Thannhauser Collection, Gift, Justin K. Thannhauser 78.2514 T16.

Plate 19. Pablo Picasso, *Le Moulin de la Galette*, autumn
1900. Oil on canvas, 88.2 x 115.5 cm (34 ¼ x 45 ½ inches).
Solomon R. Guggenheim Museum, Thannhauser
Collection, Gift, Justin K. Thannhauser 78.2514 T34.

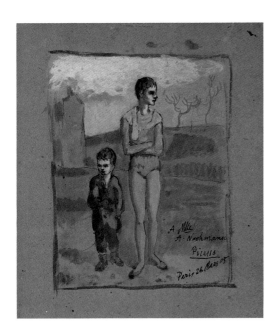

Plate 20. Pablo Picasso, *Young Acrobat and Child*
(*Jeune acrobate et enfant*), March 26, 1905. Ink and gouache
on gray cardboard, 31.3 x 25.1 cm (12 ⁵/₁₆ x 9 ⁷/₈ inches).
Solomon R. Guggenheim Museum, Thannhauser
Collection, Gift, Justin K. Thannhauser 78.2514 T42.

and the Tahitian man with a noble,
sexual animality. Indeed, Gauguin based
the man and horse pair on a section of
the West Frieze of the Parthenon
(fig. 74),[30] which indicates that he may
have perceived the Tahitian "native" not
only as earthy and sensual, but also as a
kind of timeless, heroic essence.

The artist's use of vibrant,
heightened color and broad flattened
forms conveys an air of tropical, lush
simplicity. However, Gauguin's
luxurious treatment of a male body
inserts a subtly disruptive element into
the work. Erotic representations of the
female body are rather standard fare in
Modern painting and in Gauguin's
Polynesian works; however, sexual
portrayals of the male body are less
common. Sexual stereotypes about
people of color were very much a part of
nineteenth-century consciousness, and
European settlers in the South Seas
perceived the inhabitants as possessing a
freer sexuality than their own. Gauguin
shared this perception, and while abroad
sought a utopian existence, which
included a sex life devoid of bourgeois
conventions. However, such a fiction of
eroticized, "primitive" harmony in no
way mirrors Gauguin's existence among
people that had actually destroyed their
own indigenous cultures. Gauguin did
not truly learn the language of the
Polynesians; was unable to live off the
land, requiring support from the
families of his teenage mistresses; and
concocted Polynesian myths for his art
and writing largely based on ill-
informed European texts rather than on
information he insisted came from his
"native" community.[31]

Pablo Picasso, perhaps the most
celebrated artist of the twentieth-
century, spent the beginning of
his career working through a variety
of styles indebted to those of his older
peers while painting contemporary
scenes of urban life. For example, his
Le Moulin de la Galette (1900, plate 19) is
influenced by Toulouse-Lautrec's boldly
patterned treatment of café scenes.[32]
However, the slightly feathery blur of
Picasso's forms has a greater affinity
with a brushy Impressionist stroke. The
pronounced contrast of colors and

shapes lends the painting an air of
mystery and excitement, underscoring
the slightly risqué character of the
events represented. The picture features
a plethora of brightly attired, made-up
women, whose dark eyes and brilliant
red lips seem to beckon the viewer and
the bourgeois men in top hats at left.
The eroticism in this scene of leisure is
reinforced by the ambiguous, seductive
exchange by the seated female couple,
and by the inviting smile of their
companion. Although this work depicts
a lively, exciting glimpse of nightlife, it
possesses an ominous, almost
dehumanizing, quality. The men in the
scene are virtually anonymous, although
the man second from the left has a
slightly feral face: the edges of his hat
curve upward like pointed ears, and his
long nose resembles a wolf's snout. His
bestial aspect—neither slothful as with
the females in Degas's, Toulouse-
Lautrec's, or van Gogh's work, nor noble
as with the "savage" in Gauguin's
painting—suggests a hungry, predatory
nature. The women in Picasso's work
are more clearly defined, but each seems
to be a variation on the same angular,
witchlike mannequin. This scene of
male and female pleasure evokes the
energy and titillation of a café at night,
but the interchangeability and
threatening demeanor of the figures
suggests that the encounters
experienced at the night spot may be
both superficial and dangerous.

In his *Woman Ironing* (1904, plate 21),
painted four years later, Picasso moves
from the evocation of a particular
environment of leisure to the
representation of a timeless act of
debilitating labor. Although the people
in the former painting are as anonymous
as the figure in this picture from
Picasso's Blue Period, the ironing
woman is removed from a specific place
and moment. The overall blue cast to
the image pervades the scene with
suffering, pain, and despair—emotions
further emphasized by the woman's
emaciated, bent form and vacant eyes.
Relying as the Post-Impressionists had
on color and form to trigger feeling,
Picasso uses the work-worn female body
to generalize human tragedy. His
preoccupation with the universal, rather

Plate 21. Pablo Picasso, *Woman Ironing (La Repasseuse),*
1904. Oil on canvas, 116.2 x 73 cm (45 ¾ x 28 ¾ inches).
Solomon R. Guggenheim Museum, Thannhauser
Collection, Gift, Justin K. Thannhauser 78.2514 T41.

than specific human events and emotions, is manifest in his use of stock commedia dell'arte or circus figures in much of his Blue and Rose work, characters that function as types, or who are meant to represent "everyman" (see, for example, his *Young Acrobat and Child*, 1905, plate 20). Although Picasso was impoverished as a very young artist and witnessed firsthand the plight of the urban poor, he chose to figure hardship in his early work through sentimental, pictorial signs of the eternal, rather than to describe the particulars of the penury he saw and experienced.

This appeal to the "eternal" recalls one aspect of Baudelaire's description of the modern artist's project: the need to capture a timeless truth. This quest— in various manifestations—informs much of twentieth-century art, notably that of several European artists active in the 1910s, including visionary abstract artists Vasily Kandinsky, Kazimir Malevich, and Piet Mondrian, who imbued their work with spiritual meanings. Abstraction reached a kind of apotheosis in the 1940s through 1960s with New York Abstract Expressionism and Color-field painting, both of which were celebrated by influential critic Clement Greenberg, whose analyses of the purely structural and visual relationship of forms to their material supports elevated painting to a lofty sphere uncontaminated by worldly concerns. Although Greenberg's type of formalist criticism retains some currency today, it is widely challenged by writers who analyze the imbrication of form *and* content (whether the work is representational or abstract), and who argue that all types of representation express the creator's relationship to social and psychic experience.

Notes

1. Charles Baudelaire, "The Painter of Modern Life," in *Baudelaire: Selected Writings on Art and Artists*, trans. and with an introduction by P. E. Chavet (Cambridge: Cambridge University Press, 1972), p. 423.

2. Ibid., p. 428.

3. Ibid., p. 430.

4. Ibid., p. 426.

5. Ibid., p. 411.

6. Ibid., p. 414.

7. Ibid., p. 402.

8. Robert L. Herbert, *Impressionism: Art, Leisure, and Parisian Society* (New Haven: Yale University Press, 1988), p. 305.

9. Although Manet was close to a number of the Impressionists and worked with some of them, he did not join their group or exhibit with them.

10. The Impressionists were by no means the only nineteenth-century artists to paint scenes from daily life, but their work is notable for its emphasis on then contemporary forms of entertainment. In nineteenth-century France, leisure was in the process of developing into the full-blown industry that it is today. Shortly after Napoléon III declared himself emperor in 1851, the vast reconstruction of Paris began under the supervision of Baron Haussmann. An immense network of grand boulevards was constructed to house theaters, cafés, and department stores, sites where the city's diverse population mingled, and where those with money could enjoy an array of pleasures. Paris also became a central terminus for the expanding railways, which brought peasants seeking employment from the countryside to the city, and which discharged city dwellers into the rapidly developing suburbs or into rural areas to enjoy a "country" outing or vacation. Although Paris was ravaged by the Franco-Prussian War and by civil war in 1871, the city and its environs began to flourish once again during the Third Republic. Indeed, from the mid-nineteenth through the early twentieth century, Paris was the cultural and entertainment capital of Europe.

11. Albert Boime and Richard Shiff have both discussed sketchlike technique in nineteenth-century painting. Boime argues that an "aesthetics of the sketch" arose in nineteenth-century painting whereby a loosely painted landscape *étude* (study) was seen to convey a sense of originality and spontaneity. He traces this development in academic and independent painting (see Albert Boime, *The Academy and French Painting in the Nineteenth Century* [London: Phaidon, 1971], pp. 166–81). In his

conclusion, Boime argues: "By showing that the change took place under the aegis of Academic doctrine, this study has endeavoured to construct a picture of the totality of French painting during the nineteenth century. Instead of considering this period as the scene of a heroic struggle of progressives against Academics, it shows the positive, if unintended, contribution of the Academy to the evolution of independent tendencies."

Shiff observes that the *étude* demonstrated the "effect" of chiaroscuro (contrasts of dark and light), and notes Boime's statement that in the nineteenth century "effect" went from signifying "artificial contrivance" to "natural perception" (Boime, p. 169). Shiff proceeds to ask the following: "Is impressionist painting, then, as an art of the effect, to be considered genuinely original, rather than merely suggestive of originality? . . . Does it employ the device of the *étude* as a *convention*, to relate a sense of originality and spontaneity to the viewer?" (Shiff, *Cézanne and the End of Impressionism: A Study of the Theory, Technique, and Critical Evaluation of Modern Art* [Chicago: The University of Chicago Press, 1984], p. 77).

12. Herbert, p. 304.

13. Eunice Lipton, *Looking into Degas: Uneasy Images of Women and Modern Life* (Berkeley: University of California Press, 1986), pp. 88–91. Lipton argues (p. 91) that the following factors account for the stereotype of the impoverished dancer: "Two prejudices, I believe, produced this commentary. The sexualization of their profession resulted from their being women on display; the emphasis on poverty and low parentage derived from the notion of the dancer as an artist. At first this might seem contradictory, for an emphasis on her sexuality and frivolity would seem to preclude a view of the dancer as an artist. Yet the image of poverty and mysterious or low parentage, or even the illusion that the dancer did not really work, dovetailed with contemporary attitudes about artists—their charm and ease, but particularly their conquering of harsh material odds."

14. In French, "rat" designates both the rodent and a young female dance pupil at the Opéra (see J. E. Mansion, *Harrap's Modern College French and English Dictionary*, revised by M. Ferlin and P. Forbes, ed. by D. M. Ledésert and R. P. L. Ledésert [New York: Charles Scribners' Sons, 1972], R: 8).
Degas's contemporaries noted his dancers' bestial qualities. One critic made the following remarks about the artist's *Little Fourteen-Year-Old Dancer* (ca. 1881): "I do not always ask that art be graceful, but I do not believe that its role is to represent only ugliness. Your opera rat takes after a monkey, an Aztec, a puny specimen—if she were smaller, one would be tempted to enclose her in a glass jar of alcohol" (Elie de Mont, *La Civilisation*, April 21, 1881, quoted in *The New Painting: Impressionism*

1874–1886, directed and coordinated by Charles S. Moffet, exh. cat. [San Francisco: The Fine Arts Museums of San Francisco; Washington, D.C.: National Gallery of Art, 1986], p. 361). Another writer had the following to say about the same work: "Formidable because she is thoughtless, with bestial effrontery she moves her face forward, or rather her little muzzle—and this word is completely correct because this poor little girl is the beginning of a rat" (Paul Mantz, *Le Temps*, April 23, 1881, quoted in *The New Painting*).

15. Lipton, pp. 76–84.

16. Vivian Endicott Barnett, *The Guggenheim Museum: Justin K. Thannhauser Collection* (New York: The Solomon R. Guggenheim Foundation, 1978), p. 186.

17. Mona Hadler, "Manet's Woman with a Parrot of 1866," *The Metropolitan Museum of Art Journal* 7, 1973, pp. 115–22.

18. Griselda Pollock, *Vision and Difference: Femininity, feminism and histories of art* (London: Routledge, 1988), pp. 56, 62.

19. The term Post-Impressionist was coined by the English art critic Roger Fry for a 1910–11 exhibition that included the work of Manet, Cézanne, Gauguin, Vincent van Gogh, Georges Seurat, Maurice Denis, Henri Matisse, and Picasso. Fry defined the Post-Impressionists as those artists who emphasized individual artistic expression over "accurate" representation. He believed that willed "unnaturalistic" manipulation of forms conveys "the originality of truly personal experience" (Shiff, pp. 155–57). The term Post-Impressionist is used to refer to a wide range of artists active in the late-nineteenth and early twentieth centuries.

20. See Fred Orton and Griselda Pollock, "Les donées bretonnes: la prairie de répresentation," *Art History* 3, no. 3 (September 1980), pp. 314–44.

21. Cézanne met Camille Pissarro at the Académie Suisse in 1861, and occasionally participated in the meetings of the Batignolles group, which formed around 1866 and included Degas, Manet, Claude Monet, and Renoir. Cézanne also showed with the Impressionists and intermittently painted with Pissarro in Pontoise in 1872–73. Cézanne worked with Pissarro again in 1881, and the two were joined that year by Gauguin, who also painted with Pissarro in 1883. Pissarro met Seurat in 1885, and in 1886, the latter's *A Sunday on La Grande Jatte—1884* was shown at the last Impressionist exhibition. That year, van Gogh came to Paris. In the city, he came into direct contact with the work of the Impressionists, and met Pissarro through Gauguin. In 1889, Gauguin and his friends exhibited together as the *Groupe impressioniste et synthétiste* at the Paris Universal

Exposition (see Bernard Denvir, *The Thames and Hudson Encyclopaedia of Impressionism* [London: Thames and Hudson, 1990], entry for "Batignolles," pp. 24–26; John Rewald, *The History of Impressionism*, 4th rev. ed. [New York: The Museum of Modern Art, 1973], chronology, pp. 591–607; and John Rewald, *Post-Impressionism: From van Gogh to Gauguin*, 3rd rev. ed. [New York: The Museum of Modern Art, 1978], chronology, pp. 502–07).

22. Meyer Schapiro, "The Nature of Abstract Art," in *Modern Art, Nineteenth and Twentieth Centuries: Selected Papers* (New York: George Braziller, 1982), p. 192.

23. Ibid., p. 191.

24. Schapiro also relates Seurat's figures to those of Pierre Puvis de Chavannes: "As he [Seurat] transformed the Impressionist sketchiness into a more deliberated method, so he converted the idealized imagery of Puvis into a corresponding modern scene which retained, however, something of the formality of a classic monumental style" ("Seurat" [1958], in *Modern Art, Nineteenth and Twentieth Centuries*, p. 104).

25. Van Gogh discussed his interest in peasants in his correspondence, and after visiting fellow artists Dodge MacKnight and Eugène Boch, he wrote: "The village where they are staying is *real Millet*, pure peasants and nothing else, absolutely *rustic* and homely. . . . The natives are like Zola's poor peasants, innocent and gentle beings, as we know" (LT 514, quoted in Ronald Pickvance, *Van Gogh in Arles*, exh. cat. [New York: The Metropolitan Museum of Art and Harry N. Abrams, 1984], p. 164). In another letter, after commenting about his portraits of a peasant and a poet, van Gogh stated, "In a picture I want to say something comforting, as music is comforting. I want to paint men and women with that something of the eternal which the halo used to symbolize, and which we seek to convey by the actual radiance and vibration of our coloring" (*The Complete Letters of Vincent van Gogh, with reproductions of all the drawings in the correspondence,* vol. 3 [Greenwich, Conn.: New York Graphics Society, 1958; reprinted 1978], p. 25, LT 531).

26. Orton and Pollock discuss nineteenth-century artists' interests in Japanese prints: "In the 1860s Japanese prints had seemed to offer a pictorial equivalent for the chaos of metropolitan Paris at that time; their modernity and strangeness was somehow equatable with a new experience of a new Paris. By the late 1880s they offered something else. They were seen as providing clues as to how a picture's surface could be flattened and integrated and simplified" (Fred Orton and Griselda Pollock, "Cloisonism?" [review], *Art History* 5, no. 3 [September 1982], p. 345).

27. Vincent van Gogh in an undated letter (attributed to ca. September 1888) to his brother, Theo van Gogh, in Herschel B. Chipp, with Peter Selz and Joshua C. Taylor, *Theories of Modern Art: A Source Book by Artists and Critics* (Berkeley: University of California Press, 1968), pp. 38–39. A number of nineteenth-century critics wrote about Japanese art, and like van Gogh, felt that there was something intrinsically different about the Japanese that effected their modes of representation. Commentators repeatedly explained Japanese compositional devices through causal models determined by biological, psychological, or religious conditions, and a number of these models were linked to fields of scientific exploration popular at the time. For example, Paul Dalloz, the director and founder of several newspapers, maintained that Japanese art differed radically from Western art because the Japanese actually saw the world differently. Invoking physiology, Dalloz attributed what he thought to be an intense amount of detail in Japanese works to the structure of Japanese eyes, which he argued functioned like opera glasses (as opposed to European eyes, which he compared to the camera). The collector and critic Theodore Duret favored an explanation of Japanese artistic vision based on geographical difference. He maintained that Japan received light purer and brighter than that of Europe, and that therefore, the Japanese saw fewer shadows and more highly saturated colors. Duret thus stated that while the European artist was concerned with subtle shading, the Japanese artist focused on achieving a balance of strongly contrasting colors (Elisa Evett, "The Late Nineteenth Century European Critical Response to Japanese Art: Primitivist Leanings," *Art History* 6, no. 1 [March 1983], pp. 83–85).

28. Barnett notes that R. L. Herbert believes that van Gogh's 1881 drawing of a sower and his October 1889 painting of a sower are based on an 1873 Paul LeRat engraving of Millet's *Sower* of ca. 1850 (Barnett, p. 73, note 20). Judy Sund argues that van Gogh admired and drew on Millet's work because he found it resonant with his spiritual beliefs (see Judy Sund, "The Sower and the Sheaf: Biblical Metaphor in the Art of Vincent van Gogh," *Art Bulletin* 70, no. 4 [December 1988], pp. 661–76).

29. Jennifer Blessing, catalogue entry in *From van Gogh to Picasso, From Kandinsky to Pollock: Masterpieces of Modern Art* (New York: The Solomon R. Guggenheim Foundation; Milan: Gruppo Editoriale Fabbri, Bompiani, 1990), p. 80.

30. As Barnett indicates (p. 57), this source is identified by Alfred Langer in *Paul Gauguin* (Leipzig: VEB E.A. Seeman Buch-und Kunstverlag, 1963), pp. 53–54, and Theodore Reff, review of Anthony Blunt and Phoebe Pool, *Picasso: The Formative Years*, in *Art Bulletin* 48 (June 1966), p. 266.

31. Abigail Solomon-Godeau, "Going Native," *Art in America* 77, no. 7 (July 1989), pp. 119–29, 161.

32. Barnett, p. 113.

Lisa Dennison

Paris in 1912! What could be more wonderful for a painter? A believer in signs might say that this was surely the mark of a predestined career. The year 1912 is perhaps the most glorious in the history of painting in France. This was the apogee of Cubism, and Cubism is identified with Paris, is Paris itself, the real Paris, Paris without artifice. . . . Yes, 1912 is the most Parisian moment in painting; it is a moment which will never again be recaptured.[1]

These words were written by French critic and art historian Michel Seuphor to describe Piet Mondrian's arrival in Paris from Amsterdam at the very beginning of what would indeed prove to be a landmark year in the history of Modern art.[2] Seuphor suggests that Mondrian's encounter with the art of Georges Braque and Pablo Picasso at this pivotal time crystallized the Dutchman's ambition to create "a pure plastic art" through the discovery of an underlying sense of order and harmony in Analytic Cubism at its most hermetic stage. He argues that out of the chaos of Cubism, Mondrian would begin on the path to pure abstraction: "Henceforward his values would be order, discipline, sobriety . . . recording in clear logic the whole teaching of Cubism at the very moment when the great Cubist painters halted or went backwards."[3]

Although Seuphor oversimplifies Mondrian's move toward abstraction, his recognition of 1912 as a watershed moment, representing both an apogee and a crisis point in the development of Cubism, is accurate. In this year, Cubism achieved full recognition at three major Parisian exhibitions: the *Salon des indépendants*, the *Salon d'octobre*, and most important of all, the artist-organized *Salon de la section d'or*.[4] This last exhibition, consisting of more than 180 works by thirty-two painters, was devoted exclusively to Cubism in all its manifestations and traveled to London, Berlin, Amsterdam, Vienna, Dresden, and Moscow, spreading its influence to a wide international audience. In this same year, several other factors—especially additional exhibitions in Paris (including the first presentation outside of Italy of Futurist painting, held at Galerie Bernheim-Jeune[5]) and other

European centers, the release of several now-historic publications, and the support of Guillaume Apollinaire, who acted as Cubism's public champion—assured the indomitable strength of the movement. Apollinaire proclaimed that "the Cubists, no matter to which faction they belong, appear to all of us who are concerned with the future of art to be the most serious and interesting artists of our time."[6]

Despite the growing recognition and internationalism of Analytic Cubism, its formal possibilities were narrowing rather than expanding, having reached the summit of a development that had begun in the 1890s with the work of Paul Cézanne. By late 1911, Braque and Picasso had each gone as far as possible in their analyses of both objects and space—so far that the fracturing and faceting of their subjects into small rectangular planes threatened to engulf the subject, presaging allover abstraction and undermining their commitment to Cubism as an art of representation.

But it was precisely out of this environment of crisis in 1912 that innovations occurred; from here, the revolution that Cubism had sparked quickly led in new directions that would have vast implications for twentieth-century art. Not the least among these was Picasso's daring incorporation of a piece of oilcloth printed to simulate chair caning into one of his paintings (fig. 78), thus creating the first collage, and Braque's related invention of papier collé a few months later, when he pasted pieces of imitation wood-grain wallpaper onto one of his works on paper (fig. 80). Developing the aesthetic possibilities of collage further, in the realm of three dimensions, Picasso also began his famous construction *Guitar* in 1912, thus challenging the Cubist tendency to flatten depicted space. The definition of planar sculpture was enlarged by Alexander Archipenko, who initiated his multi-media constructions inspired by the Cirque Médrano. At this time, Umberto Boccioni published his *Technical Manifesto of Futurist Sculpture* (*Manifesto tecnico della scultura futurista*), in which he encouraged the combining

Above: Fig. 76. Montmartre, Paris, ca. 1900, with Le Moulin de la Galette on the right. Courtesy Roger-Viollet.

Left: Fig. 75. The Eiffel Tower, 1889. Courtesy Roger-Viollet. ©LL-Viollet.

of unorthodox materials such as "glass, wood, cardboard, iron, cement, horsehair, leather, cloth, mirrors, and electric lights."[7] Robert Delaunay, who had his first solo show in Paris in 1912, commenced a new series of *Window* paintings, in which vibrant color, abandoned by many of his School of Paris contemporaries, played a leading role in determining pictorial construction. And Marcel Duchamp painted his controversial *Nude Descending a Staircase (No. 2)*, which he withdrew from the *Salon des indépendants* after members of the hanging committee objected to its title.[8]

Elaborating on Cubism's vocabulary and enriching its possibilities, various satellite movements, including Futurism, Cubo-Futurism, Orphism, and Rayism, erupted with explosive force during the course of 1912. Although these offshoots continued to bear some superficial resemblance to the Cubist paradigm, their conclusions were vastly different in form, intent, and content. Each of these inventions contained the seeds of further innovation, ultimately laying the groundwork for the purely abstract art that would soon emerge in Russia (Suprematism and Constructivism) and the Netherlands (Neo-Plasticism).

Elsewhere that year, the more expressionistic manifestations of art in Germany and Austria were at an equally radical stage. Drawing on the work of the Symbolists and linking often extreme emotional sentiments with images derived from the visible world, these works were characterized by violent, unnatural colors. In Munich, the second exhibition of the Blue Rider, a group founded by Vasily Kandinsky and Franz Marc, and the publication of *The Blue Rider Almanac* (*Der Blaue Reiter Almanach*) and Kandinsky's *On the Spiritual in Art* (*Über das Geistige in der Kunst*)[9] articulated the search by these artists for a common spiritual basis in the arts. And in Moscow, the Donkey's Tail, a group spearheaded by Natalia Goncharova, Mikhail Larionov, Kazimir Malevich, and Vladimir Tatlin, was hailed as the first important assertion of an independent Russian school.[10]

It is no coincidence that some of the

greatest masterpieces in the holdings of the Solomon R. Guggenheim Foundation date from 1911–13, but especially 1912. In each of the major art centers—Moscow, Munich, and Paris— works created in and around 1912 by Braque, Delaunay, Duchamp, Kandinsky, Fernand Léger, Malevich, Mondrian, and Picasso, among others, provide ample evidence of the richness and complexity of this fertile period.

Imagine the exhilaration that Mondrian must have felt upon settling in the French capital in January 1912, the year that Seuphor described as "an incomparable theater for the exhibition of innovations in a climate which knew no extremes."[11] As Roger Shattuck points out in *The Banquet Years*, a cultural history of the emergence of the avant-garde in France from 1885 to World War I, this climate was in large part fostered by the interchange and dissemination of ideas in the cafés, which in the 1860s and 1870s had been the unofficial headquarters of the Impressionists. By the end of the century, the café ritual became not only a factor in stimulating the creation of art but also a source of its iconography. This atmosphere of communal activity, in which "painters, writers, and musicians lived and worked together and tried their hands at each other's arts in an atmosphere of perpetual collaboration,"[12] carried forward into the prewar years, when the heart of artistic activity moved to Picasso's Montmartre studio in the Bateau-Lavoir.

Although Picasso and Braque were an essential part of this creative esprit de corps, frequenting galleries and museums and mixing with a wide circle of writers, painters, and sculptors, the two shared a particular self-sufficiency that isolated them from the artistic community as a whole. They rarely took part in any of the Salons or other group exhibitions. In fact, until late in 1912 neither had much contact even with the other Cubists, who for the most part lived across the Seine on the Left Bank. There, artists and writers met to formulate and promote their ideas in the Puteaux studio of Jacques Villon on Sunday afternoons, at the Courbevoie studio of Albert Gleizes on Monday evenings, at many cafés, and at the Closerie des Lilas on the Boulevard Montparnasse, which was frequented by many of the most influential younger critics, including Apollinaire and André Salmon. The circle of Frenchmen Gleizes, Henri Le Fauconnier, Léger, Jean Metzinger, and Villon was soon widened to include Roger de La Fresnaye, Marie Laurencin, Francis Picabia, Villon's two brothers, Marcel Duchamp and Raymond Duchamp-Villon, as well as the Ukrainian-born Archipenko, the Spaniard Juan Gris, and the Czech artist František Kupka.

Appropriate to the spreading internationalism of the period, it was Apollinaire—born in Rome to a Swiss-Italian father and Polish-Italian mother—who became the most enthusiastic supporter of the new French art. His "magnetism, his all-embracing enthusiasm, his very ubiquity in prewar Paris made him beyond a doubt the main impresario of the avant-garde,"[13] as well as the most respected poet/critic of his generation. Responsible for introducing Braque and Picasso in 1907, Apollinaire organized the first coherent group presentation of Cubism (the famous "Salle 41" at the 1911 *Salon des indépendants*), established a liaison between the Montmartre and Puteaux Cubists, baptized Delaunay's art as "Orphism," and in turn became its principal advocate.[14]

As a critic for the Paris daily *L'Intransigeant* from 1910 to 1914, Apollinaire reported on the Salons and gallery shows in his column "La Vie artistique" during these formative years of Modern art. In 1912, he became the principal editor of the newly founded magazine *Les Soirées de Paris* and joined a new journal, *Montjoie!*, when it was established the following year. Some of his foremost articles on Cubism appeared in these important periodicals prior to the 1913 publication of his book *The Cubist Painters: Aesthetic Meditations* (*Les Peintres cubistes: Méditations esthétiques*), which, along with Salmon's 1912 *The Young French Painting* (*La Jeune Peinture française*), pressed the notion of the style as a conceptual and intellectual one as opposed to the physical

and sensory basis of Impressionism.

Central to the discourse of the period was Cubism's relation to reality. Both Apollinaire and Salmon agreed that Cubism was an art of *representation* of a new reality, and that change, rather than permanence, was a vital element of this reality. They diverged, however, in that Apollinaire believed that this reality is not drawn from nature but from the transcendental truth that subsists beyond the scope of nature, with complete abstraction as the ultimate goal. Salmon, on the other hand, stressed the dynamic nature of reality, postulating that through intellect the Cubist artists could create a new and better reality that would be able to reflect change and progress in the world.

The belief that change is a vital element of reality was an essential concept of philosopher Henri Bergson, who developed the concept of *la durée* ("the continuous progress of the past which gnaws into the future and which swells as it advances"[15]) to express his notion of the continuous flux of time. He wrote, "The universe *endures*. The more we study the nature of time, the more we shall comprehend that duration means invention, the creation of forms, the continual elaboration of the absolutely new."[16] His ideas became the common property of critics such as Salmon and his avant-garde contemporaries, who found Bergson's approach to a reality in which the past was captured in present experience to be of great significance to the formulation of and a rationale for new pictorial and literary modes. In the words of Apollinaire, "The painter must encompass in one glance the past, the present, the future."[17]

At the meetings of the Puteaux group, conversations centered on the latest ideas in the realms of not only philosophy but of music, literature, politics, psychology, mathematics, and science, and on the analogies between these fields. It should be understood that many artists and critics who were intoxicated by the dynamic concept of the artist's role as creator of a new reality would not come to any common understanding about this reality despite

Top: Fig. 79. Georges Braque in his studio at 5, impasse de Guelma in Paris, ca. early 1912. The Granger Collection, New York.

Bottom: Fig. 80. Georges Braque, *Fruit Dish and Glass* (*Compotier et verre*), early September 1912. Charcoal and pasted paper, 61.9 x 44.5 cm (24 3/8 x 17 1/2 inches). Private collection.

Fig. 81. Vasily Kandinsky, cover for *The Blue Rider Almanac*, 1912. Courtesy Städtische Galerie im Lenbachhaus.

the accelerated exchange of ideas in the fervid intellectual climate of 1912. Rather, the interpretations of new theories were to a great degree superficial, motivated principally by an attempt to establish an a priori basis for an art that they considered intellectual. The paintings of the Cubists were not about changing the world; rather, they were the visualizations of these changes. Ultimately, Cubism is best understood as a formal development founded on empirical process, not theoretical principle.

Yet public controversy generated by Cubism's radicality prompted others in addition to Apollinaire and Salmon to publish a wide range of articles and books to explain and defend the variety of styles within the movement. Many of the artists themselves—Gleizes and Metzinger most saliently in their important volume *Cubism* (*Du cubisme*), published in Paris in December 1912—attempted to provide a theoretical basis for the movement, while the emergence of two other influential types of publications, the aesthetic manifesto in Italy and Russia and the almanac in Germany, also gave credence to the theoretical underpinnings of Modernist tenets. Futurism was initially conceived as a literary concept; the first Futurist manifesto, written by Filippo Tommaso Marinetti, was published in 1909 in the Paris newspaper *Le Figaro*. In 1910, a second manifesto laid the foundations of Futurism's visual expression, and manifestos of sculpture, music, noise, photography, theater, architecture, cinema, and politics proliferated in the next few years.[18] In Moscow in 1912, David Burliuk and his contemporaries issued their own manifesto, in which poets were encouraged to create new words from archaic word forms and fragments. Entitled *A Slap in the Face of Public Taste* (*Poschechina obshchestvennomu vkusu*), the book also included the first important Russian essay on Cubism. *The Blue Rider Almanac*, published in 1912 by Kandinsky, Paul Klee, and Marc only a few months after Kandinsky's treatise *On the Spiritual in Art*, was established as a showcase for the latest art from Paris, Moscow, Berlin, and Milan, as well as a forum for the arts in

different mediums and from different periods and cultures.

The Blue Rider actively brought together artists from Germany, Russia, and France. Delaunay and Henri Rousseau, for example, had been invited by Kandinsky to join the first exhibition of the group, held in December 1911 at the Moderne Galerie Thannhauser in Munich (which had also hosted the September 1910 exhibition of the NKVM [New Artists' Association of Munich], another international gathering organized by Kandinsky). By 1912, Delaunay had been visited in his Paris studio by Klee, August Macke, and Marc. Klee returned to Berlin deeply impressed by what he had seen; his *Flower Bed* (plate 24) of the next year reveals the influence of Cubism and Delaunay in its allover pattern of faceted forms and brilliant coloration. Marc later described Delaunay's *Window* paintings to Kandinsky as "pure tonal fugues"[19] and was himself influenced by the superimposed zones of transparent colors, adapting this technique in works such as *Stables* (1913, plate 23) to express the spirituality and harmony of the cosmos in his pantheistic vision of nature.

Many other links between major cities were established by artists, critics, dealers, and collectors during this period, so that national borders were transcended in an atmosphere of exchange and collaboration. In 1912, Delaunay exhibited at the Moderner Bund in Zurich along with Jean Arp, Klee, Kandinsky, Marc, and Henri Matisse. Gino Severini, who lived in Paris, was an important liaison with his Futurist compatriots in Rome, Milan, and Turin. The interchange of artistic influence was also broadened by certain individuals who were instrumental in bringing the most advanced art of their time to their homelands. Among them were the painter and critic Conrad Kickert, whose Circle of Modern Art (Moderne Kunstkring) in Amsterdam held annual art exhibitions of avant-garde French painting; Herwarth Walden, founder of the avant-garde Berlin gallery Der Sturm, where German Expressionism was shown alongside School of Paris works, and the

Plate 22. Vasily Kandinsky, *Improvisation 28*
(second version), 1912. Oil on canvas, 111.4 x 162.1 cm
(43 ⅞ x 63 ⅞ inches). Solomon R. Guggenheim Museum,
Gift, Solomon R. Guggenheim 37.239.

Plate 23. Franz Marc, *Stables* (*Stallungen*), 1913.
Oil on canvas, 73.6 x 157.5 cm (29 x 62 inches).
Solomon R. Guggenheim Museum 46.1037.

Plate 24. Paul Klee, *Flower Bed* (*Blumenbeet*), 1913.
Oil on cardboard, 28.2 x 33.7 cm (11 ⅛ x 13 ¼ inches).
Solomon R. Guggenheim Museum 48.1172x109.

eponymous journal, in which Futurist manifestos were published concurrently with Kandinsky's writings and a translation of Apollinaire's *Les Peintres cubistes*; and the Muscovite collectors Ivan Morozov and Sergei Shchukin, who bought seminal examples of the latest French painting.

One key to understanding this period of tremendous creativity and mutual inspiration on an international scale is the concept of simultaneity, which was new in the period.[20] In its broadest definition, simultaneity became a central theme, as well as a formal and structural principle, for some of the greatest creators of the time. Simultaneity was at once a concept, a theory, an experience, a style of painting and literature, a method of musical composition, an aesthetic system, a temporal event, and a spatial event. As Virginia Spate explains in her study of Orphism, simultaneity was an attempt to embody a change of consciousness in response to a belief that sequential modes of thought and expression were inadequate to realize the fullness and complexity of modern urban life.[21] The Simultanists thus tried to represent a sense of the unity of all beings—the interrelatedness of all things, mental events, and feelings, which might be widely separated in time and space but were brought together by the mind.

The development of the concept of simultaneity was stimulated by the impact of the technical revolution, whose advances in the realms of communication (telephone, telegraph, and cinema) and transportation (automobile and airplane) literally transformed perceptions about time and space and made a reality of the simultaneity of experience.[22] The Eiffel Tower, itself a feat of modern engineering used for radio transmission, was a soaring testimony to modernity and was celebrated by artists such as Delaunay, Marc Chagall, the Futurists, and poets Apollinaire and Blaise Cendrars. As Stephen Kern writes in *The Culture of Time and Space 1880–1918*, "The present was no longer limited to one event in one place, sandwiched tightly between past and future and limited to local surroundings. In an age of intrusive electronic communication 'now' became an extended interval of time that could, indeed must, include events around the world."[23]

The manifold developments in the various arts of the period nourished each other as well. One of the most important models for simultaneous art and poetry was found in opera when, for example, two or more voices sing separate lyrics at once, or in musical counterpoint, where different melodies play concurrently. Composers such as Béla Bartók, Claude Debussy, and Richard Strauss created simultaneities involving music in completely different tonalities, and American composer Charles Ives even experimented with sections of the orchestra playing to different tempos at the same time.[24]

In poetry, Apollinaire, Henri-Martin Barzun, and Cendrars each expressed simultaneity through different methods, exploiting the Cubist notion of fragmentation in terms of ruptured syntax and abrupt juxtapositions. In 1912 and 1913, Apollinaire wrote poems such as "Zone" and "Liens," in which distant places and times are overlapped and woven together into present experience. Also in 1912, Barzun founded a journal to present his poems and his theory of simultaneity, and, in early 1913, Cendrars published the first "simultaneous" book, *La Prose du Transsibérien et de la Petite Jehanne de France*, a poem more than six feet long that was printed in varying colors and typography on an abstract colored background designed by Sonia Terk Delaunay (fig. 83). By 1914, Apollinaire was typographically arranging his *calligrammes* to create abstract patterns and simple graphic images (see fig. 84); this exploitation of the visual and grammatical possibilities of poetry to reflect those ideas being explored in paint is reflective of the deep bond between artists and writers of this generation.[25]

Perhaps one of the greatest models of simultaneity of the period is the Cubism of Braque and Picasso. Cubism embodied simultaneity in its juxtaposition of multiple views of an object in a single image, as if the artist

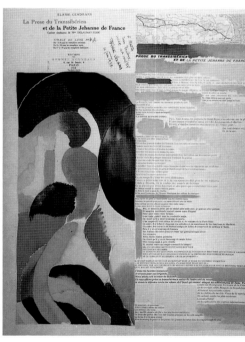

Top: Fig. 82. Guillaume Apollinaire in Picasso's studio on boulevard de Clichy in Paris, ca. 1910, probably photographed by the artist. Archives Picasso, Paris.

Bottom: Fig. 83. Sonia Terk Delaunay, design for Blaise Cendrars's *La Prose du Transsibérien et de la Petite Jehanne de France*, published in France by Pochoir in 1913. Spencer Collection, The New York Public Library, Astor, Lenox and Tilden Foundations. ©ARS, New York/ADAGP, Paris.

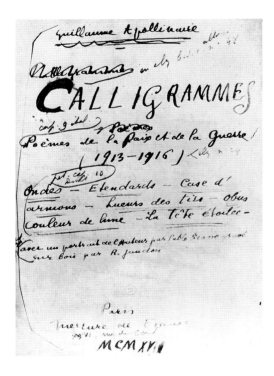

Fig. 84. Guillaume Apollinaire, frontispiece of
Calligrammes: Poèmes de la paix et de la guerre (1913–1916),
published in Paris in 1917.

has moved completely around his subject and reconstructed all of these views into one on the flat plane of the picture surface. Also prevalent in the masterful canvases of 1911 and 1912, the apogee of Analytic Cubism, is the tension established between the simultaneous plasticity of the subject and the flatness of the picture plane. In works such as *The Poet* (August 1911, plate 25), Picasso portrayed the figure faceted into small planes in order to define volume more vividly and at the same time to relate his subject more firmly to the flat picture plane. Plasticity emerged both from shading and from the rhythms created by the abutment of adjacent flat paint marks. In order to keep his depicted objects anchored to the picture plane, he also fractured the backgrounds into small planes, and confined his palette to small touches of ochers, browns, and grays that blurred—but did not obliterate—distinctions of form and setting. By 1912, Picasso's figures were barely decipherable within his compositions of fragmented rectilinear and curvilinear forms, leading to conclusions that would open a new chapter in the evolution of Cubism.

In *Paris through the Window* (1913, plate 27), Chagall accounts not only for that which is seen but also for that which is remembered or associated through physical or psychological relation. The simultaneous indoor and outdoor views in the flattened picture space, the two-headed man who looks in two directions at once, and the Chagallian device of the composite figure—here a human-faced cat—speak of discontinuity and coexistence. Chagall moved to Paris in 1910, and there he was closely associated with Robert Delaunay and Apollinaire. Apollinaire described Chagall's Cubist-influenced works of 1911–13, in which he joined together elements of his Russian-Jewish heritage with more specifically French references, as *surnaturel* in their temporal and spatial relationships.

Perhaps the most prominent application of simultaneity in painting is in the work of Delaunay, who evolved a style of painting that he called *Simultanisme* and claimed was a "new

aesthetic system representative of our epoch."[26] Two of Delaunay's most important subjects prior to 1912 were the Eiffel Tower (for example, plates 31–33) and the city, both favorite literary and artistic symbols for simultaneous experience in their embodiment of the dynamism of modern life. In his *City (La Ville)* paintings of 1911–12 (for example, plates 29–30), Delaunay treated each canvas primarily as a vehicle for experiments in constructive color. He introduced in them checkerboard zones of color applied with a pointillist brushstroke, as well as semitransparent planes of pure color that would become the hallmark of his next major stylistic advance.

In April 1912, around the time of Klee's visit to Delaunay on Kandinsky's recommendation, Delaunay embarked on a new series of *Window* paintings. These works were groundbreaking for their unprecedented emphasis on color suffused with light as the sole means of pictorial construction. Delaunay based his experiments on the work of color theorist Michel-Eugène Chevreul, who, in *The Principles of Harmony and Contrast of Colors (De la loi des contrastes simultanées des couleurs*, 1839), outlined a system that became fundamental to Georges Seurat and his colleagues. Delaunay focused in these paintings on the simultaneous interaction of juxtaposed colors. "At this time, I had ideas about a kind of painting which would exist only through color—chromatic contrasts developing in temporal sequence yet simultaneously visible. I borrowed Chevreul's scientific term: 'simultaneous contrasts.'"[27]

Simultaneous Windows (2nd Motif, 1st Part) (1912, plate 34) and *Windows Open Simultaneously (1st Part, 3rd Motif)* (1912, plate 35) represent two of his twenty-two versions of this theme. Echoing the multipaned structure of windows, the artist fuses inside and outside in a continuum of color planes. Rhythmically alternating between opaque and transparent, light and dark, the zones of color are meant to be perceived simultaneously and as such create both the image and space of these compositions. Although one can discern vestiges of the triangular form of the

Plate 25. Pablo Picasso, *The Poet* (*Le Poète*), August 1911.
Oil on canvas, 131.2 x 89.5 cm (51 ⅛ x 35 ¼ inches). Peggy
Guggenheim Collection 76.2553 PGI.

Plate 26. Georges Braque, *The Clarinet* (*La Clarinette*), summer–autumn 1912. Oil with sand on oval canvas, 91.4 x 64.5 cm (36 x 25 ⅜ inches). Peggy Guggenheim Collection 76.2553 PG7.

Eiffel Tower in the first painting, these works are not meant to be descriptive or symbolic of the natural world. Instead, they are about pure optical experience. In Delaunay's words, "I have dared to create an architecture of color, and have hoped to realize the impulses, the state of a dynamic poetry while remaining completely within the painterly medium, free from all literature, from all descriptive anecdote."[28] The oval shape of the Peggy Guggenheim Collection canvas (plate 35) dramatically presages the development of circularity in Delaunay's oeuvre. By 1913, he would begin his circular compositions, in which the representation of universal motion was depicted through spinning orbs of color and light.

Delaunay proposed a dynamic art because light, in its constant movement and change, produces color shapes. Conversely, he believed that certain combinations of colors, in harmonic contrast with each other, can reproduce this movement of light. The viewer would then apprehend the direct pictorial effect of color and light in a single instant, as a single experience, simultaneously.

The Puteaux circle, supported by the writings of Gleizes and Metzinger, were bound in their theory and practice to seek a "dynamism of form" in contrast to the more static compositions of Braque and Picasso. Léger's works demonstrate a close affinity to Delaunay's dynamic interpretation of Cubism; he, too, shared the similar goal of creating an autonomous picture structure.

In a densely structured, important transitional work, *The Smokers* (December 1911–January 1912, plate 36), Léger adopts Delaunay's device of the picture plane as a window looking out onto the cityscape, in which multiple viewpoints of figure and setting, foreground and background, are deeply interpenetrated. Interpretations vary as to whether Léger is representing two figures or two different phases of movement of a single figure, but in spite of the ambiguity the effect of movement is obvious, reinforced by the ascension of sculptural billows of smoke. The painting reveals further

similarities to Delaunay's *Eiffel Towers* in its predominant vertical axis; it also foreshadows in its upward thrust the interlocking curved planes of *Nude Model in the Studio* (1912–13, plate 37). In the *Contrast of Forms* series, begun in the latter half of 1912, Léger for the first time eliminates the distinction between representational and nonrepresentational in favor of an active surface pattern of contrasting circular and geometric shapes. Though verging on abstraction, the hierarchical arrangement of forms still contains vague suggestions of external references.

At a lecture held in conjunction with the *Section d'or* exhibition, Apollinaire coined the term Orphism to describe the works of Delaunay, Duchamp, Léger, and Picabia, all of whom he claimed were moving toward "pure painting."[29] Encouraged by requests from Kandinsky, Delaunay accompanied his new pictorial experiments with two theoretical essays written between the summer and fall of 1912, "Light" ("La Lumière") and "Note on the Construction of the Reality of Pure Painting" ("Note sur la construction de la réalité de la peinture pure"). The former was sent to Klee, who translated it and published it in *Der Sturm*, while the latter was edited by Apollinaire for the December issue of *Les Soirées de Paris*. "Note on the Construction of the Reality of Pure Painting" drew heavily on Leonardo's treatises, providing the theoretical basis for Delaunay's abstraction as well as the source for Apollinaire's own ideas on Orphism and pictorial simultaneity. This is only one instance in which Delaunay and Apollinaire found mutual inspiration in each other's work. Delaunay's essays manifest strong poetic affinities to Apollinaire in form and style, whereas Apollinaire wrote one of his most renowned poems, "Windows" ("Les Fenêtres"), based on Delaunay's paintings of that theme:

Oh Paris
From red to green all the yellow languishes
Paris Vancouver Hyères Maintenon
*   New York and the Antilles*
The window is opening like an orange
The beautiful fruit of light [30]

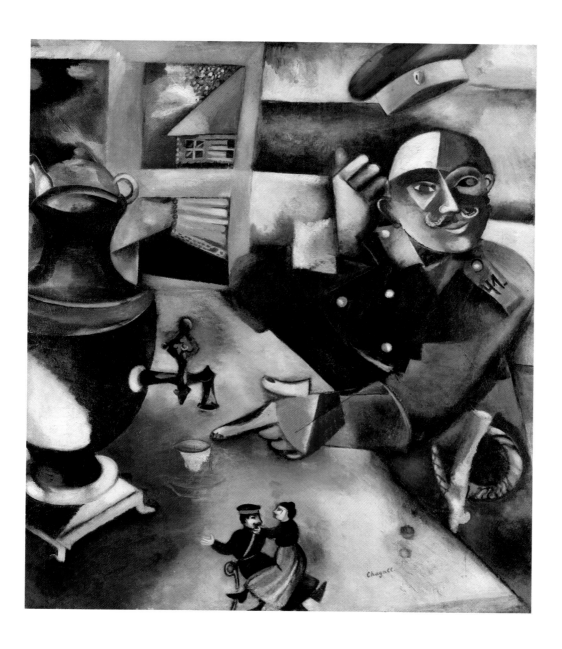

Left: Plate 27. Marc Chagall, *Paris through the Window*
(*Paris par la fenêtre*), 1913. Oil on canvas, 135.8 x 141.4 cm
(53 ½ x 55 ¼ inches). Solomon R. Guggenheim Museum,
Gift, Solomon R. Guggenheim 37.438.

Above: Plate 28. Marc Chagall, *The Soldier Drinks*
(*Le Soldat boit*), 1911–12. Oil on canvas, 109.1 x 94.5 cm (43 x
37 ¼ inches). Solomon R. Guggenheim Museum 49.1211.

Left: Plate 30. Robert Delaunay, *The City* (*La Ville*), 1911.
Oil on canvas, 145 x 112 cm (57 1/16 x 44 1/8 inches). Solomon
R. Guggenheim Museum, Gift, Solomon R. Guggenheim
38.464.

Above: Plate 29. Robert Delaunay, *Window on the City
No. 3* (*La Fenêtre sur la ville no. 3*), 1911–12. Oil on canvas,
113.7 x 130.8 cm (44 3/4 x 51 1/2 inches). Solomon R.
Guggenheim Museum 47.878.

Plate 31. Robert Delaunay, *Eiffel Tower with Trees*
(*Tour Eiffel aux arbres*), summer **1910**. Oil on canvas,
126.4 x 92.8 cm (**49 ¼ x 36 ½** inches). Solomon R.
Guggenheim Museum **46.1035**.

Plate 32. Robert Delaunay, *Eiffel Tower* (*Tour Eiffel*),
1911. Oil on canvas, **202 x 138.4** cm (**79 ½ x 54 ½** inches).
Solomon R. Guggenheim Museum, Gift, Solomon R.
Guggenheim **37.463**.

Plate 33. Robert Delaunay, *Red Eiffel Tower*
(*La Tour rouge*), **1911–12**. Oil on canvas, **125 x 90.3** cm
(**49 ¼ x 35 ⅜** inches). Solomon R. Guggenheim Museum
46.1036.

Plate 35. Robert Delaunay, *Windows Open
Simultaneously (1st Part, 3rd Motif) (Fenêtres ouvertes
simultanément { 1re partie, 3e motif }),* 1912.
Oil on oval canvas, 57 x 123 cm (22 ⅛ x 48 ⅛ inches).
Peggy Guggenheim Collection 76.2553 PG36.

Plate 34. Robert Delaunay, *Simultaneous Windows
(2nd Motif, 1st Part) (Les Fenêtres simultanées
{ 2e motif, 1re partie }),* 1912. Oil on canvas, 55.2 x 46.3 cm
(21 ⅛ x 18 ¼ inches). Solomon R. Guggenheim Museum,
Gift, Solomon R. Guggenheim 41.464a.

Left: Plate 36. Fernand Léger, *The Smokers (Les Fumeurs),*
December 1911–January 1912. Oil on canvas, 129.2 x 96.5 cm
(50 ⅞ x 38 inches). Solomon R. Guggenheim Museum,
Gift, Solomon R. Guggenheim 38.521.

Above: Plate 37. Fernand Léger, *Nude Model in
the Studio (Le Modèle nu dans l'atelier),* 1912–13. Oil on burlap,
127.8 x 95.7 cm (50 ⅜ x 37 ⅛ inches). Solomon R.
Guggenheim Museum 49.1193.

The search for a pictorial expression of simultaneity was perhaps best realized by the Futurists, who extended the notion temporally so that successive stages of movement were seen simultaneously, or so that successions of events were collapsed into a single image. Celebrating the machine, the city, and the speed, force, and energy of modern life in a burgeoning industrial age, the Futurists used what they called "force-lines" to depict the trajectory created by the movement of an object, of light, or of sound, or even the way an object would decompose according to the tendencies of its forces. They revealed the essential dynamic sensation of being, in works such as Giacomo Balla's *Abstract Speed + Sound* (1913–14, plate 39), a brightly colored composition on the theme of a speeding racing car.

One of the most explicit articulations of Futurist principles and the concept of simultaneity was espoused by Boccioni in his introduction to the 1912 Futurist exhibition catalogue at Galerie Bernheim-Jeune in Paris:

The simultaneousness of states of mind in the work of art: that is the intoxicating aim of our art. . . . In order to make the spectator live in the center of the picture, as we express it in our manifesto, the picture must be the synthesis of what one remembers and of what one sees.[31]

Boccioni's *Technical Manifesto of Futurist Sculpture* also first appeared in the catalogue of this exhibition, which included fellow Milanese artists Carlo Carrà and Luigi Russolo as well as resident Parisian Severini.

Delaunay strenuously objected to what the Futurists called "the painting of states of mind," fueling an existing polemic between the Cubists and their Italian counterparts. Drawing inspiration from Bergson, Delaunay emphasized the dynamic fluxing quality of existence, which could be portrayed through the simultaneity of contrasting colors on a painting's surface. The Futurists upheld a somewhat different interpretation of Bergson, emphasizing how the mind gathers together diverse experiences, merging successive

memories of past and present events and phenomena. The debate did not end there, however. The Futurists, in seeking to repudiate the political ineffectuality of earlier art, lambasted the classicism and "obstinate attachment to the past" of the French artists, while Apollinaire, stubbornly upholding a nationalism that persisted despite the melting pot that Paris had become, proclaimed Futurism an awkward Italian imitation of Fauvism and Cubism.

Like the Futurists, Duchamp had been involved since the previous year with portraying successive images of a figure in motion, culminating in the famous *Nude Descending a Staircase (No. 2)* (1912, now in the collection of the Philadelphia Museum of Art). In two important studies, including *Nude (Study), Sad Young Man on a Train* (1911–12, plate 38),[32] Duchamp encompasses both the forward motion of the train and that of the figure itself (identified by Duchamp as a self-portrait). On the surface, the work seems to borrow elements from Analytic Cubism, Futurism, and chronophotography. However, in a later interview, Duchamp minimized the relationship to Futurism, stating that "my interest in painting the *Nude {Descending a Staircase (No. 2)}* was closer to the Cubists' interest in decomposing forms than to the Futurists' interest in suggesting movement, or even to Delaunay's Simultanist suggestions of it. My aim was a static representation of movement—a static composition of indications of various positions taken by a form in movement—with no attempt to give cinema effects through painting."[33] The work's perceived radicality was also due to the fact that the nude had been excluded as a legitimate theme by the Cubists because it was not considered part of the iconography of modern life; in an ironic twist, Duchamp returns the nude to the liturgy in his own rejection of traditional subject matter.

Apart from *Nude Descending a Staircase (No. 2)*, 1912 was a pivotal year in Duchamp's career, in particular because he abandoned traditional painting

Plate 38. Marcel Duchamp, *Nude (Study), Sad Young Man on a Train (Nu {esquisse}, jeune homme triste dans un train),* 1911–12. Oil on cardboard, mounted on Masonite, 100 x 73 cm (39 ⅛ x 28 ¼ inches). Peggy Guggenheim Collection 76.2553 PG9.

Left: Plate 39. Giacomo Balla, *Abstract Speed + Sound*
(*Velocità astratta + rumore*), 1913–14. Oil on board, 54.5 x
76.5 cm (21 ½ x 30 ⅛ inches), including artist's painted
frame. Peggy Guggenheim Collection 76.2553 PG31.

Above: Plate 40. Gino Severini, *Sea = Dancer*
(*Mare = Ballerina*), January 1914. Oil on canvas, 105.3 x
85.9 cm (41 ½ x 33 ¹³⁄₁₆ inches), including artist's painted
frame. Peggy Guggenheim Collection 76.2553 PG32.

thereafter in favor of more experimental art forms, including mechanical drawings and Ready-mades.[34] He was, in 1912, an active participant in the Cubist circle around his brothers in Puteaux, and he visited the Futurist exhibition at Galerie Bernheim-Jeune on several occasions. However, neither Cubism nor Futurism were ultimately extreme enough for Duchamp, who wanted "to get away from the physical aspect of painting" and "to put painting once again at the service of the mind."[35] His early association with Picabia also dates from this period, and the challenging stance they took anticipated the official founding of Dada in 1916.

The Dada movement would have been unthinkable without the invention of collage in 1912. While 1912 marked the end of a long evolutionary phase of Cubism, it was also the year that ushered in a critical new phase of the Cubist aesthetic, which would culminate in the development of Synthetic Cubism. The first appearance of collage in Picasso's oeuvre was *Still Life with Chair Caning* (now in the collection of the Musée Picasso, Paris, fig. 78), executed in May of that year; in September, Braque glued imitation wood-grain wallpaper to his drawings, thus creating the first papiers collés (for example, fig. 80).

Braque's *The Clarinet* (summer–autumn 1912, plate 26), is the Guggenheim work that best exemplifies several of the tremendous innovations of this transitional stage of Cubism. Most salient among these is the use of the trompe-l'oeil technique of painted imitation wood graining. In addition, the stenciled lettering, oval format, and the incorporation of sand into the paint are all devices that subtly define spatial relationships. In this painting, the picture plane is noticeably shallower than the densely penetrated space of Braque's canvases of the previous year. The compositional planes also fall into a roughly parallel alignment with the picture plane, suggesting the new order and simplification that would emerge in Synthetic Cubism's spatially compressed, flat, and unmodulated shapes and areas of bright color.

The iconography, much of which is still tied to the artist's atelier, is made even more explicit by the inclusion of typography. The painted letters are neither in front of nor behind the illusionistic surface; rather, their position serves to define the actual two-dimensional picture plane. They exist as elements in and of themselves, not subject to pictorial distortion. And beyond that, the letters serve an associative value, providing clues to the reconstruction of the subject of the painting.

Braque's and Picasso's practice of incorporating lettering or words into their works conveys a touch of the personal, humorous, or even political, importing a new level of reality to their canvases. Similarly, the inclusion of tangible elements of everyday reality onto the surface of the canvases—scraps of newspaper, tickets, labels, and cigarette wrappers—also made specific references to the period and, in particular, to events of popular culture. The invention of collage in 1912, and its further development by Braque brought the artists a step closer to the idea of integral instead of disintegrated forms. The use of *passage*, one of the hallmarks of Analytic Cubism, gave way to contrast. A breakdown in sculptural illusion gave way to an increase in sculptural presence. It is indeed one of the seemingly contradictory implications of collage that it immediately led in two directions—to the flattened space of Synthetic Cubist painting and to relief sculpture.

Breaking with the monolithic tradition of carved or modeled sculpture, Picasso advanced the notion of collage into relief in his cardboard, string, and wire *Guitar* (now in the collection of the Museum of Modern Art, New York) sometime in the spring of 1912.[36] This construction was not predicated on a volumetric conception, but rather on the juxtaposition of almost entirely flat metal shapes, with varying degrees of shallow space between them.

Although it was a short-lived phenomenon, planar sculpture was variously interpreted by artists in France, Italy, and Russia. Drawing on Picasso's achievement, those artists all

Top left: Plate 41. Mikhail Larionov, *Glass* (*Steklo*), 1912. Oil on canvas, 104.1 x 97.1 cm (41 x 33 ¼ inches). Solomon R. Guggenheim Museum 53.1362.

Bottom left: Plate 42. Kazimir Malevich, *Morning in the Village after Snowstorm* (*Utro posle viugi v derevne*), 1912. Oil on canvas, 80.8 x 80.7 cm (31 ¼ x 31 ⅞ inches). Solomon R. Guggenheim Museum 52.1327.

Plate 43. Alexander Archipenko, *Médrano II*, 1913–14?. Painted tin, wood, glass, and painted oilcloth, 126.6 x 51.5 x 31.7 cm (49 ⅞ x 20 ¼ x 12 ½ inches). Solomon R. Guggenheim Museum 56.1445.

employed a simple vocabulary of geometric forms and a means of describing volume through intersecting planes. Their work, drawing on everyday rather than precious materials, was rough at the edges, almost makeshift, and not meant to endure.

In Paris, the mixed-media constructions of Archipenko, Henri Laurens, and Jacques Lipchitz reflected the impact of Cubism. In 1912, echoing Duchamp's *Nude Descending a Staircase (No. 2)*, Archipenko began to explore the theme of a figure in motion in a small group of mixed-media constructions based on the female jugglers and dancers of the Cirque Médrano. *Médrano I* (now destroyed), constructed of wood and glass, was dated 1912, although it may not have been begun until the following year. A controversial piece in its time, it forced the resignation of Apollinaire from his post at *L'Intransigeant*, when he was criticized for hailing this work in a review of the 1914 *Salon des indépendants* as a "most innovative and graceful exhibit."[37] Two days later, the newspaper carried a front-page illustration of *Médrano I* with the following caption: "We reproduce here the photograph of the work of art (?) praised elsewhere in this issue by our collaborator Guillaume Apollinaire, who assumes sole responsibility for his opinion."[38]

Médrano II (1913–14?, plate 43) is made of painted tin, wood, glass, and painted oilcloth. The combination of unorthodox materials pays heed to Boccioni's 1912 manifesto, while the vocabulary of tubular cone-shaped forms recalls Léger's volumes. Against a two-dimensional rectangular backdrop, the figure is given a sense of three-dimensionality in a play of solids and voids, volumes and flatness. Archipenko, who was living in Paris in this period, had remained in close contact with his Russian compatriots, and the structuring of space and use of polychromy clearly make reference to the icon painting of his native country.

Boccioni, too, began to make sculptures in 1912. True to the precepts he espoused, these works consist of a medley of incongruous elements, which he used in his attempts to make his

extension of objects into space "palpable, systematic, and plastic," because "no one can any longer believe that an object ends where another begins."[39]

The Futurists found in the collages and constructions of Picasso the means by which to express their belief in the ideas of the modern world, and in this respect so did the artists of the Russian avant-garde. In 1913, after having seen Picasso's work in Paris, Vladimir Tatlin began to make his first abstract painterly reliefs in Moscow out of metal, glass, and wood, pushing to its logical extreme the idea of Cubist collage.

A dizzying succession of events in 1912 would herald an equally momentous year in 1913. But for the continuation of this story, one must look beyond Paris. Whereas Seuphor recognized that "1912 is the most Parisian moment in painting," developments in other capitals were equally significant and revolutionary in the movements they provoked. As we have seen, 1912 in Paris represented both an apogee and a crisis point—perhaps the most drastic consequence being the development of collage, which opened to artists everywhere a wide range of aesthetic strategies that changed the course of art in the twentieth century. The year 1912 in Munich and Moscow represents an equally significant turning point, the eve of an all-important breakthrough to abstraction, the consequences of which would also be revolutionary for the art of this century. While the orientation toward non-objective art was a rather widespread and simultaneous development in several countries, many of its first manifestations appeared outside of Paris in 1913.

To return to the notion of simultaneity, one need only look at a particular month, specifically March 1912, when three exhibitions were held that testify both to the radicality of the moment and the rich cross-fertilization of the arts. These exhibitions—the *Salon des indépendants* in Paris, the second showing of the Blue Rider in Munich, and *The Donkey's Tail* in Moscow— shared a number of common

Plate 44. Alexander Archipenko, *Carrousel Pierrot*, 1913.
Painted plaster, 61 x 48.6 x 34 cm (24 x 19 ⅛ x 13 ⅛ inches).
Solomon R. Guggenheim Museum 57.1483.

contributors of all nationalities.[40] Yet they demonstrate the different types of pictorial revolutions that arose out of the different social and political climates from which they were born.

In Moscow, the Donkey's Tail was organized by a group of artists whose mission it was to declare an independent Russian school to displace the European dominance in avant-garde art. The association was formed in reaction to the Jack of Diamonds exhibitions, which first took place in 1910 (bringing together contemporary works by French, German, and Russian artists, such as Gleizes and Le Fauconnier, Kandinsky and Alexei Jawlensky, and Larionov and Goncharova) and then in January 1912 (featuring works by Erich Heckel, Ernst Ludwig Kirchner, and Max Pechstein, and a larger contingent of Parisians, including Braque and Léger). Because of the prominence and attention given to French art, Larionov and Goncharova withdrew their entries from the second exhibition, and founded the Donkey's Tail, whose 1912 exhibition consisted of 307 works by themselves, Chagall, Malevich, Tatlin, and minor members of the Moscow avant-garde. Similar to the furious storm of criticism unleashed against the Cubists in their first group showing—in Salle 41 of the 1911 *Salon des indépendants*—the public reaction to this new art was one of intense indignation and derision. Many works were in fact censured and confiscated.

Although the Russians assimilated the new artistic ideas advanced in Western Europe by the Cubists and Futurists, they also drew on traditional sources such as folk art and icon painting in order to create "a native modern idiom" to reflect the social, political, and aesthetic preoccupations of their age. Larionov's short-lived but important Rayist style of 1912–13 drew together elements of Impressionist depiction of light, Cubist fracturing, and Futurist lines of force. Like contemporaneous art movements, Rayism called for the depiction of simultaneous motion, of dynamism, and of the speed of the urban world. Yet in works such as *Glass* (1912, plate 41) Larionov was especially focused on

depicting the spatial forms that arose from the intersection of the reflected rays of different objects.

Malevich's early works were also heavily influenced by those same Western European sources. His Cubo-Futurist style of 1912, typified by *Morning in the Village after Snowstorm* (plate 42), recalls Léger's paintings of the period, which Malevich could have known from an exhibition of work by the French master held in Moscow in February 1912, or through reproductions. But the geometricized images of peasants, depicted as solid, tubular figures set in the deep landscape space of a Russian village, and the non-naturalistic metallic color and light, are not yet completely disassociated from his Neo-Primitive style.

"In 1913, trying desperately to liberate art from the ballast of the representational world, I sought refuge in the form of the square,"[41] Malevich recalled, referring to his painting of a black square on a white ground—the purest and most radically abstract painting created up to that date.[42] So marked the beginnings of the stylistic and theoretical development of what became known in 1915 as Suprematism, a pure abstract formal language based on geometry, which sought to express a universal cosmic order (see, for example, plate 67).

In this period, Kandinsky, too, strove to reach a point "at which the human state of being touches the more universal cosmic order."[43] It was Kandinsky's conviction that art was the embodiment of the spirit. He believed that the purpose of the highest art was to express inner truth, and that this could only be achieved by moving away from the representation of the objective world. The process that carried Kandinsky into the realm of the non-objective was a long and thoughtful one that he began in Murnau in 1908, and he reached his goal with the completion of his great *Improvisations* and *Compositions* between 1910 and the outbreak of World War I.[44]

An active time for Kandinsky, this phase was devoted to the preparation and publication of *The Blue Rider Almanac* and his book *On the Spiritual in*

Top left: Plate 45. Piet Mondrian, *Still Life with Ginger Pot I* (*Stilleven Met Gemberpot I*), 1911–12. Oil on canvas, 65.5 x 75 cm (25¼ x 29½ inches). Solomon R. Guggenheim Museum LN 295.76.

Bottom left: Plate 46. Piet Mondrian, *Still Life with Ginger Pot II* (*Stilleven Met Gemberpot II*), 1911–12. Oil on canvas, 91.5 x 120 cm (37½ x 47¼ inches). Solomon R. Guggenheim Museum LN 294.76.

Plate 47. Piet Mondrian, *The Sea,* 1914. Charcoal and
gouache on paper, mounted on panel; paper: 87.6 x 120.3 cm
(34 ½ x 47 ⅛ inches); panel: 90.2 x 123 x 1.3 cm
(35 ½ x 48 ⅜ x ½ inches). Peggy Guggenheim Collection
76.2553 PG 38.

Art. In December 1911, after resigning from the NKVM, Kandinsky, Alfred Kubin, Marc, and Gabriele Münter formed the Blue Rider. The group's first exhibition was held that month at the Moderne Galerie Thannhauser, including the work of Robert Delaunay, Kandinsky, Macke, Marc, and Rousseau. The show traveled to Cologne, Berlin (where Herwarth Walden added works by Klee and Jawlensky), Bremen, Hagen, and Frankfurt. The second exhibition, in 1912, again featured an international roster, including Braque, Delaunay, Goncharova, Klee, Larionov, Malevich, and Picasso.

In *On the Spiritual in Art*, Kandinsky describes his *Improvisations* of 1911–13 as "chiefly unconscious, for the most part suddenly arising expressions of events of an inner character, hence impressions of 'internal nature.'"[45] *Improvisation 28* (second version) (1912, plate 22) contains barely discernible references to certain recurrent motifs of the folk-inspired Blue Rider period—horses, riders, cannons, and castles—although these are peripheral to the inner meaning of the work, which has frequently been interpreted as a diptych with cataclysmic events on one side and a paradise of spiritual salvation on the other. The year 1913 was for Kandinsky, as it was for Malevich, a period of breakthrough to truly non-objective painting, in which his theory of correspondences between emotional experience and the formal elements of colors, forms, lines, and sounds reached its true fruition.[46]

A discussion of the emergence of abstraction would not be complete without returning to Mondrian, who we left in Paris at the threshold of 1912. Like the artists of the Puteaux circle, Mondrian assimilated the language of Cubism and made of it a style that was singularly his own. Mondrian's predisposition to the principles of flatness, frontality, and geometric form were very much a part of his Dutch heritage. Unique to his engagement with Cubism, however, was his subversion from the outset of its sculptural qualities—its simultaneous oscillation between flatness and plasticity—which he saw as a residue of

naturalism in Cubist practice. Two paintings in the Guggenheim's collection demonstrate the dramatic impact that Paris in 1912 had on his development. In *Still Life with Ginger Pot I* (1911–12, plate 45), a work that Mondrian began in the Netherlands and finished in Paris, objects that relate to his atelier are still identifiable, and light and shading are naturalistic. In remaining securely attached to external reality, the painting is traditional in appearance; indeed, its iconography relates it to seventeenth-century Dutch still lifes. However, Mondrian has begun to cautiously organize his composition in a manner that approaches Cubist practice. In the second version, *Still Life with Ginger Pot II* (1911–12, plate 46)—which he painted when he had become firmly entrenched in the Parisian scene—the sense of volume and the realistic scale of objects, as well as the local functions of contour and structure seen in the first version, are gone. The focus on the linear structure of the composition is greatly intensified: around the now truncated shape of the ginger pot, Mondrian has built a schematic network of predominantly straight lines in which the strictly balanced horizontals and verticals dominate.

Although Mondrian undermined sculptural tendencies and distilled the horizontal and vertical components of his subject matter in this important work of 1912, his first strides in the development out of Cubism and toward a truly nonrepresentational art were not begun until the following year. It is in his *Pier and Ocean* series (for example, plate 47), begun in 1914 after Mondrian returned to the Netherlands, that all objective references have been obliterated and all curved and diagonal lines banished. Here, Mondrian's subject is the internal geometry of Cubism: the linear grid functions not as an analytical tool, but as both motif and pictorial structure. Using short fragments of lines spread at fairly regular intervals across the canvas, Mondrian has in essence abstracted the Cubist grid and has made it alone the subject of the picture.

Apollinaire is the only major critic

who wrote specifically about Mondrian's work during this period. In his review of the 1913 *Salon des indépendants*, he acknowledges the new direction that Mondrian had taken away from Picasso and Braque: "Mondrian, an offshoot of the Cubists, is certainly not their imitator."[47] Apollinaire is prescient in recognizing the profound scope of these advances at the moment they were occurring. What we see even more clearly now by studying the simultaneity of artistic phenomena in this pivotal year of 1912 is that this was indeed not a period marked by imitation but rather a moment of collaboration, interchange, synthesis, and, above all, radical innovation at every turn.

Notes

1. Michel Seuphor, *Piet Mondrian: Life and Work* (New York: Harry N. Abrams, 1956), p. 93.

2. Mondrian was invited to Paris by Conrad Kikkert in December 1911, arrived in January 1912, and established his permanent residence there in May of that year.

3. Seuphor, p. 96.

4. The *28ᵉ Société des artistes indépendants* was held at the Quai d'Orsay from March 20 to May 16. The *Salon de la section d'or* was held at the Galerie de la Boëtie (64 bis, rue La Boëtie) from October 10 to 30. The *Salon d'octobre* was held from October 1 to November 8.

5. *Les Peintres futuristes italiens (Italian Futurist Painters)* was held at Galerie Bernheim-Jeune (15, rue Richepance) from February 5 to 24. It had an enormous impact on artists such as Marcel Duchamp and Fernand Léger. It subsequently traveled to the Sackville Gallery, London, the Galerie Der Sturm, Berlin, and the Galerie Georges Girous, Brussels.

6. This quote appeared in the first and only issue of the journal entitled *La Section d'or*, which accompanied the exhibition.

7. Umberto Boccioni, *Manifesto tecnico della scultura futurista*, in *Poesia*, April 11, 1912, translated in the Metropolitan Museum of Art, *Umberto Boccioni*, exh. cat. (New York: Harry N. Abrams, 1988), p. 243.

8. Duchamp recalled: "On the day before the opening Gleizes asked my brothers to go and ask me at least to change the title because he thought, after conferring with Delaunay, Le Fauconnier, and Metzinger, that it was not Cubistic in their sense. . . . A nude never descends the stairs—a nude reclines, you know. Even their little revolutionary temple couldn't understand that a nude could be *descending* the stairs. . . . So I said nothing. I said all right, all right, and I took a taxi to the show and took my painting and took it away. So it never was shown at the Indépendants of 1912, although it's in the catalog." Quoted in William C. Seitz, "What's Happened to Art? . . ." (interview with Duchamp), *Vogue*, Feb. 15, 1963, pp. 110–13, 129–31. Also quoted in Arturo Schwarz, *The Complete Works of Marcel Duchamp* (New York: Harry N. Abrams, 1969), p. 16.

9. *Über das Geistige in der Kunst* was first published by Piper of Munich in December 1911, although it was dated 1912. The second edition was published in Munich in April 1912. (See *Kandinsky in Munich: 1896–1914* [New York: Solomon R. Guggenheim Museum, 1982], p. 305.)

10. *The Donkey's Tail (Oslinyi khvost)* opened in March at the Moscow College of Painting, Sculpture, and Architecture. Also, the second *Jack of Diamonds (Bubnovyi valet)* exhibition opened in Moscow on January 12 and included works by Kandinsky, Braque, Delaunay, Léger, Picasso, Marc, Henri Matisse, and Henri Le Fauconnier.

11. Roger Shattuck, *The Banquet Years: The Origins of the Avant Garde in France, 1885 to World War I* (New York: Vintage Books, Random House, 1958; rev. ed., 1967), p. 28.

12. Ibid.

13. Leroy C. Breunig, "Introduction," in Breunig, ed., *Apollinaire on Art: Essays and Reviews 1902–1918 by Guillaume Apollinaire* (New York: Viking Press, 1972; Da Capo Press, 1988), p. xvii.

14. Shattuck, p. 280.

15. Stephen Kern, *The Culture of Time and Space 1880–1918* (Cambridge, Mass.: Harvard University Press, 1983), p. 43.

16. Christopher Gray, *Cubist Aesthetic Theories* (Baltimore: The Johns Hopkins University Press, 1953), p. 69.

17. Kern, p. 85.

18. Max Kozloff, *Cubism/Futurism* (New York: Charterhouse, 1973), p. 121.

19. Klaus Lankheit, *Unteilbares Sein, Aquarelle und Zeichnungen von Franz Marc* (Cologne: M. DuMont, 1959), p. 19. Quoted in Gustav Vriesen and Max Imdahl, *Robert Delaunay: Light and Color*, trans. by Maria Pelikan (New York: Harry N. Abrams, 1969), p. 50.

20. There are three excellent and important discussions of simultaneity in this period, to which many of the ideas here are indebted. They are in Kern, Shattuck, and Virginia Spate, *Orphism: The evolution of non-figurative painting in Paris 1910–1914* (New York: Oxford University Press, 1978; Oxford: Clarendon Press, 1979).

21. Spate, p. 20.

22. Shattuck, p. 314.

23. Kern, p. 314.

24. Ibid., p. 75.

25. James Joyce's *Ulysses* (1922) has been recognized as the work that perhaps best epitomizes the expression of simultaneity in literature, particularly as it applies to sequential time. In abandoning causal sequence in favor of a synchronicity of events in time and space, Joyce invites the reader to entertain concurrently and without synthesis various contradictory propositions and events, improvising film "montage techniques to show the simultaneous action of Dublin as a whole, not a history of the city but a slice of it out of time, spatially extended and embodying its entire past in a vast expanded present." Shattuck, p. 77.

26. Robert Delaunay, *Du cubisme à l'art abstrait*, ed. by Pierre Francastel (Paris: S.E.V.E.P.N., 1957), translated from the French by the author.

27. Robert Delaunay in his notebook, 1912, quoted by François de la Tourette, *Robert Delaunay* (Paris: C. Massin & Cie., 1950), p. 17.

28. Robert Delaunay, *Du cubisme à l'art abstrait*, p. 98. Quoted in Vriesen and Imdahl, p. 42.

29. Although much has been written about the emergence of abstraction in the works of Delaunay and the Orphists, Spate is very clear in making the distinction that "pure painting" did not necessarily mean nonrepresentational painting. Rather, it signified a type of painting that had its own internally coherent structure independent of naturalistic structural devices. See Spate, pp. 160–61.

30. Excerpted in Francis Steegmuller, *Apollinaire, Poet among the Painters* (New York: Farrar, Straus and Company, 1963), p. 241.

31. In Herschel B. Chipp, *Theories of Modern Art: A Source Book by Artists and Critics* (Berkeley: University of California Press, 1968), pp. 295–96. Boccioni's triptych *States of Mind* (1911–12), which was shown in the Bernheim-Jeune show in Paris, synthesizes the principles elucidated in this manifesto.

32. Duchamp's *Nude (Study), Sad Young Man on a Train* is a complicated picture that raises manifold art-historical questions, not the least of which is its relationship to *Nude Descending a Staircase (No. 2)*, be it a sketch, study, or a version thereof. Angelica Zander Rudenstine, in *Peggy Guggenheim Collection, Venice: The Solomon R. Guggenheim Foundation* (New York: Harry N. Abrams, 1985), accepts William Rubin's argument that *Nude (Study)* and another work, *Nude (No. 1)*, are two distinctly different studies or explorations of the problem of depicting motion. For a more detailed discussion of this debate, as well as other issues raised by this painting, see her analysis on pp. 261–68.

33. Marcel Duchamp, "Eleven Europeans in America," *The Museum of Modern Art Bulletin* 13, nos. 4–5 (1946), pp. 19–20. Quoted in Rudenstine, p. 263.

34. The year 1912 was also an important period of travel for Duchamp, who visited Barcelona on the occasion of an exhibition of his work there, and then Munich (where he painted *The Passage from the Virgin to the Bride* and *The Bride*), and finally Prague, Vienna, Dresden, and Berlin.

35. Schwarz, p. 18.

36. Recent scholarship has established that Picasso's papiers collés postdate his cardboard constructions. For a complete discussion of the dating of *Guitar*, see William Rubin, *Picasso and Braque: Pioneering Cubism*, exh. cat. (New York: The Museum of Modern Art, 1989), pp. 30–32.

37. Katherine Jánszky Michaelsen, "Early Mixed Media Constructions," *Arts Magazine* 50 (Jan. 1976), p. 72.

38. Ibid., p. 72.

39. Quoted in Chipp, p. 300.

40. For instance, Maurice de Vlaminck and Delaunay exhibited in both the *Salon des indépendants* and the Blue Rider exhibition; Marc Chagall in the *Salon des indépendants* and *The Donkey's Tail*; and Natalia Goncharova and Kazimir Malevich in *The Donkey's Tail* and the Blue Rider exhibition.

41. Kasimir [Kazimir] Malevich, "Suprematism," in *The Non-Objective World* (Chicago: Theobald, 1959), pp. 67–100, paraphrased in Chipp, p. 342. Dmitrii Sarabianov states: "We do not know exactly when the first Suprematist paintings were painted, including the *Black Square*, although they were shown at the '0.10' exhibition in 1915. However, one can hardly assume that all of these works were painted on the eve of the exhibition, so the date for *Black Square* is not necessarily 1915, just as Malevich's own designation of the year 1913 cannot be considered definitive. On the other hand, the date is not so very important when compared with the revolution the *Black Square* brought about" ("Kazimir Malevich and His Art, 1900–1930," in *Kazimir Malevich*, exh. cat. [Leningrad: Russian Museum, 1988], p. 70).

42. Although Malevich here recalls the creation of this painting as 1913, the dating is by no means certain, although it was definitely completed by December 1915, when it was shown in the *0.10* exhibition.

43. Paul Vogt, "The *Blaue Reiter*," in *Expressionism: A German Intuition 1905–1920*, exh. cat. (New York: The Solomon R. Guggenheim Foundation, 1980), p. 197.

44. Thomas M. Messer, "Introduction," in Vivian Endicott Barnett, *Kandinsky at the Guggenheim* (New York: Solomon R. Guggenheim Museum and Abbeville Press, 1983), p. 13.

45. Barnett, p. 26.

46. For a more complete discussion of the invention of abstract art and the theories that accompanied it, see "Technology Versus the Spirit: The Invention of Non-Object Art," pp. 149–77 in this book.

47. Quoted in Breunig, p. 289.

Plate 48. Vasily Kandinsky, *Black Lines* (*Schwarze Linien*),
December 1913. Oil on canvas, 129.4 x 131.1 cm
(51 x 51 ⅛ inches). Solomon R. Guggenheim Museum,
Gift, Solomon R. Guggenheim 37.241.

Technology and the Spirit
The Invention of Non-Objective Art

Michael Govan

"Non-Objectivity will be the religion of the future," wrote Hilla Rebay in 1937, the year the Solomon R. Guggenheim Foundation was chartered. "Very soon the nations on earth will turn to it in thought and feeling and develop such intuitive powers which lead them to harmony."[1] Rebay, the artist and adviser who assembled Guggenheim's collection of Modern art, had a zealous faith in the power of non-objective painting to transcend the boundaries of language and experience. She encouraged her patron to establish a museum unlike any other. In contrast to the Museum of Modern Art, founded contemporaneously in New York under the direction of the erudite Alfred H. Barr, Jr. as an encyclopedic history of the Modern movement, Guggenheim's museum was based on an idea: the spiritually redemptive power of abstract painting.

With Rebay as its first director, the Museum of Non-Objective Painting, as the Guggenheim was then called, opened in 1939 in a former automobile showroom on East Fifty-fourth Street in Manhattan. To heighten the lofty effect of the paintings, Rebay placed them in oversized frames and hung them low to the plush-carpeted floors on velour-curtained walls. The music of Bach and Beethoven was piped into the galleries through a modern sound system, accompanied by the scent of incense.

Rebay had an even more all-enveloping experience of art and environment in mind when, in 1943, she commissioned Frank Lloyd Wright to design a permanent building for the museum, one that would be "a temple to non-objectivity."[2] Wright's design—a single cantilevered spiral ramp encircling a one-hundred-foot-tall atrium beneath a broad skylighted dome—offered a metaphor for the abstract mysteries of nature and the cosmos. The building's famous inverted ziggurat structure, which the architect described as "pure optimism,"[3] has become emblematic of the utopian ideals espoused by Rebay and Guggenheim.

Non-objective painting's most articulate proponent was Russian-born painter Vasily Kandinsky. His seminal treatise *On the Spiritual in Art* (*Über das Geistige in der Kunst*, written in 1911) became a guiding light for Rebay. Guggenheim's collection grew to include over two hundred of Kandinsky's works; it also included several hundred (for example, plate 49) by German painter Rudolf Bauer, a minor follower of Kandinsky who had an intimate and influential relationship with Rebay.

The term *gegenstandslos* (literally "without object") was used in Kandinsky's writings and Bauer's many letters to Rebay. She translated it as "non-objective," and tried to popularize the use of the term.[4] Purely non-objective painting had a special distinction for Rebay, as it did for Kandinsky. It was only through the rejection of representation—the renunciation of any vestiges of the exterior material world—that painting could at once access the depth of inner life and the height of the heavenly cosmos, thus inspiring the joy of spiritual life. She wrote: "This is what these masterpieces in the quiet absolute purity can bring to all those who learn to feel their unearthly donation of rest, elevation, rhythm, balance, and beauty."[5] Rebay's dogma was pure. Sculpture was excluded from her canon because of its weighty and earthly character—however, she granted an exception to the work of Alexander Calder, whose hanging mobiles eschewed the ground and bases traditional to that medium.[6]

Rebay's and Kandinsky's quasi-religious sensibilities may seem naïve to the contemporary reader. Yet they capture the ambition of many artists searching for a visual language that could transcend the volatile and challenging cultural environment they saw around them. Before abstraction, photography had threatened to render painting altogether obsolete; the Impressionists had already discarded the rules of representational perspective for a more direct rendering of natural phenomena; the Symbolists had emphasized the representation of an internal realm of emotions over that of a more accessible visible world; and, with their invention of Cubism, Georges

Top: Fig. 85. Hilla Rebay in her Connecticut studio.

Bottom: Plate 49. Rudolf Bauer, *Invention (Composition 31)*, 1933. Oil on canvas, 130.5 x 130.5 cm (51⅛ x 51⅛ inches). Solomon R. Guggenheim Museum, Gift, Solomon R. Guggenheim 41.149.

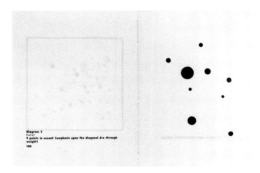

Fig. 86. Vasily Kandinsky, "Diagram 3, Point, 9 points in ascent (emphasis upon the diagonal d–a through weight)," from Kandinsky's *Punkt und Linie zu Fläche* (*Point and Line to Plane*).

Braque and Pablo Picasso (both of whom never came to embrace the idea of non-objective painting) had, almost unwittingly, opened a door to a world of visual imagery that had never before been seen.

Around 1913, pure abstraction emerged and forever changed the course of art history. To study the moment of the invention of abstract painting is to see both the world and the artists' perception of it undergoing convulsions of mind and body. Modern painters distorted, fractured, rearranged, and recolored the picture surface until it reemerged—no longer a Renaissance window on reality, but a vision unto itself as an object of contemplation and psychological effect.

Kandinsky's paintings of 1913 reveal a transition from the use of recognizable images to pure abstraction. For example, in *Painting with White Border* (plate 50) of May 1913, a central figure in a landscape is identifiable, while *Black Lines* (plate 48), painted in December, eludes such decoding. Although *Black Lines* was long considered the earliest non-objective painting, no "first" abstract painting can be identified as a model. The roots of abstraction are as diverse as its manifestations. Non-objective painting emerged simultaneously in Moscow, Paris, and the Netherlands, in each place with a different character. At first, abstraction developed among the ranks of the avant-garde. By the 1920s, however, some of its proponents found themselves leading mainstream institutions. Kandinsky, Kazimir Malevich, and other leaders of the Russian avant-garde were placed in charge of schools intended to advance the ideals of the October Revolution. In the Netherlands, Piet Mondrian's theories were spread through the publications of the De Stijl group. And in Germany, at the Bauhaus (founded by Walter Gropius in 1919), Kandinsky taught his theories of abstraction, as did Swiss painter Paul Klee, Hungarian artist László Moholy-Nagy, and other major proponents of the new style.

While some of abstract art's pioneers returned to figurative and representative styles by the late 1920s and early 1930s

(most notably Malevich), and while non-objectivity could certainly not be characterized, as Rebay proposed, as "the religion of the future," the idea of non-objective art did become the most dominant and innovative force in twentieth-century art. During and after World War II, many of abstraction's European champions, like the German Hans Hofmann, Mondrian, Moholy-Nagy, and the Russian brothers Antoine Pevsner and Naum Gabo, emigrated to the United States, where they influenced a new generation of artists. Encouraged by Rebay's and Guggenheim's crusade, as well as by exhibitions of European painting at the Museum of Modern Art and Peggy Guggenheim's Art of This Century gallery, the Europeans helped create an atmosphere in New York City that produced the Abstract Expressionists, whose work most directly launched a new chapter in non-objective art (see "Art of This Century and the New York School," pages 221–52).

Yet for all of its influence, little effort has been made by art historians to examine the invention of abstraction through an analysis of the unique cultural psychology of the twentieth century. By the late-nineteenth century, the world had been turned upside down: the industrial revolution promised the greatest change in human life since the invention of agriculture; the theories of Engels and Marx suggested revolutionary social changes to follow suit; and Nietzsche had pronounced God dead. The dramatic invention of abstract art—along with the utopian, spiritual, philosophical, and social theories that accompanied it—might be considered the single most revealing insight into the radical changes that shaped twentieth-century culture. Implicit in the leap from images representing natural appearance to images of a non-objective sort is a radical change in artists' philosophical understanding of the world around them. Why did these artists turn their eyes away from visible phenomena? What sparked that revolution in thinking? And what can be revealed about the fundamental character of our century through an examination of the invention of non-objective art?

Kandinsky's early writing, like that of many of his contemporaries, reveals the Modernists' preoccupation with the distinction of their era and their responsibility as artists to reject models of the past—to invent a new vocabulary of forms to express their world view. Ironically, the search for new forms began not with an embrace of the aesthetic of the new industrial age, but rather with a kind of regression: Kandinsky wrote of being "in sympathy" spiritually "with the Primitives."[7] Much has been written about the influence around the turn of the century of "primitive" forms of art on the advent of Modernism, especially in the work of Constantin Brancusi, Paul Gauguin, Henri Matisse, Picasso, the German Expressionists, and the Russian Primitivists. Brancusi's carved-wood sculptures (see fig. 10) provide compelling testament to the inspiration "primitive" art played in reshaping the visual language of Modern art. "Like ourselves," explained Kandinsky, the "primitives" "sought to express in their work only internal truths, renouncing in consequence all consideration of external form."[8]

Kandinsky's turn *inward* was an essential step in the development of his non-objective painting; this direction was anticipated in the work of the Symbolist painters, like Gauguin, who separated fields of color from descriptive function to express an emotional presence beyond the representation of nature. According to Symbolist poet Gustave Kahn, writing in 1886, "the essential aim of our art is to objectify the subjective (the externalization of the Idea) instead of subjectifying the objective (nature seen through the eyes of a temperament). Thus we carry the analysis of the Self to the extreme, we let the multiplicity and intertwining of rhythm harmonize with the measure of the Idea."[9] As Gauguin had sought refuge in Tahiti from a dehumanized material world, Kandinsky sought inner life as an alternative to the "nightmare of materialism"[10] of the modern world.

Mondrian, the Dutch pioneer of non-objective painting, shared Kandinsky's concern for an inner, and *abstract*,

modern life. In more cerebral terms than Kandinsky, Mondrian described an abstract inner reality of mind:

Natural (external) things become more and more automatic, and we observe that our vital attention fastens more and more on internal things. The life of the truly modern man is neither purely materialistic nor purely emotional. It manifests itself rather as a more autonomous life of the human mind becoming conscious itself.[11]

Mondrian, whose own non-objective art emerged around 1913, developed a systematic language of abstraction that has become, more than any other, synonymous with the reductivist aesthetic we associate with Modernism. Constraining the elements of line and color to essential ingredients—black horizontal and vertical lines on a white ground bounding rectangular fields of the primary colors red, yellow, and blue—Mondrian sought to represent the essence of reality rather than its particular natural appearance. He wrote:

To love things in reality is to love them profoundly; it is to see them as a microcosmos in the macrocosmos. Only in this way can one achieve a universal expression of reality. *Precisely on account of its profound love for things, nonfigurative art does not aim at rendering them in their particular appearance.*[12]

Mondrian's search for pure essential forms might be likened to Plato's parable of the cave, in which cave dwellers see only shadows of the real forms of the world outside, as in our world we see only particular manifestations projected from the realm of universal forms beyond. Plato's philosophy of universal forms was also an important source for artists of the Renaissance, who (not unlike Mondrian) were trying to reconcile in an aesthetic theory the particular imperfections of our earthly existence with their faith in a perfect universal truth. Mondrian revised Renaissance aesthetics that were "Neoplatonic" with his own theory of the "Neo-Plastic," in which he also tried to give visible form to the invisible ideal structures of nature.

Fig. 87. Piet Mondrian in meditation, 1909.

Plate 50. Vasily Kandinsky, *Painting with White Border* (*Bild mit weissem Rand*), May 1913. Oil on canvas, 140.3 x 200.3 cm (55¼ x 78⅞ inches). Solomon R. Guggenheim Museum, Gift, Solomon R. Guggenheim 37.245.

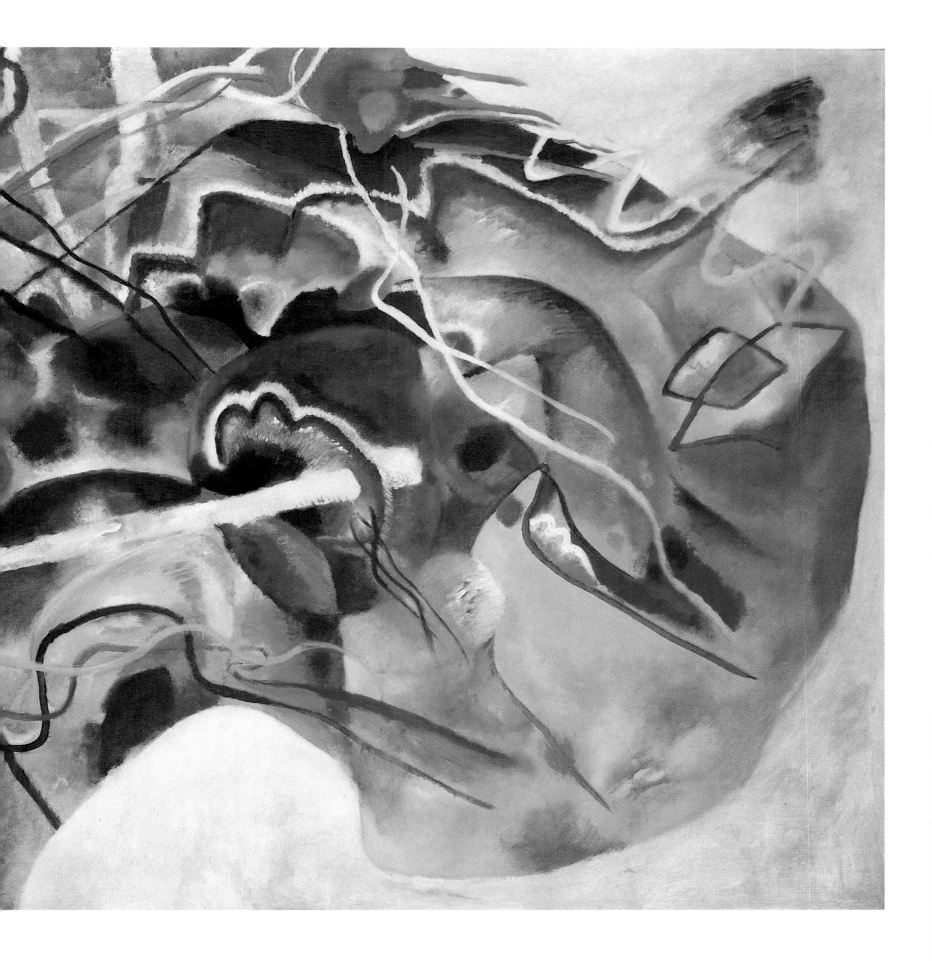

Plate 51. Vasily Kandinsky, *Dominant Curve (Courbe dominante),* April 1936. Oil on canvas, 129.4 x 194.2 cm (50 ⅞ x 76 ½ inches). Solomon R. Guggenheim Museum 45.989.

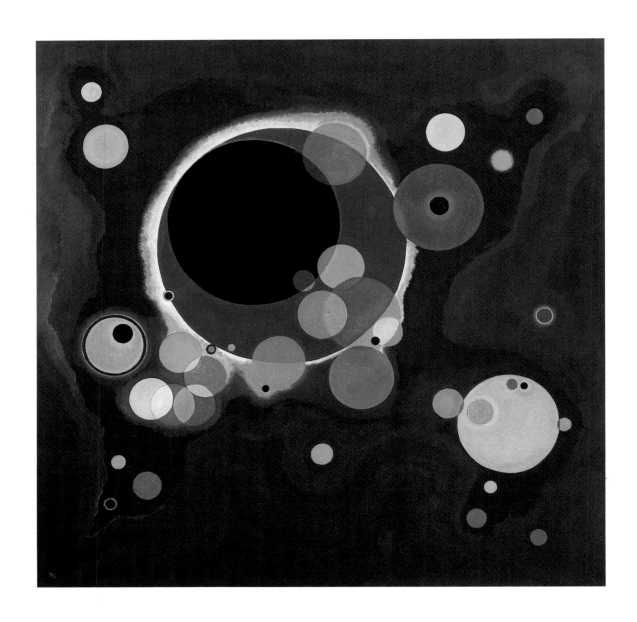

Plate 52. Vasily Kandinsky, *Several Circles (Einige Kreise),*
January–February 1926. Oil on canvas, 140.3 x 140.7 cm
(55 ¼ x 55 ⅜ inches). Solomon R. Guggenheim Museum,
Gift, Solomon R. Guggenheim 41.283.

Mondrian tried to synthesize the microcosmos and the macrocosmos, the inner and the beyond, in one universal, plastic language.

The synthesis of inner feeling with the cosmos beyond was the primary ambition of the religious/philosophical movement known as theosophy, of which both Mondrian and Kandinsky were students. Popularized by its co-founder, the Russian Helena Petrovna Blavatsky (fig. 88), in such tomes as *The Secret Doctrine: The Synthesis of Science, Religion, and Philosophy* (1888), theosophy deeply influenced, and perfectly reflected, the sensibility that sparked Mondrian's and Kandinsky's invention of non-objective painting. Mondrian joined the Theosophical Society in 1909, knew and read Blavatsky's texts, and practiced theosophical meditation (fig. 87). Rebay developed an interest in theosophy as early as age fourteen, when she attended classes held by Rudolf Steiner, theosophy's most accessible teacher and theorist.

Loosely translated from the Greek, "theosophy" means "divine wisdom," its central concern being the understanding and health of the human spirit in an individual and collective sense. The doctrine of theosophy (related to Georg Wilhelm Friedrich Hegel's more complex speculative universalism) is especially interesting in the context of the development of non-objective painting as a kind of modern mysticism in the midst of the onslaught of nineteenth-century science, from Charles Darwin's theory of evolution to Ernest Rutherford's theory of atomic structure.

The visual metaphor of clairvoyance was central to theosophical teaching. "The first point which must be clearly comprehended," remarked clairvoyant theosophist Charles W. Leadbeater in the first chapter of *Man Visible and Invisible* (1902), "is the wonderful complexity of the world around us—the fact that it includes enormously more than comes within the range of ordinary vision."[13]

Theosophy described a synthesis of science and the spirit in terms appropriated equally from ancient cultures and modern technology. Mimicking Rutherford's atomic science, Leadbeater's occult science explained that substances known as elements, like oxygen or hydrogen, are not truly elemental but ultimately can be broken down "to a set of units which are identical, except that some of them are positive and some negative."[14] These units of matter exist on several *planes of nature*, which ascend from the lowest plane, that of the physical world, to the astral and mental planes and beyond, progressively refined as they become more spiritual. Similarly, Leadbeater's experimentation in "thought-induced photography of astro-mental images," described in *Thought-Forms* (1901), a book he co-authored with his theosophical colleague Annie Besant, echoes Wilhelm Roentgen's 1895 experiments with the exposure of photographic plates to invisible X rays as a means to visually capture phenomena beyond the visible world.

Leadbeater's and Besant's intriguing books were particularly important to the development of Kandinsky's abstract painting, as art historian Sixten Ringbom has documented.[15] Their theosophical books deal with "the general subject of the aura," the cloudlike substance that emanates from man's body and extends beyond its physical confines into the mental and astral planes. Thus:

Every thought gives rise to a set of correlated vibrations in the matter of this body, accompanied with a marvellous play of color, like that in the spray of a waterfall as the sunlight strikes it, raised to the nth degree of color and vivid delicacy. The body under this impulse throws off a vibrating portion of itself, shaped by the nature of the vibrations—as figures are made by sand on a disk vibrating to a musical note—and this gathers from the surrounding atmosphere matter like itself in the fineness from the elemental essence of the mental world. We have then a thought-form pure and simple, and it is a living entity of intense activity animated by the one idea that generated it.[16]

Not only thoughts can be seen with theosophical clairvoyance, but also music:

Top: Fig. 88. Madame Helena Petrovna Blavatsky. Courtesy Theosophical University Press, Pasadena, California.

Bottom: Fig. 89. Thought-form 28, "Selfish Greed," from Annie Besant and Charles W. Leadbeater, *Thought-Forms* (1901).

Plate 53. Paul Klee, *In the Current Six Thresholds (In der Strömung sechs Schwellen),* 1929. Oil and tempera on canvas, 43.5 x 43.5 cm (17⅛ x 17⅛ inches). Solomon R. Guggenheim Museum 67.1842.

Many people are aware that sound is always associated with color—that when, for example, a musical note is sounded, a flash of color corresponding to it may be seen by those whose finer senses are already to some extent developed. . . . Every piece of music leaves behind it an impression of this nature, which persists for some considerable time, and is clearly visible and intelligible to those who have eyes to see.[17]

As a basis for his art, Kandinsky constructed an analogy to classical music, titling many of his works *Improvisations* (for example, plate 22) or *Compositions* (for example, plate 2). "A painter who finds no satisfaction in mere representation," wrote Kandinsky, "naturally seeks to apply the methods of music to his own art. And from this results that modern desire for rhythm in painting, for mathematical, abstract construction, for repeated notes of color, for setting color in motion."[18]

Kandinsky was not alone in his interest in the relationship between music and abstract painting. Mondrian loved jazz and its relation to painting, as evidenced in late works such as *Broadway Boogie Woogie* (1942–43, in the collection of the Museum of Modern Art, New York). Klee also employed musical structures, even marks of musical notation, as compositional devices in his non-objective paintings, such as *In the Current Six Thresholds* (1929, plate 53) and *New Harmony* (1936, plate 56).

What is relevant about Kandinsky's analogy to music is its relation, or lack thereof, to sight in the traditional sense. That is not to suggest that Kandinsky meant his paintings less for the eyes than other paintings, but perhaps he was implying that the visual sensation itself has other components that are not entirely visual. As smell is a major component of taste, could not hearing be part of seeing? Theosophically speaking, "sight" was not limited to the visible world.

Both *Man Visible and Invisible* and *Thought-Forms* contain illustrations of "thought-forms" and images emanating from music, which, with their accompanying explanations, are obviously sources for the clouds of color

around Kandinsky's lyrical abstract shapes (for example, in *Several Circles* [1926, plate 52] and *Dominant Curve* [1936, plate 51]). Each book also includes an illustrated "Key to the Meanings of Colours," which certainly must have influenced Kandinsky's color theory and Mondrian's early Symbolist-inspired pictures. A passage in Leadbeater's text reads almost like a play for Mondrian's triptych *Evolution* (1910–11, in the collection of the Haags Gemeentemuseum): "Light blue marks devotion to a noble spiritual ideal, and gradually rises to a luminous lilac-blue, which typifies the higher spirituality, and is usually accompanied by sparkling golden stars, representing elevated spiritual aspirations."[19]

Blavatsky placed the motto "There is no religion higher than Truth" at the beginning of *The Secret Doctrine*. Theosophy seeks to uncover the universal through a process that reveals the truth of structures—the sacred codes—beneath all visible reality. In theosophy, the traditional separation of the secular and the religious dissolves into manifestations of the same universal. The large crossed arms of the windmill Mondrian depicted in *Windmill at Night* (1907, in the collection of the Haags Gemeentemuseum), an early painting with a secular theme, is related to the cross in *Church at Domburg* (1914, in the collection of the Haags Gemeentemuseum), which is further related to the abstract "plus" and "minus" marks of later, non-objective pictures. Mondrian worked through many of his ideas on the dissolution of forms in his sketchbooks of 1912–14 (plates 57–58); he also articulated them in his writing, for, like Kandinsky, he was a prolific theorist. He began to "discern the perpendicular in everything," he wrote. "The arms of the windmill are not more beautiful to me than anything else. Seen *plastically*, they actually have a disadvantage. To the shape of the cross, particularly when in the upright position, we readily attach a particular, rather *literary* idea. The cross form, however, is constantly destroyed in the New Plastic."[20] In other words, Mondrian erases the literary/religious

Top: Plate 54. Man Ray, *Untitled,* 1923. Rayograph, gelatin-silver print, 28.8 x 23.5 cm (11 ⅜ x 9 ¼ inches). Peggy Guggenheim Collection 76.2553 PG69a.

Bottom: Plate 55. Man Ray, *Untitled,* 1927. Rayograph, gelatin-silver print, 30.4 x 25.4 cm (11 ¹⁵⁄₁₆ x 10 inches). Peggy Guggenheim Collection 76.2553 PG69b.

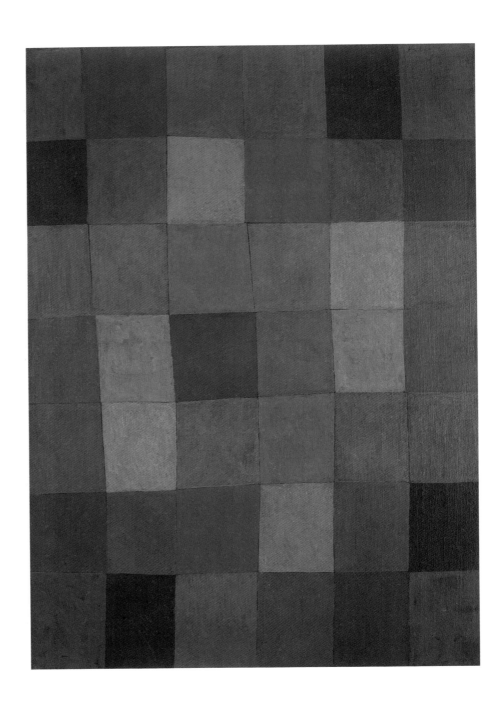

Plate 56. Paul Klee, *New Harmony (Neue Harmonie)*, 1936.
Oil on canvas, 93.6 x 66.3 cm (36⅞ x 26⅛ inches). Solomon
R. Guggenheim Museum 71.1960.

reference of the cross, incorporating it into a more universal visual system of binary marks. The progression of Mondrian's work, from early still lifes to abstractions, is demonstrated with dramatic clarity in the Guggenheim's rich collection (for example, plates 59–65).

The age-old dichotomies between body and spirit, secular and sacred, science and religion, are at the heart of Kandinsky's and Mondrian's development of non-objective painting, as they are to the general psychology of the twentieth century. Yet the dynamic between science and the spirit reflected in non-objective art is ambiguous. On the one hand, technology posed a material challenge to artists: for example, the widespread use of photography, which demystified, simplified, and mechanized the production of images of things, may have challenged artists to seek a higher, more mystical, and uniquely human vision. On the other hand, science and invention yielded new visual metaphors for artists: in his Rayographs (for example, plates 54–55), Man Ray capitalized on X-ray photography, which recorded images beneath the skin. Like the theosophical clairvoyance that inspired Kandinsky, X-ray photography suggested a new sense of vision beyond the images received by the eye. Similarly, Rutherford's 1911 description of the structure of atoms—a collection of positively charged protons orbited by negatively charged electrons—suggested an irreducible binary reality, paralleling Mondrian's painterly conception of the universe expressed in horizontal and vertical lines. Both Rutherford's and Mondrian's models reduced the particularity of the visible world to a reality of binary poles that could not be seen by the eye but could only be represented through abstract models and diagrams—or paintings.

While science has always shaken religious dogma, it has also inspired a further mystical interest in the systems of nature. In the sixteenth century, Copernicus was excommunicated because his new astronomy suggested that the earth revolved around the sun,

and therefore challenged the Church's order of the universe and man's place within it. Yet, as Rebay wrote in explaining non-objective painting, "Placing his vision outside the earth, [Copernicus] opened enormous vistas and brought to light new viewpoints with far-reaching consequences. The discovery of the possibility of placing oneself outside all former viewpoints concerning art is of equal importance to humanity."[21] Rebay rightly pointed out that the Copernican revolution is important not simply in terms of its factual results, but in terms of the mind-set that produced it. Copernicus's hypothesis (1543) was made possible by a visual system embodied in the Renaissance discovery of linear perspective. With perspectival means to map space and visual experience with illusionistic precision, artists developed the potential for a systematic, objective frame of reference, which is a prerequisite for any scientific thinking.

Even in the Renaissance, artists had an uncertain relationship to science, especially as it intersected with matters of the spirit. Leone Battista Alberti's rules of perspective, set out in *On Painting* (1436) with scientific precision, were at first rarely employed by artists with scientific rigor or results. More often, the rules of perspective were bent in the creation of compositions to stress spiritual rather than material content. Furthermore, linear perspective, stemming as it was from mathematical order, took on symbolic value as a reflection of God's spiritual perfection[22] (not unlike M. H. J. Schoenmaeker's treatise, *Plastic Mathematics* [1916], which described a Platonic universal order and inspired fellow Dutchman Mondrian's Neo-Plasticism[23]).

Copernicus's hypothesis concerning the movements of visible heavenly bodies might be compared to Rutherford's theories about the structure of invisible atoms. To the extent that linear perspective in the fifteenth century defined a relation between the artist and the visible world, the advent of non-objective art in the twentieth century defined a relation between the artist and the *invisible* world. In both cases, advances in science

Top: Plate 57. Piet Mondrian, Page from *Sketchbook I,* 1912–14. Pencil on paper, 16 x 11.5 cm (6¼ x 4½ inches). Solomon R. Guggenheim Museum, New York, Gift, David Finn and Maurice Kaplan 81.2824.

Bottom: Plate 58. Piet Mondrian, Page from *Sketchbook I,* 1912–14. Pencil and charcoal on paper, 16 x 11.5 cm (6¼ x 4½ inches). Solomon R. Guggenheim Museum, New York, Gift, David Finn and Maurice Kaplan 81.2824.

Plate 59. Piet Mondrian, *Still Life with Ginger Pot I*
(*Stilleven Met Gemberpot I*), 1911–12. Oil on canvas,
65.5 x 75 cm (25 ¼ x 29 ½ inches). Solomon R.
Guggenheim Museum LN 295.76.

Plate 60. Piet Mondrian, *Still Life with Ginger Pot II*
(*Stilleven Met Gemberpot II*), 1911–12. Oil on canvas,
91.5 x 120 cm (37 ½ x 47 ¼ inches). Solomon R.
Guggenheim Museum LN 294.76.

Plate 61. Piet Mondrian, *Composition VII*, 1913.
Oil on canvas, 104.4 x 113.6 cm (41 ⅛ x 44 ¼ inches).
Solomon R. Guggenheim Museum 49.1228.

Plate 64. Piet Mondrian, *Composition 2,* 1922. Oil on canvas, 55.6 x 53.4 cm (21 ⅞ x 21 ⅛ inches). Solomon R. Guggenheim Museum 51.1309.

Plate 63. Piet Mondrian, *Composition 1916,* 1916. Oil on canvas with wood strip at bottom edge, 119 x 75.1 cm (46 ⅞ x 29 ⅛ inches). Solomon R. Guggenheim Museum 49.1229.

Plate 62. Piet Mondrian, *Composition No. 8,* 1914. Oil on canvas, 94.4 x 55.6 cm (37 ⅛ x 21 ⅞ inches). Solomon R. Guggenheim Museum 49.1227.

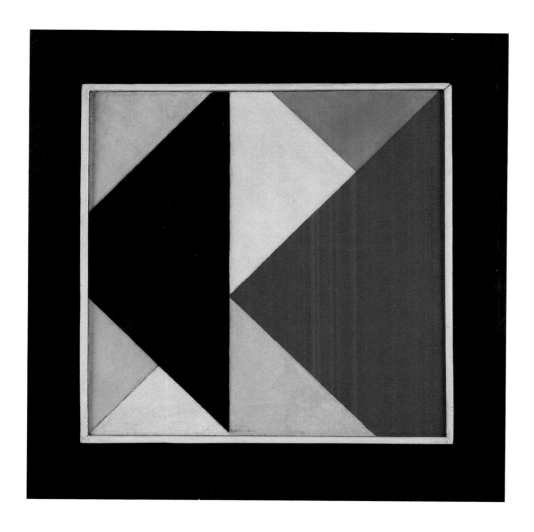

Left: Plate 65. Piet Mondrian, *Composition IA*, 1930. Oil on canvas (lozenge), 75.2 x 75.2 cm (29 ⅝ x 29 ⅝ inches). Solomon R. Guggenheim Museum, Hilla Rebay Collection 71.1936R96.

Above: Plate 66. Theo van Doesburg, *Counter-Composition XIII (Contra-Compositie XIII)*, 1925–26. Oil on canvas, 50 x 50 cm (19 ⅝ x 19 ⅝ inches). Peggy Guggenheim Collection 76.2553 PG41.

and art had radical implications for the way in which the structure of the world was understood and represented.

Modernism, embodied in the development of non-objective art, responded most directly to intertwined phenomena in the Western world at around the turn of the century, all of which might be considered outgrowths of overwhelming advancements in science and technology: the crisis in religious belief, Marxist revolutions, and the emergence of theosophy. Technology, according to twentieth-century philosopher Martin Heidegger, is both a means to an end and a human activity—in both the instruments, procedures, and methods that define it, and the attitude it reflects. Its essence lies in the process of classification and the development of models (representations) by which humanity achieves mastery over the substance of the world. It is the ability through scientific thinking to form a "world picture" as an objective model (a fundamentally subjective process) that coincides with the loss of belief embedded in Nietzsche's decree, "God is dead."

Malevich's introduction of Suprematism in 1915 perfectly embodied the complex psychological condition within which non-objective art was born. *Black Square* (1915, in the collection of the State Tretiakov Gallery, Moscow), the first Suprematist painting, was hung in the upper corner of a room, the place in a Russian home traditionally reserved for a religious icon. With it, Malevich presented, as he called it, a "single bare, frameless, icon of our times."[24] Malevich's Suprematism was, like Kandinsky's and Mondrian's art, a search for a universal language that resolved the conflict between a technological and a spiritual existence. In works such as *Untitled* (ca. 1916, plate 67), Malevich fashioned his geometric constructions (inspired, like his colleague Vladimir Tatlin's Constructivist sculptures, by modern images of airplanes and factories) with deliberate, painterly marks, expressing the intuitive and spiritual aspects of his science. Malevich's square icon was both a substitute for traditional religious

faith, in crisis as it was challenged by the new industrial, technological world, and a guardian of the human spirit in the face of such change.

El Lissitzky, Gabo, and Pevsner took the relationship between science, technology, and art even further. Perhaps more than any other artists of the Russian avant-garde, they fully embraced the new industrial age. Lissitzky's early non-objective paintings (for example, *Untitled*, 1919–20, plate 68) are indebted to Suprematism. Only a few years after the October Revolution, however, he expanded his artistic output to include sculpture, architecture, photography, and industrial, poster, and theater design, attempting to harness the power of abstract art to further the goals of the new Communist society. Sculptors Pevsner and Gabo also subscribed for a time to the tenet that art should be placed in service of the Revolution, and, like Lissitzky, were important members of the Constructivist group. Pevsner's *Anchored Cross* (1933, plate 73), in which he combined industrial materials and shapes with the image of the Russian Orthodox cross, exemplifies the meeting of science, religion, and art in abstraction. Gabo's *Column* (ca. 1923, plate 74) derives its architectural form from mathematical and scientific compositional devices. It is one of the first sculptures to utilize plastic—at the time, one of the newest material inventions of advancing technology.

Moholy-Nagy's earliest experiments in plastic influenced his use of perspective and transparency in oil paintings such as *T1* (1926, plate 69) and *AXL II* (1927, plate 70). The invention of Plexiglas in 1936 provided Moholy-Nagy with the ideal medium to realize his quasi-scientific exploration of the formal properties of light and space. He found that the malleable material could be bent, incised, and painted to form a hybrid of painting and sculpture that the artist called "space modulators." Ever-changing effects of transparency and the shadows cast by plastic forms in real space (for example, in *B-10 Space Modulator*, 1942, plate 71, and *Dual Form with Chromium Rods*, 1946, plate 72) introduced new elements

Plate 67. Kazimir Malevich, *Untitled*, ca. 1916. Oil on
canvas, 53 x 53 cm (20 ⅞ x 20 ⅞ inches). Peggy Guggenheim
Collection 76.2553 PG42.

Plate 68. El Lissitzky, *Untitled,* ca. 1919–20. Oil on canvas,
79.6 x 49.6 cm (31 5/16 x 19 1/2 inches). Peggy Guggenheim
Collection 76.2553 PG43.

into his exploration of a human perception of the universe. Moholy-Nagy also carried his concerns about light and space into the realm of photography, capturing light, space, and time on the chemical surface of his "photograms."

Kandinsky inscribed the limits of the power of science and technology at the edge of matter, noting that no "principle can be laid down for those things which lie beyond, in the realm of the immaterial. That which has no material existence cannot be subjected to a material classification."[25] Instead, a "non-matter" related to the spirit can only be reached "by the way of *inner* knowledge."[26] For Kandinsky, theosophy's synthesis of scientific means and primitive religion provided a base from which to challenge materialistic science.

Heidegger, in confronting the "danger" of technology, quotes the German Romantic poet Friedrich Hölderlin: "But where danger is, grows / The saving power also." Heidegger implies that the "saving power" may be pursued through the philosopher's *thought*, and through *art*:

Because the essence of technology is nothing technological, essential reflection upon technology and decisive confrontation with it must happen in a realm that is, on the one hand, akin to the essence of technology and, on the other hand, fundamentally different from it. Such a realm is art. But certainly only if reflection on art for its part, does not shut its eyes to the constellation of truth after which we are questioning.[27]

By delineating the edge of matter and materialistic science and exploring its counterpart, found in thought and emotion (and in the cosmos beyond), Kandinsky's and Mondrian's non-objective painting touched the essence of technology and science: its vision. The essence of technology is, like theosophical clairvoyance, a kind of divine wisdom.

Any systematic theory or world view, including theosophy, may fall prey to the danger of mastery over materials. In his theories, Kandinsky was careful to avoid the artist's natural mastery over substance or the escapism of art for art's sake, writing, "The artist must have something to say, for mastery over form is not his goal but rather the adapting of form to its inner meaning."[28] The process is an investigation rather than an exposition. And, as Heidegger states, "the more questioningly we ponder the essence of technology, the more mysterious the essence of art becomes."[29]

The "subject" of Kandinsky's non-objective art is the inner being made manifest in the mysterious process of subjective inspiration by means of an intimate knowledge of pure color and form in painting. In developing his non-objective art, Kandinsky was attempting to retrieve the spirit without turning his back on the modern technological age.

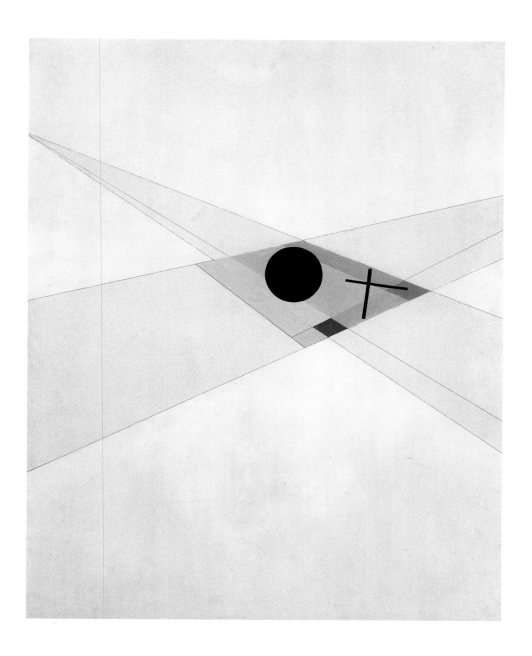

Left: Plate 69. László Moholy-Nagy, *T1*, 1926. Oil on
Trolitan, 139.8 x 62.9 cm (55 x 24¾ inches). Solomon R.
Guggenheim Museum, Gift, Solomon R. Guggenheim
37.354.

Above: Plate 70. László Moholy-Nagy, *AXL II*, 1927.
Oil on canvas, 94.1 x 73.9 cm (37 x 29⅛ inches). Solomon R.
Guggenheim Museum, Gift, Mrs. Andrew P. Fuller
64.1754.

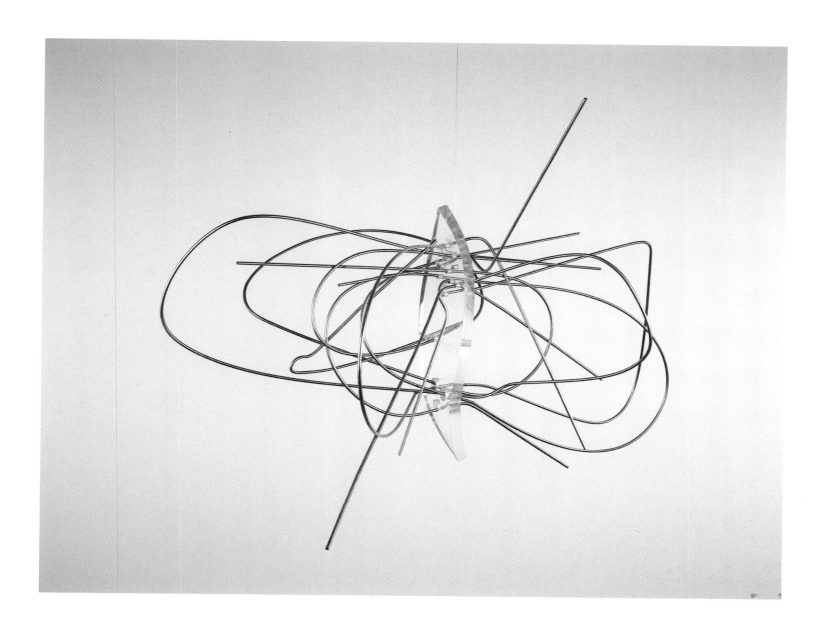

Left: Plate 71. László Moholy-Nagy, *B-10 Space
Modulator*, 1942. Oil on incised molded Plexiglas, mounted
with chromium clamps 5.1 cm (2 inches) from white
plywood backing; Plexiglas: 45.1 x 30.5 cm (17 ¾ x
12 inches). Solomon R. Guggenheim Museum 47.1063.

Above: Plate 72. László Moholy-Nagy, *Dual Form with
Chromium Rods*, 1946. Plexiglas and chrome-plated steel
rods, 92.7 x 121.6 x 55.9 cm (36 ½ x 47 ⅞ x 22 inches).
Solomon R. Guggenheim Museum 48.1149.

Notes

1. Hilla Rebay, "The Beauty of Non-Objectivity," in *Second Enlarged Catalogue of the Solomon R. Guggenheim Collection of Non-Objective Paintings* (New York: The Solomon R. Guggenheim Foundation, 1937), p. 13.

2. Quoted in Joan M. Lukach, *Hilla Rebay: In Search of the Spirit in Art* (New York: George Braziller, 1983), p. 62.

3. Wright's discussion of his conception of the museum, as well as Rebay's responses, can be found in *Frank Lloyd Wright: The Guggenheim Correspondence*, selected by Bruce Brooks Pfeiffer (Fresno: The Press at California State University; Carbondale: Southern Illinois University Press, 1986).

4. Rebay rigorously used the term "non-objective" as opposed to "abstract" painting to refer to the art she espoused, thereby stressing the subtle but critical difference between the two. Abstraction, to Rebay and others, is derived from reality—a reduction of its content, but in the final analysis still a reference to specific things. On the other hand, non-objective painting has no real referent and therefore is pure and simple. Rebay did acquire abstractions, such as works by Picasso, but only as precursors to non-objective painting.

The term "non-objective" never became commonplace in the vocabulary of art historians and critics, who have preferred the term "abstraction" to refer both to abstractions and compositions-without-object. Conceptually, the difference between the two terms is great, but in practice the line between abstraction and non-objectivity is thin—defined perhaps by an artist's intent rather than the visual impression.

I once asked art historian Ernst Gombrich what he perceived as the fundamental difference between representational and purely non-objective painting. His one-word answer— "Scale"—was at first disappointing but then seemed suggestive of the viewer's response to such art. Any time the viewer identifies a real referent in an image, his or her senses place that image in a context and assign to it an estimated scale. Modernist representational painting (works by Marc Chagall or the Surrealists, for example) often relies on plays of scale. Perhaps Gombrich intended to suggest the unique quality of an image without any scale.

In his art and writings, Kandinsky made an analogy between music and painting, suggesting the possibility of interpreting images without the usual frame of reference that suggests scale. Rebay's defining of non-objective painting is important primarily because of the metaphorical potential of an image without scale. Kandinsky himself tried to use the term "concrete" to refer to his purely pictorial compositions (in *Kandinsky: Complete Writings on Art*, ed. by Kenneth C. Lindsay and Peter Vergo, vol. 2 [Boston: G. K. Hall & Co., 1982], p. 830):

Abstract or non-figurative or non-objective art (which I myself most prefer to call concrete) differs from older forms of expression and from Surrealism today by reason of the fact that it does not set out from an object, but itself "invents" its forms of expression in very different ways.

For the purposes of this essay, the distinction between a distortion or abstraction of reality, and pure non-objectivity is critical. However, because "non-objective" remains cumbersome the terms "non-objective" and "abstraction" are used interchangeably.

5. Rebay, "The Beauty of Non-Objectivity," p. 13.

6. Rebay, however, did not collect Calder. While the work of Calder, as well as of Brancusi, has become closely identified with the Guggenheim, these sculptures were added to the collection by the museum's second director, James Johnson Sweeney.

7. Wassily Kandinsky, *Concerning the Spiritual in Art*, trans. by M. T. H. Sadler (New York: Dover Publications, 1977), p. 1. Reprint of *The Art of Spiritual Harmony* (London: Constable and Company, 1914).

8. Ibid.

9. Quoted in Herschel B. Chipp, *Theories of Modern Art: A Source Book by Artists and Critics* (Berkeley: University of California Press, 1968), p. 50

10. Kandinsky, p. 2.

11. Quoted in Chipp, p. 321.

12. Quoted in Chipp, p. 359.

13. C. W. Leadbeater, *Man Visible and Invisible* (Wheaton, Ill.: The Theosophical Publishing House, 1987), p. 6.

14. Ibid., p. 7.

15. See Sixten Ringbom, *The Sounding Cosmos: A Study in the Spiritualism of Kandinsky and the Genesis of Abstract Painting* (Abo, Finland: Abo Akademi, 1970).

16. Annie Besant and C. W. Leadbeater, *Thought-Forms* (Wheaton, Ill.: The Theosophical Publishing House, 1969), p. 8. Reprint (Adyar, India: The Theosophical Publishing House, 1925).

17. Ibid., p. 67.

18. Kandinsky, p. 19.

19. Leadbeater, p. 69.

20. Piet Mondrian, "Natural Reality and Abstract Reality," in Harry Holtzman and Martin S. James, *The New Art–The New Life: The Collected Writings of Piet Mondrian* (Boston: G. K. Hall & Co., 1986), p. 99.

21. Hilla Rebay, "Definition of Non-Objective Painting," in *Solomon R. Guggenheim Collection of Non-Objective Paintings* (Charleston, S.C.: Carolina Art Association, 1936), p. 8.

22. See Samuel Y. Edgerton, Jr., *The Renaissance Rediscovery of Linear Perspective* (New York: Basic Books, 1975).

23. For a description of the relationship between the theories of Schoenmaeker and Mondrian, see H. L. C. Jaffe, *De Stijl 1917–1931, The Dutch Contribution to Modern Art* (Amsterdam: Meulenhoff, 1956), p. 57.

24. Quoted in Jane Sharp, "The Critical Reception of the *0.10* Exhibition: Malevich and Benua," in *The Great Utopia: The Russian and Soviet Avant-Garde, 1915–1932* (New York: Guggenheim Museum Publications, 1992), p. 44.

25. Kandinsky, p. 12.

26. Ibid., p. 13.

27. Martin Heidegger, "The Question Concerning Technology," in *The Question Concerning Technology and Other Essays* (New York: Harper and Row, 1977), pp. 34–35.

28. Kandinsky, p. 54.

29. Heidegger, p. 35.

Plate 73. Antoine Pevsner, *Anchored Cross* (*La Croix
ancrée*), 1933. Marble, brass painted black, and crystal,
84.6 cm (33 ¹⁄₁₆ inches) long (diagonally), 25.2 cm
(9 ¹⁵⁄₁₆ inches) deep. Peggy Guggenheim Collection
76.2553 PG60.

Plate 74. Naum Gabo, *Column,* ca. 1923. Perspex, wood, metal, and glass, 104.5 (41 ⅛ inches) high, 75 cm (29 ½ inches) in diameter. Solomon R. Guggenheim Museum 55.1429.

Plate 75. Max Ernst, *The Antipope*, December 1941–
March 1942. Oil on canvas, 160.8 x 127.1 cm (63¼ x
50 inches). Peggy Guggenheim Collection 76.2553 PG80.

Peggy's Surreal Playground

Jennifer Blessing

Peggy Goes to London, Guggenheim Jeune Gallery

Surrealism was the perfect playground for Peggy Guggenheim. Hemmed in by the proprieties of the New York Jewish aristocracy in which she was raised, Guggenheim escaped to Europe in 1920 and was in Paris to witness the birth of Surrealism. Her engagement with the movement in the 1920s was limited to social contacts with predominantly literary figures; it was not until she decided to open a gallery in London in 1938 that she became actively involved with the artistic community.

The name of the gallery, Guggenheim Jeune, made punning reference to the established Galerie Bernheim-Jeune in Paris, while fostering the mistaken assumption that Peggy Guggenheim was the daughter of Solomon R. Guggenheim, an important collector of non-objective painting in New York, though in fact he was her uncle.[1] This joke was not at all appreciated by Solomon's very serious adviser, Baroness Hilla Rebay von Ehrenwiesen, who chided Peggy in the opening salvo of what was to be a long-running antagonism between the two women. "It is extremely distasteful at this moment, when the name of Guggenheim stands for an ideal in art, to see it used for commerce," she wrote.[2]

Guggenheim Jeune became a model for Peggy Guggenheim's history-making gallery venture in New York City during World War II, Art of This Century. Many of her exhibitions in England became prototypes for American shows: at both galleries she favored Surrealists, showed the work of sculptors and emerging artists, and made no attempt to censor potentially controversial art, perhaps even seeking to promote it.[3]

In March 1939, Guggenheim decided to found a museum of twentieth-century art in London. When London became an untenable site, Guggenheim moved to Paris, intending to open her museum in a townhouse there. With a list of must-haves in hand, she went on a shopping spree, determined to "buy a picture a day" as the rest of Europe prepared for war.[4] Her intentions caused tremendous consternation for Solomon Guggenheim's and Rebay's French envoy, Yvanhoé Rambosson, who in July 1939 had begun to organize the Centre d'Etudes Artistiques Solomon R. Guggenheim to advance the study and exhibition of non-objective painting in Europe. In January 1940, Rambosson informed Rebay of Peggy Guggenheim's plans and urged a counteroffensive. On March 9, he wrote in distress to his patron, arguing that Solomon must take action to secure their position in the face of the oncoming enemy, Solomon's troublesome niece: "It must be so in the interest of the Art we are defending, because I would awfully fear that if Mrs. Peggy G. were alone to act, she might partly deviate the movement on a wrong way—it is almost certain, if one considers the artists she is encouraging till now."[5]

Peggy and the Personality of Surrealism

While Guggenheim insisted that her collection was to be "historical and unprejudiced,"[6] and that she personally preferred no particular style, her heart belonged to Surrealism, which was exactly what frightened the Rebay contingent. From André Breton's initial codification of the movement in 1924, when he published his notorious *Manifesto of Surrealism* (*Manifeste du surréalisme*), one of Surrealism's main goals was liberation from repression of all kinds: social, political, psychological, and sexual. Surrealism's transgression of established bourgeois norms, which was derived from Dada practices that resulted from post–World War I disillusionment, allowed for, in theory, the spontaneous expression of any repressed desire or whim. Guggenheim came of age in the adventurous atmosphere of 1920s Paris and took full advantage of the license that her wealth afforded her. She told an interviewer in 1976, "I was the original liberated woman. . . . I did everything, was everything; I was totally free financially, emotionally, intellectually, sexually."[7] In the early 1920s, she attempted a modicum of conventional marriage and motherhood, but in 1928 she left her husband and children, eventually alighting in London. She shocked her mother, among others, when she lived with a succession of lovers and indulged in affairs with Surrealist artists such as E. L. T. Mesens and Yves Tanguy, and artist/art historian Roland Penrose. In England, Guggenheim obtained her reputation as a "voracious consumer of men,"[8] which was not a particular liability in Surrealist circles because many of their investigations focused on Woman and her sexual desire.

In 1928, Breton—an avid student of Sigmund Freud's teachings and during World War I an intern at a neuropsychiatric center—published "Research on Sexuality," transcripts of informal discussions he conducted among Surrealist poets and artists about their sexual practices.[9] Couching prying questions in the guise of scientific inquiry, Breton foreshadowed Masters and Johnson by bringing quotidian sexual customs and opinions into the detached domain of the printed page. Breton asked the men what age they preferred their female partners to be, their favorite positions, and what they thought of women who engaged in "coquetry." The merits and demerits of women simulating orgasm were discussed, as were various fantasies such as watching two women making love, participating in a ménage à trois, and having sex with nuns. One poet asked what excited the men most, which elicited a litany of female body parts from the participants.[10] This inquiry, as well as the Surrealists' notorious enthusiasm for the Marquis de Sade, was scandalously provocative and contributed to their popular reputation as sexually licentious.

Based on this evidence alone, the role of women in Surrealism would seem to be limited to a position as mute object of desire. The situation, however, was somewhat more complicated. Breton, as self-appointed mouthpiece for the movement, took the lead in articulating the poetic concept of Woman, which suggested the individual woman's role as muse and inspiration for the male artist. In his first manifesto of Surrealism, he describes a marvelous castle inhabited by his guests, poet

friends, and "gorgeous women": ". . . the solitude is vast, we don't often run into one another. And anyway, isn't what matters that we be the masters of ourselves, the masters of women, and of love too?"[11] Though characterized as a fantasy, the castle is also Breton's model community of like-minded souls, clearly one in which men create and women provoke creation.

Among the Surrealists' practical concerns were free love and women's liberation from domestic responsibility. Both were advocated as refutations of bourgeois restrictions, although organized protests of existing day-to-day conditions were frowned upon. The Surrealists focused instead on the mythopoeic concept of the marvelous woman. As art historian Whitney Chadwick has explained, they conceived of woman as *femme-enfant* (naïf, fairy princess, unconscious medium) or *femme fatale* (seductress, deceptive performer, sorceress).[12] Despite the limitations of Breton's theoretical model of a mythical muse, many women actively participated in the Surrealist movement as writers and artists, especially in the 1930s. The gamut of the roles for women that appealed to the Surrealists is illustrated by the sign for Breton's short-lived gallery, Gradiva, which he opened in 1937 and named for the protagonist—a sculpture that came to life—of a story analyzed by Freud.[13] Below each letter of Gradiva was the name of a female mascot. For example, "G comme Gisèle" stood for Gisèle Prassinos, a fourteen-year-old poet *femme-enfant*; A for artist Alice Paalen; D for photographer Dora Maar; and V for Violette Nozières, a condemned patricide whom the Surrealists defended.[14]

The Surrealists were also sympathetic to the Papin sisters, who gouged out the eyes of their employer, as well as a number of other criminally insane women. Although in many ways the Surrealists' attitude about the insane was enlightened, they maintained a romantic notion of madness, which they saw as a privileged state that accessed the unrepressed operations of the unconscious and hence as a model of creativity. Their conjunction of insanity

and femininity—through their exaltation of the madwoman—came out of a cultural trope pervasive beyond the realm of Surrealism. (The conceptualization of hysteria, for example, was founded upon the female patient.[15]) Perhaps because women were believed to be more emotional and disposed to psychological disorders, they—along with "primitive" peoples, children, and the insane—were considered to have more integrated psyches, untouched by the rationality that society demanded of "civilized" adult males.[16] Thus, the Surrealists were fascinated by both the art made by these "outsiders" and the people themselves. The movement's journals contain photographic essays about their art production, ethnological and psychological articles, and images of the individuals themselves presented as if they were more documents to be studied.[17]

The Surrealists delighted in the marvelous—the exotic and erotic that stunned the senses through its unusualness, shocking the viewer into a new outlook or expanding the boundaries of his imagination.[18] Their desire for unique experiences led to innovation in all realms of expression, from theater and cinema, to painting techniques, to clothing and food. Seeking to integrate oppositions—the waking and dreaming states as well as the worlds of art and life—they proposed a new kind of existence, a new reality in surreality, which they visualized as a multifarious *gesamtkunstwerk*. While some male artists, such as Salvador Dalí, extended their art into life by conceiving of themselves as a kind of living performance spectacle, it was more often women who invented themselves as marvelous, dramatic extravagances.[19] Surrealist women artists frequently presented themselves as works of art, whether in self-portraits or for someone else's camera, suggesting that the creation of dramatis personae became a vehicle for women's expression (it continues to be manifested today in the work of artists such as Laurie Anderson, Eleanor Antin, and Cindy Sherman).[20]

With a manner of dress that verged on the marvelous, a mode of behavior outside bourgeois boundaries in terms of her boldness and sexual libertinage, and a history of insanity in her family, which she herself emphasized, Guggenheim participated in this spectacular masquerade, predisposing herself to the Surrealists and their art.[21] Although she also collected abstract work, she was not inclined to its spiritual program or its self-proclaimed spokesperson, Rebay. This disinclination became outright conflict when Guggenheim came to New York City in 1942.

Peggy's Collection of Surrealist Art

In the last months before Paris fell, Guggenheim combed artists' studios and received picture dealers in her hotel bedroom, working assiduously to amass a collection of important works exemplifying the period since 1910. An examination of Guggenheim's signal Surrealist works gives voice to the central concerns of the movement and perhaps also to the taste of its patron.

The Surrealist collection that Guggenheim created, in toto, outlines a vast explosion of cultivated sexual obsession. A landscape of desire emerges in which the female body takes center stage, whether directly in a realistic rendition or obliquely through abstract references. Oscillating from the vaguely feminine biomorphic curves of a relief by Jean Arp to the anatomically complete depictions of women in paintings by Ernst or Dalí, Surrealism was grounded in the body, most often the female body. Underlying the movement's notions of the working of the unconscious and its machinations in the realm of sexual desire were the ideas of Freud, which were disseminated through various Surrealist journals and more popular media. Some artists were intimately familiar with Freud's original writings; for example, the work of Ernst, who had studied psychoanalytic texts, reflects an advanced understanding of Freudian concepts.[22]

The crude sexual symbolism that pervades Freud's *The Interpretation of Dreams* (1900) is one of the hallmarks of Surrealist compositions. By 1929, oppositional Surrealist writer Georges

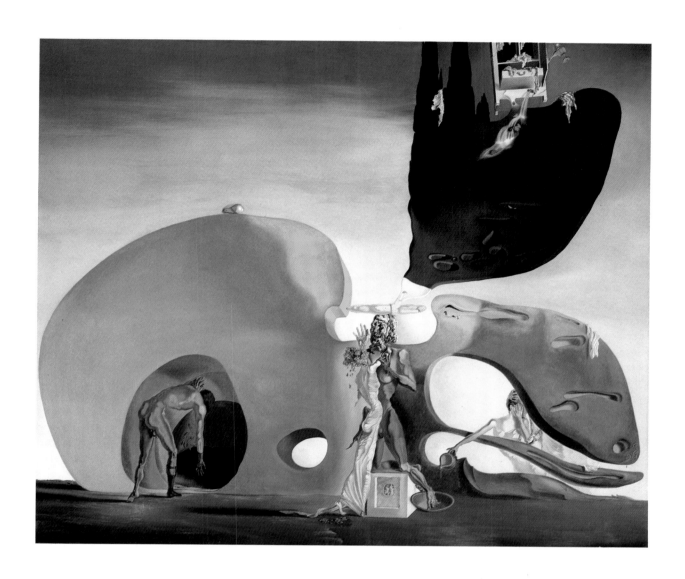

Plate 76. Salvador Dalí, *Birth of Liquid Desires*
(*La Naissance des désirs liquides*), 1931–32. Oil and collage
on canvas, 96.1 x 112.3 cm (37 ⅞ x 44 ¼ inches).
Peggy Guggenheim Collection 76.2553 PG100.

Plate 77. Max Ernst, *Little Machine Constructed by Minimax Dadamax in Person (Von minimax dadamax selbst konstruiertes maschinchen)*, 1919–20. Hand printing (?), pencil and ink frottage, watercolor, and gouache on paper, 49.4 x 31.5 cm (19 ½ x 12 ⅛ inches). Peggy Guggenheim Collection 76.2553 PG70.

Bataille could write, on the symbolism of flowers, that "the value given to pointed or hollowed-out objects is fairly well-known."[23] Surrealists canonized the Comte de Lautréamont's famous late-nineteenth-century literary image, "He is as handsome . . . as the fortuitous encounter on a dissecting table of a sewing machine and an umbrella,"[24] making it the motto for their practice of using provocative and absurd juxtapositions that usually bore sexual connotations. In a 1926 film, Marcel Duchamp hybridized Lautréamont and Freud in his question, "Have you ever put the marrow of your sword into the frying pan of your beloved?"[25]

Dada artists had used sexual innuendo in their absurd mechanomorphic constructions, dryly equating the structure of a human body or the act of intercourse with tools and instruments, or engine parts. Francis Picabia's *The Child Carburetor* (1919, plate 78)[26] and Ernst's *Little Machine Constructed by Minimax Dadamax in Person* (1919–20, plate 77), works that Guggenheim acquired, employ the obvious symbolism of Duchamp's riddle: in Picabia's construction, piercing needle and spindle forms create the analogy; in the Ernst, a faucet is equated with a penis. Both of the works exemplify the Dadaists' delight in puns and word games. Picabia's vaguely scientific phrases ("dissolution de prolongation" and "flux et reflux des résolutions") have sexual connotations. Ernst's inscription—"Little machine constructed by minimax dadamax in person for fearless pollination of female suckers at the beginning of the change of life and for other such fearless functions"—is less ambiguous yet still absurd.[27] In these and other works, the artists wittily underline the subliminal meanings of technical language—for example, the suggestiveness of the distinctions "male" and "female" used for plumbing apparatuses or electrical devices.

The ironic sexual play in Dada art was taken up by the Surrealists, along with its inherent ambivalence toward the machine and women.[28] The Surrealists, however, added a psychoanalytic dimension to the use of sexual metaphors. Frequently, they visualized the unconscious mind as a landscape in which desires and traumas are metaphorically embodied in the figures and objects inhabiting the fictive space. In Paul Delvaux's *The Break of Day* (1937, plate 81)[29] and Dalí's *Untitled* (1931, plate 79), an uncanny sense of the real is maintained through conventional recession into space and the presence of familiar forms, which are unfamiliarly juxtaposed. In both canvases, the object of desire is a woman who is equated with nature: Delvaux repeats the same *femme-arbre* (tree-woman) four times, and Dalí's head of a woman is composed of a pile of seashells, her hair seeming to ooze into a molten mass. Dalí's desolate landscape echoes Tanguy's lunar terrain in *The Sun in Its Jewel Case* (1937, plate 80), but Tanguy departs from recognizable imagery, creating anthropomorphoid bodies that suggest individual beings. Tanguy preserves a sense of corporeality by the modeling of the abstract forms and the shadows they cast; the bone and antennae shapes ground the bodies in an organic environment. Balls are couched in sockets; nodules make physical contact with corpuses, suggesting a primeval sexuality. The shadow-casting ray emanations of the figure in the right middleground are reminiscent of Joan Miró's symbology of sexual evanescences, as well as of Duchamp's.

In *Seated Woman II* (1939, plate 83), Miró eschews the conventional perspective and modeling employed by Delvaux, Dalí, and Tanguy, yet his imagery is still tied to the female form. The ferocity of this woman is articulated in her toothy grin, jutting jaw, angular breasts, and streaming hair. Her sexual vitality is bound up with this ferocity: despite her nominally seated position she appears to be in an ecstatic frenzy, waving her arms, her kaleidoscopic eye reeling. Her sexuality is stressed through her prominently revealed breasts, body hair, and the vaginal emblem on her collar. Gone is the static muse of Dalí and Delvaux, replaced by the voracious *femme fatale*, the flip side of Surrealism's conception of Woman.

Plate 78. Francis Picabia, *The Child Carburetor* (*L'Enfant carburateur*), 1919. Oil, enamel, metallic paint, gold leaf, pencil, and crayon on stained plywood, 126.3 x 101.3 cm (49 ¼ x 39 ⅞ inches). Solomon R. Guggenheim Museum 55.1426.

Left: Plate 79. Salvador Dalí, *Untitled*, 1931. Oil on
canvas, 27.2 x 35 cm (10 ¹¹⁄₁₆ x 13 ¾ inches).
Peggy Guggenheim Collection 76.2553 PG99.

Above: Plate 80. Yves Tanguy, *The Sun in Its Jewel Case*
(*Le Soleil dans son écrin*), 1937. Oil on canvas, 115.4 x 88.1 cm
(45 ⁷⁄₁₆ x 34 ¹¹⁄₁₆ inches). Peggy Guggenheim Collection
76.2553 PG95.

Plate 81. Paul Delvaux, *The Break of Day* (*L'Aurore*), July 1937. Oil on canvas, 120 x 150.5 cm (47 ¼ x 59 ¼ inches). Peggy Guggenheim Collection 76.2553 PG103.

Plate 82. Pablo Picasso, *On the Beach* (*La Baignade*), February 12, 1937. Oil, conté crayon, and chalk on canvas, 129.1 x 194 cm (50 ¹³⁄₁₆ x 76 ⅛ inches). Peggy Guggenheim Collection 76.2553 PG5.

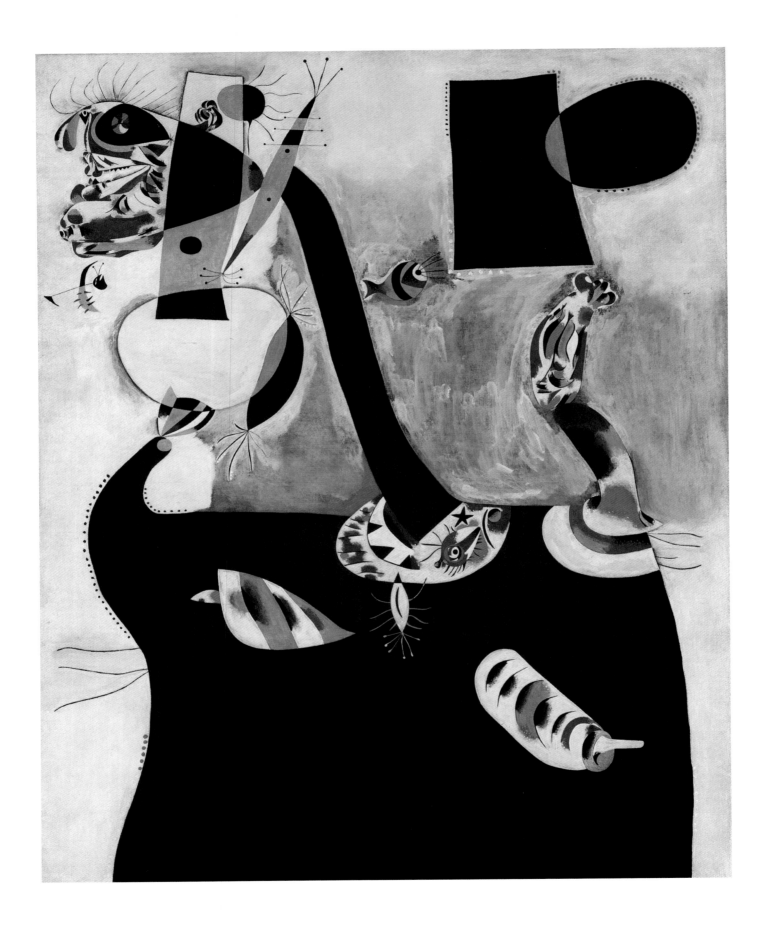

Plate 83. Joan Miró, *Seated Woman II (Femme assise II)*,
February 27, 1939. Oil on canvas, 162 x 130 cm (63 ¼ x
51 ¹⁄₁₆ inches). Peggy Guggenheim Collection 76.2553 PG93.

Pablo Picasso's *On the Beach* (1937, plate 82) schematically maintains the fictive space of "realistic" works by Surrealists such as Dalí, although here it is occupied by fantastic monster-women, their sculptural construction determined by erotic zones. These bodies are a mass of parts: projectile breasts, giant buttocks, looming wombs and vulvas. Despite the arcadian theme, their innocent visages, and their childlike play with a toy boat, the women's apparently gargantuan size, strange insectoid craning necks, fragmentation, and vestigial hands are vaguely threatening. The voyeur on the horizon, who embodies the viewer's fear, brings to mind the spectral man peaking from behind a rock in Dalí's *Untitled*.[30] The image of the male voyeur spying the abundant gifts of a nude female is a traditional theme, typically represented in morality tales such as Diana spied upon by Actaeon, or Susanna and the Elders. The peeker in these images is a stand-in for the male viewer of the picture; both have the exquisite delight of watching without being seen, which puts them in a position of power.[31] Freud's entire account of the genesis of sexuality in the individual is predicated on sight, specifically on the male child's discovery that the mother does not have a penis, thus introducing the fear of castration (his might be removed like mommy's was). Voyeurism yields the pleasure of reliving that moment of discovery, which is both frightening in its implicit threat and delightful in its reassertion that the male spectator is not himself "castrated" as the female subject appears to be.[32] The theoretical complexity of the issue of the voyeur in Surrealist art is beyond the scope of this essay. However, the acknowledgment that vision has a sexual component and is interrelated with issues of power is requisite to an examination of such works as *On the Beach*.[33]

While Picasso and Dalí literally represent the scopophiliac in their paintings, Ernst, in his collage *The Postman Cheval* (1932, plate 84), creates a voyeuristic experience that requires the viewer to consciously act as a Peeping Tom. The structure of collage itself, in which pieces of paper or other materials are layered onto a support, can arouse curiosity by raising the question of what is hidden beneath the layers. For *The Postman Cheval*, Ernst cut holes in a sheet of marbleized paper, behind which the tantalizing suggestions of a young woman can be seen. Also attached to the surface is an envelope from which a lascivious postcard pokes out, and through its window female bodies are discernible. Joseph Cornell's *Swiss Shoot-the-Chutes* (1941, plate 85), though not blatantly sexual, also elicits the viewer's desire to look, requiring his or her active participation to achieve this goal. Object-toys like this one illuminate two central Surrealist preoccupations: the grounding of the work in material reality, exemplified by the use of the found object, and the focus on the body, not only as object of representation, but as a living, responsive subject, from whom physical participation is sought. *Swiss Shoot-the-Chutes* is activated by removing a ball from the lower door on the side panel and inserting it into the upper one, initiating its rolling descent along slats in the box and ringing the bells hidden in the case. The front panel of the construction is riddled with holes like those in Ernst's collage, some permitting the viewer to see the interior of the box, where there is an image of a woman's head and a mirror, others blocked by clippings of cows, skiers, and more women. Regulated by Cornell's Swiss-cheeselike membrane, the viewer-voyeur strains to see into the holes. An insert of the Wolf, eyes bulging, and Little Red Riding Hood suggests a predator's sight of a little girl, with its ominous foreshadowing of violence, in this construction in which modalities of vision are emphasized.

Because it exists as a three-dimensional object, a sculpture broadens the participation of the viewer, who can move around it, thereby experiencing a relationship between its mass and the viewer's own body. Guggenheim demonstrated the sensuality of the physical response to sculpture when she explained why she bought her first piece, Arp's *Head and Shell* (ca. 1933, plate 86): "I fell so in love with it that I asked to take it in my

Left: Plate 84. Max Ernst, *The Postman Cheval* (*Le Facteur Cheval*), 1932. Paper and fabric collage with pencil, ink, and gouache on paper, 64.3 x 48.9 cm (25 ⅜ x 19 ¼ inches). Peggy Guggenheim Collection 76.2553 PG74.

Above: Plate 85. Joseph Cornell, *Swiss Shoot-the-Chutes*, 1941. Box construction, 53.8 x 35.2 x 10.5 cm (21 ¹/₁₆ x 13 ¹³/₁₆ x 4 ⅛ inches). Peggy Guggenheim Collection 76.2553 PG127.

Top: Plate 86. Jean Arp, *Head and Shell* (*Tête et coquille*), ca. 1933. Polished brass, 19.7 cm (7 ¼ inches) high. Peggy Guggenheim Collection 76.2553 PG54.

Bottom: Plate 87. Constantin Brancusi, *Bird in Space* (*L'Oiseau dans l'espace*), 1932–40. Brass, 134.7 cm (53 inches) high. Peggy Guggenheim Collection 76.2553 PG51.

hands. The instant I felt it, I wanted to own it."[34]

Since the creation of the first Western sculptures-in-the-round, stone and bronze idols were equated with the human body. While this equation is obvious in naturalistic sculpture, abstract work maintains the correlation not only when it incorporates the suggestion of body parts, such as the multiple breast forms of Arp's pink limestone *Crown of Buds I* (1936, plate 88), but simply by the fact of its physical mass. Metaphors of presence and absence classically denote the male and female genitalia, as Freud's study of sexual symbolism sustains. And traditional sculpture, including many Surrealist objects, emphasizes the language of presence by its preoccupation with phallus forms that seem to serve as fetish objects warding against the fear of castration also described by Freud. Alberto Giacometti's *Model for a Square* (1931–32, plate 89), which Guggenheim bought in Paris in 1940, was a kind of game board in which the various "male" and "female" components resting on pegs could be moved, suggesting a chesslike diversion as a metaphor for human relations.[35] This work was a model for a much larger outdoor installation in stone, dominated by the central glyph that epitomizes a phallic fetish (the pieces were executed in plaster, as shown in fig. 91, but the installation remained unrealized).[36] Constantin Brancusi's *Bird in Space* (1932–40, plate 87), which the artist arrived at through working with images of a magic bird, also operates as a phallic emblem.[37]

Transgression against bourgeois norms of propriety and expected behavior was a central strategy of Surrealist practice that is grounded in Breton's Freudian-derived mandate to dredge up repressed traumas, dreams, and desires and expose them in art. In Surrealism, the transgressive act was most frequently literalized in the image of the nude female body, perhaps because of a socially constructed notion of its sacrosanctity that would heighten the shock and titillation of representations of its violation.[38] Moreover, the Surrealists relied heavily

on Freud, whose story of the genesis of sexuality was filled with images of brutality—the horror of castration, and its symbolization in the blinding of Oedipus, for example—that wound the thread of violence so tightly to sexuality. This climate promoted the *femme fatale* represented by the ultimate castrating figure, the female praying mantis, who eats her mate after copulation. Giacometti depicted the aftermath of a preventative annihilation of the mantis-woman in his *Woman with Her Throat Cut* (1932 [cast 1940], plate 90), a headless insectoid that rests on the floor like a squashed bug.[39] The threat of castration also pervades much of Dalí's work. In *Birth of Liquid Desires* (1931–32, plate 76), a painting rife with Freudian implications, the central couple makes clear a motif repeated in the artist's work—a father figure sexually united with a muse who can be identified as both Gradiva and Gala, Dalí's lover.[40]

Peggy Goes to New York, Art of This Century Gallery

When Paris fell, Guggenheim was forced to flee to the south of France, where she arranged for the transfer of her collection and the move of her family to New York as the conflict was escalating. In addition, Breton, Jacqueline Lamba, and their daughter, as well as Ernst were able to leave Europe through her assistance. Ernst was a particularly difficult case since he had been interned in France as an enemy alien. It was at this time that Guggenheim and the artist began a liaison that eventually resulted in their short-lived marriage in New York, where they arrived on July 14, 1941. According to Guggenheim, Ernst's painting *The Antipope* (1941–42, plate 75) is a manifestation of their complicated relationship.[41] Her identification of figures representing Ernst, herself, and her daughter Pegeen has been supplemented by the suggestion of the presence of a representation of Leonora Carrington, with whom Ernst was romantically involved. The artist's axiomatic themes in this work have been described by Angelica Rudenstine as "the universal issues of power,

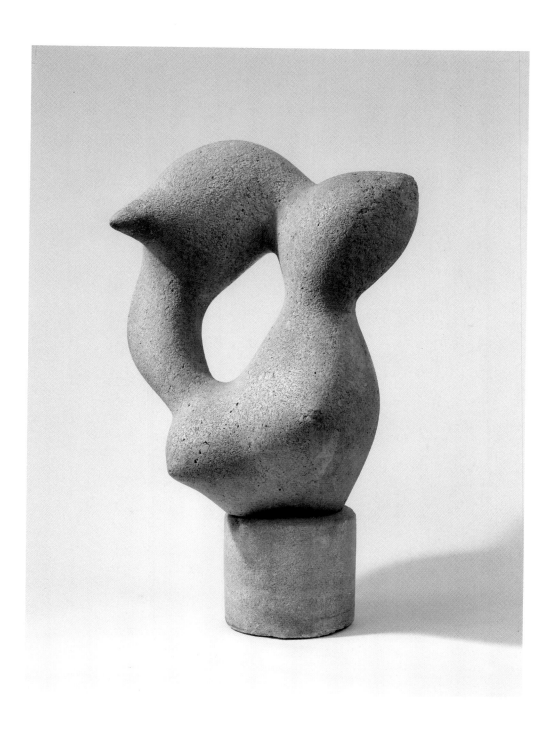

Plate 88. Jean Arp, *Crown of Buds I* (*Couronne de bourgeons I*), 1936. Limestone, 49.1 cm (19 ⅛ inches) high. Peggy Guggenheim Collection 76.2553 PG56.

Plate 90. Alberto Giacometti, *Woman with Her Throat Cut* (*Femme égorgée*), 1932 (cast 1940). Bronze, 23.2 (9 ⅛ inches) high. Peggy Guggenheim Collection 76.2553 PG131.

Top: Fig. 92. The Surrealist Gallery in Art of This Century, Peggy Guggenheim's New York gallery designed by Frederick Kiesler. Photo of 1942 by Berenice Abbott.

Bottom: Fig. 93. The Abstract Gallery in Art of This Century, photographed in 1942 by Berenice Abbott. In the background toward the left is Kandinsky's *Dominant Curve* (1936).

manipulation, and potential destructiveness in sexual relations."[42]

Settling in New York for the duration of the war, Guggenheim continued editing her collection catalogue, which she had begun in Europe. Determined to finally open the museum she had been planning, she hired the visionary architect Frederick Kiesler to design an environment appropriate to her collection, "a place where people who are doing something really new can show their work."[43] On October 20, 1942, her Art of This Century museum-gallery opened in the space that two tailors had occupied at 30 West Fifty-seventh Street, garnering national attention.

By hiring Kiesler—whom she called "the most advanced architect of the century"[44]—Guggenheim faced off against her uncle and his adviser Rebay, who in 1939 had opened their Museum of Non-Objective Painting in a former car showroom at 24 East Fifty-fourth Street. In fact, in the 1930s Rebay had herself considered hiring Kiesler to design an exhibition space in Rockefeller Center. Perhaps Solomon's and Rebay's engagement in June 1943 of the world-famous architect Frank Lloyd Wright, whom they commissioned to build a freestanding edifice to replace the Fifty-fourth Street venue, was precipitated by Peggy Guggenheim's museum-gallery success. By calling her space a museum (she charged admission for a while), enlisting the services of an architect known for his set design and theatrical window displays, and challenging him to devise a new method of exhibiting art, Guggenheim created a sensational splash that seemed to deliberately challenge her uncle and Rebay.[45]

Kiesler designed four galleries for Art of This Century.[46] The most conventional—illuminated by daylight—served as the painting library, a study center for Guggenheim's "permanent collection," and the space for changing exhibitions. Kiesler felt that walls were repressive; thus, the partitions of the Abstract Gallery, consisting of ultramarine stretched-canvas sheets battened down with cord, appeared to float since they did not

meet either the floor or ceiling (figs. 93, 100). Paintings, mounted on tripods suspended by cord, seemed to hover in space, adding to the gallery's gravity-defying atmosphere. For an automatic-display or kinetic gallery, Kiesler designed various mechanisms that incorporated dynamic movement and allowed the viewing of art in limited space: an automatically activated, enclosed conveyor belt spotlighting individual Klee paintings at prescribed intervals, which the viewer could override by pushing a button; a giant wheel controlling the rotation of works from Duchamp's *Box in a Valise*, visible through a peephole (fig. 95); and a box with a viewer-controlled diaphragm that opened to reveal Breton's poem-object *Portrait of the Actor A. B.* This corridor area became notorious as the "penny-arcade peep show" section of the gallery,[47] an appropriate appellation since all of these devices involved the spectator in the act of voyeurism that is embodied in Surrealist works like those of Ernst and Cornell discussed above.

Considered the most unconventional of the spaces, the Surrealist Gallery (figs. 92, 94) exhibited frameless paintings mounted on baseball bats— Kiesler likened them to outstretched arms[48]—that protruded from the curving gumwood walls. A mind-altering experience was created by a tape recording of a roaring train; lights timed to alternately illuminate different sides of the black room further dislocated the visitor. Kiesler's sympathy for Surrealism's bodily metaphors is manifested in his rationale for the lighting, which he installed because "it's dynamic, it pulsates like your blood."[49] The Surrealists created this kind of disorienting environmental installation, an all-encompassing physical experience of surreality, for various exhibitions including the 1938 *International Surrealist Exhibition* (*Exposition internationale du surréalisme*) in Paris and *First Papers of Surrealism*, which opened in New York less than a week before Art of This Century did. Surrealist art's shocking juxtapositions, which could be suggested through automatism, trances, or drugs, were

Top: Fig. 94. Max Ernst and Peggy Guggenheim in the Surrealist Gallery of Art of This Century, October 1942.

Bottom: Fig. 95. Peggy Guggenheim in the kinetic gallery of Art of This Century in 1942. The visitor turned the large wooden wheel while looking through a small hole; fourteen reproductions from Marcel Duchamp's *Box in a Valise* (*Boîte-en-valise*) appeared sequentially. Photo by Berenice Abbott.

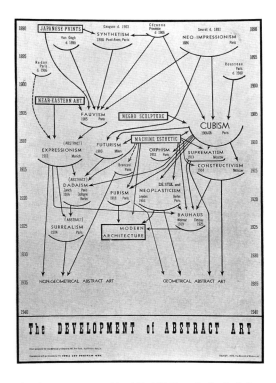

Fig. 96. Chart prepared by Alfred H. Barr, Jr. for the jacket of the exhibition catalogue *Cubism and Abstract Art*, published by the Museum of Modern Art, New York, 1936. Courtesy The Museum of Modern Art, New York.

magnified in these environments in which the visitor walked down a lane of macabre street-walking mannequins, trudged through leaves and twigs, used flashlights to see the art in the dark, became entangled in a web of string, or was surrounded by children playing ball. At Art of This Century, the viewer's physical experience was enhanced by a number of devices Kiesler created to respond to the "new aspect of correlating the visitor to the painting,"[50] among them specially designed movable chairs and display stands adjustable to eighteen positions. Although Guggenheim may have attempted to maintain impartiality by having both an abstract and Surrealist gallery in her "museum," most attention was given to Kiesler's surreal effects. Indeed, the gallery became known as "that madhouse of surrealism."[51]

Art of This Century apparently caused a ripple of anxiety among Solomon Guggenheim's contingent, an indication of which may be "The Violent Art of Hanging Pictures," an article written by Edgar Kaufmann, Jr., a Wright acolyte.[52] Ostensibly a review of a number of innovative art-exhibition facilities, including the yet-to-be-built Wright museum, the article critiques Kiesler's system, arguing that in Art of This Century's moving exhibits and gravity-denying design "display rather than art is on view," while Wright's plan "respects the essentials of picture viewing." Kaufmann concluded that his hero's scheme promised to be better: "If the Museum of Non-Objective Art is built, one of the sanest and most ingenuous efforts to find a better way to show pictures will be at hand for comparison."[53]

The antagonism between the two Guggenheim camps went beyond mere competition for preeminence in the New York art world. What for Peggy was an effort "to establish her place in the history of modern art" seems to have been, for Rebay, a holy war.[54] Their distinct visions of the significance of this art determined the form that their collections and exhibition spaces took and reflect larger differences within the art world. During the period in which

the two Guggenheim collections were formed, the contemporary art community—artists, collectors, critics, and curators—were struggling to name, categorize, and champion new developments. Rebay's and Guggenheim's rivalry—fueled by their desire to disseminate the art of their time in a particular package—mirrored the concerns of their constituencies. In 1936, the founding director of the Museum of Modern Art, Alfred H. Barr, Jr., had presented the young history of twentieth-century art as an inexorable drive to abstraction, which was divided into two different paths, "non-geometric abstract art," resulting from the strands of Expressionism, Surrealism, and Brancusi, versus "geometric abstract art," devolving from De Stijl and Neo-Plasticism, the Bauhaus, and Constructivism.[55] This scheme of categorization and nomination remains to this day rather inelegant and controversial, yet it illuminates the nascent dialectical paradigm for thinking about Modern art, which was at the core of the rivalry between Guggenheim and Rebay.

The distinction between their two positions started at the etymological level, as evident in their descriptions of their respective collections. Hilla Rebay used the term "non-objective" to distinguish art that is generated directly from the artist's imagination, yet is not abstract in that it is not derived from the observable world. Surrealism was defined by Breton as "the future resolution of these two states, dream and reality, which are seemingly so contradictory, into a kind of absolute reality, a *surreality*."[56] Guggenheim refused to use the term "non-objective" even to describe the non-Surrealistic portion of her collection, preferring to call those works "nonrealistic" or, occasionally, "abstract."[57]

The lines of division between these two camps—Rebay and non-objectivity versus Guggenheim and Surrealism—are as murky and difficult to untangle as the web of Barr's chart (fig. 96). Some artists could be claimed by both contingents, and Guggenheim attempted a modicum of equanimity in her support. There is evidence, however, that the competition between the two collectors (and their supporters) was perceived as a battle for supremacy and the continuation of the species. Apollonian non-objectivity, the force of light, seemed to counter Surrealism's powers of Dionysian darkness.[58] Whereas non-objective artists rejected the representation of the material world in striving to depict the immaterial and to describe the essence of enlightened principles like harmony and goodness through the spiritual intensity of forms and colors,[59] Surrealists focused on material reality by rendering oneiric worlds grounded in skewed yet familiar terrain, or by examining objects themselves and their properties.[60] Apollonian non-objectivity was intended to illuminate, synthesizing through reason, using music as a model for clarity, and attempting to represent truth; Dionysian Surrealism was obsessed with the irrational and explored nocturnal fantasies and the most debased aspects of culture, whether that meant hunting at a flea market for objects to be "found" or representing excrement in a painting. Non-objective artists strove for integration and synthesis in their work, while Surrealists used violent fragmentation to force a shock of guilty recognition upon the viewer. Vasily Kandinsky, whose ideas influenced Rebay's articulation of non-objectivity, wrote that paintings should appeal to the soul, their colors causing a "spiritual vibration"[61]; Breton, from whom Peggy Guggenheim commissioned an introduction to her collection catalogue, argued that Surrealism should liberate the unconscious and unleash the repressed.

Non-objective philosophy focused on the lofty life of the mind in order to transcend corporeality and commune with the cosmos, seemingly conceiving of the body as an impediment. Surrealist art was grounded in the human form, through representing the figure as well as through the viewer's experience of the work of art in relation to his or her own body, which was especially emphasized in movable sculpture and participatory installations. Non-objective intentions

were to be taken with dead seriousness, whereas Surrealism was often whimsical and humorous. As Rebay wrote, "The pictures of non-objectivity are the key to a world of unmaterialistic elevation. Educating humanity to respect and appreciate spiritual worth will unite nations more firmly than any league of nations."[62] She saw her museum as "the Temple of Non-objectivity," while Guggenheim called hers "a research laboratory."[63] The Museum of Non-Objective Painting presented Rebay's idea of unequivocally pure paintings in soothing surroundings—gray-velour-covered walls, plush carpeting, incense, and piped-in Bach. Guggenheim, on the contrary, mounted exhibitions such as *Natural, Insane, Surrealist Art*, in which she displayed driftwood, roots, and jawbone fragments (with teeth) in her cacophonous gallery, with its recorded train noise and flashing lights.

Rebay refused to include sculpture in the collection of the Museum of Non-Objective Painting, while the subtitle of Guggenheim's catalogue reads *Objects-Drawings-Photographs-Paintings-Sculpture-Collages 1910 to 1942.*[64] Sculpture was too corporeal for Rebay's brand of non-objectivity. It could never transcend its material limitations and privilege the sublime realm of the higher faculties.[65]

In 1946, the young artist Ad Reinhardt (who showed at Art of This Century) visualized a variation of Barr's flowchart in the form of a tree in which the upright, living branches are filled with leaves labeled with the names of artists, many of whom exhibited with Guggenheim (fig. 97).[66] The leaves on a branch that is breaking off the tree are marked with artists that Reinhardt, and presumably his colleagues, felt were retrograde. Although Guggenheim (not being an artist) is not mentioned by name, Rebay is depicted as a bird pecking on the tree. Instead of being a vital member of the growing branches, she is almost a scavenger. Reinhardt's cartoon represents another volley in the partisan battle for primacy and indicates that Guggenheim was perceived as an advocate of the art of the future through her support of young artists.

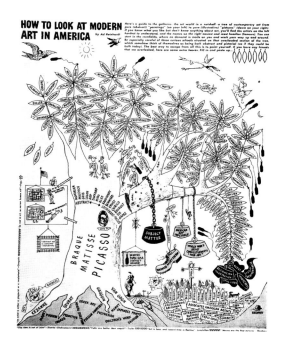

Fig. 97. Ad Reinhardt, "How to Look at Modern Art in America," published in *P.M.*, June 2, 1946.

Peggy's Contributions to American Art

Just as she had done in London, Guggenheim brought a number of firsts to New York: she held the premier exhibition of Arp's work and the first international collage show, just as she had mounted the first Kandinsky exhibition in London, among others. But she is perhaps best known for her financial subsidization and exhibition of the nascent New York School of Abstract Expressionists, giving solo shows to William Baziotes, David Hare, Hans Hofmann, Robert Motherwell, Jackson Pollock, Mark Rothko, and Clyfford Still, many of whom came of age as artists under Surrealism's influence. In fact, Guggenheim felt that her promotion of Pollock was her "most honorable achievement."[67] In 1981, Lee Krasner summarized Guggenheim's accomplishment:

Art of This Century was of the utmost importance as the first place where the New York School could be seen. . . . Her Gallery was the foundation, it's where it all started to happen. There was nowhere else in New York where one could expect an open-minded reaction. Peggy was invaluable in founding and creating what she did.

In a 1977 interview, Hare remarked:

There were only three places in New York during the early 1940s: Julien Levy, Pierre Matisse, and Peggy. She was the only one who showed contemporary Americans: of course she was important. She gave people a chance to show, to see, to be seen . . . she supported you, and it was vital.[68]

Guggenheim envisioned "serving the future instead of recording the past,"[69] and with this mandate she exhibited the work of many young, undiscovered artists. While a number of these painters and sculptors gained lasting prominence, others have been forgotten or lost to history. Guggenheim set a precedent for showing the work of women in her gallery in London, which she continued in New York: almost 40 percent of the artists who exhibited at Art of This Century were female, and more than one-quarter of the solo shows were devoted to women. Many of these artists, however, are unknown today,[70] although most rated leaves on the living section of Reinhardt's tree.[71] Among those Guggenheim exhibited who remain familiar are Louise Bourgeois, Leonora Carrington, Léonor Fini, Frida Kahlo, Louise Nevelson, Meret Oppenheim, and Dorothea Tanning. Despite well-known uncharitable statements about women, Guggenheim had long supported their artistic endeavors. She gave novelist Djuna Barnes a monthly stipend throughout her life and provided for her in her will; she helped poet and artist Mina Loy with a number of ventures; and she lent Berenice Abbott the money to open her first photography studio.

Guggenheim held two exhibitions at Art of This Century devoted exclusively to the work of female artists. The juried *Exhibition by 31 Women*, the third show at the newly opened gallery, caused one journalist to remark, "Already this gallery is living up to its promise of uncovering troublesome new talents."[72] The second exhibition, *The Women*, took place at the end of the gallery's third season. A sampling of the reviews indicates the climate within which both shows were received. One journalist condescendingly suggested that "other all-female organizations should look-in" on the exhibition; while another used cooking metaphors to describe the "giggly" endeavors of the group.[73] Much attention was given to the inclusion of Gypsy Rose Lee's surrealistic collage box construction, and many snipes connecting striptease, Eros, and art were made.[74] The typical reviewer used the occasion to disparage women artists—such as referring to the participants as the wives of famous artists—and to criticize Surrealism. One critic wrote:

Surrealism is about 70 per cent hysterics, 20 per cent literature, 5 per cent good painting and 5 per cent is just saying "boo" to the innocent public. There are . . . plenty of men among the New York neurotics but . . . still more women among them. Considering the statistics the doctors hand out, and considering the percentages listed above . . . it is obvious the women ought to excel at surrealism. At all events, they do.[75]

Plate 91. Marino Marini, *The Angel of the City* (*L'Angelo della città*), 1948 (cast 1950?). Bronze, 172 cm (67 ¹¹/₁₆ inches) high. Peggy Guggenheim Collection 76.2553 PG183.

Right: Fig. 98. Peggy Guggenheim on her bed with
Alexander Calder's *Silver Bedhead* (1945–46), photographed
by Roloff Beny in 1956.

Although Guggenheim's and her advisers' intentions may have been admirable, the ghettoization of women into exhibitions designated by the artists' sex rather than the nature of their art may have facilitated the journalists' focus on gender, rather than production. Georgia O'Keeffe, for one, sensed the disadvantages of a women's exhibition when she icily informed Peggy Guggenheim, "I am not a woman painter."[76] Guggenheim participated in the Surrealist's separatist categories in mounting the shows just discussed, as well as *Exhibition of Paintings and Drawings by Children*, *The Negro in American Life* (an exhibition of photographs of, not by, black Americans), and *Natural, Insane, Surrealist Art*, which perpetuated the axiomatic position of sane white adult males—who were not themselves categorized—as the standard from which the "others" diverged.[77] Nevertheless, Guggenheim regularly integrated the work of women into the group exhibitions at Art of This Century, and devoted solo shows to female artists, some of whom were important figures in the New York art world, among them Irene Rice Pereira, Janet Sobel, and Hedda Sterne. She also collected the work of women artists, though much of this art was given away or sold over the years.[78]

Peggy Goes to Venice, The Peggy Guggenheim Collection

As World War II drew to a close, Guggenheim yearned to return to Europe, which she had always preferred to the United States. Eventually settling in Venice, she brought to the city a wealth of art barely known in Italy, just as she had enlivened London's cultural backwater, and then New York's. In all of these places, she was subjected to the uncomprehending criticism of local guardians of conservative standards: in London, the director of the Tate Gallery denied that the sculptures arriving for one of her exhibitions were art, permitting British customs officials to tax them as raw material[79]; in New York, supporters of domestic realist painting considered Surrealism to have "an unwholesome, if not pernicious, influence" on American art[80]; and in Italy, local officials rejected what they deemed her "arte degenerata" the day before her collection was slated to travel to Turin for an exhibition.[81]

In Venice, Guggenheim raised eyebrows, as usual, for her profligate behavior. She bought a palazzo with an infamous past to house her collection, held court with an endless parade of celebrities, and generally behaved with her trademark wanton abandon. She continued to collect art, supporting local emerging artists as she had in London and New York. One of her most prized acquisitions was a sculpture of an ecstatic man on horseback, Marino Marini's *The Angel of the City* (1948 [cast 1950?], plate 91), which she placed prominently at the canal entrance to the house. The conspicuous, erect phallus of the rider was detachable—Guggenheim removed it on holy days in deference to the nuns who passed before the palazzo in floating processions, initiating rumors that she had replacement parts of various sizes.[82] The sculpture became a mascot for Guggenheim and her collection: at her 1976 exhibition at the Galleria Civica d'Arte Moderna in Turin a photo blow-up of the sculpture was juxtaposed with Man Ray's photograph of Guggenheim (fig. 90); and the collector standing next to the sculpture was a prized snapshot for tourists. The stories about the Marini sculpture were repeated with delight by Guggenheim, who loved to be considered a Casanova as much as the public loved to make her one.

In Venice, she finally established the museum that had been her goal since 1939—the Peggy Guggenheim Collection—entertaining the hoards who came to look both at her Surrealist art and the marvelous woman who had brought it together. One of her favorite poses for photographs epitomizes Peggy Guggenheim's self-presentation as a fabulous, surreal woman: in it the collector is captured wearing a slinky Fortuny sheath in her boudoir, surrounded by her Alexander Calder marine headboard and her numerous earrings mounted on the wall as trophies of a modern fetishist (fig. 98).[83]

Fig. 99. The Palazzo Venier dei Leoni, Venice, which houses
the Peggy Guggenheim Collection. Photo by David Heald.

Notes

I would like to gratefully acknowledge the assistance of Ward Jackson, Archivist of the Solomon R. Guggenheim Museum, and Lisa Panzera, Curatorial Assistant. I would also like to thank interns Chrystine de la Verrière and Madhavi Menon, and volunteer Sergio Borges Allan.

1. Melvin P. Lader, "Peggy Guggenheim's Art of This Century: The Surrealist Milieu and the American Avant-Garde, 1942–1947," Ph.D. dissertation, University of Delaware (available from University Microfilms International, Ann Arbor, Mich.), 1981, pp. 23–24; Joan M. Lukach, *Hilla Rebay: In Search of the Spirit in Art* (New York: George Braziller, 1983), p. 132.

2. Peggy Guggenheim, *Out of This Century: Confessions of an Art Addict* (London: André Deutsch Limited, 1979), p. 171.

3. Lader, p. 31. For descriptions of Guggenheim's exhibitions, see the appendix of Angelica Zander Rudenstine, *Peggy Guggenheim Collection, Venice: The Solomon R. Guggenheim Foundation* (New York: Harry N. Abrams and the Solomon R. Guggenheim Foundation, 1985), pp. 746–801.

4. Guggenheim, *Out of This Century*, p. 209.

5. Quoted in Lukach, p. 131.

6. Guggenheim, *Out of This Century*, p. 214.

7. Quoted in John H. Davis, *The Guggenheims: An American Epic* (New York: William Morrow and Company, 1978), p. 434.

8. Davis, p. 408. He also mentions that Guggenheim claimed she slept with one thousand men before her younger sister Hazel reached that number only because she had "started earlier." When her autobiography *Out of This Century* was published in 1946, reviewers called Guggenheim "nymphomaniacal" and "'an urge on wheels' in quest of an 'orgasm a day.'" In addition, Herbert Read compared her to Casanova (all in Jacqueline Bograd Weld, *Peggy: The Wayward Guggenheim* [New York: E. P. Dutton, 1986], pp. 346–48 [note the adjective of the title]). Aline B. Saarinen called her "the appasionata of the avant-garde" in *The Proud Possessors* (New York: Random House, 1958), pp. 326–43.

9. "Recherches sur la sexualité: Part d'objectivité, déterminations individuelles, degré de conscience," *La Révolution surréaliste*, no. 11 (March 15, 1928), pp. 32–40; translated in José Pierre, ed., *Investigating Sex: Surrealist Research 1928–1932*, trans. by Malcolm Imrie, afterword by Dawn Ades (London: Verso, 1992), pp. 1–34. The group consisted of Louis Aragon, Jacques Baron, J.-A. Boiffard, André Breton, Marcel Duhamel, Man Ray, Max Morise, Pierre Naville, Marcel Noll, Benjamin Péret, Jacques Prévert, Raymond Queneau, Georges Sadoul, Yves Tanguy, and Pierre Unik.

10. The closest this group came to a woman's voice in the proceedings was when one participant admitted that he asked his partner what she desired. "Talk about complications!" exclaimed Breton. Quoted in Whitney Chadwick, *Women Artists and the Surrealist Movement* (Boston: Little, Brown and Company, 1985), p. 103. The discussion that follows is indebted to Dr. Chadwick's work.

11. André Breton, *Manifesto of Surrealism*, in *Manifestoes of Surrealism*, trans. by Richard Seaver and Helen R. Lane (Ann Arbor, Mich.: The University of Michigan Press, 1969), p. 17.

12. In *Women Artists* (pp. 13–65), Chadwick discusses the contradictions and discrepancies between Breton's stated goals and real actions vis-à-vis women. For an example of Breton's symptomatic attitude toward the female artist, note his characterization of Frida Kahlo as "a young woman endowed with all the gifts of seduction, one accustomed to the company of men of genius" (quoted in Chadwick, *Women Artists*, p. 87). Breton's goal was not so much the bettering of women's daily lives, but rather reducing competing demands so as to foster their undistracted concentration on the male genius. See also Tyler Stovall, "Paris in the Age of Anxiety," in Sidra Stich, *Anxious Visions: Surrealist Art*, exh. cat. (Berkeley: University Art Museum; New York: Abbeville Press, 1990), p. 214.

13. Sigmund Freud, "Delusions and Dreams in Jensen's *Gradiva*," in *The Standard Edition of the Complete Psychological Works of Sigmund Freud*, vol. 9, ed. and trans. by James Strachey (London: The Hogarth Press, 1959), pp. 3–93.

14. Chadwick, *Women Artists*, pp. 50–55. See also Chadwick, "Masson's *Gradiva*: The Metamorphosis of a Surrealist Myth," *Art Bulletin* 52 (Dec. 1970), pp. 415–22.

15. For a discussion of the relationship between Surrealism and psychoanalysis, including conceptions of the madwoman, see Elisabeth Roudinesco, "Surrealism in the Service of Psychoanalysis," in *Jacques Lacan and Co.: A History of Psychoanalysis in France, 1925–1985*, trans. by Jeffrey Mehlman (Chicago: The University of Chicago Press), 1990, pp. 3–34.

The Surrealists' interest in the science of mental disorders is shown in their commemoration of the fiftieth anniversary of Jean-Martin Charcot's 1878 "discovery" of hysteria. In *La Révolution surréaliste* (no. 11 [March 15, 1928], pp. 20–22), they republished photographs of one of Charcot's female patients in various "attitudes passionelles," poses representing the different stages of the disease. The same phrase was used to mean sexual positions in Breton's "Research on Sexuality," which appeared in the same issue of *La Révolution surréaliste*.

16. One example of this thinking is Alfred H. Barr, Jr.'s comment in his exhibition catalogue *Cubism and Abstract Art* (New York: The Museum of Modern Art, 1936, p. 179) that the Surrealist artists "turned, rather, to primitive art as a revelation of unspoiled group expression and to the art of the insane and of children as the uninhibited expression of the individual."

17. The Surrealists supported the incipient designation "art" for ritual objects used in tribal cultures. See James Clifford, "On Collecting Art and Culture," in *The Predicament of Culture: Twentieth-Century Ethnography, Literature, and Art* (Cambridge, Mass.: Harvard University Press, 1988), pp. 215–51, especially the section entitled "A Chronotrope for Collecting," pp. 236–46. Note that Guggenheim and Ernst both amassed extensive collections of "primitive" objects, which they greatly augmented in New York City during World War II. Guggenheim's collection of "primitive" art has not been adequately studied.

The Surrealists' support of the production of traditionally excluded populations ascribed to it a measure of legitimacy denied in conservative, establishment circles, and, by extension, allowed the "outsider" artists some access to dominant culture. Yet their art was often categorized as exotic and naïve, which, though intended as a compliment of sorts, still perpetuated an idea of inferiority. For the Surrealists' complex position vis-à-vis "primitive" art and culture, see Clifford, "On Ethnographic Surrealism," in *The Predicament of Culture*, pp. 117–51.

18. In a whimsical chronology of his youth that exemplifies the Surrealist imaginary, Ernst listed some of his fantastical investigations: "(1906–1914) Excursions in the world of marvels, chimeras, phantoms, poets, monsters, philosophers, birds, women, lunatics, magi, trees, eroticism, stones, insects, mountains, poisons, mathematics and so on" (Ernst, "Some Data on the Youth of M. E.," *Beyond Painting* [New York: Wittenborn, Schultz, 1948], p. 29).

19. Another masculine example is Marcel Duchamp's alter ego Rrose Sélavy. I would argue that the male artist's persona has been perceived as separate from his costume or disguise, while the female artist's identity has been derived from, or presumed to be equivalent to, the costume. In support of this assumption, note references to women's appearances in Surrealist histories, for example, Marcel Jean, with Arpad Mezei, *The History of Surrealist Painting*, trans. by Simon Watson Taylor (New York: Grove Press, 1960), p. 280; as well as reproductions of photographs *of* female artists rather than works *by* them (see, for example, the entries on artists in Erika Billeter and José Pierre, *La Femme et le*

Plate 92. Léonor Fini, *The Shepherdess of the Sphinxes,* 1941. Oil on canvas, 46.2 x 38.2 cm (18 3/16 x 15 1/16 inches). Peggy Guggenheim Collection 76.2553 PG118.

surréalisme, exh. cat. [Lausanne: Musée Cantonal des Beaux-Arts, 1987]; and *La Femme surréaliste,* special issue of *Obliques* [Paris], nos. 14–15 [Oct.–Dec. 1977]). The female artist also takes on a costume or disguise as a conscious artistic gesture. A theoretical model for this reading can be found in Mary Ann Doane, "Film and the Masquerade: Theorizing the Female Spectator," in *Femme Fatales: Feminism, Film Theory, Psychoanalysis* (New York: Routledge, 1991), pp. 17–32.

20. Kahlo and Léonor Fini are just two of the Surrealists whose self-portraits and self-presentation suggest consciously created personas. Guggenheim respected both artists' work, if not Fini's "vedette manner." See Guggenheim, *Out of This Century,* pp. 235, 359. Fini's *The Shepherdess of the Sphinxes* (1941, plate 92) was exhibited at Peggy Guggenheim's Art of This Century gallery.

21. Weld (p. 158) writes, "Peggy stood out in the crowd, gotten up in wild, extravagant, and often grotesque jewelry and dramatic, if not flattering, outfits." See also the description of Guggenheim and her party guests on p. 255. The first chapter of Guggenheim's autobiography is devoted to a review of her forebears' eccentricities. She begins (p. 2) with a comment about her grandfather, "Most of his children were peculiar, if not mad." She then outlines various strange behaviors: her aunt was a compulsive consumer of Lysol; an uncle chewed charcoal; another attempted to murder his family. Crimes of passion always fascinated the Surrealists. Two of the infant children of Guggenheim's sister Hazel apparently died under such circumstances (Weld, "Medea," pp. 78–81). According to Guggenheim, Tanguy called her sister "La Noisette" (Guggenheim, *Out of This Century,* p. 181).

22. See Elizabeth M. Legge, *Max Ernst: The Psychoanalytic Sources* (Ann Arbor, Mich.: UMI Research Press, 1989).

23. Georges Bataille, "The Language of Flowers," reprinted in Bataille, *Visions of Excess: Selected Writings, 1927–1939,* ed. and trans. by Allan Stoekl, with Carl R. Lovitt and Donald M. Leslie, Jr. (Minneapolis: University of Minnesota Press, 1985), pp. 10–14. Freud outlined a dream he called "The Language of Flowers" in *The Interpretation of Dreams,* with which Bataille was undoubtedly familiar.

24. Quoted in Maurice Nadeau, *The History of Surrealism,* trans. by Richard Howard, introduction by Roger Shattuck (Cambridge, Mass.: The Belknap Press of Harvard University Press, 1989), p. 25.

25. The sentence was inscribed in French ("Avez vous déja mis la moëlle de l'épée dans le poêle de l'aimée?") on a disc that appeared in Duchamp's film *Anemic Cinema.* See Arturo

Schwarz, *The Complete Works of Marcel Duchamp* (New York: Harry N. Abrams [1969]), fig. 140, p. 322, cat. no. 289, p. 495.

26. Peggy Guggenheim owned *The Child Carburetor* in the early 1940s. It is now in the collection of the Solomon R. Guggenheim Museum. For its provenance, see Angelica Zander Rudenstine, *The Guggenheim Museum Collection Paintings 1880–1945,* vol. 2 (New York: The Solomon R. Guggenheim Foundation, 1976), p. 591.

27. Translation from *Handbook: Peggy Guggenheim Collection,* texts by Lucy Flint and Elizabeth C. Childs (New York: The Solomon R. Guggenheim Foundation, 1986), p. 120.

28. Harold Foss Foster mentions this ambivalence in his discussion of the machinistic work of Duchamp, Ernst, and Picabia in "Surrealism in the Service of Psychoanalysis: A Reading of the Surreal as the Uncanny," unpublished Ph.D. dissertation, City University of New York, 1990, p. 169.

29. This painting had a special significance for Guggenheim. In *Out of This Century* (p. 191), she recalled sleeping with Penrose under the Delvaux: "I was so thrilled; I felt as though I were one of the women." She bought the painting from Mesens in London in 1938 (see Rudenstine, *Peggy Guggenheim Collection, Venice,* p. 215).

30. That the voyeur is male is known from two preparatory drawings. See Rudenstine, *Peggy Guggenheim Collection, Venice,* pp. 624–25.

31. While in the fables mentioned the perpetrators are punished, the pictures usually downplay or ignore that episode of the stories.

32. See Sigmund Freud, "Medusa's Head," in *The Standard Edition of the Complete Psychological Works of Sigmund Freud,* vol. 18, pp. 273–74, and "Fetishism," in vol. 21, pp. 152–57.

33. Film theorists have pioneered the development of psychoanalytical interpretations of representation. For an overview of critical texts, starting with Laura Mulvey's groundbreaking "Visual Pleasure and Narrative Cinema," see *Screen, The Sexual Subject: A Screen Reader in Sexuality* (London: Routledge, 1992).

34. Quoted in Lader, p. 26.

35. Rudenstine, *Peggy Guggenheim Collection, Venice,* pp. 329–35. The wooden model was made by Jean Ipoustéguy, who worked from Giacometti's plaster version. Some of the pieces that should rest on pegs are now nailed down, and the two stele forms are angled incorrectly.

36. Michael F. Brenson sees this figure as a woman in his "The Early Work of Giacometti:

1925–35," unpublished Ph.D. dissertation, Johns Hopkins University, 1974; cited by Rudenstine, *Peggy Guggenheim Collection, Venice*, p. 335. Psychoanalyst Jacques Lacan, who associated with the Surrealists both professionally and personally, argued that woman herself represents the phallus (see Lacan, "The Meaning of the Phallus," in *Feminine Sexuality: Jacques Lacan and the école freudienne*, ed. by Juliet Mitchell and Jacqueline Rose, trans. by Rose [New York: W. W. Norton & Company and Pantheon Books, 1985], pp. 74–85). Thus, a reading of the form as woman or phallus is not exclusive but rather, mutually supportive.

37. The Peggy Guggenheim Collection's *Maiastra* (1912[?]) is an example of Brancusi's magic bird. The various versions of his *Princess X* and *Torso of a Young Man* are archetypal examples of fetishistic sculpture, which were considered obscene representations of penises when first shown. They both present the female form as phallic, supporting a Lacanian reading (see note 36, above).

38. See Susan Rubin Suleiman's analysis of transgression as a modernist literary device in her *Subversive Intent: Gender, Politics, and the Avant-Garde* (Cambridge, Mass.: Harvard University Press, 1990), pp. 72–87.

39. See Rosalind Krauss's interpretation in "Giacometti," in *"Primitivism" in 20th Century Art*, vol. 2, ed. by William Rubin, exh. cat. (New York: The Museum of Modern Art, 1984), pp. 503–33.

40. Rudenstine, *Peggy Guggenheim Collection, Venice*, pp. 198–205, identifies the various figures in the painting and their relationship to Dalí's obsession with the Freudian conceptualization of castration and impotence.

41. Guggenheim, *Out of This Century*, pp. 261–62.

42. See Rudenstine, *Peggy Guggenheim Collection, Venice*, pp. 312–18, for the quote as well as an interpretation of the painting. On Guggenheim's first visit to Ernst's studio, in the winter of 1938–39, she purchased a work by Carrington, *The Horses of Lord Candlestick*, rather than one by Ernst (Guggenheim, *Out of This Century*, p. 216; this painting is no longer in the collection). In Ernst's *Attirement of the Bride* (1940, Peggy Guggenheim Collection), the bride (who has been associated with Carrington) wears a red-orange feathered cape reminiscent of Ernst's costume in Carrington's *Portrait of Max Ernst* (ca. 1939; reproduced in Chadwick, colorplate 20).

43. Guggenheim, quoted in Adelaide Kerr, "In House That Peggy Built, Paintings Dangle From the Ceiling, and the Walls Often Curve," *Times Dispatch* (Richmond, Va.), November 2, 1942.

44. Guggenheim, *Out of This Century*, p. 270.

45. Lukach (p. 155), notes that Guggenheim's gallery name implied "a direct challenge to Uncle Solomon's 'Art of Tomorrow'" (part of Solomon Guggenheim's collection was exhibited in the 1939 show *Art of Tomorrow* at his Fifty-fourth Street museum). In *A Not-So-Still Life* (New York: St. Martin's/Marek, 1984, pp. 224–25), Jimmy Ernst, Max's son, claims that, through artists employed at "the 'Rebay' museum," he learned that Hilla Rebay was "interfering with Peggy's New York plans by threatening likely real estate firms if they cooperated with us in the search for a gallery location anywhere in midtown Manhattan."

46. For descriptions, see Cynthia Goodman, "Frederick Kiesler: Designs for Peggy Guggenheim's Art of This Century Gallery," *Arts* 51 (June 1977), pp. 90–95; Lader, pp. 115–25; Rudenstine, *Peggy Guggenheim Collection, Venice*, pp. 762–70; and Goodman, "The Art of Revolutionary Display Techniques," in Lisa Phillips, *Frederick Kiesler*, exh. cat. (New York: Whitney Museum of American Art in association with W. W. Norton & Company, 1989), pp. 57–83.

47. "Isms Rampant: Peggy Guggenheim's Dream World Goes Abstract, Cubist, and Generally Non-Real," *Newsweek*, November 2, 1942, p. 66. Goodman, "Frederick Kiesler," p. 94, notes the aptness of the peep-show analogy since Kiesler had been explicitly incorporating aspects of this mode of presentation in his work since the 1920s.

48. Goodman, "Frederick Kiesler," p. 93.

49. Quoted in "Isms Rampant," p. 66.

50. Goodman, "Frederick Kiesler," p. 93.

51. Gallery notice in *Cue*, January 16, 1943. Goodman, "Frederick Kiesler," p. 92, states that "Kiesler's design for Art of This Century was the major Surrealist architectural project built in the United States."

52. Edgar Kaufmann, Jr., "The Violent Art of Hanging Pictures," *Magazine of Art* 39 (March 1946), pp. 108–13. Kaufmann had convinced his parents to hire Wright, resulting in the architect's 1936 masterpiece Falling Water.

53. Kaufmann, pp. 109, 112–13. Wright's model for the Solomon R. Guggenheim Museum was unveiled in August 1945.

54. Guggenheim, *Out of This Century*, p. 324. Rebay often referred to her museum as a religious temple.

55. Barr's influential catalogue *Cubism and Abstract Art* included on its jacket an esoteric chart diagramming the diffusion of influence in early twentieth-century art. He extended this paradigm through the face-off of two important 1936 exhibitions, the aforementioned *Cubism and Abstract Art* and its antipode *Fantastic Art, Dada, Surrealism*. In the catalogue *Fantastic Art, Dada, Surrealism* (Alfred H. Barr, Jr., ed., exh. cat., New York: The Museum of Modern Art, 1936, p. 9), Barr wrote, "*Cubism and Abstract Art*, was, as it happens, diametrically opposed in both spirit and esthetic principles" to *Fantastic Art, Dada, Surrealism*. In Barr's framework, Surrealism, a secondary phenomenon, was subsumed under abstract art, not vice versa. Within Surrealism he made the formal distinction between automatic and dream painting, privileging the former.

56. Breton, *Manifesto of Surrealism*, p. 14. Rebay objected to Breton's conceptualization of reality when she stated, "Surrealism came in only recently, through such painters who invented this senseless title to stupefy the public. (Realism cannot be unearthly)." See Rebay, "The Beauty of Non-Objectivity," in *Second Enlarged Catalogue of the Solomon R. Guggenheim Collection of Non-Objective Paintings* (New York: The Solomon R. Guggenheim Foundation, 1937), p. 8.

57. See, for example, Peggy Guggenheim, ed., *Art of This Century* (New York: Art of This Century, 1942), p. 9; and Guggenheim, *Out of This Century*, p. 276.

58. In *Cubism and Abstract Art* (p. 19), Barr identified Apollo with the lineage of abstraction and Dionysus with the trends resulting in Surrealism.

59. A possible exception to non-objective artists' rejection of the real is their employment of biological metaphors or planetary, astronomic ones. Yet in each case a spiritual aspiration lies beneath the micro- or macrocosmic world that is evoked.

60. In "Genesis and Perspective of *Surrealism*," in Guggenheim, ed., *Art of This Century*, p. 26, Breton refers to "the great physico-mental stream of Surrealism." "What is admirable about the fantastic," he also wrote, "is that there is no longer anything fantastic: there is only the real" (*Manifesto of Surrealism*, p. 15). Rebay disapproved of what she saw as a frantic emphasis on objective reality: "The sensation of the object has outlived itself. The minds are tired of too much reality, brought to us confusingly and without effort. There is no rest unless we lift our eyes to the sky whose purity and endlessness demands no meaning from our harassed intellect" (see Rebay, "The Beauty of Non-Objectivity," p. 9).

61. Wassily Kandinsky, *Concerning the Spiritual in Art* (1911), trans. by M. T. H. Sadler (New York: Dover Publications, 1977), p. 24. The Solomon R. Guggenheim Foundation published

its own translations of *Concerning the Spiritual in Art* and Kandinsky's *Point and Line to Plane* (1926) in 1946 and 1947, respectively. The latter publication was the first translation into English.

62. Hilla Rebay, "Definition of Non-Objective Painting," in *Solomon R. Guggenheim Collection of Non-Objective Paintings* (Charleston, S.C.: Carolina Art Association, 1936), p. 8. Conversely, she had the gravest doubts about the Surrealists' aspirations: "They effectively put together sensational attractions which are usually of decidedly bad taste" (Rebay, "The Beauty of Non-Objectivity," p. 8).

63. Quoted in Lukach, p. 62, and Lader, p. 126, respectively.

64. Guggenheim, ed., *Art of This Century*, title page.

65. The ethereal work of Alexander Calder was an exception to this injunction.

66. Ad Reinhardt, "How to Look at Modern Art in America," *P.M.*, June 2, 1946; reprinted in *Ad Reinhardt*, with text by Yve-Alain Bois, exh. cat. (New York: Rizzoli, 1991), p. 110. Guggenheim preserved this cartoon in a scrapbook, now in the Peggy Guggenheim Archives, the Solomon R. Guggenheim Foundation.

67. Guggenheim, *Out of This Century*, p. 347. She wrote, p. 303, that Pollock was the "spiritual offspring" of James Johnson Sweeney (who became the Solomon R. Guggenheim Museum's director in 1952) and herself.

68. The gallery was also significant to young American artists because it provided them with unusual access to European works. Motherwell said in 1982:

Peggy's place was unique in several ways. It could be treated as a place to browse, and it was designed to be treated that way. . . . You were invited to take the pictures in your hands—like a print or a book—and move them back and forth so that you could see a line or a surface more clearly in different kinds of light. It was a small place, intimate, and everything was meant to be used, and she felt strongly about that.

All three quotes cited in Rudenstine, *Peggy Guggenheim Collection, Venice*, p. 799.

69. October 1942 press release for the opening of Art of This Century, quoted in Lader, p. 126.

70. Only a small portion of this discrepancy can be ascribed to Guggenheim's inclusion of certain artists due to personal rather than professional reasons.

71. In mourning the closing of Peggy's gallery in 1947, Clement Greenberg included a list of

important artists: "Her departure is in my opinion a serious loss to living American art. . . . In the three or four years of her career as a New York gallery director she gave first showings to more serious new artists than anyone else in the country (Pollock, Hare, Baziotes, Motherwell, Rothko, [Rudolph] Ray, De Niro, [Virginia] Admiral, [Marjorie] McKee, and others). I am convinced that Peggy Guggenheim's place in the history of American art will grow larger as time passes and as the artists she encouraged mature" (in *The Nation*, May 31, 1947, quoted in Rudenstine, *Peggy Guggenheim Collection, Venice*, p. 798). It is interesting to note that both women on this list are not well-known. Chadwick's book acts as a corrective to the lack of notoriety of many of the female Surrealist artists.

72. R. F. [Rosamund Frost], "Thirty-Odd Women," *Art News* 41 (Jan. 15–31, 1943), p. 20.

73. *Art News* 44 (July 1–31, 1945), p. 26; and Robert M. Coates, "The Art Galleries," *The New Yorker* 18 (Jan. 15, 1943), p. 56: "Thirty-one ladies . . . have got together and cooked up a mess of paintings, collages, constructions, and so on, all highly spiced with surrealism. . . . The main attraction for many visitors will be the contribution of Gypsy Rose Lee, a sort of collage *en coquille* . . ."

74. For example, Ben Wolf, "Bless Them," *The Art Digest* 19 (July 1, 1945), p. 13: "Gypsy Rose Lee, versatile daughter of Eros, originally scheduled to strip her soul in the above company . . ."

75. Henry McBride, "Women Surrealists: They, Too, Know How to Make Your Hair Stand on End," *New York Sun*, January 8, 1943, p. 28.

76. Quoted in Jimmy Ernst, p. 236.

77. At Guggenheim Jeune in 1939, she had also held *André Breton Presents Mexican Art*, cited by Weld, p. 446.

78. Guggenheim notes in *Out of This Century*, pp. 344–45, that in 1950 her "basement was stacked with the overflow of" her collection. She mentions Virginia Admiral and Janet Sobel in the list of artists whose work she bought at Art of This Century shows, thus filling her cellar.

79. See Guggenheim, *Out of This Century*, pp. 172, 174; and Rudenstine, *Peggy Guggenheim Collection, Venice*, p. 750. The decision was eventually overturned after significant protest was voiced.

80. Painter George Biddle, quoted in Lader, pp. 78–79.

81. See Weld, p. 368; and Guggenheim, *Out of This Century*, pp. 330, 374.

82. Guggenheim, *Out of This Century*, pp. 334–35. Weld, p. 375, notes that eventually a phallus was permanently attached after the removable one was stolen.

83. Her presentation of earrings in a manner similar to her collection of art has a Surrealist precedent in the "photocomplex" of jewelry that appeared in the October 15, 1929 issue of *Variétés*, with the caption "Fétichisme aujourd'hui." Foster (p. 173) discusses this reproduction in the context of his conceptualization of modernist fetishism.

Following two pages: Willem de Kooning,
Composition, 1955 (detail).

Art of This Century and the New York School

Diane Waldman

In March 1939, a year and a half after she opened the Guggenheim Jeune gallery in London, Peggy Guggenheim decided to found a museum of Modern art. She persuaded Herbert Read, a prominent critic and art historian, to give up his job as editor of *Burlington Magazine* and become the museum's director. Plans for an autumn opening were well under way when World War II erupted. Concerned about her collection, which included works by Robert Delaunay, Vasily Kandinsky, Paul Klee, André Masson, Joan Miró, and Pablo Picasso, among others, Guggenheim stored it for a brief period in Grenoble, France; in July 1941, she brought it to New York, where it became the foundation of a new enterprise—Art of This Century, which was to serve as a museum to display her collection and as a gallery dedicated to introducing artists to the public. Art of This Century opened in October 1942 to great fanfare and was an instantaneous, if controversial, success. It featured sensational spaces designed by the Romanian-born architect and designer Frederick Kiesler, a participant in the De Stijl movement, who had been brought to her attention by Howard Putzel. Putzel, a West Coast art dealer, was one of several people who advised her on her collection (the others being André Breton, Marcel Duchamp, Max Ernst, and Nellie van Doesburg, the widow of Theo van Doesburg). Kiesler installed the collection in two main galleries, one for Surrealism, the other for abstract and Cubist art. Unframed Surrealist paintings jutted out on baseball bats from curved walls, while the abstract and Cubist works were suspended on cords (fig. 100). In each gallery, sculpture was placed on biomorphic-shaped wooden pedestals.

The opening of Peggy Guggenheim's gallery and the presence in New York of many of Europe's legendary painters and poets who had fled due to the war—among them Breton, Ernst, and Masson—gave young, unrecognized American artists a taste of the heady international scene that prevailed in Paris before the war. Robert Motherwell, who met Guggenheim shortly after she opened her New York

gallery, said that it was he who introduced her to William Baziotes. They and their colleague Jackson Pollock were invited by Guggenheim to participate in her *Exhibition of Collage*, which was held at the gallery from April 16 to May 15, 1943, although none had worked in the medium before. Baziotes made a collage entitled *The Drugged Balloonist* (now in the collection of the Baltimore Museum of Art) for the show, but the work remains an exception in his oeuvre. Motherwell recalled that he and Pollock worked together on collage in Pollock's studio and that "Pollock became more and more tense and vehement as he tore up papers, pasted them down, even burned their edges, splashed paint over everything, quite literally like something in a state of trance."[1] While Pollock incorporated elements of collage in his drawings and paintings that postdate the exhibition, he produced relatively few independent works in that medium. Motherwell, however, went on to develop a substantial body of collages that, like his paintings, are poetic, sensual, and passionate. Many of the great themes that he developed in his paintings first began to take shape in the collages, such as *Personage (Autoportrait)* (1943, plate 94), that he produced beginning in 1943. Collage became an integral part of Motherwell's oeuvre, separate in intent and meaning from his equally formidable paintings.

In London before the war, Read had planned to hold a "Spring Salon" to encourage new talent. Peggy revived the concept for her New York gallery and selected a jury of such notable figures as artists Duchamp and Piet Mondrian; museum directors Alfred H. Barr, Jr., James Thrall Soby, and James Johnson Sweeney; Putzel; and herself. The first *Spring Salon for Young Artists* was held from May 18 to June 26, 1943, and included Baziotes, Matta, Motherwell, and Ad Reinhardt, among others. Persuaded by Mondrian that the young Pollock showed talent, and encouraged by Matta and Putzel, she offered him a one-year contract with the gallery; he would receive a modest stipend in exchange for work. Guggenheim also commissioned Pollock to paint a mural

Top: Fig. 101. Peggy Guggenheim and Jackson Pollock, standing in front of the mural Peggy commissioned in 1943 for her New York apartment. Photo by Mirko Lion.

Bottom: Fig. 102. Herbert Read. Photo courtesy Karole Vail.

Left: Fig. 100. Abstract Gallery at Art of This Century, with Theo van Doesburg's *Composition in Gray (Rag-time)* (1919) in the foreground.

Plate 93. Joseph Cornell, *Untitled (Grand Hôtel de l'Observatoire)*, 1954. Box construction and collage, 46.5 x 33 x 9.8 cm (18 5/16 x 12 15/16 x 3 7/8 inches). Solomon R. Guggenheim Museum, Partial gift, C. and B. Foundation, by exchange 80.2734.

for her home, and thus provided him and his artist wife, Lee Krasner, with vital financial support during a difficult period in their lives. Guggenheim considered Baziotes, Motherwell, and Pollock the outstanding artists in the first *Spring Salon*. Between 1943 and 1946, she gave solo exhibitions to them as well as to other important Americans, including Mark Rothko and Clyfford Still. Guggenheim purchased work from these exhibitions and added an impressive collection of younger American painters and sculptors to her already substantial collection of European Modern art. Her reputation for acquiring vast amounts of art in a short period of time was infamous. In her autobiography, *Out of This Century* (the first version of which was published in 1946), Guggenheim stated that when she lived in Paris in 1940, she deliberately set out to acquire a painting a day. Her appetite for art continued unabated in New York, as did her proclivity for moving in the fast lanes of the avant-garde.[2] Although she closed her gallery in May 1947 to return to Europe, Art of This Century filled a void at a critical time in the history of American art.

Prior to Peggy Guggenheim's arrival, the New York art scene was in flux. Many of the younger Americans working in New York during the Depression years practiced a form of figuration known as Social Realism. Others were members of the American Abstract Artists, an association founded in New York in 1936 and dedicated to the principles of European geometric abstraction, in particular the work of Mondrian and the De Stijl movement; the association gained added prestige from Mondrian's presence in New York from 1940 until his death in 1944. Neither the politically and socially oriented Depression-era American-scene painting, which depicted the downtrodden urban masses and glorified rural life, nor the programmatic non-objective painting of the American Abstract Artists proved to have a lasting effect on the young American avant-garde working for the most part in New York City. Instead, they were increasingly impressed by two of this century's most important European movements, Cubism and Surrealism. The Cubist innovations of Picasso and Georges Braque were a particular source of inspiration. The Cubists' fragmentation of the figure and their emphasis on compressing volume into two-dimensional space had a great impact on the Americans, who were historically predisposed to flatness and frontality. However, it was the Surrealists who gained in importance, when many of the movement's leading figures, among them Breton, Ernst, Masson, and Matta took up residence in New York. Their active involvement in the New York art scene, their zealous commitment to the subconscious, and their belief in automatism (the suspension of the conscious mind in order to release subconscious imagery) influenced virtually every major painter and sculptor of the New York School. For the fledgling Americans it was an exhilarating time, which gave them the freedom and challenge they needed to invent a brilliant new American art.

The Surrealist influence on the young American artists began to emerge in the early 1930s and grew in importance throughout the decade. As early as November 1931, the first significant Surrealist exhibition, *Newer Super-Realism*, was organized by [Arthur Everett] Chick Austin at the Wadsworth Atheneum in Hartford, Connecticut. The dealer Julien Levy showed some of the same works as the Wadsworth had in an exhibition entitled *Surréalisme* at his New York gallery in January 1932. Levy played a major role in establishing the movement in New York, presenting its leading figures throughout the 1930s and publishing the anthology *Surrealism* in 1936. That same year, Alfred H. Barr, Jr. presented the historic exhibition *Fantastic Art, Dada, Surrealism* at the Museum of Modern Art in New York.

For Joseph Cornell and Arshile Gorky, Americans who were influenced by Surrealism in the early 1930s, the presence of the Surrealist artists and poets in exile in New York during the war years was particularly significant: the personal encouragement of Breton

Plate 94. Robert Motherwell, *Personage (Autoportrait)*, December 9, 1943. Paper collage, gouache, and ink on board, 103.8 x 65.9 cm (40 ⅞ x 25 ¹⁵⁄₁₆ inches). Peggy Guggenheim Collection 76.2553 PG155.

Plate 95. Mark Rothko, *Sacrifice*, April 1946. Watercolor, gouache, and india ink on paper, 100.2 x 65.8 cm (39 7/16 x 25 7/8 inches). Peggy Guggenheim Collection 76.2553 PG154.

and others was invaluable to them at a critical time in their careers. Cornell's *Untitled (Grand Hôtel de l'Observatoire)* (1954, plate 93) and *Swiss Shoot-the-Chutes* (1941, plate 85), among other of his box constructions, combine the Surrealists' fondness for chance with strange and unexpected juxtapositions of objects. Of all of the Americans, it was Cornell who most faithfully subscribed to the writings of a major Surrealist precursor, the Comte de Lautréamont. "Beautiful as the fortuitous meeting, on a dissection table, of a sewing machine and an umbrella,"[3] the celebrated passage from his fantasy novel *Les Chants de Maldoror* (1874), was interpreted by Cornell in his collages and box constructions. Yet while utilizing the Surrealist technique of disorientation in time and space, suggested by the random juxtaposition of objects and images, Cornell's box constructions of this period also reveal a disarming naïveté entirely at odds with the black humor and disturbing, often grotesque effects deliberately cultivated by many of the Surrealist painters and poets. Moreover, his appreciation of other European Modernists like Mondrian and his fondness for the trompe-l'oeil still lifes of the nineteenth-century American painter William Harnett helped give his work its distinctive quality and separated him from mainstream Surrealism.

Although Surrealist imagery, with its sexually charged subject matter and ambiguous thematic content, figured prominently in the work of Willem de Kooning, Motherwell, Pollock, and others, it was the Surrealists' concept of automatism that radically altered the course of American art. Automatism, linked with Freudian notions of the subconscious, liberated the Abstract Expressionists from the external world of objective reality and freed them to explore in their own work the irrational, chance, and accident. Unlike the Surrealists, who remained committed to representation, narrative, and illusionism, many of the Abstract Expressionists used automatism as their point of departure in the formation of a radical new abstract imagery.

Automatism made it possible for them to transcend representational subject matter, consolidate process and end product, and fuse inner vision and external phenomena.

Gorky, too, made effective use of the Surrealist idiom, often linking sexually symbolic imagery with automatic drawing or painting. *Untitled* (1944, plate 96) is in many ways different from his more painterly canvases. Here, Gorky adapted his leanest style to canvas, using a sort of rude drawing and giving scant attention to detail or exquisite effects. Line is urgent and abrupt in *Untitled*, while in many drawings and paintings of the period it is full of liquid grace; there is anger and defiance in the work, while in others there is harmony. Of this and related paintings of the same year, Gorky said, "Any time I was ready to make a line somewhere, I put it somewhere else. And it was always better."[4] *Untitled* is a tough and demanding work in which Gorky begins to explore line in a manner that anticipates by several years Pollock's allover imagery.

Pollock's paintings of 1938–41 are filled with images of snakes, skulls, and plant and animal forms. One of the most important images favored by Pollock was the eye, which figures prominently in *The Moon Woman* (1942, plate 98); its usage indicates his familiarity with its role in Surrealist iconography and Jungian philosophy (Pollock was in Jungian analysis for eighteen months beginning in 1939 and continued therapy until 1943) as a symbol of the union between inner and external states of being. Pollock continued to use archetypal symbols in the 1940s, as in such major paintings as *Eyes in the Heat* (1946, plate 99), one of seven paintings from the *Sounds in the Grass* series. (*Croaking Movement* [1946, plate 100] is also part of the series.) *Sounds in the Grass* signaled an important transition in Pollock's oeuvre. During the winter of 1946–47, Pollock began to drip and pour enamel and aluminum paint onto large unprimed canvases laid out on the floor of his studio. Pollock's drip technique involved his entire body as he circled his canvases, pouring and splashing

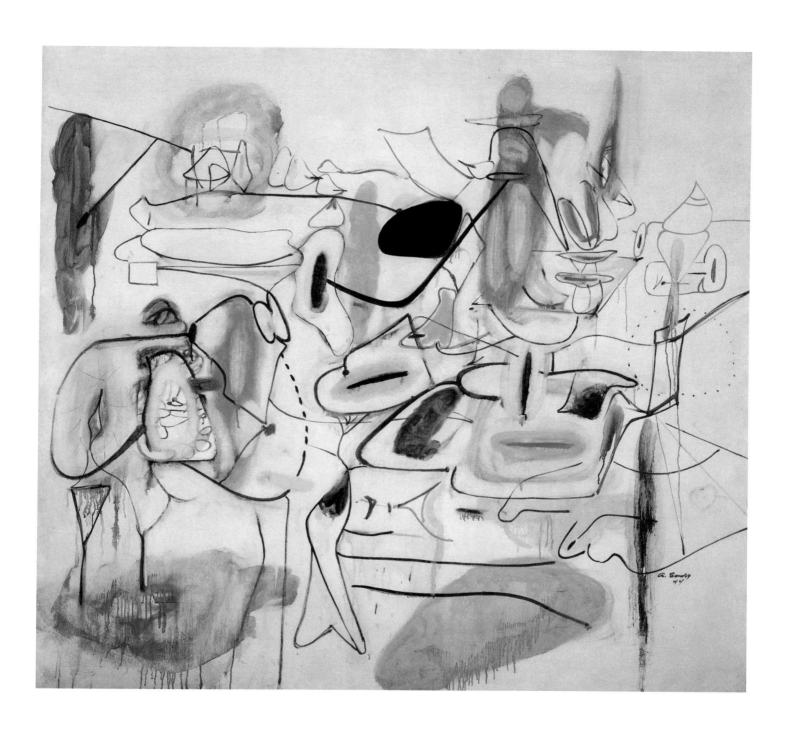

Plate 96. Arshile Gorky, *Untitled*, summer 1944. Oil on canvas, 167 x 178.2 cm (65 ¾ x 70 ³⁄₁₆ inches). Peggy Guggenheim Collection 76.2553 PG152.

Plate 97. Clyfford Still, *Jamais*, May 1944. Oil on canvas, 165.2 x 82 cm (65 ⅟₁₆ x 32 ¼ inches). Peggy Guggenheim Collection 76.2553 PG153.

paint from every direction. His methods eventually led him to favor mural-sized canvases over easel pictures.

In his classic drip paintings of 1947–50, such as *Enchanted Forest* (1947, plate 101) and *Alchemy* (1947, plate 103), Pollock created a sense of continuous movement and an illusion of shallow space that extends behind the picture plane and often laterally beyond the edges of the composition. At the same time, he called attention to the flatness of the field. As in *Eyes in the Heat*, there is implicit in many later canvases, such as *Ocean Greyness* (1953, plate 102), a vortex motion that may derive from the way in which he worked. This whirling or circular motion occurs despite Pollock's emphasis on flatness, and sets up a tension in many of his best drip paintings that relieves them of the stasis that would otherwise occur as the result of his allover imagery. Pollock used his revolutionary drip technique to capitalize to the utmost on chance and spontaneous effects. His allover drip paintings are remarkable for their powerful, dynamic abstract imagery and large scale.

During the early 1940s, Rothko and Adolph Gottlieb also developed a body of archetypal images based upon the Jungian theory of the collective unconscious. Like many of their fellow New York artists, both subscribed to the Surrealist belief in dream imagery and the power of the subconscious to reveal hidden truths. In keeping with these beliefs, Rothko created a series of images that, like *Sacrifice* (1946, plate 95), indicate his interest in myth. In 1941, Gottlieb began a series of pictographs in which he used a grid pattern derived from Cubist scaffolding, combined with a highly charged vocabulary of signs and symbols. Images of the human anatomy such as eyes, a hand, and teeth, as well as other body parts form the vocabulary of his image-symbols, which Gottlieb believed had universal significance in the human collective unconscious. While Rothko was later to shift his emphasis from the visible world and mythic imagery to the inner world of the imagination, Gottlieb continued to employ the grid with its compartments of recognizable

motifs throughout the 1930s. During the late 1940s and early 1950s, Gottlieb's work took on an increasingly abstract quality, but he never relinquished his interest in nature and organic phenomena. *W* (1954, plate 104) and other paintings that indicate his development of abstract shapes from pictographic imagery retain an aura of the mythic and the archaic, while *Mist* (1961, plate 105) contains a palpable physical dimension that links his work to the Impressionists and the world of the senses.

Certain of Still's works of the 1940s, such as *Jamais* (1944, plate 97) are classic examples of Surrealist-inspired painting. Although Still ultimately rejected European tradition, the shape, color, and space evident in this canvas became the primary features of his later work. For artists like Motherwell, the Surrealist concept of automatism translated easily into painterly gesture and symbolism. Motherwell's *Elegy to the Spanish Republic No. 110* (1971, plate 111) is one of a series of nearly two hundred paintings that the artist began in 1948 to celebrate freedom and pay tribute to the Spanish people. Generally, the ovoid forms balanced by linear brushstrokes suggest the male and female. Their bold yet pliable shapes are a manifestation of human life and fragility.

In 1946, the critic Robert Coates, writing for the *New Yorker*, used the term "abstract expressionism" to describe the work of some of the New York–based painters. The term stuck but was amplified by others. In 1952, the critic Harold Rosenberg invented the term "action painting" to emphasize the importance of the act of painting. Rosenberg described the canvas as an arena and the image that resulted from the act of painting as an event. Rosenberg wrote that the "new painting has broken down every distinction between art and life."[5] He furthermore believed that action painting was part of an existential experience that led to a struggle for self-creation and a crisis in painting. Self-creation could be achieved by capturing the primary experience, the moment of inspiration. Painting was to be direct, immediate, spontaneous.

Plate 99. Jackson Pollock, *Eyes in the Heat*, 1946.
Oil (and enamel?) on canvas, 137.2 x 109.2 cm
(54 x 43 inches). Peggy Guggenheim Collection
76.2553 PG149.

Plate 100. Jackson Pollock, *Croaking Movement*, 1946.
Oil on canvas, 137.2 x 112 cm (54 x 44 ¹/₈ inches). Peggy
Guggenheim Collection 76.2553 PG148.

Plate 98. Jackson Pollock, *The Moon Woman*, 1942.
Oil on canvas, 175.2 x 109.3 cm (69 x 43 ¹/₁₆ inches).
Peggy Guggenheim Collection 76.2553 PG141.

Plate 102. Jackson Pollock, *Ocean Greyness*, 1953.
Oil on canvas, 146.7 x 229 cm (57 ³/₄ x 90 ¹/₈ inches).
Solomon R. Guggenheim Museum 54.1408.

Plate 103. Jackson Pollock, *Alchemy,* 1947.
Oil, aluminum (and enamel?) paint, and string on canvas,
114.6 x 221.3 cm (45 ⅛ x 87 ⅛ inches). Peggy Guggenheim
Collection 76.2553 PG150.

Above: Plate 104. Adolph Gottlieb, *W*, 1954. Oil with
sand on canvas, 182.9 x 91.5 cm (72 x 36 inches). Solomon R.
Guggenheim Museum 54.1401.

Left: Plate 105. Adolph Gottlieb, *Mist*, 1961. Oil on
canvas, 182.9 x 121.9 cm (72 x 48 inches). Solomon R.
Guggenheim Museum, Gift, Susan Morse Hilles 78.2401.

Left: Plate 106. Mark Rothko, *Untitled (#18)*, 1963.
Oil on canvas, 175.6 x 163.5 cm (69 ⅛ x 64 ⅛ inches).
Solomon R. Guggenheim Museum, Gift of The Mark
Rothko Foundation, Inc. 86.3421.

Above: Plate 107. Mark Rothko, *Untitled (Black on Grey)*,
1970. Acrylic on canvas, 203.3 x 175.5 cm (80 ⅛ x
69 ⅛ inches). Solomon R. Guggenheim Museum, Gift of
The Mark Rothko Foundation, Inc. 86.3422.

Left: Plate 108. Willem de Kooning, *Composition*, 1955.
Oil, enamel, and charcoal on canvas, 201 x 175.6 cm (79 ⅛ x
69 ⅛ inches). Solomon R. Guggenheim Museum 55.1419.

Above: Plate 109. Willem de Kooning, . . . *Whose Name
Was Writ in Water*, 1975. Oil on canvas, 195 x 223 cm
(76 ¾ x 87 ¾ inches). Solomon R. Guggenheim Museum,
By exchange 80.2738.

Plate 110. Franz Kline, *Painting No. 7*, 1952. Oil on canvas, 146 x 207.6 cm (57½ x 81¼ inches). Solomon R. Guggenheim Museum 54.1403.

Plate 111. Robert Motherwell, *Elegy to the Spanish Republic No. 110*, Easter Day 1971. Acrylic with pencil and charcoal on canvas, 208.5 x 289.8 cm (82 x 114 inches). Solomon R. Guggenheim Museum, Gift, Agnes Gund 84.3223.

Although the term action painting became too unwieldy to describe artists as diverse in sensibility and method as Cornell and Gorky, de Kooning and Rothko, it is a valid measure of the belief in the creative act born at the moment of inspiration and the unfolding drama that takes place in the arena of painting. It is an outgrowth of the belief in the subconscious and in the vehicle of automatism first proposed by the Surrealists and central to the art of each of the artists of the New York School. The Abstract Expressionist movement constitutes the first truly international American style. The artists who emerged during this period were challenged by the possibility of forging a new and heroic American art. Their work exemplifies a spirit of adventure and a grandeur of vision unparalleled in earlier twentieth-century American art.

In general terms, two groups emerged whose work defines the period: the first, the action painters like de Kooning, Franz Kline, and Pollock, to whom gesture was essential; the second, the painters Barnett Newman, Rothko, and Still, who used color as metaphor. The painters in the latter group purified their art by rejecting the seductive qualities of paint and by ridding their canvases of complex relationships of color, form, and structure. Two works by Rothko—*Number 18 (Black, Orange on Maroon)* (1963, plate 106) and *Untitled (Black on Grey)* (1970, plate 107)—exemplify the tendency among the group to reduce color to its essence and make it become volume, form, space, and light. Having emptied their paintings of the superfluous, they were able to express both the material reality of abstract painting and the incorporeal reality of the sublime.

De Kooning is primarily known for his *Women* series of paintings, but they are bracketed by two series of works, comprised of abstract images, that complement his interest in the figure. Around 1946, he began a series of black paintings that incorporated symbolic forms with abstract shapes and silhouettes of subjects taken from everyday life. While de Kooning used Surrealist-inspired imagery in these and later works of the 1940s, he was never committed to that movement. Nor was his work ever totally abstract, because his subject matter remained wedded to the real world from which, for him, all imagery stemmed.

Shortly after he completed his *Women* series, de Kooning began to search for a new theme. *Composition* (1955, plate 108) contains only marginal references to the female figure. Here, as before, she is torn apart and rearranged as part of an abstract image. Color and brushstroke are newly independent and all but freed from form. *Composition* is a highly original painting in that it signals the unique direction de Kooning's work was taking. In abandoning, if temporarily, the subject of the figure, he embraced the subject of abstraction without relinquishing his commitment to the visible world. By 1955, the image of the woman had virtually disappeared, replaced by landscape images based on urban and suburban themes.

In 1961, de Kooning moved from his studio in New York to The Springs in East Hampton. There, he began a series of bold new paintings that differed dramatically from their predecessors. The beaches, marshes, scrub oaks, and potato fields of The Springs were the basis for these new paintings. In works like . . . *Whose Name Was Writ in Water* (1975, plate 109), atmosphere fuses with and transfigures form. In these paintings, de Kooning's preoccupation with the sensations and reflections of color and light may be compared to that of Claude Monet late in his life. Yet even in such landscape-oriented paintings as these, fragments of the figure or of objects in the landscape are evident. Color may or may not suggest a figure, the grass, or the sky; freed from depiction, liberated from shape and contour, these paintings reveal a new dimension in de Kooning's oeuvre. Exuberant, free, and innovative, they are a late great flowering of his art.

In canvases such as *Painting No. 7* (1952, plate 110), de Kooning's friend Kline produced a body of work in which he balanced a series of muscular black shapes against white grounds. Kline's fierce forms have often been compared to architectural structures,

Plate 112. Hans Hofmann, *The Gate*, 1959–60. Oil on
canvas, 190.7 x 123.2 cm (75⅛ x 48½ inches). Solomon R.
Guggenheim Museum 62.1620.

Plate 113. Morris Louis, *Saraband*, 1959. Acrylic resin on canvas, 257 x 378.5 cm (101 ⅛ x 149 inches). Solomon R. Guggenheim Museum 64.1685.

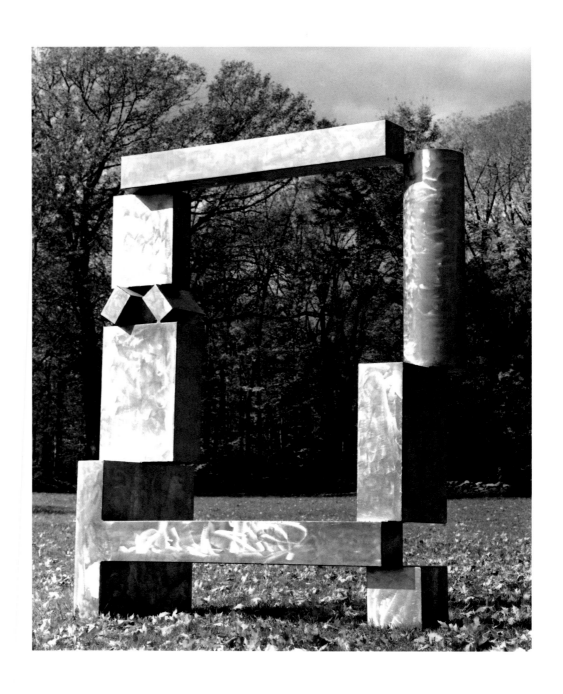

Plate 114. David Smith, *Cubi XXVII*, March 1965.
Stainless steel, 282.9 x 222.9 x 86.4 cm (111 3/8 x 87 1/4 x
34 inches). Solomon R. Guggenheim Museum,
By exchange 67.1862.

while his bold brushwork has been seen as a modern enactment of the drama of the New York skyline, with its starkly silhouetted skyscrapers, massive steel girders, and strong contrasts of black and white. Kline and many of his colleagues, de Kooning, Motherwell, and Pollock among them, experimented with black and white because it afforded them a new opportunity to explore vital form relationships that were different in intent and in effect from the form relationships in the work of Newman, Rothko, and Still. Because gesture was either paramount or a coefficient of color for the former painters, they retained the element of line and contour in their work. The latter group, on the other hand, downplayed or eliminated line altogether in order to free color to act on its own.

Hans Hofmann, an influential painter, teacher, and theorist, came to the United States from Germany in 1932 and worked and taught in New York and Provincetown, Massachusetts. In *The Gate* (1959–60, plate 112), richly textured brushstrokes, crisp geometric forms, and brilliant color demonstrate the artist's belief in the "push and pull" of the canvas. Hofmann created tension and depth within the space of the canvas by establishing a dialogue between his active painterly brushstrokes and his equally dominant rectangles. He resolved the potential conflict between his vigorous brushstrokes and his vivid color by aligning his rectangles to the edges of the picture plane. Hofmann thus created a vital dialogue between two seeming opposites, that of painterly expressionism and bold geometry. In this respect, his paintings stand somewhat apart from either of the two main tendencies of Abstract Expressionism, but in so doing they add another dimension to the painting of the New York School.

Although the New York School produced fewer important sculptors than it did painters, the sculptors of the group exemplify the spirit of adventure, lyricism, austerity, and, as Motherwell noted, a "spontaneity and lack of self-consciousness."[6] The sculptures in David Smith's *Cubi* series (plate 114, for

example) are among the finest he produced. Smith assembled and welded the works in this series with methods similar to those he had employed earlier in his career. Preparatory drawings and collages were created before the final assembly and welding. As soon as each element was joined, the constructions were roughly buffed to produce variegated surfaces and an iridescent sheen. For the first time, Smith was able to incorporate light into his work, as it played off the surface of each sculpture to create a resplendent luster. Powerful and individualized, Smith's sculpture captures the heroic vision evidenced throughout the work of the New York School.

Isamu Noguchi was also drawn to Surrealism and to what he called "the sublime rationality of the irrational,"[7] a trait that is also common to Eastern aesthetics, as noted by the critic Shuzo Takiguchi. Noguchi's use of archetypal motifs and sensual materials, as in *Lunar* (1959–60, plate 116), are the result of Western and Eastern influences; his successful marriage of both traditions resulted in a body of sculpture that has a unique place among the art of the New York School.

Subsequent generations of artists amplified the vision of the Abstract Expressionists. Artists as diverse as Morris Louis, Robert Rauschenberg, and John Chamberlain extended the color forms of Still and the painterly gestures of de Kooning. Louis was among a group known as Color-field painters, who began to experiment with pouring and staining paint directly onto unprimed canvas. Among Louis's most successful paintings are his *Veils*, such as *Saraband* (1959, plate 113), a series in which expansive areas of translucent color were poured in successive layers onto the canvas and overlapped to fill most of the painting field. Whereas Louis and the other Color-field painters emphasized the primacy of abstract painting, its color, shape, and size, Rauschenberg and Chamberlain expanded the two-dimensional possibilities of the painted surface into the three-dimensional reality of forms assembled from the real world. Chamberlain's monumental sculpture

Plate 115. John Chamberlain, *Dolores James*, 1962.
Welded and painted automobile parts, 193 x 246.4 x 99.1 cm
(76 x 97 x 39 inches). Solomon R. Guggenheim Museum
70.1925.

Plate 116. Isamu Noguchi, *Lunar*, 1959–60. Anodized
aluminum with wood, 189.2 x 61 x 29.5 cm (74 ½ x 24 x
11 ⅛ inches). Solomon R. Guggenheim Museum 61.1596.

Dolores James (1962, plate 115), faithful to the painterly, gestural aesthetic of the New York School, capitalizes on the readymade—the automobile—to make a pithy statement on the nature of American society and on the automobile as an emblem of the American dream.

The vital dialogue begun by these and other artists of the New York School in the 1940s continues unabated today. Many of the New York School artists were first shown by Peggy Guggenheim, and became aware of Surrealism through Art of This Century. Their lasting importance is a tribute to her patronage and vision.

Notes

1. Quoted in Herta Wescher, *Collage*, trans. by Robert E. Wolf (New York: Harry N. Abrams, 1968), pp. 299–300.

2. Peggy Guggenheim, *Out of This Century: Confessions of an Art Addict* (London: André Deutsch Limited, 1979), p. 209.

3. Translated in Anna Balakian, *Surrealism: The Road to the Absolute* (Chicago: The University of Chicago Press, 1986), p. 191.

4. Quoted in Jerry Tallmer, "Watch That Paint," *New York Post*, June 7, 1980, p. 13.

5. Harold Rosenberg, "The American Action Painters," *Art News* 51, no. 8 (December 1952), p. 23.

6. Quoted in *The School of New York*, exh. cat. (Beverly Hills: Frank Perls Gallery, 1951), p. 3.

7. Quoted in Shuzo Takiguchi, Saburo Hasegawa, and Isamu Noguchi, *Noguchi* (Tokyo, 1953), p. 28.

Following two pages: Joseph Kosuth,
'Titled (Art as Idea as Idea)' {Water}, 1966 (detail).

-ter (wâ′ter), ...
...in to Icel. *vatr*
...lan, water, L. ...
E. *wet*: cf. *hy*...
...hich in a more ...
...kes, rivers, etc. ...
...odorous, tastel...
...ygen, H_2O, fre...
...or 100° C.; a...

. [AS. *wæter*

, Goth. *watō*,

nda, a wave, w

dra, otter[1], *una*

or less impure s

and which in

ess liquid, a

ezing at 32° F.

pecial form or

Against the Grain
*A History of Contemporary Art
at the Guggenheim*

Nancy Spector

Since its inception in 1937, the Solomon R. Guggenheim Foundation has made it a priority to acquire art of the immediate present, amassing an extensive collection that reflects the avant-garde tendencies of the twentieth century. From the 1960s, when Modernist monuments began to be viewed as historical artifacts, the Guggenheim's approach to the presentation and preservation of art evolved into a two-part program, one aspect of which commemorates, resuscitates, and often revises elements of the recent art-historical past; the other focuses on the immediate present with an eye toward future developments. Hence, exhibitions of the last thirty years have included surveys of historical movements such as German Expressionism, retrospectives devoted to artists such as Constantin Brancusi and Oskar Kokoschka, as well as radical explorations of contemporary trends.

The Guggenheim's relationship to contemporary art has, however, been tempestuous; the history of its contemporary programming is one of conflict and controversy that constitutes, ultimately, a map of the most progressive and polemical developments in postwar art. In the course of the museum's efforts to engage and exhibit important new work, it has encountered serious difficulties in interpretation and presentation; this is not surprising given the radical nature of the new art forms, many of which were devised to subvert existing conventions and value systems.

Aspects of these art forms, in particular Pop art, Minimalism, and Post-Minimalism, were explored in several significant exhibitions organized by the Guggenheim during the 1960s and early 1970s. By focusing on the critical and curatorial issues raised in conjunction with these shows, it is possible to construct a history of postwar art that encompasses far more than chronology and description. It is in the slippages of meaning, the clashes over content, the dissensions of artists, and the disputes over aesthetic decisions that the critical implications of avant-garde activity come to light. When examined in retrospect, these conflicts describe the all-too-brief historical moments when the avant-garde truly broke with tradition—before it was subsumed into the mainstream culture that it initially assailed.

The Institutionalization of Contemporary Art

As with any museum, the history of the Guggenheim is, ultimately, a history of its directors and curators—their visions, their values, their perspectives. The museum's initial premise was based on Hilla Rebay's passion for the potential spiritual dimension of non-objective painting. While the predilection for abstract art has not diminished throughout the institution's history, an appreciation for alternate modes of expression has evolved as each successive administration sets its own policy. James Johnson Sweeney, Rebay's successor as director, expanded on her rather narrow and idiosyncratic program to include sculpture and representational art. In 1962, during Thomas M. Messer's tenure as director, the Guggenheim hired as its curator Lawrence Alloway, a young British art critic and historian who had served as deputy director of London's Institute of Contemporary Art from 1954 to 1957. In 1952, as a member of the Independent Group—a consortium of architects, artists, historians, and designers created to analyze and utilize the myriad facets of contemporary culture—Alloway fostered an appreciation for the diverse cultural phenomena that fall outside the realm of fine art: product design, glossy magazines, advertising, technology, cinema, comic books, and the like.[1] "The missile and the toaster," wrote Alloway in 1959, "the push-button and the repeating revolver, military and kitchen technologies, are the natural possession of the media—a treasury of orientation, a manual of one's occupancy of the twentieth century."[2] Alloway is credited with having originated the term "Pop art" in reference to visual material that is "industrialized [and] mass produced," as opposed to that which is "unique [and] luxurious."[3] Though he initially adopted this appellation in order to differentiate "high" from "low" culture in defense of

Left: **Fig. 103. Daniel Buren,** *Inside (Center of Guggenheim),* 1971. Acrylic on cloth, 20 x 9.1 m (65 feet 7½ inches x 29 feet 9¼ inches). Collection of the artist. Installed at the Solomon R. Guggenheim Museum for one day before the opening of the *Guggenheim International Exhibition, 1971.*

Top: **Fig. 104.** Former Guggenheim Director Thomas M. Messer.

Bottom: **Fig. 105.** Lawrence Alloway (right) during installation of the 1966 exhibition *Systemic Painting.* Photo by Paul Katz.

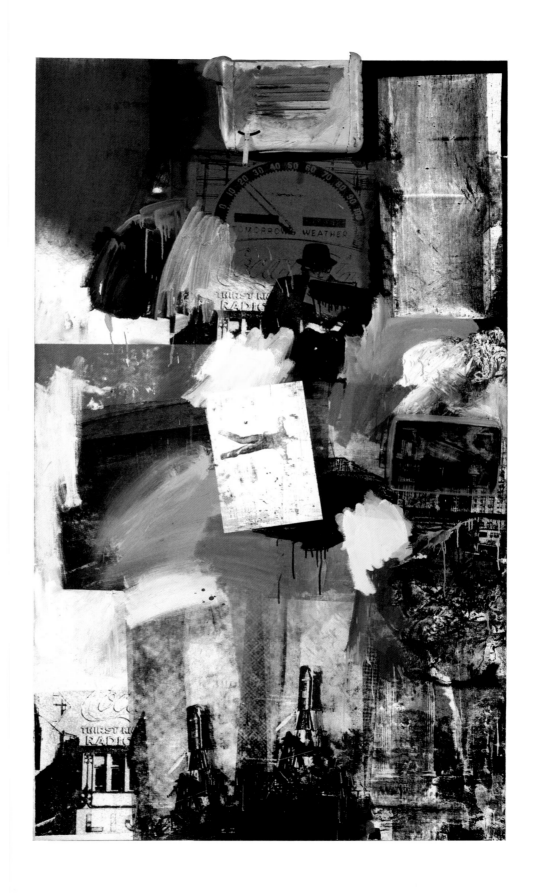

Plate 117. Robert Rauschenberg, *Untitled*, 1963.
Oil, silkscreen, ink, metal, and plastic on canvas, 208.3 x
121.9 cm (82 x 48 inches). Solomon R. Guggenheim
Museum, Purchased with funds contributed by Elaine and
Werner Dannheisser and The Dannheisser Foundation
82.2912.

the latter's creative potential, the term has since come to define an aesthetic movement of the late 1950s and 1960s with roots in England, America, France, and Germany.[4] Premised on the appropriation of commercial imagery and the imitation of industrial fabrication, Pop art evoked, celebrated, and in more provocative cases ironically criticized the mercantile dimension of culture and its perpetuation of mass consumption.

Given Alloway's innovative approach to the interpretation and display of art, his appointment to the Guggenheim—an institution dedicated almost exclusively to high Modernism—seems an unexpected and fortuitous gesture. His liberal and broadly inclusive aesthetic orientation could not have been more dissimilar from Rebay's quest for the metaphysical essence of painting, yet his belief in the far-ranging communicative aspects of art was in some ways analogous to her faith in its redemptive possibilities. The key similarity between Alloway and Rebay, however, is that both were motivated by their intimate acquaintances with contemporary artists and well conversant in—if not catalysts for—the theoretical justifications for specific aesthetic manifestations.

With his introductory exhibition at the Guggenheim, *Six Painters and the Object*, Alloway addressed the area with which he is most closely associated, popular imagery as it is illustrated in fine art. Initially conceived in August 1962 as a comprehensive survey of this burgeoning trend in American art, the show was held in March 1963, the earliest full-scale museum exhibition to investigate the phenomenon.[5] Half a year earlier the Sidney Janis Gallery had mounted *The New Realists*, considered to be the first American show to deal explicitly with Pop imagery. Named after the French movement Nouveau Réalisme, which was founded in 1960 by a diverse group of artists including Arman, Yves Klein, Daniel Spoerri, and Jean Tinguely, whose works incorporate the quotidian object and the flotsam of everyday life, the exhibition featured both European and American artists. It was at this point of convergence, when

an international affinity for commodity culture was recognized, that nationalistic biases arose and Pop art was segregated along geographic boundaries.[6]

The artists selected for *Six Painters and the Object* were solely Americans—in fact, Jim Dine, Jasper Johns, Roy Lichtenstein, Robert Rauschenberg, James Rosenquist, and Andy Warhol were all based in New York—even though Alloway initially intended a comprehensive national survey. A preliminary prospectus of the exhibition included sculptural works by Claes Oldenburg, Ed Ruscha's oversized word paintings, and figurative cutouts by Alex Katz.[7] Perhaps in response to the rambling, multimedia nature of the Janis Gallery exhibition or to curatorial restrictions at the Guggenheim, Alloway ultimately created a narrow framework through which to examine Pop art, one that seems strangely at odds with his prior affiliations and convictions. After conceiving an exhibition that would consist of both two- and three-dimensional works, he limited his choices to painters who represented—instead of actually presented—the object as a sign, a visual code for the culture of which it is intrinsically a part. "What these six artists have in common," he wrote in the catalogue, "is the use of objects drawn from the communications network and the physical environment of the city."[8] Although each of these artists was also known for his sculptures and three-dimensional assemblages, all of the thirty-three works in the show were paintings, some with "moderate collage elements."[9] "The painter committed to the surface of his canvas and to the process of translating objects into signs," Alloway explained, "does not have a wide-ranging freedom in which everything becomes art and art becomes anything."[10] What Alloway seems to have been implying with this statement was that the limitations of the technique guaranteed aesthetic quality. In other words, the translation of popular culture into a mimetic reflection of itself manifest in oil on canvas brought the realm of the "low" into that of the fine arts, and thus

Fig. 106. Cover of the 1963 exhibition catalogue *Six Painters and the Object*, designed by Herbert Matter.

Plate 118. Roy Lichtenstein, *Preparedness*, 1968. Oil and
Magna on canvas, three panels; 304.8 x 183 cm (120 x
72 inches) each; 304.8 x 548.7 cm (120 x 216 inches) overall.
Solomon R. Guggenheim Museum 69.1885.a–.c.

worthy for display in a museum. A letter sent by Messer to other potential museum venues describing the basic tenor of the exhibition corroborates such a view:

"Six Painters and the Object" . . . is to include the best in the general area of what has been described variously as New realism, Pop Art, etc. Not to mislead you by the terminology, let me explain further that the exhibition is envisaged quite unlike others of this kind. It would not be too much to say that it will attempt to set right the mixed presentations that have occurred in many places by stressing the pure painting forms in separation from the crowded assemblages of objects and other tendencies with which these have often been associated.[11]

This redemptive attitude is substantiated in Alloway's catalogue text, a portion of which traces the artistic practice of quotation from popular sources to the eighteenth century in an attempt to validate and contextualize current practices. Alloway even quotes Sir Joshua Reynolds on the subject of excerpting from the past: "It is generally allowed, that no man need be ashamed of copying the ancients: their works are considered as a magazine of common property."[12] In documenting the dissemination of mass-produced imagery and its importance for the development of Modern art, Alloway admitted that the notion of uniqueness was no longer imperative to aesthetic theory. However, from his vantage point in 1963, he did not fully comprehend the implications of this realization, the significance of which would be played out more fully in the 1980s with the emergence of a Postmodernist "appropriation" art that categorically denied the existence of "originality."

The Guggenheim's formalist approach to Pop art, which was elaborated upon and enhanced by Diane Waldman in her large-scale Lichtenstein exhibition in 1969, circumscribed the way in which the aesthetic was understood, processed, and presented. This underscores just how much the museum was a product of its time, caught between the desire to embrace the new and the need to legitimize the

unfamiliar within an art-historical context.[13] Pop art's unabashed flirtation with commercial vocabulary, its flippant repetitiveness, and its disregard for previous aesthetic precedent raised issues that major cultural institutions were not prepared to analyze, let alone interpret for the general public. It will never be conclusively determined whether Pop art was reactionary in its seeming complicity with the market—with its assertion of itself as a commodity not unlike the Campbell's Soup cans and comic books it usurped for its subject matter—or truly subversive in its parodic, parasitical engagement with the politics of consumption. It is more likely that Pop art will be perceived as a dialectical phenomenon—as a critical enterprise that exploited the cultural drift into late capitalism and an artistic stance that was, at times, seduced by its own charms. Warhol's career provides the consummate paradigm for the Pop generation. As voyeur, antiartist, cultural scavenger, celebrity, and ironic commentator, Warhol reflected the best and worst of postwar American culture. "Andy Warhol," claimed Carl Andre, "was the perfect mirror of his age and certainly the artist we deserved."[14] The veritable canonization of Warhol after his premature death in 1987— embodied in the Museum of Modern Art's massive, posthumous retrospective of the artist and the adulatory reviews it evoked—demonstrates how institutional endorsement can determine the manner in which a body of work is interpreted. Warhol's flagrant homosexuality, the camp aesthetic of his early drawings of shoes, perfumes, and female movie stars, the homoerotic content of his depictions of young boys and transvestites, and the quasi-pornographic quality of his films were played down, if not omitted, from MoMA's supposedly definitive analysis of the artist.[15] Using the Guggenheim's important early presentations of Pop and MoMA's reassessment of the movement as brackets around a twenty-five year period, it becomes apparent that institutionalized Pop art was and continues to function on a relatively benign level.

Plate 119. Andy Warhol, *Orange Disaster*, 1963. Acrylic
and silkscreen enamel on canvas, 269.2 x 207 cm
(106 x 81 ½ inches). Solomon R. Guggenheim Museum,
Gift, Harry N. Abrams Family Collection 74.2118.

Fig. 107. Cover of the 1966 exhibition catalogue *Systemic Painting*, designed by Herbert Matter.

The manner in which Pop art strategies were recuperated by artists working in the late 1970s and 1980s to investigate the mechanisms of the culture industry resuscitated the critical dimensions of the movement. Artists such as Félix González-Torres, Barbara Kruger, Jenny Holzer, and Haim Steinbach—all of whom are represented in the Guggenheim Museum's collection—incorporate the techniques of mass-media transmission into their works in order to expose and undermine the coercive elements of representation, the way it is disseminated, and the way it constructs and perpetuates desire.

Contemporary Art and the Institution

In addition to *Six Painters and the Object*, Alloway organized relatively small thematic exhibitions that traced specific currents in contemporary art: *The Shaped Canvas* (December 1964), *Eleven from the Reuben Gallery* (January 1965), *Word and Image* (December 1965–January 1966), and *The Photographic Image* (January–February 1966). Guided by an instinct for the topical and a predilection for narrative closure, Alloway submitted various aesthetic tendencies to analytical categorization. In 1966, for instance, he mounted an exhibition, *Systemic Painting*, devoted to a form of American abstract painting premised on a new conception of planar space, the use of monochromatic color fields or structural modules, which often utilized predetermined systems. "In all these works," explained Alloway, "the end-state of the painting is known prior to completion (unlike the theory of Abstract Expressionism)."[16] Dubbed "systemic painting" by Alloway, the reductive, early work by artists such as Al Held, Ellsworth Kelly (for example, *Blue, Green, Yellow, Orange, Red* [1966, plate 121]), Robert Mangold, Agnes Martin, Kenneth Noland, and Frank Stella has also become known as Color-field painting, Hard-edge painting, Post-painterly abstraction, and Cool-Art. Although not discussed by Alloway as such, the rigorous economy of formal means found in such painting served as the counterpart to Minimalist sculpture, then a burgeoning movement receiving precursory critical attention.[17] Following

Systemic Painting and Alloway's tenure at the Guggenheim, the museum's exhibition programming shifted to reflect the insights of its new curators, Waldman and Edward Fry, as well as the increasing predominance of a Minimalist aesthetic in American art.

Between 1970 and 1975, the Guggenheim presented four comprehensive solo exhibitions devoted to young artists—Andre, Mangold, Robert Ryman, and Brice Marden— whose radical abbreviations of form and content (for example, plates 120 and 122) distinguished them from the generation of gestural Abstract Expressionists that preceded them.[18] Though disparate in intent, the work of these artists shares a reductivist sensibility—traceable to Malevich's *White on White* series of 1918 and revived in Rauschenberg's all-white paintings of 1951—that pushes art to the zero degree.[19] Andre's austere carpets of metal tiles, Mangold's subtly rendered geometric distortions, Marden's sequential panels of color and texture, and Ryman's painterly meditations in white were not, however, conceived as nihilistic propositions. As extreme, and in some cases insurgent, extensions of Clement Greenberg's critical doctrine of Modernist art—which requires absolute formal specificity within each aesthetic discipline—these works exist as distillations of painting and sculpture.[20] They are not, however, simply exercises in self-reflexivity. The sparseness of detail in each artist's work does not preclude the presence of subjectively determined content or poetic associations.

The question of what, in essence, was required for a work of art to be considered "Minimal" during the late 1960s and early 1970s is relevant when reviewing what the Guggenheim selected as its representative exhibitions. The term "Minimal art" came into common usage in 1965 after the aesthetician Richard Wollheim discussed the polemic posed by works of art that required little effort in their creation, such as Marcel Duchamp's Ready-mades or Ad Reinhardt's highly muted "black" paintings.[21] Responding to the oft-voiced complaint that art created in a Minimal mode does not

Plate 120. Robert Ryman, *Classico 4,* 1968. Acrylic on
paper, mounted on foamcore; 12 sections of paper,
76.2 x 56.5 cm (30 x 22 ¼ inches) each, 228.6 x 226 cm
(90 x 89 inches) overall. Solomon R. Guggenheim Museum,
Panza Collection 91.3845.a–.l.

Plate 121. Ellsworth Kelly, *Blue, Green, Yellow, Orange,*
Red, 1966. Oil on canvas, five panels, 152.3 x 121.9 cm (60 x
48 inches) each. Solomon R. Guggenheim Museum 67.1833.

reveal the artist's hand, let alone talent, Wollheim argued that a work of art can be determined merely by an artist's decision, thereby establishing the conceptual basis of much contemporary reductivist work. Known variously as ABC art, Primary Structures, and Literalist art, the painting and sculpture most frequently labeled Minimalist encompasses the phenomenological "presence" of Robert Morris's geometric, plywood sculptures and Richard Serra's metal barriers (for example, plate 124), the "specificity" of Donald Judd's serial containers, the analytic nature of Sol LeWitt's three-dimensional grids, the lattice patterns of Martin's canvases (for example, plate 123), the luminosity of Dan Flavin's fluorescent installations, the slick lacquered fiberglass surfaces of John McCracken's planks, and so on. In other words, the category is broad and ill-defined. The classification "Minimalist" was employed primarily during the 1960s and 1970s to describe a style—a clean, rational, and often industrial look that relied on mathematical formulas, predetermined progressions, and rigid, geometric configurations. Revisionist efforts have been made to understand the critical implications of the genre as manifest in the work of its principal protagonists: Andre, Judd, LeWitt, Morris, and Serra.[22] For example, Rosalind Krauss has posited a phenomenological reading of Minimalism, making the claim that the new sculpture did not engage the viewer on a private, psychological level, nor did it affect instantaneously, but rather, through time, activated the viewer's perceptual capabilities to such an extent that one became aware of one's own body as a perceiving being in relation to the work of art.[23] Anna Chave has questioned the supposedly neutral content of Minimalism in her investigation of the authoritative rhetoric surrounding the art, its abundant references to male sexuality, and its rapid assimilation into the American corporate landscape.[24] For Craig Owens, the dialectic between the aesthetic object and the critical writing that emerged during the 1960s—Judd, Morris, and Robert Smithson all wrote

theoretical texts explicating current cultural phenomena—indicated the advent of a Postmodernist sensibility.[25] Brian Wallis has also offered a Postmodernist, quasi-political reading of Minimalism, noting that Minimalism "constitutes a significant cultural and epistemological shift which continues to be explored in contemporary art practice . . . a shift from a visual to a semiotic, linguistic or verbal field."[26] He construes Minimalism to have been "a response to the socio-political conditions of the Sixties—the Vietnam War and the civil-rights movement," while linking its formal characteristics—seriality and industrial appearance—to "late capitalist mass-production."[27] Hal Foster concurs with these notions, arguing that within Minimalism are contained the early rumblings of discontent that led to the critical rupture with Modernism that has defined much of today's most radical art. Discussing the "crux" of Minimalism, Foster claims that, Janus-like, the movement simultaneously functioned as the culmination of Modernist, purist aesthetics and the commencement of Postmodernist self-reflexive criticism that involved an examination of the institutional and discursive conditions of art itself.[28] "Now as an analysis of perception," Foster argues, "Minimalism is also an analysis of the conditions of perception."[29] This ultimately led, he claims, to a critique of the very spaces in which art is exhibited and the conventional modes of aesthetic display as well as a denunciation of art's inextricable links to the market. Citing Benjamin H. D. Buchloh's study of the Ready-made paradigm in contemporary art, Foster sees Minimalism as one interval in the "genealogy of presentational strategies" that extends from Duchamp.[30]

While the retrospective reading of Minimalism as a critique (or at least a catalyst for the critique) of the institutions and discourses that frame it is, in essence, correct, the initial transition from Modernist abstraction to self-conscious critical intervention was not always a smooth one. The various factions within the group of artists

Plate 122. Robert Mangold, *Circle In and Out of a*
Polygon 2, 1973. Acrylic and black pencil on canvas, 183.4 x
184 cm (72 ³⁄₁₆ x 72 ⁷⁄₁₆ inches). Solomon R. Guggenheim
Museum, Panza Collection 91.3771.

Plate 123. Agnes Martin, *White Stone*, 1965. Oil and
graphite on canvas, 182.6 x 182.6 cm (71 ⅞ x 71 ⅞ inches).
Solomon R. Guggenheim Museum, Gift, Mr. Robert Elkon
69.1911.

labeled Minimalist, their transmutations of style and technique, and their discrete theoretical approaches precluded the emergence of any one decisive consensus. Additionally, the moment that Minimalism began to receive relatively mainstream attention, there emerged a counter-aesthetic known variously as Anti-Form, Post-Minimal, or Process Art that found its inspiration in the human body, the random occurrence, the process of improvised artistic creation, and the liberating qualities of nontraditional materials such as industrial felt (for example, Robert Morris's *Untitled* [1970, plate 126]), molten lead, wax, fiberglass (for example, Eva Hesse's *Expanded Expansion* [1969, plate 125]), and rubber.[31] Simultaneously, a strictly conceptual approach to art as a linguistic proposition evolved that challenged all formal, empirical characteristics of painting and sculpture. Tensions and conflicts were revealed throughout the period, often in exhibition reviews and artists' own commentaries. Judd, for example, assailed then-current art critical terminology, while weakly recalling Duchamp, when he wrote: "'Non-art,' 'anti-art,' 'non-art art,' and 'anti-art art' are useless. If someone says his work is art, it's art."[32] This open-ended declaration of artistic freedom was hardly representative of the times, for critics, curators, and artists themselves were grappling with the very definition of art as well as its political, cultural, and economic implications. In partial response to Judd's statement, for instance, Conceptual artist Joseph Kosuth pointed out in "Art After Philosophy" that "formalist critics and artists alike do not question the nature of art." He added:

Being an artist now means to question the nature of art. If one is questioning the nature of painting, one cannot be questioning the nature of art. If an artist accepts painting (or sculpture) he is accepting the tradition that goes with it. That's because the word art is general and the word painting is specific. Painting is a kind of art. If you make paintings you are already accepting (not questioning) the nature of art.[33]

In works such as *'Titled (Art as Idea as Idea)' {Water}* (1966, plate 127), Kosuth began to employ language itself as his medium. What resulted was a rigorously conceptual art devoid of all morphological presence; intellectual provocation replaced perception as words displaced images and objects.

The *Guggenheim International Exhibition, 1971*—an exhibition devoted to the work of twenty-one contemporary artists from eight countries—served unwittingly as a forum for such dissent and brought the conflicts between institutional-critical art and the museums that harbored it to the fore. Jointly curated by Waldman and Fry, the exhibition was the sixth invitational of its kind. Initiated in 1956, the series represented the museum's attempt to survey up-to-date aesthetic achievements on a global scale, while honoring well-known figures such as Giacometti, Antoni Tàpies, and Robert Motherwell.[34] Prior to 1971, no particular effort was made to feature specific styles; artists included in the 1964 and 1967 shows ranged from Öyvind Fahlström, Lucio Fontana, Joan Miró, Louise Nevelson, and Isamu Noguchi to Larry Bell, John Chamberlain, Kelly, and Tony Smith. The 1971 *International* focused exclusively on contemporary work, underscoring the recent emergence of a Post-Minimalist sensibility involving process-oriented art, Conceptual Art, Earthworks, and an overall de-materialization of the aesthetic object. This exhibition followed a spate of other international museum and gallery shows that recognized and explored the new art forms, often in ways that complemented their ephemeral, purely cerebral nature; in 1969, for example, the Kunsthalle Bern organized *When Attitude Becomes Form/Works—Concepts—Processes-Situations—Information*; the Whitney Museum of American Art mounted *Anti-Illusion: Procedures/Materials*; and the Museum of Contemporary Art in Chicago hosted *Art by Telephone*. That same year, the Guggenheim featured a number of the artists included in these and other focal exhibitions—Bruce Nauman, Gerhard Richter, Serra, and Gilberto Zorio—in

Top: Fig. 108. Diane Waldman with Richard Serra during installation of the *Guggenheim International Exhibition, 1971.*

Bottom: Fig. 109. Donald Judd during installation of the *Guggenheim International Exhibition, 1971.*

Plate 124. Richard Serra, *Strike (to Roberta and Rudy),*
1969–71. Hot-rolled steel plate, on edge, 243.8 x 731.5 x
2.5 cm (96 x 288 x 1 inches). Solomon R. Guggenheim
Museum, Panza Collection 91.3871.

its own selection of emerging talent sponsored by the Theodoron Foundation.[35] But unlike those other theme-oriented survey shows, the Guggenheim's group exhibition did not attempt to contextualize the art, an effort only broached in the 1971 *International*, which included work by Andre, Victor Burgin, Hanne Darboven, Walter De Maria, Jan Dibbets, Flavin, Michael Heizer, Judd, On Kawara, Kosuth, LeWitt, Richard Long, Mario Merz, Morris, Nauman, Ryman, Serra, and Lawrence Weiner.[36] Each artist was invited to create installations uniquely conceived for the Guggenheim's demanding architecture or to contribute individual, representative pieces. Dutch artist Dibbets requested that in his absence photographs be taken of the garden window of the rotunda every five minutes for the duration of December 21, the shortest day of 1970 (see fig 110). Slides and prints documenting the passage of time were presented in the exhibition. Flavin created an installation of fluorescent tubes whose light cascaded from bay to bay.[37] Morris devised an interactive environment in which viewers were instructed by tape recordings to execute a number of activities with either a ball, rope, or pole (see fig. 112). LeWitt provided instructions for five wall drawings (see fig. 111). Judd constructed a sculpture from gray steel sheeting that was bolted together to form two concentric circles that conformed exactly to the sloping ramp of Wright's spiral rotunda. Weiner was represented by the two texts he submitted to the exhibition catalogue, "Flanked Beside" and "Done Without." Merz laced the interior of the Guggenheim's ascending spiral with neon numerals that, in accordance with the structural progression of the Frank Lloyd Wright design, advanced in increments based on the Fibonacci mathematical sequence.[38]

It was a work proposed by the French artist Daniel Buren—a monumental 20-by-10-meter striped, woven cotton banner suspended from the rotunda skylight—that forced a confrontation between the aesthetic, theoretical, and ideological tenets practiced among this representative group of artists. For Buren, the striped blue-and-white fabric, the two vertical ends of which were coated in white paint, embodied the two poles of his critical project: an attack on Modernist painting, and Duchamp's Ready-made as "its radical historical other."[39] As a neutral, redundant emblem that is repeated in different, but arbitrary, color combinations throughout his oeuvre, the stripe parodies painting, yet offers nothing but its own effigy. It is its own reality rather than a representation of it. And as a prefabricated object viewed within the context of the museum, it recalls Duchamp's ironic exposure of art's inextricable dependency on institutional support for its legitimatization, while, in turn, exposing the rampant institutionalization of Duchamp's own project. By expanding on the possibilities for the production and display of his stripes, Buren disrupts the rarified atmosphere of the museum, an act that he explains as follows:

It is established that the proposition {the striped work}, in whatever location it be presented, does not "disturb" that location. The place in question appears as it is. It is seen in its actuality. This is partly due to the fact that the proposition is not distracting. Furthermore, being its own subject matter, its own location is the proposition itself, which makes it possible to say, paradoxically: the proposition in question "has no real location." In a certain sense, one of the characteristics of the proposition is to reveal the "container" in which it is sheltered.[40]

Buren had described the banner without providing specific dimensions prior to his arrival in New York for the exhibition, and when it was installed (fig. 103) just one day before the opening of the *International*, the work caused an uproar. A number of artists seriously contested the inclusion of the piece in that it obstructed the view of their works and they threatened to withdraw from the show. Noting that it had not provided Buren with an unconditional commitment to exhibiting the banner, and since the work had never been seen in concert

Plate 125. Eva Hesse, *Expanded Expansion*, 1969. Fiberglass
and rubberized cheesecloth, three units; eight-pole unit:
310 x 457.2 cm (122 x 180 inches); five-pole unit: 310 x
304.8 cm (122 x 120 inches); three-pole unit: 310 x 152.4 cm
(122 x 60 inches). Solomon R. Guggenheim Museum,
Gift, Family of Eva Hesse 75.2138.a–.c.

Plate 126. Robert Morris, *Untitled*, 1970. Felt,
variable dimensions. Solomon R. Guggenheim Museum,
Panza Collection 91.3804.

wa-ter (wâ′tẽr), *n.* [AS. *wæter* = D. *water* = G. *wasser,* akin to Icel. *ratn,* Goth. *watō,* water, also to Gr. ὕδωρ, Skt. *udan,* water, L. *unda,* a wave, water; all from the same root as E. *wet*: cf. *hydra, otter*[1], *undine,* and *wash.*] The liquid which in a more or less impure state constitutes rain, oceans, lakes, rivers, etc., and which in a pure state is a transparent, inodorous, tasteless liquid, a compound of hydrogen and oxygen, H_2O, freezing at 32° F. or 0° C., and boiling at 212° F. or 100° C.; a special form or variety of this liquid, as rain, or (often in *pl.*) as the liquid ('mineral water') obtained from a mineral spring (as, "the *waters* of Aix-la-Chapelle".

Plate 127. Joseph Kosuth, *'Titled (Art as Idea as Idea)' {Water},* 1966. Photostat, accompanied by documentation of printed definition with pencil mounted on cardboard; photostat: 121.9 x 121.9 cm (48 x 48 inches); documentation: 14.3 x 11.4 cm (5 ⅝ x 4 ½ inches). Solomon R. Guggenheim Museum, Gift, Leo Castelli, New York 73.2066.1–.2.

with the other works in the show, the museum attempted to orchestrate a compromise: a striped banner Buren had designed for the outside of the building would be displayed as planned during the *International*, and Buren would have a solo show immediately following the exhibition. Because the artist's project depended on the dialectic between interior and exterior presentation, this solution was untenable to Buren, and he refused to participate unless on his terms. Pressured by the other artists' protests and, no doubt, sympathetic to their desire for the unmitigated visibility of their works, the museum removed both banners from the exhibition. "This issue," explained Waldman, "was one of incompatibility: there was simply no way of reconciling Buren's project with the work in the exhibition."[41] Buchloh has pointed out in his discussion of the incident that even though the artists' complaints were valid, the intensity of their reaction was most likely premised on the fact that Buren's project betrayed specific characteristics of their work that had become obsolete.[42] The emphatic manner in which the banner sliced through the rotunda created great architectural tension, activating a spatial void so commanding in its presence that the impact of art exhibited along the walls was in many cases compromised. On both a metaphoric and empirical level, the banner challenged the dominating character of Frank Lloyd Wright's structure as well as the institutional framework of the museum itself.[43] Conversely, Flavin and Judd designed works that conformed exactly to the descending curvilinear ramps of the spiral, as if they were acquiescing to the ideological, economic, and cultural control asserted by the institution.

The conflicts that arose at the *International* as a result of the artists' territorial tendencies as well as their fundamental theoretical discrepancies are indicative of the critical differences among the various aesthetic movements of the time. Minimalism undermined the notion that art exists as an autonomous entity by including human perception as an integral part of the work itself, subsequently making the location in which this perception occurs another determining factor of the aesthetic experience. Recognizing that the physical circumstances in which a work is viewed contributes to the way it is comprehended, artists such as Flavin, Morris, Nauman, and Serra produced site-specific installations. What remained relatively unanalyzed, however, were the social, political, and economic conditions underlying places for exhibition usually construed as neutral or as benign cultural environments. Also unquestioned were issues of spectatorship and reception— to whom, for instance, are the works of art directed; does the art take into account the gender, religion, or social class of its viewers; or does the artist investigate his or her mode of production in terms of its economic implications. As divergent artistic trends emerged out of, and in contradistinction to, Minimalism, these inquiries began to be pursued and continue to be so today. At the *International*, Buren's banner represented a move away from the formal constraints of Minimalism, his agenda being far more conceptually and critically motivated. Additionally, but less controversially, De Maria's contribution—a hollowed aluminum swastika resting on the floor and containing a metal ball—addressed and undermined the notion of the art institution as a neutral container, an objective repository for cultural artifacts. Entitled *Museum Piece* (1966, plate 129), this ironic work emulates a child's game but the horrific implication of its current iconographic meaning makes any reference to recreation utterly perverse. Beyond allusions to amusement, De Maria's haunting sculpture evokes issues of collective cultural memory, a territory embraced and inscribed by the museum itself as an institution devoted to the preservation of historical memorabilia. As an archive of assorted visual objects, the museum has traditionally been considered nonpartisan in terms of economic or political issues, its only domain being that of quality. But like any social institution, it intersects with

Fig. 110. Jan Dibbets, instructions for *The Shortest Day of 1970 Photographed from Sunrise to Sunset*, the Solomon R. Guggenheim Museum, New York, 1971, for the *Guggenheim International Exhibition, 1971.*

BAY # 38

VERTICAL, PARALLEL LINES, NOT TOUCHING
DRAWN FREEHAND, AT RANDOM USING
FOUR COLORS (BLACK, YELLOW, RED & BLUE)
WHICH ARE UNIFORMLY DISPERSED, WITH
MAXIMUM DENSITY, COVERING THE ENTIRE
WALL SURFACE.

BAY # 37

LINES, NOT SHORT, NOT STRAIGHT,
CROSSING AND TOUCHING, DRAWN AT
RANDOM USING FOUR COLORS (BLACK,
YELLOW, RED & BLUE) WHICH ARE UNI-
FORMLY DISPERSED, WITH MAXIMUM
DENSITY, COVERING THE ENTIRE WALL
SURFACE.

BAY # 36

SHORT LINES (ABOUT TWO INCHES LONG)
DRAWN AT RANDOM, USING FOUR COLORS
(BLACK, YELLOW, RED & BLUE), NOT TOUCHING,
WHICH ARE UNIFORMLY DISPERSED, WITH
MAXIMUM DENSITY, COVERING THE ENTIRE
SURFACE OF THE WALL, EXCLUDING THE
DOORS.

BAY # 35

LINES, NOT LONG, NOT STRAIGHT, NOT
TOUCHING, DRAWN AT RANDOM USING
FOUR COLORS (BLACK, YELLOW, RED &
BLUE) WHICH ARE UNIFORMLY DISPERSED
WITH MAXIMUM DENSITY, COVERING THE
ENTIRE WALL SURFACE.

BAY # 34

STRAIGHT LINES, APPROXIMATELY
6" LONG, TOUCHING AND CROSSING DRAWN
FREE HAND AT RANDOM, USING FOUR
COLORS (BLACK, YELLOW, RED & BLUE) WHICH
ARE UNIFORMLY DISPERSED, WITH MAX-
IMUM DENSITY, COVERING THE ENTIRE
WALL SURFACE.

prevailing political ideologies and economic realities, its purported neutrality providing a mask for its own complicity with dominant social values and its reliance upon public patronage. It is, therefore, impossible for the contents and programs of a museum to be considered as entities entirely separate from the institution's financial profile and social obligations. Both the museum and the objects in its collection have their unique histories and neither should be hidden from view, though traditionally that has been the practice. In the case of De Maria's sculpture, the Guggenheim attempted to mitigate the impact of the work by denying its immediate and exclusive reference to Nazism and pointing out the status of the swastika as a universal symbol in a statement it issued to accompany the piece. As a matter of principle, the Guggenheim Museum had rarely relied on didactic material to explicate the aesthetic experience, but when the piece provoked several complaints, it seemed necessary to ease the situation.[44] While De Maria's intentions for the work remain unclear, it inevitably functions as a critical device by forcing the institution in which it is exhibited to confront its own, often convoluted, role as cultural interpreter.

The Guggenheim was once again compelled to face these issues when, immediately following the International, Messer canceled the Conceptual artist Hans Haacke's exhibition, scheduled to open in April 1971, on the grounds that portions of the show were "inappropriate for presentation."[45] The objectionable works proposed for the Guggenheim, all premised on Haacke's investigation of existing social systems, consisted of a visitors' poll containing ten demographic questions about age, gender, education, and the like, and ten questions regarding current cultural and political issues (for example, "Do you sympathize with Women's Lib?" and "In your opinion, should the general orientation of the country be more or less conservative?"), as well as two documentary presentations of major Manhattan real-estate holdings.[46] The work that caused the most apprehension recorded and illustrated the myriad

properties amassed by Harry Shapolsky, a well-connected, infamous New York slumlord, through information gleaned from the New York County Clerk's office. Comprised of maps, 142 photographs of building façades and empty lots, data sheets listing their addresses, the corporations or individuals holding title, the date of acquisition, and so on, the piece identifies a strategy of real-estate investment dependent upon the exploitation of the lower class by a complex, interdependent network of interested parties that thinly veils the private individual at its core. However discriminating the work appeared, it did not include any evaluative commentary, a fact that the artist stressed in his defense of the project. When Messer expressed concern over what he construed to be a "muckraking venture" that might lead to charges of libel, Haacke offered to substitute fictitious names for all references. The museum, nevertheless, rescinded its offer for an exhibition, citing the overtly political nature of the work as cause.[47] "It is well understood," wrote Messer in his letter to Haacke, "that art may have social and political consequences but these, we believe, are furthered by indirection and by the generalized, exemplary force that works of art may exert upon the environment, not, as you propose, by using political means to achieve political ends." Advocating the metaphoric aspects of art that affect by allusion and suggestion, Messer dismissed Haacke's art for its specificity and its unabashed directness. As with De Maria's sculpture, and to some extent with Pop art, the museum sought to sustain the supposedly neutral tenor of its discourse through the repression of controversial content. Though Haacke disavowed Messer's description of his project as overtly political, claiming the work to be nothing more than the explication of a particular social system, the issue at hand was more far-reaching. What emerged from the Haacke controversy were questions regarding the degree to which a museum, as an institution in the public realm, could be considered a private "sanctuary"; whether all art forms and their institutional presentation might be interpreted as political in that they inexorably respond to (or against) prevalent ideologies; and to what extent the Guggenheim, or any city museum, could extricate itself from the urban power structures centered around class systems, segregation, and economic inequity. If laced with picture after picture of crumbling tenements and litter-strewn empty lots, the pristine white walls of the museum on Fifth Avenue would have only served to reinforce the geographic and financial discrepancies operative in the city.

The Haacke affair created a controversy that reverberated throughout the art world; petitions were signed against the Guggenheim's act of "censorship" and artists demonstrated outside the museum. Fry, the curator responsible for the show, was dismissed when he opposed the administration's decision and issued a public statement in favor of the artist. Haacke himself achieved a notoriety that far exceeded what the exhibition itself would have earned for him. His real-estate project became, through its denunciation, an art-historical entity, a work martyred to the cause of rebellious art, a progeny of Duchamp's urinal.

For the Guggenheim, the Haacke scandal was, like the Buren debacle, a somber event. In retrospect, these incidents embody the dialectical and polemical nature of contemporary art that endeavored to disrupt the supposedly seamless, neutral façade of the museum from within the very frame of the institution. This frame does not just connote the physical environment in which work is exhibited and appreciated as aesthetic phenomena, but also refers to the discourses through which art is inscribed and circumscribed, the social and economic system through which it is acquired, and the theoretical foundations from which it emerges and, subsequently, perpetuates. In other words, the sophisticated, subversive nature of Haacke's and Buren's projects made it virtually impossible for the museum to comfortably exhibit and condone them since they undermined the institution's very premise.[48] Ultimately, as with any

avant-garde gesture, such work has now been incorporated into, if not embraced by, the institutions it attempted to expose and subvert. In some cases, museums themselves have become more critically reflexive by questioning their own complicity with hegemonic cultural values and examining their place within the larger social fabric. Their self-directed investigations are manifest in a shift in programming to include more artists whose work inspires such critique, exhibitions that reflect the multicultural flavor of society or reexamine inherited art-historical convention, and publications that articulate the theoretical questions at hand. For the Guggenheim Museum, this has been a slow but invigorating process. The exhibition *Jenny Holzer*, in which incisive, often acerbic, statements about our various and indeterminate cultural realities circled around the rotunda's spiral in one continuous LED sign (fig. 119), was one example of the museum's continuous effort to explore and confront the issues intrinsic to important contemporary art.[49] By 1989, when the show was mounted, most of the art-viewing public had become familiar with such critical, self-reflexive work. The exhibition, therefore, caused little to no controversy. If it had been organized twenty years earlier, however, this show of a woman's monumental object/text that interrogates our very belief systems and the language used to discuss them would have undoubtedly provoked great institutional tension. The question remains, however, whether art without conflict can incite and motivate in ways that still seem vital to our cultural survival.

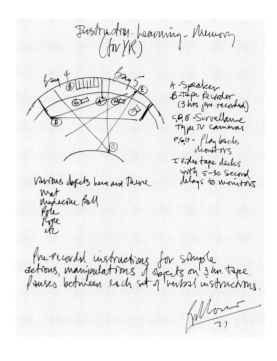

Left: Fig. 111. Sol LeWitt, instructions for *Five Wall Drawings*, 1971, for the *Guggenheim International Exhibition, 1971.*

Above: Fig. 112. Robert Morris, instructions for *Instruction-Learning-Memory*, 1971, for the *Guggenheim International Exhibition, 1971.*

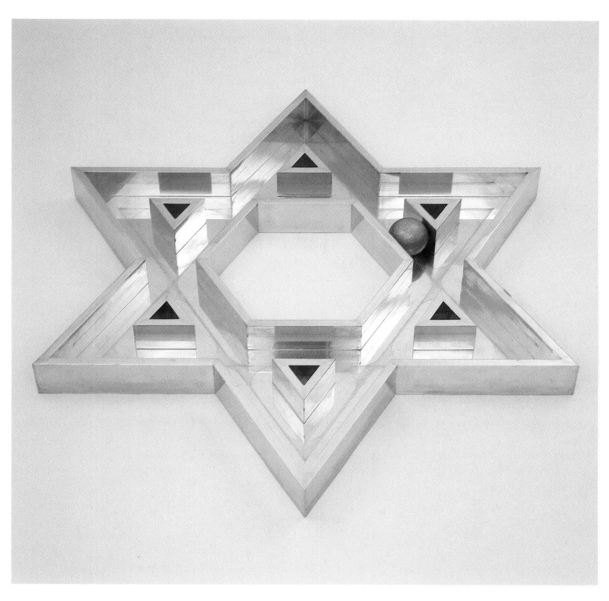

Left: Plate 128. Walter De Maria, *Cross*, 1965–66.
Aluminum, 10.2 x 106.7 x 55.9 cm (4 x 42 x 22 inches).
Solomon R. Guggenheim Museum 73.2033.

Center: Plate 129. Walter De Maria, *Museum Piece*, 1966.
Aluminum, 10.2 x 91.5 x 91.5 cm (4 x 36 x 36 inches).
Solomon R. Guggenheim Museum 73.2034.

Right: Plate 130. Walter De Maria, *Star*, 1972.
Aluminum, 10.2 x 111.8 x 127 cm (4 x 44 x 50 inches).
Solomon R. Guggenheim Museum 73.2035.

1. While involved with the Independent Group, Alloway and fellow member John McHale organized a series of public lectures, examples of which are indicative of the association's concerns: "Probability and Information Theory and Their Application to the Visual Arts," "Advertising 2, Sociology in the Popular Arts," "Fashion and Fashion Magazines," and "Aesthetics and Italian Product Design." In addition to discussions and symposia, the Independent Group participated in and curated exhibitions, the most renowned being *This is Tomorrow Today* held at the Whitechapel Art Gallery in 1956. Included in this groundbreaking show was an installation designed by Independent Group members McHale, Richard Hamilton, and John Voelcker that consisted of an architectural environment crammed with a multitude of visual stimuli gleaned from popular culture—film posters, a life-sized image of Marilyn Monroe, a giant beer bottle, and optical illusions—accompanied by an audio collage created from jukebox recordings combined with the taped sounds of previous visitors to the exhibit. An immense cardboard cutout of a sci-fi robot clutching a barely clad, futuristic Fay Wray framed the entrance to the installation.

2. Lawrence Alloway, "The Long Front of Culture," in *This is Tomorrow Today; The Independent Group and British Pop Art*, exh. cat. (New York: The Institute for Art and Urban Resources, The Clocktower, 1987), p. 33. Reprinted from *Cambridge Opinion*, no. 17 (1959).

3. Lawrence Alloway and Robert Adams, "Personal Statement," *Ark*, no. 19 (March 1957), pp. 28–29.

4. For an overview of the evolution of British Pop art and its reception in relation to analogous but not equivalent developments in American art, see Lynne Cooke, "The Independent Group: British and American Pop Art, a 'Palimpcestuous' Legacy," *Modern Art and Popular Culture: Readings in High and Low* (New York: The Museum of Modern Art and Harry N. Abrams, 1990), pp. 192–216. Andreas Huyssen discusses the critical debate surrounding the attention to popular culture in Germany during the 1960s, in "The Cultural Politics of Pop," in Paul Taylor, ed., *Post-Pop Art* (Cambridge, Mass.: MIT Press, 1989), pp. 45–77; reprinted from *New German Critique*, no. 4 (1975).

5. The Washington Gallery of Modern Art (Washington, D.C.) mounted the exhibition *The Popular Image* in April 1963. Curated by Alice Denney, it included works by George Brecht, Jim Dine, Jasper Johns, Roy Lichtenstein, Claes Oldenburg, Robert Rauschenberg, James Rosenquist, Andy Warhol, Robert Watts, John Wesley, and Tom Wesselmann. The catalogue essay by Alan R. Solomon, "The New Art" (reprinted in *Art*

International 7, no. 7 [September 1963], pp. 37–43), posits these artists as apolitical champions of all that is popular and entertaining in American culture: "Instead of rejecting the deplorable and grotesque products of the modern commercial industrial world—the world of the hard sell and all it implies . . . —these new artists have turned with relish and excitement to . . . television commercials, comic strips, hot dog stands, billboards, junk yards, hamburger joints, used car lots, juke boxes, slot machines and supermarkets. They have done so not in the spirit of . . . social criticism . . . but out of an affirmative and unqualified commitment to . . . a fantastic new wonderland, or, more properly, Disneyland." This analogy between 1960s America and Disneyland has familiar echoes in Jean Baudrillard's treatise on the American cultural landscape (*America*, trans. by Chris Turner [London: Verso, 1988]), which he likens to Disneyland.

6. The catalogue for *The New Realists* was written by poet/critic John Ashbery, Pierre Restany, the French critic who originated the term Nouveau Réalisme, and gallery owner Sidney Janis. A prejudice toward the American incarnation of Pop art is clearly stated in at least two reviews of the show: T. B. H. [Thomas B. Hess], "New Realists at Janis Gallery," *Art News* 61 (December 1963), p. 12, and S. T. [Sidney Tillim], "The New Realists at Janis Gallery," *Arts Magazine* 37 (December 1962), pp. 43–44. "The European entries," wrote Hess, "look feeble in this line-up." "Americans," claimed Tillim, "dominate the exhibition. . . . There is nothing Surreal, nothing coated with ennui, about the Americans. They give you the thing itself—pow!" Conversely, Restany argued in a separate article that the American version of Nouveau Réalisme was far weaker than its European counterpart in that it merely made a fetish of the object through trompe-l'oeil. "I ask myself," he claimed, "if one will speak about Lichtenstein and Warhol in two or three years." See Restany, "Le Nouveau Réalisme à la Conquête de New York," *Art International* 7, no. 1 (January 1963), pp. 29–36.

7. In the Solomon R. Guggenheim Museum Exhibition Archives.

8. Lawrence Alloway, *Six Painters and the Object*, exh. cat. (New York: The Solomon R. Guggenheim Foundation, 1963), p. 7.

9. Ibid.

10. Ibid.

11. Letter in the Solomon R. Guggenheim Museum Exhibition Archives (emphasis mine).

12. Alloway, *Six Painters and the Object*, p. 10.

13. Waldman emphasized the abstract elements

of Lichtenstein's style in her catalogue essay on the artist. She suggests that it is critical "to see the formal aspect of his paintings and to understand that it was not the imagery that was solely important. I wasn't denying that it fed his painting, but for me, at the time and still, the best of Pop art is both about its subject and its formal properties." Unpublished interview with Lewis Kachur, October 24, 1986. Manuscript in the Solomon R. Guggenheim Museum Archives.

14. Quoted in Kynaston McShine, ed., *Andy Warhol: A Retrospective*, exh. cat. (New York: The Museum of Modern Art, 1989), p. 436. The present essay was completed prior to the exhibition *Hand-Painted Pop: American Art in Transition, 1955–62*, which opened in December 1992 at the Museum of Contemporary Art in Los Angeles. While the exhibition focused exclusively on the painterly quality of early Pop art, its accompanying catalogue examines the conceptual, economic, and social contexts in which the work was created through essays such as Kenneth E. Silver's "Modes of Disclosure: The Construction of Gay Identity and the Rise of Pop Art," and David Deitcher's "Unsentimental Education: The Professionalization of the American Artist."

15. For further discussion regarding the reception of Warhol, see my article "Andy and After," *Artscribe*, no. 76 (summer 1989), pp. 7–8.

16. Lawrence Alloway, *Systemic Painting*, exh. cat. (New York: The Solomon R. Guggenheim Foundation, 1966), p. 19. Reprinted in Gregory Battcock, ed., *Minimal Art: A Critical Anthology* (New York: E. P. Dutton, 1968), pp. 37–60. In reaction to Clement Greenberg's rigid, formalist reading of such abstract painting, Alloway insisted that the variations and fluctuations within each system imparted emotional and iconographical content. For him, systems were entirely open-ended: "A system is not antithetical to the values suggested by such art-world clusters as humanist, organic, and process. On the contrary, while the artist is engaged with it, a system is a process. . . . The predictive power of the artist, minimized by the prestige of gestural painting, is strongly operative" (p. 19).

17. In his catalogue text, Alloway indicated that he had planned to exhibit "systemic" sculpture as well when he initially conceived the show in 1964, but the Jewish Museum had dedicated the exhibition *Primary Structures* to such work during the spring of 1966. See Alloway, *Systemic Painting*, p. 21, note 8.

18. The first three of these exhibitions were curated by Diane Waldman, and *Brice Marden* by assistant curator Linda Shearer.

19. The art-historical sources for Minimalism are myriad; prototypes for 1960s monochrome

painting can be found in the art of Aleksandr Rodchenko, Barnett Newman, Ad Reinhardt, Mark Rothko, Yves Klein, and Piero Manzoni. For a brief critical text on the lineage of reductivist art, see Barbara Rose, "ABC Art," *Art in America* 53, no. 5 (October–November 1965), pp. 57–69; reprinted in Battcock, pp. 274–97.

20. For an in-depth discussion about the generation of artists who, following Stella's black-stripe paintings and aluminum shaped canvases, embraced Greenberg's formalist dictum but later, having taken the notions of flatness and self-reflexivity to the logical conclusion of the blank monochrome, explored the "objecthood" of art, see Thierry de Duve, "The Monochrome and the Blank Canvas," in Serge Guilbaut, ed., *Reconstructing Modernism: Art in New York, Paris, and Montreal 1945–1964* (Cambridge, Mass.: MIT Press, 1990), pp. 244–310.

21. Richard Wollheim, "Minimal Art," *Arts Magazine* 39, no. 4 (January 1965), pp. 26–32. Reprinted in Battcock, pp. 387–99.

22. The work of Larry Bell, Walter De Maria, and Dan Flavin may also be considered in this category. Although Minimalism is generally regarded as a three-dimensional genre, the contemporaneous work of many painters—Alan Charlton, Bob Law, Mangold, Marden, Martin, and Ryman—demands like consideration. For reappraisals of Minimalism, see in particular Rosalind Krauss's *The Originality of the Avant-Garde and Other Modernist Myths* (Cambridge, Mass.: MIT Press, 1985); *Passages in Modern Sculpture* (New York: Viking Press, 1977); and "Richard Serra/Sculpture," in *Richard Serra/Sculpture*, exh. cat. (New York: The Museum of Modern Art, 1986), pp. 15–39.

23. It was precisely this temporal aspect of Minimalism that had incited Michael Fried's now infamous attack against the genre. Finding the introduction of temporality a threat to the Modernist vision of pure presence, of instantaneous comprehension, Fried condemned what he considered to be a contamination of sculpture by the theatrical. A follower of Greenberg's denunciation of the interdisciplinary in art, he could not condone the breakdown of rigid aesthetic categories. See Fried, "Art and Objecthood," *Artforum* 5, no. 10 (June 1967), pp. 12–23. Revised version in Battcock, pp. 116–47.

24. Anna Chave, "Minimalism and the Rhetoric of Power," *Arts Magazine* 64, no. 5 (January 1990), pp. 44–63.

25. Craig Owens, "Earthwords," *October* 10 (fall 1979), pp. 121–30.

26. Quoted in Lynne Cooke, "Minimalism Reviewed," *Burlington Magazine* 131, no. 1038 (September 1989), p. 643.

27. Quoted in Frances Colpitt, *Minimal Art: The Critical Perspective* (Ann Arbor: UMI Research Press, 1990), p. 134.

28. Hal Foster, "The Crux of Minimalism," in Howard Singerman, ed., *Individuals: A Selected History of Contemporary Art 1945–1986*, exh. cat. (Los Angeles: The Museum of Contemporary Art, 1986), pp. 162–83.

29. Ibid., p. 177.

30. Ibid., p. 178. See Benjamin H. D. Buchloh, "Allegorical Procedures: Appropriation and Montage in Contemporary Art," *Artforum* 21, no. 1 (September 1982), pp. 43–56.

31. In 1968, Morris, who, along with Judd, had articulated the formal and theoretical tenets of Minimalist sculpture in their critical texts, published his prolegomenon to an aesthetic sensibility that seemed the utter antithesis of Minimalism. See Robert Morris, "Anti-Form," *Artforum* 6, no. 8 (April 1968), pp. 33–35. Ever the observer and catalyst, Morris was no doubt participating in artistic developments here and abroad affected by Joseph Beuys in Germany, Mario Merz and Gilberto Zorio in Italy, and Hesse, Serra, Bruce Nauman, Smithson, and others in the United States.

32. Reprinted in *Donald Judd: Complete Writings 1959–1975* (Halifax: The Press of the Nova Scotia College of Art and Design; New York: New York University Press, 1975), p. 190.

33. Joseph Kosuth, "Art After Philosophy," and "Art After Philosophy, Part II," *Studio International* 178, no. 915 (October 1969), pp. 134–37, and no. 916 (November 1969), pp. 160–61. Reprinted in Ursula Meyer, *Conceptual Art* (New York: E. P. Dutton, 1972), p. 161.

34. The first three of the exhibitions were selected by an international committee and awards were bestowed on particular artists. In 1964, Alloway assembled the group of invited artists, while three judges—Hans Hofmann, Arnold Rüdinger, and Werner Haftmann—were engaged to grant awards of excellence. By 1967, when Fry (who was not yet an associate curator at the Guggenheim) organized the survey *Sculpture from Twenty Nations* as the fifth *International*, the notion of awards had been transferred into museum-purchase prizes.

35. Beginning in 1969, the Theodoron Foundation, comprised of anonymous members, supported a series of small invitational exhibitions of young artists and the purchase of one work by each participant. The first show, featuring Dan Christensen, Barry Flanagan, Nauman, Richter, James Seawright, Serra, John Walker, Peter Young, and Zorio, and the second, in 1971, with Power Boothe, Ron Cooper, Billy Bryant Copley, Mary Corse, Guy Dill, Andrew Gerndt, Harriet Korman, Dona Nelson, Michael Singer, and George Trakis, were curated by Fry and Waldman. The third and last exhibition, in 1977, featuring John Duff, Steve Gianakos, Darryl Hughto, Michael Hurson, Mary Miss, Elizabeth Murray, Katherine Porter, Allen Ruppersberg, and James Surls was curated by assistant curator Linda Shearer. These showcases for emerging talent were revived in 1978 with Exxon Corporation–supported exhibitions, which, held annually until 1986, alternated between presentations of international and exclusively American artists.

36. Given that Waldman took responsibility for the European and American sections of the exhibition, all but two of the selections were hers; Fry chose Brazilian artist Antonio Dias and Japanese artist Jiro Takamatsu. Although the list of participants is impressive for its breadth, the fact that the majority of artists are American did not go unnoticed by the critics. However, as in any group show, the list of omissions is instructive as to matters of taste and institutional policy but remains, ultimately, an act of futility. One can ask, for instance, why Vito Acconci, Beuys, Mel Bochner, Dan Graham, Douglas Huebler, Dennis Oppenheim, and Smithson were not included, but this remains merely an exercise in naming. The absence of Hesse is less disconcerting in that the museum organized her memorial retrospective a year later.

37. Flavin re-created this piece, extending it throughout the entire rotunda, for the Guggenheim's 1992 exhibition marking the reopening of the museum after an extensive renovation and expansion.

38. Since 1970, Merz has incorporated the Fibonacci formula of mathematical progression into his works. Originally conceived by the medieval monk Leonardo da Pisa (known as Fibonacci) and explicated in his *Liber Abacci* of 1202 and 1228, the formula is a sequence in which each number equals the sum of the two numbers that precede it: 1, 1, 2, 3, 5, 8, 13 . . . His observations were based on the reproduction of rabbits beginning with one pair and expanding, ultimately, to infinity. Corresponding to biological, spatial, and temporal dimensions, Fibonacci progressions relate to the proliferation and growth of organic materials—leaves, reptile skins, deer antlers, pinecones, seashells—items or images that Merz often uses in his art.

39. This description of Buren's project is borrowed from Benjamin H. D. Buchloh, "Conceptual Art 1962–1969," *October* 55 (winter 1990), p. 137.

40. Daniel Buren, "Beware," *Studio International* 179, no. 920 (May 1970), pp. 100–04. Reprinted in Meyer, p. 74.

41. See "Gurgles Around the Guggenheim," *Studio International* 181, no. 934 (June 1971), pp. 246–250, in which Waldman's response to the occurrences at the *Guggenheim International* and Buren's detailed defense of his project are published. The quote is from p. 248.

42. Benjamin H. D. Buchloh, "Formalism and Historicity—Changing Concepts in American and European Art Since 1945," in *Europe in the Seventies: Aspects of Recent Art*, exh. cat. (Chicago: The Art Institute of Chicago, 1977), pp. 82–111. In this essay, he claims that the American approach to art during the early to mid-1970s tended to be formalist in its focus on the physical attributes of a work, while the European critical practice of historicity situated an art work within its sociopolitical climate. The following (from pp. 91–92) summarizes his thesis:

Both concepts {formalism and historicity} have to be regarded as the opposite ends of an axis on which art activities seem to be permanently shifting according to their own and to historical conditions. Of course neither of them could be called specific per se to European and American art of the recent decades, but it seems that at precisely the point where the major European artists of the present like Buren, Broodthaers, Richter . . . developed an entirely changed notion of the artist's relation to history— which was around 1965—a strong current of formalist identification with art seems to have been representative for the American situation.

43. In Buchloh's (and Buren's) opinion, Wright's design for the museum is, in effect, quite polemical. "It could be argued," Buchloh explained, "that Wright's museum seriously questions and 'exposes' the historical character of easel painting for whose exhibition and installation it was paradoxically constructed." See Buchloh, "Formalism and Historicity," p. 102.

44. In her review of the *International*, Barbara Rose claimed that De Maria's piece embodied the "perverse and ironic relationship American art bears to American society in this moment of bad faith." See Rose, "Gobbledygook at the Guggenheim," *New York Magazine* 4 (March 8, 1971), p. 48.

45. Letter to Hans Haacke from Thomas Messer dated March 19, 1971, in the Solomon R. Guggenheim Museum Archives. In this correspondence, Messer states his misgivings about the exhibition; the show was officially canceled on April 1.

46. The poll is described in the statement that Haacke issued on April 3, 1971, after being notified of the cancellation of his exhibition.

Statement in the Solomon R. Guggenheim Museum Archives. Haacke had created a similar poll the year before for MoMA's *Information* exhibition. This poll only asked one question: "Would the fact that Governor Rockefeller has not denounced President Nixon's Indochina policy be a reason for you not to vote for him in November?"

47. For a detailed analysis of Haacke's canceled exhibition at the Guggenheim, see Rosalyn Deutsche, "Property Values: Hans Haacke, Real Estate and the Museum," in *Hans Haacke: Unfinished Business*, exh. cat. (New York: The New Museum of Contemporary Art, 1986), pp. 20–37. The catalogue also includes reproductions of a portion of the controversial work, *Shapolsky et al. Manhattan Real Estate Holdings, a Real-Time Social System, as of May 1, 1971*, which exists today in an edition of two. See pp. 92–97. The cancellation generated a debate between Haacke and Messer that was published in a number of art magazines and discussed in several editorial pieces. The exhibition catalogue provides a comprehensive bibliography.

48. This critical approach can be described as a deconstructive process about which Jacques Derrida has written: "The movements of deconstruction do not destroy structures from the outside. They are not possible and effective, nor can they take accurate aim, except by inhabiting those structures." Quoted by Craig Owens in "From Work to Frame, Or is There Life After 'The Death of the Author,'" in *Implosion: Ett postmodernt perspektiv/A Postmodern Perspective*, exh. cat. (Stockholm, 1988), p. 209.

49. The exhibition was curated by Waldman.

The Institution as Frame
Installations at the Guggenheim

Clare Bell

If traditional sculpture has been considered in terms of "the deployment of bodies in space,"[1] site-specific art—work created and installed by its maker with its physical surroundings in mind—may be thought about as the propulsion of space onto bodies. It *frames* looking in a particular place and at a particular time, attaching as much importance to the context in which art is shown as to the art object itself. Site-specific installations pose a direct challenge to the longstanding notion of art as a self-contained entity enjoying the status of a precious object. Such installations have broadened the scope of art to include terrains where the spontaneous, the phenomenological, the theatrical, the collaborative, the political, and the personal can converge.

Site-specific art has matured into an art form with far-reaching implications, but its evolution has not followed a direct course. As early as 1909, with the advent of Italian Futurism, and continuing through the 1920s with the international Dada movement, artists began to counteract art's tendency to become a static icon. Since then, artists have reconsidered art in terms of its ephemeral, temporal, and spatial qualities, investigating the very processes and systems through which it is made and presented as well as introducing the use of unconventional materials and settings.

A direct precedent to site-specific art is found in the work of the American Allan Kaprow, who, with other artists of his generation, sought a form of artistic expression that fused the visual arts with everyday life. In a 1958 article entitled "The Legacy of Jackson Pollock," Kaprow seized on the liberating qualities he saw in Pollock's gestural drip paintings of the 1940s and early 1950s as a way to identify new territory in which art could exist. "Anywhere is everywhere and you can dip in and out when and where you can," wrote Kaprow about Pollock's canvases. "What we have then is a type of art which tends to lose itself out of bounds, tends to fill our world with itself."[2] The theatricality that Kaprow observed in Pollock's work, along with the theories of chance the younger artist

learned from avant-garde composer John Cage, with whom he began studying in 1956 at the New School for Social Research in New York, led him to experiment with a type of performance he eventually termed Happenings.[3] The name was adopted by critics at the time to describe this elusive art form, which was embraced by several practitioners. Happenings were conceived by artists and carried out by players who performed simple, seemingly meaningless activities, such as sweeping or standing in line. Performers and audience members often interacted with each other and with various objects, typically newspapers and other items of urban detritus, that were placed in the same space. Happenings have been described as a "theater of effect,"[4] intended to be experienced piecemeal, outside the bounds of character, time, and place. They were critical in helping to establish an art form that reached beyond the confines of the picture frame or sculpture base into culture at large. As much recent theory developed by feminists shows, the emphasis on spectacle displaced conventional iconographic readings—which seek to fix meaning—in favor of the continuous reinvention of meaning elicited by the viewer's gaze. With any gaze come infinite points of reference, leading to manifold readings of the art at hand. Gender, sexuality, religion, ethnic background, race, and class are all inseparable from what constitutes a look. Happenings activated their environments, promoting the involvement of the audience in the action/making process, and thus broke down the boundaries between object and spectator by melding them into one.

In the 1960s, with the advent of Minimalism, Process Art, and Earthworks, artists such as Eva Hesse, Donald Judd, Robert Morris, Richard Serra, and Tony Smith created simple geometric sculptures that were intended to elicit similar, fundamental responses from all viewers. (The emergence in the 1970s of Body Art, which involved fetishizing or mutilating the artist's own body or subjecting it to various

Above: Fig. 115. Joseph Beuys, photographed in 1979 at the Solomon R. Guggenheim Museum during installation of *Joseph Beuys*. Photo by Bernard Gotfryd.

Left: Fig. 114. Joseph Beuys, *The Pack*, 1969. Volkswagen bus with 20 sleds, each carrying felt, fat, and a flashlight. Collection Herbig. Installed at the Solomon R. Guggenheim Museum for the 1979–80 exhibition *Joseph Beuys*. Photo by Mary Donlon.

physical ordeals or stimuli, further identified the body as the site for artistic investigation.) Many artists associated with Minimalism experimented with Earthworks (also called Land Art), in which art is sited outdoors, often in vast areas such as meteor craters or fields. Many of these projects were so expansive, and located in places so remote, that they were seen only in the photographs that documented their existence. They usually involved the alteration of the landscape; and all were subject to the effects of the elements. As John Beardsley has noted:

Land art helped to restore to sculpture a sense that the surroundings—and most particularly the landscape—were all-important both in the formulation of a work and in its perception. Sited sculpture emerged in the wake of this restoration and can be said to have descended in part from land art.[5]

In an influential 1967 essay, critic Michael Fried attacked the blending of theater with the art object, writing, "There is a war going on between the theatrical and modernist painting, between the theatrical and the pictorial."[6] Fried believed that Minimalist works, which he described as "literalist art," were so intent on asserting their own "objecthood" that they could never be experienced as true paintings or sculptures. In contending with artists such as Morris, Smith, and Anne Truitt, Fried concluded that their work "amounts to nothing other than a plea for a new genre of theater; and theater is now the negation of art. Whereas in previous art 'what is to be had from the work is located steadily within [it],' the experience of literalist art is of an object in a situation—one which, virtually by definition, includes the beholder."[7] Fried's argument—that the work of art must take precedence over the viewer in order for the visual arts to remain intact and separate from the performing arts—was highly disputed among artists and critics. Fried's line of thought underscores the understanding that time and place contribute to differing experiences of objects by individuals. In doing just

that, site-specific works have succeeded in moving art beyond the strict Modernist canon, which deemed that art could be understood as a universal experience.

Installations designed for conventional exhibition spaces such as museums and galleries have been crucial to the development of site-specific art. Such installations have fostered an essential dialogue between art and the art institution by activating architectural spaces so that they no longer remain discreet and supposedly neutral presences. The Guggenheim Museum made its first foray into showing installations with the *Guggenheim International Exhibition, 1971* (see "Against the Grain," pages 257–86). Beginning with *Joseph Beuys* in 1979, and continuing through the present, the museum has mounted several installations designed specifically for the spaces of the Frank Lloyd Wright building. In so doing, the Guggenheim has provided an important site in which to broaden definitions of art.

When his work was installed at the Guggenheim in 1979, Joseph Beuys commented, "My concern is for the transformation of substance, rather than the traditional aesthetic understanding of beauty. If creativity relates to the transformation, change, and development of substance, then it can be applied to everything in the world, and is no longer art."[8] Like Marcel Duchamp, who believed that anyone could be an artist and spent the better part of his career exposing the futility of defining what art is, Beuys preached that art is unfixed and open to everyone. Beuys's varied oeuvre consisted of live performance pieces that sometimes involved the use of animals; "social-sculptures," works made from felt, copper, fat, and a variety of relics, which Beuys described as part of "how we mould and shape the world in which we live"[9]; public "actions," often political in intent, which generated many artifacts; and junk items and personal effects the artist presented in vitrines.

Although his work shared traits with the Post-Minimal experiments of contemporary American artists, who were also using items like felt and metals, their intentions were quite different. American artists were involved with unconventional materials and formats in an effort to demystify traditional artistic practice, while Beuys assumed the ancient role of shaman, heightening a sense of mysticism and a peculiar inclination toward ritual in his oeuvre. Shrouded in autobiographical references of mythic proportions, Beuys's work was unique and highly elusive. His account of being rescued in the Crimean tundra by the nomadic clan called the Tartars after his German fighter plane was shot down during World War II was legendary in European and American art circles (although the episode has been questioned as fact by some historians). His claim that he was taught to survive the freezing temperatures by swaddling himself in fat and felt lent a fascination to his use of those materials in his art. The mythic speech Beuys used to describe his work personalized and romanticized his art in terms that were quintessentially heroic. It also imbued it with a symbolic quality that seemed closer in line with the more grandiose mythological themes reminiscent of Abstract Expressionist paintings from the 1940s and 1950s, not to mention the art of the distant past. Because of the outspoken disdain he held for the art world and for capitalist culture in general, his art production was considered to be politically charged by admirers and detractors alike.

Beuys, who was born in Kleves, Germany in 1921 and who died in 1986, had visited the United States only a few times before the Guggenheim's retrospective presentation opened to the public on November 2, 1979. He came to New York twice in 1974; once for an exhibition at the Ronald Feldman Gallery that consisted of an empty room; the next time for a show at the René Block Gallery, where he confined himself with a live coyote and proceeded to engage the animal in a pseudo-dialogue. Beuys had refused an invitation to show his work at the Museum of Modern Art in New York in protest of United States involvement in Vietnam. Thus, his exhibition at the Guggenheim, initiated as early as the summer of 1976, a year after the final withdrawal of American troops from Vietnam, was the first major showing of his work in the United States. The installation marked a critical moment in the reception of Beuys's work in America, exposing the misunderstandings surrounding his oeuvre while further explaining its intentions and expanding its influence.

Guggenheim director Thomas M. Messer recognized the importance to Beuys of exercising complete control over the way his work was shown and the context in which it would appear. When he proposed the project to the institution's Board of Trustees, Messer noted that "it was clear from the onset that Joseph Beuys and his deputies would have to be given a free hand to shape the project and that this in turn would require a measure of uninhibited functioning that far exceeded the norm."[10] Messer queried British curator Caroline Tisdall, Beuys's close friend, on the prospect of a Beuys show, and she served as the curator for the presentation and the author of its accompanying catalogue. Given the nature of Beuys's art—his use of such idiosyncratic substances as fat, honey, asphalt, and felt as well as more substantial objects like bathtubs, cages, and automobiles—the installation was devised to speak to the transformation of the modern art museum as much as it was meant to capture the changeability of Beuys's materials and his artistic formulations.

Beuys conceived the installation as a series of interrelated tableaux that would be placed in the bays on Wright's ramps. Plans for what he termed *Stations* appeared in Tisdall's correspondence to Messer beginning in 1978. These *Stations*, wrote Tisdall, would "give access to a reading of development, rather than the 'straight chronology.'"[11] Designed to induce a feeling of harmony and continuous movement within the museum, Beuys's *Stations* were disturbing in their deliberate conflation of Christianity, the Holocaust, and art. They emphatically recalled both the "Stations of the Cross" in the Christian Church and the

Following two pages: Fig. 116. On wall: Richard Long, *River Avon Mud Circle*, 1986. Mud on painted plasterboard wall, 5.3 m (17 feet 4 inches) diameter. Temporary installation. **On floor:** Richard Long, *Chalk Circle*, 1986. Chalk rocks, 5.6 m (18 feet 3 inches) diameter. San Francisco Museum of Modern Art. Installed in the High Gallery of the Solomon R. Guggenheim Museum for the 1986 exhibition *Richard Long*. Photo by David Heald.

to mark his passage. Often, the forms he creates are as elusive as the crush of grass or earth beneath his feet or mounds of stones or twigs he piles together at certain intervals along the way. Photographs are taken by the artist to mark each expedition.

In his 1986 one-person show, organized by guest-curator Rudi Fuchs, Long created a contemplative environment of circular rock and slate floor sculptures within the museum (see fig. 116). For these works, the artist supplied diagrams and written accounts about the placement of each rock or piece of slate in relationship to the ones around it, specifying what their ultimate diameters must be in the final configuration. He also created mud wall drawings and included black-and-white photographs of various walks he had taken throughout the world. The simple geometric forms in the photographs and other works in the installation echoed the architectural designs found in Wright's terrazzo floor, the skylight, and the sweeping curves of the building's shell. Discussing Long's work in the exhibition's catalogue, Fuchs sums up the defining principles underlying Long's oeuvre, commenting, "Impermanence lies at the very heart of Richard Long's conviction as an artist. It has rendered possible the idea of walking as his comprehensive art form, containing all the other forms through which his art chooses to express itself."[14] With his earthen materials and organic shapes, Long intended, as Wright had, to link the inside of the building with the environment outside.

That same winter, a collaborative piece designed by artists Oldenburg and Coosje van Bruggen and architect Frank O. Gehry was installed at the Guggenheim. A larger-than-life red Swiss Army knife, it recalled in scale numerous Pop art public sculptures of the 1960s created by Oldenburg, an artist born in Stockholm, Sweden whose family settled in the United States in 1934. Typically, Oldenburg's early works were based on commonplace objects that the artist would transform into large, sagging vinyl forms stuffed with kapok and placed on the wall or floor. With the assistance of van Bruggen,

over a period of time he began to enlarge many to the scale of architecture. *The Knife Ship*, as this object was called, was motorized and took up a large portion of rotunda floor (fig. 117). It was comprised of eight oars, each ten feet long, which jutted out from either side of the knife's red casing. When one of the knife's blades was fully extended it reached over thirty feet into the air. A parody of Wright's "corkscrew" museum, the gigantic corkscrew of *The Knife Ship* stood motionless while the two blades continually crisscrossed each other. Though not originally intended for the Wright space (the object had been used in 1985 as the central piece in a performance that took place on the Grand Canal in Venice, Italy), the playful yet imposing presence of *The Knife Ship* turned the museum into a theater of the uncanny, fusing two monumental presences, art object and edifice, to form a new reality. Wrote van Bruggen, "Since Oldenburg's own concern is with the tension between 'thing-ness' and abstraction, the subject of buildings opened up a new, abstract manipulation of forms."[15]

In September 1989, Mario Merz, a leading proponent of Arte Povera, mounted his largest presentation of work to date in the United States, in an exhibition organized by Germano Celant for the Guggenheim. Arte Povera ("poor" art) was a catch-all term coined by Celant in 1967 to describe the work of a select group of international artists who were drawing their materials from nature. Beuys and Long, for instance, were among a number of artists who fell under the rubric in the late 1960s. Other artists associated with the movement included New York–based artist Eva Hesse, Dutch artist Jan Dibbets, and several other Americans and Europeans. Merz and fellow Turin-based artists Giovanni Anselmo, Giulio Paolini, and Giuseppe Penone comprised the core of the Italian contingent Celant identified with Arte Povera. Celant wrote that these artists had "chosen to live within direct experience." Their work, he continued, drew "from the substance of the natural event—that of the growth of a plant,

Following two pages: **Fig. 117. Claes Oldenburg, Coosje van Bruggen, and Frank O. Gehry,** *The Knife Ship*, 1986. Wood, steel, paint, and motor; closed: 2.4 x 12.3 x 3.2 m (8 feet x 40 feet 3 inches x 10 feet 6 inches); with blades, corkscrew, and oars open: 9.7 x 25.3 x 9.7 m (31 feet 8 inches x 83 feet x 31 feet 10 inches). The Museum of Contemporary Art, Los Angeles. Installed at the Solomon R. Guggenheim Museum for the 1986–87 exhibition *The Knife Ship from "Il Corso del Coltello."* Photo by David Heald.

The Knife Ship
from "Il Corso del Coltello"

This exhibition is sponsored by a generous grant from Gruppo GFT.

the chemical reaction of a mineral, the movement of a river . . . the fall of a weight."[16] While Celant maintained that Arte Povera was an international style, today the term is most often used to identify works by the Italian artists.

Born in 1925, Merz is chiefly involved with notions of progression and infinite growth, and his nearly thirty years of artistic production lies at the forefront of the Arte Povera spirit of creativity. Concerned with biological and sensory occurrences, his works are expandable and fluid. He has fashioned igloos from items like clamped shards of glass, sandbags, melted wax, twigs, and branches. Other works include helical glass tables covered with fresh fruits and vegetables, and umbrellas and rubberized raincoats pierced by neon tubes. In all, these works reflect the semi-intangible nature of all things.

For the 1971 *Guggenheim International Exhibition*, Merz arranged neon tubes formed into a group of numbers, known as a Fibonacci series, on the outer parapet wall of the Guggenheim. A Fibonacci series is an infinite sequence in which the first two numbers are *1* and the rest are the sum of the two numbers that precede it. Because a Fibonacci series may be considered a mathematical abstraction of a spiral, Merz used it as a way of calling attention to the progression of the Guggenheim's shape. In his 1989 retrospective exhibition at the museum, this work appeared once again on the outer wall.

Unlike most monographic exhibitions, in which an artist's works are made to fit into a linear chronology, the placement of Merz's works in the museum was kaleidoscopic (fig. 118). Some of the objects in the show were pieces that had been reworked by Merz over an extended period of time. Another segment had been refabricated for the Guggenheim installation. The final portion included pre-existing objects that the artist changed completely for the presentation. Slippery in its chronology (as with the Beuys exhibition a decade earlier), the Merz installation, much like his individual pieces, felt more like a habitat than the charted presentation of an artist's development.

It seems fitting that Jenny Holzer's 1989 installation at the Guggenheim would mark a decisive transition in the museum's history. Though the installation was conceived by Diane Waldman during Messer's tenure, it was not mounted until December 1989, by which time Thomas Krens had become director. And Holzer's installation was the final presentation at the Guggenheim before it closed to the public in February 1990 to undergo a two-year renovation and expansion project.

Holzer, born in Gallipolis, Ohio in 1950, is a visual artist as well as a social activist. Through her language-based work, she attempts to call into question systems of power in Western culture. Holzer first came to prominence with a group of offset posters printed with her *Truisms*, a series of deadpan sentences describing clashing ideological values. The sentences were placed in alphabetical order so as not to give one any more weight than the next. She had begun to clandestinely paste up unsigned posters around Manhattan in 1977. The *Truisms* were followed in 1979 by another poster project, *The Inflammatory Essays*. This time Holzer used colored sheets of paper, each printed with a paragraph of urgent, confrontational writing. Moving from posters to mediums such as enamel and bronze plaques, Holzer formulated texts for *The Living Series* in 1982.

If anonymity marked the first phase of Holzer's artistic production, public recognition of her work characterized the next. In 1982, Holzer was invited by the Public Art Fund in New York to display messages or computer-generated images on the Spectacolor Board in Times Square. Other artists who participated in *Messages to the Public* at various times included Ida Applebroog, David Hammons, Edgar Heap-of-Birds, Alfredo Jaar, and Barbara Kruger. Although each of their works had different intentions and spoke to a variety of concerns, it was clear that all of these artists were deeply involved with the politics of identity and of remaking culture.

Following the presentation of her work on the Spectacolor Board, Holzer

began *The Survival Series*, creating texts specifically for smaller computerized light boards. Eventually she discovered LED (light-emitting diode) display boards, and began to program them with the series. She also used peel-off stickers and tractor caps to display her messages. Texts from *The Survival Series* usually appeared outdoors and many could be seen on public-announcement signboards located in various cities. In 1985, "Protect Me From What I Want," a text from *Survival*, was displayed on the Spectacolor Board. Selections from *Truisms* and *Survival* were seen on the marquee for Caesar's Palace in Las Vegas in 1986; some, like "Money Creates Taste," underscored the sensibilities of the gambling industry. All of these public projects served to establish Holzer as an artist whose undertaking could not be ignored. She soon became familiar to the general public, which began to recognize her still-unsigned work on the street and read about her exploits in the press.

Holzer had made the transition from outdoor spaces to the interiors of galleries and museums several years before her installation at the Guggenheim. Series such as *Under a Rock* (1986) and *Laments* (1989) were conceived for spaces designated to display art. The former series dealt with feelings about dying, while the latter conjured up the sense of death itself. She thought people would spend more time reading these than the outdoor messages, which were designed to catch the fleeting attention of a passerby. Granite benches were used for the first time in *Under a Rock*. They were engraved with the same texts that moved across an LED sign positioned nearby. Inscribed marble and granite sarcophagus forms and vertical LEDs in virtual darkness comprised *Laments*, an installation that opened at the Dia Art Foundation in New York in 1989.

When her 530-foot-long LED sign wound its way down the outside of the Guggenheim's parapet, the bays of five of the museum's ramps left bare, it was clearly unlike anything she or the museum had shown before (fig. 119). For the first time, she included texts from every series on one LED sign. Different typefaces and light patterns were used to distinguish the individual series from each other, but the program did not follow a preconceived order.

During preparations for the Guggenheim's show, Holzer gave birth to her daughter, Lili, and she wrote a new text centering on her convictions and fears about motherhood. *Child Text*, which premiered on the LED sign at the Guggenheim, was later developed into a body of writing for her installation at the Venice Biennale in the summer of 1991. She was the first female artist to have a solo exhibit at the American Pavilion.

Flashing and streaming colorful texts—ranging from conflicting statements about morality, issues of quality, and the macabre that often accompanies daily existence, to somber references to the AIDS epidemic, to the artist's own damning and passionate reactions as a mother—Holzer's LED signboard at the Guggenheim ran for one hour and forty-five minutes and continued nonstop until the museum closed each evening. The sinuous current of multicolored lights created a fantastic spectacle. It demanded, provoked, seduced, amused, annoyed, dazzled. It was often difficult to read, though mesmerizing to watch. Its unrelenting presence in the museum's space destabilized the viewer's gaze and as a result it resisted slippage into the realms of indifference or the sublime. The hold that representation maintains on how we come to know the world was thrown emphatically off guard.

Benches were also an important element of Holzer's installation. Two sets, one in white granite and placed in the High Gallery, the other of red granite and positioned in a circular grouping on the rotunda floor (fig. 120), were etched, tombstone fashion, with statements that also appeared on the signboard, making the charged statements pulsating overhead seem lasting and permanent.

There had been few shows at the museum devoted to the work of women artists, and the decision to mount a show of Holzer's work signaled a critical passage in the Guggenheim's history.[17]

The museum's reopening in the summer of 1992 provided another occasion for a site-specific work, this time to inaugurate the newly renovated spaces of the Wright rotunda. Dan Flavin's *Untitled (to Tracy, to celebrate the love of a lifetime)*, a work dedicated to his fiancée (now wife), was comprised of a series of pink, yellow, green, and blue industrial fluorescent-light tubes placed in differing configurations throughout all seven ramps of the rotunda, highlighting each bay (fig. 121). The piece reprised and expanded Flavin's installation for the 1971 *Guggenheim International Exhibition*, at which time its dedication read *(to Ward Jackson, an old friend and colleague who, during the fall of 1957 when I finally returned to New York from Washington and joined him to work together in this museum, kindly communicated)*; Jackson, an artist in his own right, is the museum's longtime archivist.[18] For the 1992 installation, Flavin added an immense column of pink fluorescent rods joining floor and skylight.

Flavin, who was born in Jamaica, New York in 1933, pioneered the use of fluorescent-light tubes as an art medium and has used them since 1961. He worked as an assistant at the Guggenheim just before the opening of the Wright building in 1959. The artist holds the Guggenheim edifice in high regard, and through this work sought to reorient perceptions of Wright's architecture through subtle permutations in ambience rather than by interfering with its physical structure. The oblique transformation Flavin intended to produce with this concentration of soft light was offset by the verticality of the pink totem, which suggested a phallus in the way it seemingly penetrated the skylight. Like all site-specific art, Flavin's piece cannot be separated from the cultural, social, and political matrix in which it existed. A reminder of patriarchal power and its stranglehold on how we come to know the world, Flavin's installation offered important insights into the challenge to dismantle its grip on us. As the museum continues to inspire and embrace site-specific art, that art will serve an all-important function—to encourage us to search out important aspects of our own lives and the lives of those around us in ever more meaningful ways.

Following eight pages: **Fig. 119. Jenny Holzer,** Selections from *Truisms, Inflammatory Essays, The Living Series, The Survival Series, Under a Rock, Laments,* and new writing, 1989. LED display board. Site-specific installation at the Solomon R. Guggenheim Museum for the 1989–90 exhibition *Jenny Holzer.* Photo by David Heald.

Fig. 120. Jenny Holzer, Selections from *The Survival Series* and *The Living Series,* 1989. Granite benches. Site-specific installation at the Solomon R. Guggenheim Museum for the 1989–90 exhibition *Jenny Holzer.* Photo by David Heald.

Fig. 121. Dan Flavin, *Untitled (to Tracy, to celebrate the love of a lifetime),* 1992, expanded version of *Untitled (to Ward Jackson, an old friend and colleague who, during the fall of 1957 when I finally returned to New York from Washington and joined him to work together in this museum, kindly communicated),* 1971. Fluorescent light, variable dimensions. Solomon R. Guggenheim Museum, Partial gift of the artist in honor of Ward Jackson 72.1985. Installed at the Solomon R. Guggenheim Museum for the 1992 exhibition *Dan Flavin.* Photo by David Heald.

Fig. 122. Rebecca Horn, *Paradiso,* 1993. Glass funnels, pumping system, lightning machines, fox machines, water, and dye. Solomon R. Guggenheim Museum, Gift of the artist. Installed at the Solomon R. Guggenheim Museum for the 1993 exhibition *Rebecca Horn: The Inferno-Paradiso Switch.* Photo by Lee Ewing.

Notes

1. See Rosalind Krauss's discussion of Gotthold Lessing's essay "Laocoön; or On the Limits of Painting" (1766) in her introduction to *Passages in Modern Sculpture* (Cambridge, Mass.: MIT Press, 1990), pp. 1–3.

2. Allan Kaprow, "The Legacy of Jackson Pollock," *Art News* 57, no. 6 (Oct. 1958), p. 26.

3. In the spring of 1959, Kaprow performed *Something to Take Place, a Happening* at Rutgers University in New Brunswick, New Jersey, where he was teaching. A year earlier, he presented several junk-filled environments at Hansa Gallery (210 Central Park South, New York City). Others involved with Happenings during the late 1950s and 1960s included Jim Dine, Red Grooms, Claes Oldenburg, and Robert Whitman.

4. Michael Kirby, ed., *Happenings: An Illustrated Anthology* (New York: E. P. Dutton, 1965), p. 19.

5. John Beardsley, *Earthworks and Beyond: Contemporary Art in the Landscape*, expanded edition (New York: Abbeville Press, Cross River Press, 1989), p. 103.

6. Michael Fried, "Art and Objecthood," *Artforum* 5, no. 10 (June 1967), p. 20.

7. Ibid., p. 15.

8. Acoustiguide transcript for the exhibition, *Joseph Beuys*, Solomon R. Guggenheim Museum Archives, p. 5.

9. Quoted in Caroline Tisdall, *Joseph Beuys*, exh. cat. (New York: Solomon R. Guggenheim Museum, 1979), p. 7.

10. Quoted in the Institute for Foreign Cultural Relations, Stuttgart, *Joseph Beuys: Drawings, Objects and Prints*, exh. cat. (Stuttgart, 1989), p. 25.

11. Letter from Tisdall to Messer, January 24, 1978, quoted in ibid., p. 29.

12. Concurrent with *Joseph Beuys*, an exhibition of photographs, posters, and slide projections developed by several F.I.U. students was also on view, in the now-defunct smaller side galleries of the Monitor building. The student exhibition took place from December 11, 1979–January 2, 1980, and a four-page brochure describing the teachings of F.I.U. was printed.

13. John Russell, "The Shaman as Artist," *The New York Times Magazine* (Oct. 28, 1979), p. 40.

14. R. H. Fuchs, *Richard Long*, exh. cat. (New York: Solomon R. Guggenheim Foundation; London: Thames and Hudson, 1986), p. 45.

15. Coosje van Bruggen, "Waiting for Dr. Coltello: A Project by Coosje van Bruggen, Frank O. Gehry, and Claes Oldenburg," *Artforum* 23, no. 1 (Sept. 1984), p. 88.

16. Germano Celant, *Art "Povera"* (New York: Praeger, 1969), p. 225.

17. In addition to the installation *Jenny Holzer*, other exhibitions at the Guggenheim devoted to women artists have included: *Alice Mattern Memorial* (opened October 1945, closing date unknown); *Hilla Rebay* (November 2, 1948–January 16, 1949); *Chryssa* (November 14–December 17, 1961); *Eva Hesse: A Memorial Exhibition* (December 7, 1972–February 11, 1973); *Helen Frankenthaler Tiles* (May 2–June 1, 1975); *Ree Morton; Manipulations of the Organic* (February 8–March 24, 1985); [Helen] *Frankenthaler: Works on Paper 1949–1984* (February 22–April 21, 1985); *Hannelore Baron* (May 19–July 23, 1989); *Rebecca Horn: The Inferno-Paradiso Switch* (June 25–September 26, 1993, fig. 122).

18. See Cornelia Lauf, "Dan Flavin," in *Guggenheim Museum: A to Z* (New York: Guggenheim Museum, 1992), p. 84.

Exhibitions

Solomon R. Guggenheim's collection of non-objective paintings was exhibited publicly from 1936. The foundation that bears his name was chartered in 1937, and, under its auspices, the Museum of Non-Objective Painting opened in 1939; its name was changed to Solomon R. Guggenheim Museum in 1952. This history includes exhibitions mounted by the foundation as well as those organized by other institutions and shown at the Guggenheim. Peggy Guggenheim Collection exhibitions are included from 1979, the year that the foundation assumed full responsibility for its operation. The Guggenheim Museum SoHo opened in 1992.

In the following exhibition history, the abbreviation S.R.G.M. stands for the Solomon R. Guggenheim Museum, New York, N.Y.; G.M.S. for the Guggenheim Museum SoHo, New York, N.Y.; and P.G.C. for the Peggy Guggenheim Collection, Venice. Numbers at the beginning of entries are used for the museum's record keeping; the letter т indicates that an exhibition was organized by the Solomon R. Guggenheim Museum for presentation elsewhere. A bibliography of books and catalogues published by the foundation begins on page 330.

1936

1-т. Charleston, S.C., Carolina Art Association, Gibbes Memorial Art Gallery, *Solomon R. Guggenheim Collection of Non-Objective Paintings*, March 1–April 12 (catalogue).

2-т. Chicago, Ill., The Arts Club of Chicago, *Paintings by Rudolf Bauer from the Collection of Solomon R. Guggenheim*, May 12–June 6 (checklist).

1937

3-т. Philadelphia, Pa., Philadelphia Art Alliance, *Solomon R. Guggenheim Collection of Non-Objective Paintings*, Feb. 8–28 (second enlarged catalogue).

1938

4-т. Charleston, S.C., Gibbes Memorial Art Gallery, *Solomon R. Guggenheim Collection of Non-Objective Paintings*, March 12–April 17 (third enlarged catalogue).

1939

5-т. Baltimore, Md., The Baltimore Museum of Art, *Solomon R. Guggenheim Collection of Non-Objective Paintings*, Jan. 6–29 (fourth catalogue).

6-т. Paris, Galerie Charpentier, *Réalités nouvelles* (including selections from the Solomon R. Guggenheim Foundation): "1ʳᵉ Exposition (1ʳᵉ Série), Oeuvres des artistes français," June 15–28; "1ʳᵉ Exposition (2ᵐᵉ Série), Oeuvres des artistes étrangers," June 30–July 15; "2ᵐᵉ Exposition, Oeuvres des artistes dont la tendance inobjective s'est volontairement arrêtée avant 1920"; "Oeuvres des artistes après 1920" (list of participating artists).

New York, N.Y., Museum of Non-Objective Painting, *Art of Tomorrow*, opened June 1.

1940

7. New York, N.Y., Museum of Non-Objective Painting, *Three American Non-Objective Painters: I. Rice Pereira, Balcomb Greene, Gertrude Greene*, Jan. 3–Feb. 14.

8. New York, N.Y., Museum of Non-Objective Painting, *Eight American Non-Objective Painters: Penrod Centurion, John Ferren, Gerome Kamrowski, Hilla Rebay, Rolph Scarlett, Charles Smith, John von Wicht, Jean Xceron*, Feb. 15–March 30.

9. New York, N.Y., Museum of Non-Objective Painting, *Charles G. Shaw: Thirteen Recent Paintings*, April 1–May 13.

10. New York, N.Y., Museum of Non-Objective Painting, *Twelve American Non-Objective Painters: Emil Bisttram, Florence Brillinger, Manuel Essman, Robert Gribboek, Noah Grossman, Lawren Harris, Raymond Jonson, Hanany Meller, Agnes Pelton, Rouben Samberg, Rolph Scarlett, Charles Smith*, May 14–June 27.

11. New York, N.Y., Museum of Non-Objective Painting, *Three American Non-Objective Painters: Penrod Centurion, Dwinell Grant, Noah Grossman*, June 28–Aug. 5.

12. New York, N.Y., Museum of Non-Objective Painting, *Six American Non-Objective Painters: Penrod Centurion, Dwinell Grant, Lawren Harris, Raymond Jonson, Rouben Samberg, Stuart Walker*, Aug. 6–Sept. 30.

13. New York, N.Y., Museum of Non-Objective Painting, *Twelve American Non-Objective Painters: Florence Brillinger, Penrod Centurion, Josette Coeffin, Dwinell Grant, Noah Grossman, Hanany Meller, I. Rice Pereira, Hilla Rebay, Mary Ryan, Rolph Scarlett, Charles Smith, Jean Xceron*, Oct. 1–Nov. 13.

14-т. Brooklyn, N.Y., Lincoln Gallery, Abraham Lincoln High School, *Non-Objective Art from the Solomon R. Guggenheim Foundation*, Oct. 13–27.

15. New York, N.Y., Museum of Non-Objective Painting, *Ten American Non-Objective Painters: Penrod Centurion, Josette Coeffin, Manuel Essman, Noah Grossman, Hanany Meller, Marie Menken, I. Rice Pereira, Mary Ryan, Rolph Scarlett, Charles G. Shaw*, Nov. 14–Dec. 31.

1941

16. New York, N.Y., Museum of Non-Objective Painting, *American Non-Objective Painters*, Jan. 1–Feb. 10.

17. New York, N.Y., Museum of Non-Objective Painting, *Charles G. Shaw: Twenty-six New Paintings*, Feb. 11–March 9.

18. New York, N.Y., Museum of Non-Objective Painting, *Ten American Non-Objective Painters: Florence Brillinger, Olga Egeressy, Thomas Eldred,*

Edward Landon, Lloyd R. Ney, Mary Ryan, Rolph Scarlett, Roland St. John, Edna Tacon, Paul Tacon, March 11–April 22.

19-т. Portland, Oreg., Pacific Arts Association, Lincoln High School, *Fifteen Non-Objective Paintings from the Solomon R. Guggenheim Foundation*, April 7–23; Eugene, Oreg., University of Oregon, April 28–May 11; Corvallis, Oreg., Oregon State College, May 12–30; Los Angeles, Calif., Chouinard Art Institute, July; San Diego, Calif., Fine Arts Gallery, Aug.; Institute, W. Va., West Virginia State College, Sept.; Massillon, Ohio, The Massillon Museum, Oct.; Normal, Ill., Illinois State Normal University, Nov.; Hazleton, Pa., Hazleton Undergraduate Center, The Pennsylvania State College, Feb. 1942.

20. New York, N.Y., Museum of Non-Objective Painting, *Paintings and Constructions by Ladislas Moholy-Nagy*, April 24–May 25.

21-т. Norton, Mass., Wheaton College, *Thirteen Non-Objective Paintings from the Solomon R. Guggenheim Foundation*, May–June; Washington, D.C., The Catholic University of America, July 25–Aug. 10; South Hadley, Mass., Mount Holyoke Friends of Art, Dwight Art Memorial, Mount Holyoke College, Oct. 3–24; Boise, Idaho, The Boise Art Association, Boise Art Gallery, Nov.; Dallas, Tex., Dallas Museum of Fine Arts, Jan. 4–24, 1942; Pullman, Wash., The State College of Washington, Feb. 22–March 25, 1942; Des Moines, Iowa, Des Moines Association of Fine Arts, April 1942; Detroit, Mich., Women's City Club of Detroit, May 1942.

22. New York, N.Y., Museum of Non-Objective Painting, *Eight American Non-Objective Painters: Florence Brillinger, Werner Drewes, Dwinell Grant, Maude I. Kerns, Edward Landon, Ted Price, Mary Ryan, Rolph Scarlett*, May 27–June 29.

23. New York, N.Y., Museum of Non-Objective Painting, *Eight American Non-Objective Painters: Thomas Eldred, Dwinell Grant, Noah Grossman, Marguerite Hohenberg, Ladislas Moholy-Nagy, Otto Nebel, I. Rice Pereira, Rolph Scarlett*, July 25–closing date unknown.

24-т. Bennington, Vt., Bennington College, *Twenty-seven Non-Objective Paintings from the Solomon R. Guggenheim Foundation*, Oct.; Iowa City, Iowa, The State University of Iowa, Jan. 6–26, 1942; Birmingham, Ala., Birmingham Art Club, Public Library, Feb. 1942; Minneapolis, Minn., The University Gallery, University of Minnesota, March 2–31, 1942.

25. New York, N.Y., Museum of Non-Objective Painting, *American Non-Objective Painters*, Nov.

26. New York, N.Y., Museum of Non-Objective Painting, *American Non-Objective Painters*, Dec.

1942

27. New York, N.Y., Museum of Non-Objective Painting, *Guest Exhibition: Drawings and Woodblock Prints by Mary Ryan, John Sennhauser, Charles Smith*, Jan. 1–Feb. 27.

28. New York, N.Y., Museum of Non-Objective Painting, *Ten American Non-Objective Painters: Noah Grossman, Marguerite Hohenberg, Charles Johnson, Hyman Koppelman, Hans Kraus, Edward Landon, Grischa Metlay, John Sennhauser, Edna Tacon, Paul Tacon*, March 1–May 10.

29. New York, N.Y., Museum of Non-Objective Painting, *Twelve American Non-Objective Painters: Lucille Autorino, Penrod Centurion, Noah Grossman, Marguerite Hohenberg, Gerome Kamrowski, H. Felix Kraus, Joseph Manfredi, Ladislas Moholy-Nagy, Michael Schlazer, John Sennhauser, Charles G. Shaw, Edna Tacon*, May 11–June 20.

30. New York, N.Y., Museum of Non-Objective Painting, *Fifth Anniversary Exhibition*, June 25–Oct. 31.

31-T. Summit, N.J., Summit Art Association, *Non-Objective Paintings from the Solomon R. Guggenheim Foundation*, Nov. 1–15.

32. New York, N.Y., Museum of Non-Objective Painting, *American Non-Objectives*, Nov. 1, 1942–Jan. 30, 1943 (checklist).

1943

33-T. Cazenovia, N.Y., Cazenovia Junior College, *Nine Non-Objective Paintings from the Solomon R. Guggenheim Foundation*, Jan. 12–Feb. 15.

34. New York, N.Y., Museum of Non-Objective Painting, *American Non-Objectives, Third Group Show Commemorating the Fifth Anniversary of the Solomon R. Guggenheim Foundation*, Feb. 7–June 13 (checklist).

35-T. Savannah, Ga., Telfair Academy of Arts and Sciences, *Non-Objective Art from the Solomon R. Guggenheim Foundation*, March 10–April 10.

36. New York, N.Y., Museum of Non-Objective Painting, *Loan Exhibition*, June 15–Oct. 14 (checklist).

37. New York, N.Y., Museum of Non-Objective Painting, *Loan Exhibition*, Oct. 15–closing date unknown (checklist).

1944

38-T. Washington, D.C., Arts Club of Washington, *Forty-five Paintings from the Solomon R. Guggenheim Foundation*, Jan.

39. New York, N.Y., Museum of Non-Objective Painting, *Loan Exhibition*, April 18–closing date unknown (checklist).

40. New York, N.Y., Museum of Non-Objective Painting, *Loan Exhibition*, Oct. 15–closing date unknown (checklist).

41-T. Cazenovia, N.Y., Cazenovia Junior College, *Selections from the Solomon R. Guggenheim Foundation*, Nov. 11, 1944–Jan. 1945.

1945

42-T. Fort Worth, Tex., Fort Worth Association, Public Library, *Selections from the Solomon R. Guggenheim Foundation*, Jan. 6–March 21.

43. New York, N.Y., Museum of Non-Objective Painting, *In Memory of Wassily Kandinsky*, March 15–April 29 (two catalogues).

44. New York, N.Y., Museum of Non-Objective Painting, *Loan Exhibition*, June 6–closing date unknown (checklist).

45-T. Scranton, Pa., Everhart Museum, *Art of Tomorrow*, June 15–Sept. 15 (checklist).

46. New York, N.Y., Museum of Non-Objective Painting, *Alice Mattern Memorial*, Oct.–closing date unknown (checklist).

47-T. Chicago, Ill., The Arts Club of Chicago, *Wassily Kandinsky Memorial Exhibition*, Nov. (checklist).

48. New York, N.Y., Museum of Non-Objective Painting, *Loan Exhibition*, Dec. 5–closing date unknown (checklist).

49-T. Milwaukee, Wis., Milwaukee Art Institute, *Wassily Kandinsky Memorial Exhibition*, Dec. 1945–Jan. 1946.

1946

50-T. Savannah, Ga., Telfair Academy of Arts and Sciences, *Selections from the Solomon R. Guggenheim Foundation*, Feb. 9–26; traveled in part to Augusta, Ga., Augusta Art Club, March; Athens, Ga., Southern Art Association, April.

51-T. Anniston, Ala., United Service Organizations, Inc. (USO), *Seventeen Paintings from the Solomon R. Guggenheim Foundation*, April.

52-T. Utica, N.Y., Munson-Williams-Proctor Institute, *Thirty-five Non-Objective Paintings from the Solomon R. Guggenheim Foundation*, April 7–28.

53-T. Pittsburgh, Pa., Department of Fine Arts, Carnegie Institute, *Memorial Exhibition of Paintings by Wassily Kandinsky (1866–1944)*, April 11–May 12 (catalogue).

54. New York, N.Y., Museum of Non-Objective Painting, *Loan Exhibition*, June 5–Oct. 14 (checklist).

55. New York, N.Y., Museum of Non-Objective Painting, *Loan Exhibition*, Oct. 15, 1946–Feb. 10, 1947 (checklist).

1947

56. New York, N.Y., Museum of Non-Objective Painting, *Loan Exhibition*, Feb. 12–closing date unknown (checklist).

57. New York, N.Y., Museum of Non-Objective Painting, *In Memoriam Laszlo Moholy-Nagy*, May 15–July 10 (catalogue).

58. New York, N.Y., Museum of Non-Objective Painting, *Loan Exhibition*, July 15–closing date unknown (checklist).

59. New York, N.Y., Museum of Non-Objective Painting, *Loan Exhibition*, Oct. 15–closing date unknown (checklist).

60-T. Zurich, Kunsthaus Zürich, *Solomon R. Guggenheim Foundation: Zeitgenössische Kunst und Kunstpflege in U.S.A.*, Oct. 15–Dec. 15 (catalogue); (selections shown previously in Paris, Palais des Beaux-Arts, *Deuxième Salon des réalités nouvelles*, July 18–Aug. 17); Karlsruhe, Kunsthalle, as *Gegenstandlose Malerei in Amerika*, March 18–April 18, 1948 (no catalogue); Munich, Kunstrunde, May–June 1948 (no catalogue); Mannheim, Städtische Kunsthalle Mannheim, July 1948 (catalogue); Frankfurt am Main, Kunstkabinett, Aug.–Sept. 1948 (henceforth no catalogue); Kassel, Staatliche Kunstsammlungen, Oct. 1948; Braunschweig, Galerie Otto Ralfs, Nov. 1948; Hamburg, Kunstrunde, Dec. 1948; Hannover, Landesmuseum, Jan. 1949; Düsseldorf, Kunsthalle, 1949 (specific dates unknown); Essen, 1949 (institution and dates unknown); Karlsruhe, Kunsthalle, July 1949; Bremerhaven, Firma Nordkunst, Nov. 19–Dec. 25, 1949; Munich, Amerika-Haus, 1950 (specific dates unknown); Bremerhaven, Amerika-Haus, June–Aug. 1950; Hamburg, Amerika-Haus, Sept. 1950; Bremen, Amerika-Haus, Oct. 1950; Hamburg, Amerika-Haus, Nov. 1950; Braunschweig, Amerika-Haus, Dec. 1950.

1948

61. New York, N.Y., Museum of Non-Objective Painting, *Hilla Rebay*, Nov. 2, 1948–Jan. 16, 1949 (catalogue).

1949

62. New York, N.Y., Museum of Non-Objective Painting, *European Painters: Otto Nebel, Friedrich Vordemberge-Gildewart, Lotte Konnerth, Hannes Beckmann*, Jan. 18–Feb. 20 (checklist).

63. New York, N.Y., Museum of Non-Objective Painting, *New Exhibition, American Non-Objective Painters: Jordan Belson, Ilya Bolotowsky, Kenneth Campbell, Svend Clausen,*

Hohannesian, Ibram Lassaw, Alice T. Mason, Lloyd Ney, Hilla Rebay, Rolph Scarlett, Zahara Schatz, Charles Smith, Lucia Stern, Robert Wolff, Jean Xceron, Feb. 22–May 29 (checklist).

64. New York, N.Y., Museum of Non-Objective Painting, *Tenth Anniversary Exhibition*, May 31–Oct. 10.

65. New York, N.Y., Museum of Non-Objective Painting, *Loan Exhibition*, Oct. 11, 1949–Feb. 15, 1950 (checklist).

1950
66. New York, N.Y., Museum of Non-Objective Painting, *Loan Exhibition*, Feb. 21–June 11 (checklist).

67. New York, N.Y., Museum of Non-Objective Painting, *Loan Exhibition*, June 20–Oct. 9 (checklist).

68-T. Nantucket Island, Mass., Kenneth Taylor Galleries of the Nantucket Foundation, Inc., *Selections from the Solomon R. Guggenheim Foundation*, July.

69. New York, N.Y., Museum of Non-Objective Painting, *Loan Exhibition*, Nov. 14, 1950–March 1951 (checklist).

1951
70. New York, N.Y., Museum of Non-Objective Painting, *Loan Exhibition*, April 3–June 17 (checklist).

71-T. Avon, Conn., Avon Old Farms School, *Selections from the Solomon R. Guggenheim Foundation*, May.

72-T. Cazenovia, N.Y., Cazenovia Junior College, *Selections from the Solomon R. Guggenheim Foundation*, Oct. 1–14; Ithaca, N.Y., New York State College of Home Economics, Cornell University, Oct. 22–Nov. 9; Delaware, Ohio, Lyon Art Hall, Ohio Wesleyan University, Nov. 15–Dec. 9; Columbia, Mo., University of Missouri, Dec. 13, 1951–Jan. 21, 1952; Tallahassee, Fla., The University Museum and Art Gallery, Florida State University, Jan. 31–Feb. 22, 1952; Jacksonville, Ala., State Teachers College, March 4–26, 1952; Troy, N.Y., Faculty Club, Rensselaer Polytechnic Institute, April 22–May 15, 1952 (selections shown also at the Emma Willard School and the Troy Public Library); New Paltz, N.Y., State Teachers College, State University of New York, May 22–June 22, 1952.

73. New York, N.Y., Museum of Non-Objective Painting, *Loan Exhibition*, Nov. 27, 1951–closing date unknown (checklist).

1952
74. New York, N.Y., Museum of Non-Objective Painting, *Evolution to Non-Objectivity*,

April 29–closing date unknown (checklist).

75. New York, N.Y., Museum of Non-Objective Painting, *Group Exhibition: Gianni Dova, Elinor Evans, Ben Joppolo, Alberto Martini, Dale McKinney, J. Jay McVicker, Samuel Olkinetzky, Cesare Peverelli, Mauro Reggiani*, fall.

76-T. New Paltz, N.Y., State Teachers College, State University of New York, *Eighteen Non-Objective Paintings from the Solomon R. Guggenheim Foundation*, Oct. 10–Nov. 3; Garden City, N.Y., Adelphi College, Nov. 7–Dec. 1; Endicott, N.Y., Harpur College, Dec. 5–23; Summit, N.J., Jan. 16–Feb. 2, 1953.

1953
77-T. Rome, Galleria Origine, *Mostra Fondazione R. Solomon Guggenheim* [sic], Jan. 24–Feb. 20 (catalogue). Selections shown previously in Paris, Palais des Beaux-Arts de la Ville de Paris, *Septième Salon des réalités nouvelles*, July 18–Aug. 17, 1952.

78. S.R.G.M., *A Selection*, Feb. 4–May 3 (checklist).

79. S.R.G.M., *Selection II*, May 13–Nov. 22 (checklist).

80. S.R.G.M., *Sixty Years of Living Architecture: The Work of Frank Lloyd Wright*, Oct. 22–Dec. 13 (catalogue).

81. S.R.G.M., *Interim Exhibition of Museum Collection*, Dec. 2–13.

82. S.R.G.M., *Younger European Painters: A Selection*, Dec. 3, 1953–May 2, 1954; traveled to Minneapolis, Minn., Walker Art Center, Aug. 8–Sept. 24, 1954; Portland, Oreg., Portland Art Museum, Oct. 8–Nov. 14, 1954; San Francisco, Calif., San Francisco Museum of Art, Nov. 26, 1954–Jan. 23, 1955; Dallas, Tex., Dallas Museum of Fine Arts, Feb. 1–27, 1955; Fayetteville, Ark., University of Arkansas, March 7–April 9, 1955; Dayton, Ohio, The Dayton Art Institute, April 15–May 13, 1955; Andover, Mass., Addison Gallery of American Art, Phillips Academy, Oct. 1–31, 1955; Hanover, N.H., Carpenter Art Galleries, Dartmouth College, Nov. 5–Dec. 18, 1955; South Hadley, Mass., Dwight Art Memorial, Mount Holyoke College, Jan. 3–31, 1956; Middletown, Conn., Davison Art Center, Wesleyan University, Feb. 7–March 31, 1956 (catalogue).

1954
83. S.R.G.M., *Interim Exhibition of Museum Collection*, Jan. 5–March 21.

84. S.R.G.M., *Selection III*, March 31–May 5 (checklist).

85-T. Toronto, The Art Gallery of Toronto, *A Loan Exhibition from the Solomon R. Guggenheim Museum, New York*, April 2–May 9 (catalogue).

86. S.R.G.M., *Younger American Painters: A Selection*, May 12–Sept. 26; traveled to Portland, Oreg., Portland Art Museum, Sept. 2–Oct. 9, 1955; Seattle, Wash., Henry Gallery, University of Washington, Oct. 16–Nov. 13, 1955; San Francisco, Calif., San Francisco Museum of Art, Nov. 15, 1955–Jan. 22, 1956; Los Angeles, Calif., Los Angeles County Museum, Feb. 1–29, 1956; Fayetteville, Ark., University of Arkansas, March 9–April 10, 1956; New Orleans, La., Isaac Delgado Museum of Art, April 15–May 20, 1956 (catalogue).

87. S.R.G.M., *Selection IV*, Oct. 6, 1954–Feb. 27, 1955 (checklist).

88-T. Vancouver, Vancouver Art Gallery, *The Solomon R. Guggenheim Museum: A Selection from the Museum Collection*, Nov. 16–Dec. 12 (catalogue).

1955
89. S.R.G.M., *Interim Exhibition of Museum Collection*, March 1–13.

90-T. Boston, Mass., Institute of Contemporary Art, *Selected Paintings from the Guggenheim Museum*, March 9–April 17.

91. S.R.G.M., *Robert Delaunay*, March 22–May 22; traveled to Boston, Institute of Contemporary Art, June 2–30 (checklist).

92-T. Greensboro, N.C., Woman's College of the University of North Carolina, *Supplementary Exhibition of Drawings*, April 1–15; Atlanta, Ga., Georgia Institute of Technology, April 21–May 5; University, Ala., University of Alabama, May 11–25; Dallas, Tex., The Dallas Museum of Fine Arts, June 1–30; Tulsa, Okla., Philbrook Art Center, July 8–Aug. 5; Long Beach, Calif., Municipal Art Center, Aug. 15–Sept. 15; Reno, Nev., University of Nevada, Sept. 23–Oct. 7; Eugene, Oreg., University of Oregon, Oct. 18–Nov. 1; Seattle, Wash., Henry Gallery, University of Washington, Nov. 11–Dec. 30; Missoula, Mont., Montana State University, Jan. 9–21, 1956; remainder of tour canceled.

93-T. Montreal, The Montreal Museum of Fine Arts, *A Selection from the Solomon R. Guggenheim Museum, New York*, June 4–July 3 (catalogue).

94. S.R.G.M., *Alberto Giacometti*, June 8–July 17 (checklist).

95. S.R.G.M., *Selection V*, July 27–Oct. 9 (checklist).

96. S.R.G.M., *Constantin Brancusi*, Oct. 26, 1955–Jan. 8, 1956; traveled to Philadelphia, Pa., Philadelphia Museum of Art, Jan. 27–Feb. 26, 1956 (checklist).

1956
97. S.R.G.M., *Selection VI*, Jan. 25–May 1 (checklist).

98-T. Oberlin, Ohio, Allen Memorial Art Museum, *Supplementary Exhibition of Watercolors*, March 1–21; Cedar Rapids, Iowa, Coe College, March 28–April 19; Albion, Mich., Albion College, April 28–May 12; Hanover, N.H., Carpenter Art Galleries, Dartmouth College, May 21–June 15; Brunswick, Maine, Bowdoin College Museum of Fine Arts, June 24–July 22; University Park, Pa., The Pennsylvania State University, Nov. 1–21; Washington, D.C., Howard University, Nov. 30–Dec. 21; Savannah, Ga., Telfair Academy of Arts and Sciences, Jan. 3–24, 1957; New Orleans, La., Newcomb College, Tulane University, Feb. 2–23, 1957; University, Miss., Fine Arts Center, University of Mississippi, March 3–24, 1957; Lexington, Ky., University of Kentucky, April 2–23, 1957; Collegeville, Minn., St. John's University, May 3–24, 1957; Grand Rapids, Mich., Grand Rapids Art Gallery, June 1–23, 1957.

99-T. Cornish, N.H., Picture Gallery, Saint-Gaudens Memorial, *Painters of Today*, Aug. 3–Sept. 4 (checklist).

1957
100-T. Kalamazoo, Mich., Kalamazoo Institute of Arts, *Supplementary Exhibition of Drawings*, Feb. 3–24; Cedar Rapids, Iowa, Coe College, March 1–31; Beloit, Wis., Beloit College, April 5–28; Duluth, Minn., College of St. Scholastica, May 5–31; Laramie, Wyo., The University of Wyoming, June 10–Aug. 16; Bozeman, Mont., Montana State College, Sept. 22–Oct. 13; Caldwell, Idaho, The College of Idaho, Oct. 20–Nov. 10; Davis, Calif., University of California, Nov. 17–Dec. 15; Fayetteville, Ark., Arts Center Gallery, University of Arkansas, Jan. 5–26, 1958; Notre Dame, Ind., Art Gallery, University of Notre Dame, Feb. 2–23, 1958; South Hadley, Mass., Dwight Art Memorial, Mount Holyoke College, March 2–23, 1958.

101. S.R.G.M., *Jacques Villon, Raymond Duchamp-Villon, Marcel Duchamp*, Feb. 20–March 10; traveled to Houston, Tex., The Museum of Fine Arts, Houston, March 23–April 21 (catalogue with checklist insert).

102. S.R.G.M., *Guggenheim International Award, 1956*, March 27–June 7 (checklist). Entries judged in Paris shown at Musée National d'Art Moderne, Nov. 28–Dec. 15, 1956.

103-T. Williamstown, Mass., Lawrence Art Museum, Williams College, *Selection of American Paintings from the Solomon R. Guggenheim Museum*, April 8–28; Middletown, Conn., Davison Art Center, Wesleyan University, May 1–31.

104-T. London, Tate Gallery, *An Exhibition of Paintings from the Solomon R. Guggenheim Museum, New York*, April 16–May 26; The Hague, Haags Gemeentemuseum, June 25–Sept. 1; Helsinki, Ateneumin Taidekokoelmat, Sept. 27–Oct. 20; Rome, Galleria Nazionale d'Arte Moderna,

Dec. 5, 1957–Jan. 8, 1958; Cologne, Wallraf-Richartz-Museum, Jan. 26–March 30, 1958; Paris, Musée des Arts Décoratifs, April 23–June 1, 1958 (separate catalogue published by each museum).

105-T. Brussels, Palais des Beaux-Arts, *45 Oeuvres de Kandinsky provenant du Solomon R. Guggenheim Museum, New York*, May 17–June 30; Paris, Musée National d'Art Moderne, Nov. 15, 1957–Jan. 5, 1958; London, Tate Gallery, Jan. 15–Feb. 28, 1958; Lyon, Musée des Beaux-Arts, March 8–April 6, 1958; Oslo, Kunstnernes Hus, April 18–May 4, 1958; Rome, Galleria Nazionale d'Arte Moderna, May 15–June 30, 1950 (separate catalogue published by each museum).

106. S.R.G.M., *Recent Acquisitions and Loans*, June 12–Aug. 11 (checklist).

107. S.R.G.M., *Recent Acquisitions and Loans II*, Aug. 21–Dec. 1 (checklist).

108. S.R.G.M., *Piet Mondrian: The Earlier Years*, Dec. 11, 1957–Jan. 26, 1958; traveled to San Francisco, Calif., San Francisco Museum of Art, Feb. 6–April 14, 1958 (catalogue with checklist).

1958
109. S.R.G.M., *Sculptures and Drawings from Seven Sculptors*, Feb. 12–April 27 (checklist).

110-T. Portland, Maine, The Portland Museum of Art, *Supplementary Exhibition of Prints, 1958–1959*; Hamilton, N.Y., Colgate University; Cedar Rapids, Iowa, Coe College; Superior, Wis., State Teachers College; University Park, Pa., The Pennsylvania State University; Scranton, Pa., Marywood College; Charlotte, N.C., Mint Museum of Art; Athens, Ga., The University of Georgia; Talladega, Ala., Talladega College; Ypsilanti, Mich., Eastern Michigan College; Saratoga Springs, N.Y., Skidmore College.

111. S.R.G.M., *Recent Accessions*, May 14–Aug. 3 (checklist).

112. S.R.G.M., *Selections*, Aug. 13–Oct. 5 (checklist).

113-T. Baltimore, Md., The Baltimore Museum of Art, *Sixteen Paintings by Wassily Kandinsky from the Solomon R. Guggenheim Museum*, Sept. 20–Oct. 31.

114. S.R.G.M., *Guggenheim International Award, 1958*, Oct. 22, 1958–Feb. 23, 1959 (catalogue).

1959
115. S.R.G.M., *Twenty Contemporary Painters from the Philippe Dotremont Collection, Brussels*, April 1–May 24 (catalogue).

116. S.R.G.M., *Some Recent Gifts*, April 1–May 24 (checklist).

117-T. Toronto, The Art Gallery of Toronto, *Paintings by Kandinsky from the Collection of the Solomon R. Guggenheim Museum*, April 24–May 24.

118. S.R.G.M., *Inaugural Selection*, Oct. 21, 1959–June 19, 1960 (checklist).

119-T. Boston, Mass., Museum of Fine Arts, *A Salute to the Guggenheim Museum, Selected Works*, Oct. 30–Dec. 13 (checklist).

1960
120-T. Ann Arbor, Mich., The University of Michigan Museum of Art, *Images at Mid-Century*, April 13–June 12 (catalogue).

121-T. Chicago, Ill., The Arts Club of Chicago, *Sculpture and Drawings by Sculptors from the Solomon R. Guggenheim Museum*, April 19–May 19 (checklist with reproductions).

122-T. Lexington, Ky., University of Kentucky, *European Paintings from the Solomon R. Guggenheim Museum*, May 8–June 19 (catalogue).

123. S.R.G.M., *Before Picasso; After Miró*, June 21–Oct. 20 (catalogue with checklist).

124. S.R.G.M., *Guggenheim International Award, 1960*, Nov. 1, 1960–Jan. 29, 1961 (catalogue).

1961
125. S.R.G.M., *Paintings from the Arensberg and Gallatin Collections of the Philadelphia Museum of Art*, Feb. 7–April 16 (catalogue).

126. S.R.G.M., *Exhibition of Ceramic Mural by Miró* (*Untitled*, 1960, lent by Harvard University, Cambridge, Mass., prior to permanent installation), March 30–April 16.

127. S.R.G.M., *Acquisitions, 1953–1961*, April 19–May 21.

128. S.R.G.M., *One Hundred Paintings from the G. David Thompson Collection*, May 26–Aug. 27 (catalogue).

129. S.R.G.M., *Modern Masters from the Collection of the Solomon R. Guggenheim Museum*, Aug. 30–Oct. 8 (catalogue with checklist).

130. S.R.G.M., *Raymond Parker*, Aug. 30–Oct. 8 (checklist).

131. S.R.G.M., *Alfred Jensen*, Aug. 30–Oct. 8 (checklist).

132. S.R.G.M., *Elements of Modern Art*, Oct. 3–Nov. 12; reinstalled Jan. 9–25, 1962 (catalogue, *Elements of Modern Painting*, with checklist insert).

133. S.R.G.M., *American Abstract Expressionists and Imagists*, Oct. 13–Dec. 31 (catalogue).

134-T. Philadelphia, Pa., Philadelphia Museum of Art, *Guggenheim Museum Exhibition: A Loan Collection of Paintings, Drawings, and Prints from the Solomon R. Guggenheim Museum, New York*, Nov. 2, 1961–Jan. 7, 1962 (catalogue).

135. S.R.G.M., *Chryssa*, Nov. 14–Dec. 17 (checklist).

1962

136. S.R.G.M., *Sculpture from the Museum Collection*, Jan. 9–Feb. 25.

137. S.R.G.M., *Acquisitions, 1961*, Jan. 9–Feb. 25.

138. S.R.G.M., *Jan Müller, 1922–1958*, Jan. 11–Feb. 25; traveled to Boston, Mass., Institute of Contemporary Art, March 16–April 22 (catalogue).

139. S.R.G.M., *Fernand Léger: Five Themes and Variations*, Feb. 28–April 29 (catalogue).

140. S.R.G.M., *Antoni Tàpies*, March 22–May 13 (catalogue).

141. Minneapolis, Minn., University Gallery, University of Minnesota, *The Nineteenth Century: One Hundred Twenty-five Master Drawings*, March 26–April 23; traveled to S.R.G.M., May 15–June 28 (catalogue).

142. S.R.G.M., *Philip Guston*, May 3–July 1; traveled to Amsterdam, Stedelijk Museum, Sept. 21–Oct. 15; London, Whitechapel Art Gallery, Jan. 1–Feb. 15, 1963; Brussels, Palais des Beaux-Arts, March 1–31, 1963; Los Angeles, Calif., Los Angeles County Museum of Art, May 21–June 30, 1963 (catalogue).

143-T. Laguna Beach, Calif., Laguna Beach Art Association, *Elements of Modern Art* (selections from the Solomon R. Guggenheim Museum, circulated by the American Federation of Arts), July 1–30; Salt Lake City, Utah Museum of Fine Arts, Aug. 13–Sept. 3; Washington, D.C., The Phillips Collection, Sept. 17–Oct. 8; Oak Ridge, Tenn., Oak Ridge Community Art Center, Oct. 22–Nov. 12; Durham, N.C., Duke University, Nov. 26–Dec. 17; Oswego, N.Y., State University College Student Union, Jan. 1–22, 1963; Nashville, Tenn., Vanderbilt College, Feb. 5–25, 1963; Greensboro, N.C., Woman's College of the University of North Carolina, March 10–30, 1963; Charleston, Ill., Paul Sargent Gallery, Eastern Illinois University, April 13–May 4, 1963; Clinton, N.Y., Hamilton College, May 18–June 8, 1963; Tampa, Fla., University of Southern Florida, June 22–July 22, 1963; Memphis, Tenn., Brooks Memorial Art Gallery, Sept. 10–30, 1963; Lake Charles, La., Art Association of Lake Charles, Oct. 14–Nov. 4, 1963; Saratoga Springs, N.Y., Hathorn Gallery, Skidmore College, Nov. 18–Dec. 9, 1963; Grand Rapids, Mich., Grand Rapids Art Gallery, Jan. 3–24, 1964; Saginaw Mich., The Saginaw Museum,

Feb. 7–28, 1964 (catalogue, *Modern Art: An Introductory Commentary*, reprint of *Elements of Modern Painting*, for exhibition no. 132).

144. S.R.G.M., *Summer Selection, 1962*, July 3–Sept. 30 (checklist).

145. S.R.G.M., *Modern Sculpture from the Joseph H. Hirshhorn Collection*, Oct. 3, 1962–Jan. 20, 1963 (catalogue).

1963

146-T. Pasadena, Calif., The Pasadena Art Museum, *Vasily Kandinsky, 1866–1944: A Retrospective Exhibition*, Jan. 15–Feb. 15; San Francisco, Calif., San Francisco Museum of Art, March 1–April 1; Portland, Oreg., The Portland Art Museum, April 15–May 15; San Antonio, Tex., Marion Koogler McNay Art Institute, June 1–July 1; Colorado Springs, Colo., Colorado Springs Fine Arts Center, July 15–Aug. 25; Baltimore, Md., The Baltimore Museum of Art, Sept. 19–Oct. 20; Columbus, Ohio, The Columbus Gallery of Fine Arts, Nov. 5–Dec. 5; St. Louis, Mo., Washington University Art Gallery, Dec. 22, 1963–Jan. 6, 1964; Montreal, The Montreal Museum of Fine Arts, Feb. 5–March 5, 1964; Worcester, Mass., Worcester Art Museum, March 20–April 20, 1964 (catalogue).

147. S.R.G.M., *Vasily Kandinsky, 1866–1944: A Retrospective Exhibition*, Jan. 25–April 7; traveled to Paris, Musée National d'Art Moderne, April 29–June 24; The Hague, Haags Gemeentemuseum, July 1–Aug. 30; Basel, Kusthalle Basel, Sept. 7–Nov. 7 (catalogue).

148-T. Worcester, Mass., Worcester Art Museum, *Aspects of Twentieth-Century Painting Lent by the Solomon R. Guggenheim Museum, New York*, Feb. 7–April 7 (catalogue).

149. S.R.G.M., *Six Painters and the Object*, March 14–June 2; traveled to Los Angeles, Calif., Los Angeles County Museum of Art, July 24–Aug. 20; Minneapolis, Minn., Minneapolis Institute of Art, Sept. 3–29; Ann Arbor, Mich., University of Michigan Museum of Art, Oct. 9–Nov. 3; Waltham, Mass., Rose Art Museum, Brandeis University, Nov. 18–Dec. 29; Pittsburgh, Pa., Jan. 17–Feb. 23, 1964; Columbus, Ohio, The Columbus Gallery of Fine Arts, March 8–April 5, 1964; La Jolla, Calif., Art Center in La Jolla, April 20–May 17, 1964 (catalogue).

150. S.R.G.M., *Five Mural Panels Executed for Harvard University by Mark Rothko*, April 9–June 2.

151. S.R.G.M., *Museum Collection, Spring, 1963*, April 19–June 2 (checklist).

152. S.R.G.M., *Coins by Sculptors*, May 7–Aug. 26; traveled to Philadelphia, Pa., The Philadelphia National Bank, Sept. 20–27; Waltham, Mass., Brandeis University Library,

Oct. 21–Nov. 10; Philadelphia, Pa., Great Eastern Numismatic Society, Dec.

153. S.R.G.M., *Cézanne and Structure in Modern Painting*, June 6–Oct. 13 (catalogue with checklist insert).

154. S.R.G.M., *Morris Louis, 1912–1962: Memorial Exhibition*, Sept. 25–Oct. 27 (catalogue).

155. S.R.G.M., *Francis Bacon*, Oct. 18, 1963–Jan. 12, 1964; traveled to Chicago, Ill., The Art Institute of Chicago, Jan. 24–Feb. 23, 1964 (catalogue).

156. S.R.G.M., *20th-Century Master Drawings*, Nov. 6, 1963–Jan. 5, 1965; traveled to Minneapolis, Minn., University Gallery, University of Minnesota, Feb. 3–March 15, 1964; Cambridge, Mass., The Fogg Art Museum, Harvard University, April 6–May 24, 1964 (catalogue).

1964

157. S.R.G.M., *Guggenheim International Award, 1964*, Jan. 16–March 9; traveled to Honolulu, Hawaii, Honolulu Academy of Fine Arts, May 14–July 5; Berlin, Haus am Lützowplatz, Aug. 21–Sept. 15; Ottawa, The National Gallery of Canada, Oct. 5–Nov. 9; Sarasota, Fla., John and Mable Ringling Museum of Art, Jan. 16–March 14, 1965; Buenos Aires, Museo Nacional de Bellas Artes, April 20–May 20, 1965 (catalogue).

158. Washington, D.C., The Washington Gallery of Modern Art, *Vincent van Gogh: Paintings, Watercolors, and Drawings*, Feb. 1–March 18; traveled to S.R.G.M., April 2–June 28 (catalogue).

159-T. Tulsa, Okla., Philbrook Art Center, *Elements of Modern Art II* (selections from the Solomon R. Guggenheim Museum, circulated by the American Federation of Arts), March 1–22; Nashville, Tenn., Vanderbilt University, April 5–26; Charleston, W. Va., Charleston Civic Center, May 10–31; Muskegon, Mich., Hackley Art Gallery, June 14–July 5; Charleston, S.C., Gibbes Art Gallery, Sept. 27–Oct. 18; Saratoga Springs, N.Y., Hathorn Gallery, Skidmore College, Nov. 1–23; Philadelphia, Pa., Tyler School of Fine Art, Temple University, Dec. 6–27; Austin, Tex., Laguna Gloria Art Museum, Jan. 10–31, 1965; Norfolk, Va., Old Dominion College, Feb. 14–March 7, 1965; East Lansing, Mich., Kresge Art Center, Michigan State University, March 21–April 11, 1965; Montclair, N.J., Montclair Art Museum, May 2–30, 1965.

160. S.R.G.M., *Selections from the Museum Collection*, April 2–June 28.

161. S.R.G.M., *Frederick Kiesler: Environmental Sculpture*, May 5–June 28 (catalogue).

162. S.R.G.M., *Van Gogh and Expressionism*, July 1–Sept. 13 (catalogue with checklist insert).

163. S.R.G.M., *Albert Gleizes, 1881–1953: A Retrospective Exhibition*, Sept. 15–Nov. 1; traveled to Paris, Musée National d'Art Moderne, Dec. 5, 1964–Jan. 31, 1965; Dortmund, Museum am Ostwall, March 13–April 25, 1965 (catalogue).

164-T. San Francisco, Calif., San Francisco Museum of Art, *Albert Gleizes, 1881–1953: A Retrospective Exhibition*, Sept. 17–Nov. 1; St. Louis, Mo., City Art Museum of St. Louis, Nov. 19–Dec. 20; Champaign-Urbana, Ill., Krannert Art Museum, University of Illinois, Jan. 9–Feb. 21, 1965; Columbus, Ohio, The Columbus Gallery of Fine Arts, March 11–April 8, 1965; Ottawa, The National Gallery of Canada, April 23–May 23, 1965; Buffalo, N.Y., Albright-Knox Art Gallery, June 1–Aug. 30, 1965; Chicago, Ill., The Arts Club of Chicago, Sept. 20–Oct. 30, 1965 (same catalogue as previous exhibition).

165. S.R.G.M., *American Drawings*, Sept. 17–Oct. 27; traveled to Ann Arbor, Mich., University of Michigan Museum of Art, Nov. 11–Dec. 13; Grand Rapids, Mich., Grand Rapids Art Museum, Jan. 10–Feb. 7, 1965; Minneapolis, Minn., University Gallery, University of Minnesota, Feb. 24–March 21, 1965; Seattle, Wash., Seattle Art Museum, April 8–May 2, 1965; Denver, Colo., The Denver Art Museum, June 6–July 4, 1965; Dallas, Tex., Dallas Museum of Fine Arts, July 25–Aug. 22, 1965; Columbus, Ohio, The Columbus Gallery of Fine Arts, Sept. 12–Oct. 10, 1965; Champaign-Urbana, Ill., Krannert Art Museum, University of Illinois, Nov. 14–Dec. 5, 1965 (catalogue).

166. S.R.G.M., *Alexander Calder: A Retrospective Exhibition*, Nov. 6, 1964–Jan. 31, 1965; half of exhibition traveled to St. Louis, Mo., Washington University Gallery of Art, Feb. 21–March 26; Toronto, The Art Gallery of Toronto, April 30–May 30; half of exhibition traveled to Milwaukee, Wis., Milwaukee Art Center, Feb. 25–March 28; Des Moines, Iowa, Des Moines Art Center, April 28–May 30; entire exhibition traveled to Paris, Musée National d'Art Moderne, July 1–Oct. 15 (catalogue with checklist insert).

167. S.R.G.M., *The Shaped Canvas*, Dec. 9–29 (checklist with introductory essay and several reproductions).

1965
168. S.R.G.M., *Eleven from the Reuben Gallery*, Jan. 6–28 (pamphlet with introductory essays and several reproductions).

169-T. Caracas, Ateneo de Caracas, Jan. 10–Feb. 10, and Museo de Bellas Artes, Jan. 10–24, *Evaluación de la pintura latinoamericana, años '60*, preliminary version of exhibition *The Emergent*

Decade, organized by the Solomon R. Guggenheim Museum and Cornell University (checklist).

170. S.R.G.M., *Gustav Klimt and Egon Schiele*, Feb. 5–April 25 (catalogue).

171. S.R.G.M., *William Baziotes: A Memorial Exhibition*, Feb. 5–March 21; traveled to Cincinnati, Ohio, Cincinnati Art Museum, April 9–May 2; Reading, Pa., The Reading Public Museum and Art Gallery, May 23–June 27; Santa Barbara, Calif., Santa Barbara Museum of Art, July 13–Aug. 22; Milwaukee, Wis., Milwaukee Art Center, Sept. 9–Oct. 10; Waltham, Mass., Rose Art Center, Brandeis University, Nov. 1–30; Utica, N.Y., Munson-Williams-Proctor Institute, Dec. 11, 1965–Jan. 11, 1966; Columbus, Ohio, The Columbus Gallery of Fine Arts, Jan. 27–Feb. 28, 1966; Washington, D.C., The Corcoran Gallery of Art, March 15–April 15, 1966; Minneapolis, Minn., The Minneapolis Institute of Arts, May 15–June 15, 1966; Dallas, Tex., Dallas Museum of Fine Arts, July 4–Aug. 4, 1966; Akron, Ohio, Akron Art Institute, Oct. 10–Nov. 14, 1966 (catalogue).

172. S.R.G.M., *Illustrations for Opera by Gramatté and Lissitzky*, March 23–April 25.

173. S.R.G.M., *Paintings from the Collection of the Solomon R. Guggenheim Museum*, April 30–Oct. 3 (catalogue).

174. S.R.G.M., *Masterpieces of Modern Art, by Courtesy of the Thannhauser Foundation*, April 30–Oct. 3 (catalogue with insert of addenda to the exhibition).

175. Rotterdam, Museum Boymans-van Beuningen, *de Staël*, May 27–July 11; traveled to Kunsthaus Zürich, July 28–Sept. 5; Boston, Museum of Fine Arts, Oct. 1–Nov. 7; Chicago, Ill., The Art Institute of Chicago, Jan. 7–Feb. 13, 1966; S.R.G.M., Feb. 24–April 17, 1966 (catalogue).

176. S.R.G.M., *Some Recent Gifts*, June.

177. S.R.G.M., *Some Recent Gifts II*, July 20–Aug. 29.

178. S.R.G.M., *Jean Xceron*, Sept. 8–Oct. 10; traveled to Providence, R.I., Museum of Art, Rhode Island School of Design, April 7–May 1, 1966; Athens, Zappeion Palace, Oct. 3–30, 1966 (catalogue).

179. Ithaca, N.Y., Andrew Dickson White Museum, Cornell University, *The Emergent Decade: Latin American Painters and Painting in the 1960's*, Oct. 8–Nov. 8; Dallas, Tex., Dallas Museum of Fine Arts, Dec. 18, 1965–Jan. 18, 1966; Ottawa, The National Gallery of Canada, April 1–May 1, 1966; S.R.G.M., May 20–June 19, 1966; Champaign-Urbana, Ill.,

Krannert Art Museum, University of Illinois, Sept. 16–Oct. 9, 1966; Lincoln, Mass., DeCordova Museum, Nov. 6–Dec. 4, 1966; Sarasota, Fla., John and Mable Ringling Museum of Art, April 9–May 7, 1967. Organized by the Solomon R. Guggenheim Museum and Cornell University (related publication and brochure with checklist).

180. S.R.G.M., *Edvard Munch*, Oct. 15, 1965–Feb. 20, 1966 (catalogue).

181. S.R.G.M., *Word and Image*, Dec. 8, 1965–Jan. 2, 1966 (checklist with introductory essay).

1966
182. S.R.G.M., *The Photographic Image*, Jan. 12–Feb. 13 (checklist with introductory essay).

183. S.R.G.M., *European Drawings*, Feb. 24–April 17; traveled to Minneapolis, Minn., University Gallery, University of Minnesota, May 10–31; Lincoln, Mass., DeCordova Museum, June 26–Sept. 4; Providence, R.I., Museum of Art, Rhode Island School of Design, Sept. 14–Oct. 8; Ottawa, The National Gallery of Canada, Nov. 28–Dec. 25; Milwaukee, Wis., Milwaukee Art Center, Jan. 5–Feb. 5, 1967; Atlanta, Ga., The High Museum of Art, March 1–31, 1967; Dallas, Tex., Dallas Museum of Fine Arts, April 15–May 15, 1967; Champaign-Urbana, Ill., Krannert Art Museum, University of Illinois, May 28–June 25, 1967; Raleigh, N.C., The North Carolina Museum of Art, July 15–Aug. 20, 1967 (catalogue).

184. S.R.G.M., *Vasily Kandinsky, 1901–1914* (museum collection and loans), April 19–Sept. 18; loans returned, exhibition reinstalled Nov.; reinstalled Dec. 4, 1966–Feb. 12, 1967.

185. S.R.G.M., *Barnett Newman: The Stations of the Cross: lema sabachthani*, April 23–June 19 (catalogue).

186. S.R.G.M., *Museum Collection*, April 23–Sept. 18.

187. S.R.G.M., *Gauguin and the Decorative Style*, June 23–Oct. 23 (catalogue with checklist insert).

188-T. Richmond, Va., Virginia Museum of Fine Arts, *Masterpieces from the Collection of the Solomon R. Guggenheim Museum*, circulated in the Virginia Museum's "Artmobile," Sept. 15, 1966–Jan. 15, 1967.

189. S.R.G.M., *Systemic Painting*, Sept. 21–Nov. 27 (catalogue).

190. S.R.G.M., *Jean Dubuffet 1962–66*, Oct. 27, 1966–Feb. 5, 1967 (catalogue).

191. S.R.G.M., *Vasily Kandinsky: Painting on*

Glass (Hinterglasmalerei), Anniversary Exhibition, Dec. 4, 1966–Feb. 12, 1967 (catalogue).

1967

192. S.R.G.M., *Paul Klee, 1879–1940: A Retrospective Exhibition*, Feb. 17–April 30; traveled to Basel, Kunsthalle Basel, June 3–Aug. 16 (separate catalogue published by the two museums).

193-T. Pasadena, Calif., The Pasadena Art Museum, *Paul Klee, 1879–1940: A Retrospective Exhibition*, Feb. 21–April 2; San Francisco, Calif., San Francisco Museum of Art, April 13– May 14; Columbus, Ohio, The Columbus Gallery of Fine Arts, May 25–June 25; Cleveland, Ohio, The Cleveland Museum of Art, July 5–Aug. 13; Kansas City, Mo., William Rockhill Nelson Gallery of Art, Sept. 1–30; Baltimore, Md., The Baltimore Museum of Art, Oct. 24–Nov. 19; St. Louis, Mo., Washington University Gallery of Art, Dec. 3, 1967–Jan. 5, 1968; Philadelphia, Pa., Philadelphia Museum of Art, Jan. 15– Feb. 15, 1968. Organized by the Solomon R. Guggenheim Museum in collaboration with the Pasadena Art Museum (catalogue).

194. S.R.G.M., *Joseph Cornell*, May 4–June 25 (catalogue).

195. S.R.G.M., *Selections from the Museum Collection*, May 4–June 25.

196. S.R.G.M., *Museum Collection, Seven Decades, A Selection*, June 28–Oct. 1 (checklist).

197. S.R.G.M., *Guggenheim International Exhibition, 1967: Sculpture from Twenty Nations*, Oct. 20, 1967–Feb. 4, 1968; traveled to Toronto, Art Gallery of Ontario, Feb. 24–March 27, 1968; Ottawa, The National Gallery of Canada, April 26–June 9, 1968; Montreal, The Montreal Museum of Fine Arts, June 20–Aug. 18, 1968 (catalogue).

198-T. New York, N.Y., The Metropolitan Museum of Art, *Selections from the Solomon R. Guggenheim Museum*, Nov. 16, 1967–March 31, 1968.

1968

199. S.R.G.M., *Neo-Impressionism*, Feb. 9–April 7 (catalogue).

200. New York, Whitney Museum of American Art, Feb. 14–March 31, and Solomon R. Guggenheim Museum, Feb. 14–April 7, *Adolph Gottlieb* (joint exhibition); traveled to Washington, D.C., The Corcoran Gallery of Art, April 26–June 2; Waltham, Mass., Rose Art Museum, Brandeis University, Sept. 9– Oct. 20 (catalogue).

201. S.R.G.M., *Paul Feeley (1910–1966): A Memorial Exhibition*, April 11–May 26 (catalogue).

202. S.R.G.M., *Acquisitions of the 1930's and 1940's: A Selection of Paintings, Watercolors and Drawings in Tribute to Baroness Hilla von Rebay, 1890–1967*, April 11–May 26 (catalogue).

203. S.R.G.M., *Harold Tovish*, May 15–June 30 (checklist).

204. S.R.G.M., *Recent Acquisitions*, May 30– Sept. 8.

205. S.R.G.M., *Rousseau, Redon, and Fantasy*, May 31–Sept. 8 (catalogue with checklist insert).

206. San Francisco, Calif., San Francisco Museum of Art, *Julius Bissier, 1893–1965: A Retrospective Exhibition*, Sept. 18–Oct. 27; traveled to Washington, D.C., The Phillips Collection, Nov. 18–Dec. 22; Pittsburgh, Pa., Museum of Art, Carnegie Institute, Jan. 20–Feb. 23, 1969; Dallas, Tex., Dallas Museum of Fine Arts, March 19–April 20, 1969; S.R.G.M., May 16–June 29, 1969 (catalogue).

207-T. Columbus, Ohio, The Columbus Gallery of Fine Arts, *Paintings from the Solomon R. Guggenheim Museum*, Oct. 5, 1968–Sept. 7, 1969 (catalogue).

208. S.R.G.M., *A Selection of Works by Vasily Kandinsky (1866–1944) from the Museum Collection*, Oct. 8, 1968–Jan. 12, 1969.

209. S.R.G.M., *Mastercraftsmen of Ancient Peru*, Oct. 19, 1968–Jan. 11, 1969; traveled to Los Angeles, Calif., Los Angeles County Museum of Art, March 11–June 1, 1969 (catalogue).

210. Los Angeles, Calif., The UCLA Art Galleries, *Jean Arp (1886–1966): A Retrospective Exhibition*, Nov. 10–Dec. 5; traveled to Des Moines, Iowa, Des Moines Art Center, Jan. 11–Feb. 16, 1969; Dallas, Tex., Dallas Museum of Fine Arts, March 12–April 13, 1969; S.R.G.M., May 16–June 29, 1969 (monograph by H. Read, *The Art of Jean Arp*).

1969

211. S.R.G.M., *Works from the Peggy Guggenheim Foundation*, Jan. 16–March 23 (catalogue).

212. S.R.G.M., *Vasily Kandinsky, Selections from the Solomon R. Guggenheim Museum Collection*, Feb. 14–March 9.

213. S.R.G.M., *American Paintings from the Museum Collection*, March 28–May 11.

214. S.R.G.M., *Vasily Kandinsky: Thirteen Paintings from the Museum Collection*, March 28–May 11.

215. S.R.G.M., *David Smith*, March 29–May 11; traveled to Dallas, Tex., Dallas Museum of Fine Arts, June 25–Sept. 1; Washington, D.C.,

The Corcoran Gallery of Art, Oct. 18–Dec. 7 (catalogue).

216. S.R.G.M., *European Paintings from the Museum Collection*, April 25–May 11.

217. S.R.G.M., *Nine Young Artists, Theodoron Awards*, May 24–June 29 (catalogue with checklist).

218. Chicago, Ill., Museum of Contemporary Art, *Laszlo Moholy-Nagy*, May 31–July 12; traveled to Santa Barbara, Calif., Santa Barbara Museum of Art, Aug. 2–Sept. 21; Berkeley, Calif., University Art Museum, University of California, Oct. 2–Nov. 2; Seattle, Wash., Seattle Art Museum, Nov. 20, 1969–Jan. 4, 1970; S.R.G.M., Feb. 20–April 19, 1970 (catalogue).

219-T. New York, N.Y., Art Gallery, Center for Inter-American Relations, *Latin American Paintings from the Collection of the Solomon R. Guggenheim Museum*, July 2– Sept. 14 (catalogue).

220. S.R.G.M., *Selected Sculpture and Works on Paper*, July 8–Sept. 14 (catalogue).

221. S.R.G.M., *Collection: From the Turn of the Century to 1914*, Sept. 16–Oct. 12.

222. S.R.G.M., *Larger Paintings from the Museum Collection*, Sept. 18, 1969–Jan. 21, 1970.

223. S.R.G.M., *Roy Lichtenstein*, Sept. 19–Nov. 9; traveled to Kansas City, Mo., Nelson-Atkins Gallery of Art, Dec. 19, 1969–Jan. 18, 1970; Chicago, Ill., Museum of Contemporary Art, Feb. 7–March 22, 1970; Seattle, Wash., Seattle Art Museum, April 10–May 17, 1970; Columbus, Ohio, Columbus Gallery of Art, July 9–Aug. 30, 1970 (catalogue).

224. Philadelphia, Pa., Philadelphia Museum of Art, *Constantin Brancusi, 1876–1957: A Retrospective Exhibition*, Sept. 25–Nov. 2; S.R.G.M., Nov. 21, 1969–Feb. 15, 1970; Chicago, Ill., The Art Institute of Chicago, March 14–April 26, 1970 (catalogue); Bucharest, Muzeul de Arta R.S.R., June 6–Aug. 20, 1970 (separate catalogue). Organized by the Solomon R. Guggenheim Museum, The Art Institute of Chicago, and the Philadelphia Museum of Art.

225-T. Cincinnati, Ohio, Cincinnati Art Museum, *Paintings from the Guggenheim Museum: A Loan Exhibition of Modern Paintings Covering the Period 1949–1965*, Oct. 3, 1969–March 29, 1970 (catalogue).

226. S.R.G.M., *Vasily Kandinsky, 1866–1944: A Selection*, Oct. 14–Dec. 21; reinstalled Jan. 19– Feb. 8, 1970.

227. S.R.G.M., *Collection: From the First to the*

Second World War, 1915–1939, Dec. 13, 1969–Jan. 18, 1970.

1970

228. S.R.G.M., *Kandinsky, Klee, Feininger: 3 Bauhaus Painters*, Feb. 17–April 19.

229. S.R.G.M., *Sculpture Selections from the Museum Collection*, Feb. 19–April 5.

230. S.R.G.M., *Younger Artists from the Museum Collection*, April 21–Sept. 9.

231. Berkeley, Calif., University Art Museum, University of California, *Pol Bury*, April 28–May 31; St. Paul, Minn., The College of St. Catherine, and Minneapolis, Minn., Walker Art Center, Aug. 2–Sept. 10; Iowa City, Iowa, University of Iowa Museum of Art, Sept. 20–Oct. 31; Chicago, Ill., The Arts Club of Chicago, Nov. 24, 1970–Jan. 2, 1971; Houston, Tex., Institute for the Arts, Rice University, Jan. 25–March 7, 1971; S.R.G.M., April 15–June 6, 1971. Organized by the Solomon R. Guggenheim Museum and the University Art Museum (catalogue; Guggenheim Museum published an insert listing deletions and additions to the exhibition).

232. S.R.G.M., *Selections from the Guggenheim Museum Collection, 1900–1970*, May 1–Sept. 13 (fully illustrated handbook, *Selections from the Guggenheim Museum Collection, 1900–1970*).

233. S.R.G.M., *Francis Picabia: A Retrospective Exhibition*, Sept. 18–Dec. 6; traveled to Cincinnati, Ohio, Cincinnati Art Museum, Jan. 6–Feb. 7, 1971; Toronto, The Art Gallery of Ontario, Feb. 26–March 28, 1971; Detroit, Mich., The Detroit Institute of Arts, May 12–June 27, 1971 (catalogue).

234. S.R.G.M., *Carl Andre*, Sept. 29–Nov. 22; traveled to St. Louis, Mo., City Art Museum of St. Louis, May 13–June 27, 1971 (catalogue).

235. Ottawa, The National Gallery of Canada, *Joaquín Torres-García: 1879–1949*, Oct. 2–Nov. 1; traveled to S.R.G.M., Dec. 12, 1970–Jan. 31, 1971; Providence, R.I., Museum of Art, Rhode Island School of Design, Feb. 16–March 31, 1971 (catalogue).

236. S.R.G.M., *The Artist Responds to Crisis: A Sketch for an Exhibition*, Oct. 29–Dec. 3.

237. S.R.G.M., *Contemporary Japanese Art: Fifth Japan Art Festival Exhibition*, Dec. 2, 1970–Jan. 24, 1971; traveled to Philadelphia, Pa., Philadelphia Civic Center, Feb. 26–March 28, 1971; Berkeley, Calif., University Art Museum, University of California, May 25–June 27, 1971 (catalogue).

238. S.R.G.M., *Fangor*, Dec. 18, 1970–Feb. 7, 1971; traveled to Fort Worth, Tex., Fort Worth Art Center Museum, April 4–May 9, 1971;

Berkeley, Calif., University Art Museum, University of California, July 6–Aug. 22, 1971 (catalogue).

1971

239. S.R.G.M., *Guggenheim International Exhibition, 1971*, Feb. 12–April 11 (catalogue).

240. S.R.G.M., *Cubist Painters from the Museum Collection*, April 15–June 6.

241. S.R.G.M., *Selections from the Museum Collection and Recent Acquisitions, 1971*, June 11–Sept. 12 (handbook published for exhibition no. 232, with printed insert of addenda).

242. S.R.G.M., *A Summer with Children*, exhibition of the Guggenheim Museum's summer program in the arts for inner-city children, Sept. 10–19.

243. S.R.G.M., *Ten Young Artists: Theodoron Awards*, Sept. 24–Nov. 7 (catalogue and checklist).

244. S.R.G.M., *Piet Mondrian, 1872–1944: Centennial Exhibition*, Oct. 8–Dec. 12; traveled to Bern, Kunstmuseum Bern, Feb. 9–April 9, 1972 (catalogue).

245. S.R.G.M., *Robert Mangold*, Nov. 19, 1971–Jan. 2, 1972 (catalogue).

246. Washington, D.C., National Gallery of Art, *The Drawings of Rodin*, Nov. 20, 1971–Jan. 23, 1972 (catalogue); traveled to S.R.G.M., *Rodin Drawings: True and False*, March 10–May 7, 1972 (catalogue with checklist insert).

247. S.R.G.M., *John Chamberlain: A Retrospective Exhibition*, Dec. 22, 1971–Feb. 20, 1972 (catalogue).

248. S.R.G.M., *Museum Collection: Contemporary Prints and Drawings, Selections from the Permanent Collection and New Acquisitions of the 50's and 60's*, Dec. 24, 1971–March 10, 1972.

1972

249. S.R.G.M., *Ten Independents: An Artist-Initiated Exhibition*, Jan. 14–Feb. 27 (catalogue with checklist insert).

250. S.R.G.M., *Robert Ryman*, March 3–April 30 (catalogue).

251. S.R.G.M., *Classics in the Collection*, May 9–Aug. 27.

252. S.R.G.M., *Kandinsky at the Guggenheim Museum*, May 12–Sept. 5; traveled to Los Angeles, Calif., Los Angeles County Museum of Art, Oct. 3–Nov. 19; Minneapolis, Minn., Walker Art Center, May 5–July 15, 1973 (catalogue).

253. S.R.G.M., *Recent Acquisitions*, May 16–Aug. 27.

254. S.R.G.M., *Museum Pieces of the Post-War Era*, Sept. 7–Oct. 15 (checklist).

255. S.R.G.M., *A Year with Children*, Sept. 13–28.

256. S.R.G.M., *Amsterdam Paris Düsseldorf*, Oct. 6–Nov. 26; traveled to Pasadena, Calif., The Pasadena Art Museum, Feb. 20–April 8, 1973; Dallas, Tex., Dallas Museum of Fine Arts, May 2–June 3, 1973 (catalogue).

257. S.R.G.M., *Joan Miró: Magnetic Fields*, Oct. 26, 1972–Jan. 21, 1973 (catalogue).

258-T. Cleveland, Ohio, Cleveland Museum of Art, *Masterpieces from the Solomon R. Guggenheim Museum*, Nov. 15, 1972–Feb. 11, 1973 (catalogue).

259. Berkeley, Calif., University Art Museum, University of California, *Ferdinand Hodler*, Nov. 22, 1972–Jan. 7, 1973; traveled to S.R.G.M., Feb. 2–April 8, 1973; Cambridge, Mass., Busch-Reisinger Museum, Harvard University, May 1–June 22, 1973 (catalogue).

260. S.R.G.M., *Collection Exhibition*, Dec. 7, 1972–Feb. 22, 1973.

261. S.R.G.M., *Eva Hesse: A Memorial Exhibition*, Dec. 7, 1972–Feb. 11, 1973; traveled to Buffalo, N.Y., Albright-Knox Art Gallery, March 8–April 22, 1973; Chicago, Ill., Museum of Contemporary Art, May 19–July 8, 1973; Pasadena, Calif., The Pasadena Art Museum, Sept. 18–Nov. 11, 1973; Berkeley, Calif., University Art Museum, University of California, Dec. 12, 1973–Feb. 3, 1974 (catalogue).

1973

262. S.R.G.M., *American Painters through Two Decades from the Museum Collection*, Feb. 23–April 1.

263-T. Rochester, N.Y., Memorial Art Gallery of the University of Rochester, *Works from the Solomon R. Guggenheim Museum Collection*, Jan. 19–July 30.

264-T. Albany, New York, Albany Institute of History and Art, *Works from the Solomon R. Guggenheim Museum Collection*, Feb. 10–July 29.

265. S.R.G.M., *Jean Dubuffet: A Retrospective*, April 26–July 29 (catalogue); traveled to Paris, Centre National d'Art Contemporain, Sept. 27–Dec. 20 (catalogue).

266. S.R.G.M., *Selections from the Guggenheim Museum Collection: Recent Acquisitions 1972–73*, Aug. 9–Sept. 3.

267-T. Danville, Ky., Centre College of Kentucky, *Postwar Painting from the Solomon R. Guggenheim Museum*, Sept. 5, 1973–June 3, 1974.

268. S.R.G.M., *Richard Hamilton*, Sept. 14–Nov. 4 (catalogue); traveled to Cincinnati, Ohio, The Contemporary Arts Center, Jan. 7–Feb. 14, 1974; Munich, Städtische Galerie im Lenbachhaus, March 15–April 15, 1974; Tübingen, Kunsthalle Tübingen, May 10–June 30, 1974; Berlin, Nationalgalerie, July 16–Aug. 26, 1974 (catalogue).

269. S.R.G.M., *A Year with Children*, Sept. 21–Oct. 14 (folder with checklist).

270. University Park, Pa., Museum of Art, The Pennsylvania State University, *Cuno Amiet, Giovanni Giacometti, Augusto Giacometti: Three Swiss Painters*, Sept. 23–Nov. 4; traveled to Utica, N.Y., Museum of Art, Munson-Williams-Proctor Institute, Nov. 18–Dec. 30; Cambridge, Mass., Busch-Reisinger Museum, Harvard University, Feb. 1–March 9, 1974; S.R.G.M., April 5–June 23 (catalogue).

271. S.R.G.M., *Futurism: A Modern Focus: The Lydia and Harry Lewis Winston Collection, Dr. and Mrs. Barnett Malbin*, Nov. 16, 1973–Feb. 3, 1974 (catalogue).

272. S.R.G.M., *Kasimir Malevich*, Nov. 16, 1973–Jan. 13, 1974; traveled to Pasadena, Calif., The Pasadena Art Museum, Feb. 4–March 25, 1974 (catalogue).

1974
273. S.R.G.M., *The Graphic Work of Kandinsky*, Jan. 17–Feb. 24; traveled under the auspices of the International Exhibitions Foundation to Cincinnati, Ohio, Cincinnati Art Museum, April 1–30; Little Rock, Ark., Arkansas Arts Center, May 15–June 15; San Antonio, Tex., Marion Koogler McNay Art Institute, July 1–31; Houston, Tex., The Museum of Fine Arts, Houston, Aug. 15–Sept. 15; Fort Worth, Tex., Fort Worth Art Center, Oct. 1–31; Kansas City, Mo., William Rockhill Nelson Gallery and Atkins Museum of Fine Arts, Nov. 15–Dec. 15; Davenport, Iowa, Davenport Municipal Art Gallery, Jan. 4–Feb. 2, 1975; Detroit, Mich., The Detroit Institute of Arts, Feb. 15–March 16, 1975; Worcester, Mass., Worcester Art Museum, April 1–30, 1975; Washington, D.C., The Phillips Collection, May 15–June 15, 1975 (catalogue).

274. S.R.G.M., *Within the Decade: Selections from the Guggenheim Museum Permanent Collection*, Feb. 12–March 24.

275. S.R.G.M., *Alberto Giacometti: A Retrospective Exhibition*, April 5–June 23 (catalogue); traveled in part to Minneapolis, Minn., Walker Art Center, July 13–Sept. 1; Cleveland, Ohio, Cleveland Museum of Art, Sept. 24–Oct. 28; Ottawa, The National Gallery of Art, Nov. 15, 1974–Jan. 5, 1975; Des Moines, Iowa, Des Moines Art Center, Jan. 27–March 2, 1975 (catalogue); Montreal, Musée d'Art Contemporain, March 27–May 4, 1975 (catalogue).

276. S.R.G.M., *Concentrations I: Nine Modern Masters from the Guggenheim Museum and Thannhauser Collections*, July 4–Sept. 8.

277. S.R.G.M., *Ilya Bolotowsky*, Sept. 20–Nov. 11; traveled to Washington, D.C., The National Collection of Fine Arts, Dec. 21, 1974–Feb. 17, 1975 (catalogue).

278. S.R.G.M., *Jean Dubuffet: Recent Acquisitions and Permanent Collection*, Oct. 1–20.

279. S.R.G.M., *Soto: A Retrospective Exhibition*, Nov. 8, 1974–Jan. 26, 1975; traveled to Washington, D.C., Hirshhorn Museum and Sculpture Garden, Sept. 26–Nov. 9 (catalogue).

280. S.R.G.M., *Masters of Modern Sculpture: The Lydia and Harry Lewis Winston Collection (Dr. and Mrs. Barnett Malbin) and the Guggenheim Museum Collection*, Nov. 19, 1974–Feb. 4, 1975.

281. S.R.G.M., *A Year with Children*, Nov. 22, 1974–Jan. 5, 1975 (folder and checklist).

1975
282. S.R.G.M., *Max Ernst: A Retrospective Exhibition*, Feb. 14–April 20 (catalogue); traveled to Paris, Grand Palais, May 15–Sept. 8 (catalogue).

283. S.R.G.M., *Brice Marden*, March 7–April 27 (catalogue).

284. S.R.G.M., *Helen Frankenthaler Tiles*, May 2–June 1.

285. S.R.G.M., *Recent Acquisitions*, May 2–June 1.

286. S.R.G.M., *Museum Collection: Recent American Art*, May 11–Sept. 7.

287. S.R.G.M., *Marc Chagall*, June 8–Sept. 28. Organized by the International Exhibitions Foundation (catalogue).

288. S.R.G.M., *Jiří Kolář*, Sept. 12–Nov. 9 (catalogue).

289. S.R.G.M., *František Kupka, 1871–1957: A Retrospective*, Oct. 10–Dec. 7; traveled to Zurich, Kunsthaus Zürich, Jan.–March 1976 (catalogue and brochure).

290. S.R.G.M., *A Year with Children*, Nov. 21–Dec. 14 (checklist).

291. S.R.G.M., *Aristide Maillol: 1861–1944*, Dec. 19, 1975–March 21, 1976 (catalogue).

1976
292-T. Columbus, Ohio, The Columbus Gallery of Fine Arts, *Aspects of Postwar Painting in America*, Jan. 15–Feb. 29 (checklist).

293. S.R.G.M., *Twentieth-Century American Drawing: Three Avant-Garde Generations*, Jan. 23–March 23; traveled to Baden-Baden, Staatliche Kunsthalle Baden-Baden, May 27–July 11; Bremen, Kunsthalle Bremen, July 18–Aug. 29 (catalogue).

294. S.R.G.M., *Scott Burton: Pair Behavior Tableaux*, Feb. 24–April 5 (brochure).

295. S.R.G.M., *The Guggenheim Museum Collection: Paintings 1880–1945*, April 9–Oct. 3 (related collection catalogue and checklist).

296. S.R.G.M., *Constantin Brancusi*, April 15–May 9.

297. S.R.G.M., *Salvador Dalí*, May 25–July 11.

298. S.R.G.M., *Jean Arp: 1877–1966*, July 14–Aug. 22 (checklist).

299. S.R.G.M., *Frederick Kiesler*, Aug. 24–Sept. 12.

300. S.R.G.M., *Horia Damian: The Hill*, Sept. 16–Oct. 10 (catalogue).

301. S.R.G.M., *Joseph Schillinger: Salute to the Cooper-Hewitt Opening*, Oct. 5–Nov. 28.

302. S.R.G.M., *Acquisition Priorities: Aspects of Postwar Painting in America*, including "Arshile Gorky: Works 1944–1948," Oct. 15, 1976–Jan. 16, 1977 (catalogue and checklist).

303-T. Winston-Salem, N.C., Wake Forest University Art Gallery, *European Art from the Solomon R. Guggenheim Museum*, Oct. 19, 1976–May 20, 1977.

304. S.R.G.M., *A Year with Children*, Oct. 29–Nov. 14.

305. S.R.G.M., *Piet Mondrian at the Guggenheim Museum*, Nov. 19, 1976–April 7, 1977.

1977
306. Chicago, Ill., The Art Institute of Chicago, *James Ensor: A Retrospective*, Nov. 6, 1976–Jan. 3, 1977; S.R.G.M., Jan. 28–April 11. Organized by the Solomon R. Guggenheim Museum and the Art Institute of Chicago (catalogue).

307. S.R.G.M., *Recent Acquisitions*, Feb. 4–27.

308. S.R.G.M., *Nine Artists: Theodoron Awards*, March 4–April 7 (catalogue).

309. S.R.G.M., *Kenneth Noland: A Retrospective*, April 15–June 19; traveled to Washington, D.C., Hirshhorn Museum and Sculpture Garden and the Corcoran Gallery of Art, Sept. 29–Nov. 27; Toledo, Ohio, The Toledo Museum of Art, Jan. 22–March 8, 1978; Denver, Colo., The Denver Art Museum, March 23–May 7, 1978 (catalogue).

310. S.R.G.M., *Klee at the Guggenheim Museum*, June 24–Sept. 5; traveled to Montreal, Musée d'Art Contemporain, Sept. 18–Oct. 23; Quebec, Musée du Québec, Nov. 3–Dec. 4; Milwaukee, Wis., Milwaukee Art Center, Feb. 2–March 18, 1978; Berkeley, Calif., University Art Museum, University of California, April 11–June 4, 1978; Cleveland, Ohio, Cleveland Museum of Art, July 6–Sept. 3, 1978; Baltimore, Md., The Baltimore Museum of Art, Sept. 26–Nov. 19, 1978; Richmond, Va., Virginia Museum of Fine Arts, Jan. 1–Feb. 18, 1979 (catalogue and newsletter).

311. S.R.G.M., *American Postwar Painting from the Guggenheim Collection*, July 1–Sept. 11.

312. S.R.G.M., *Forty Modern Masters*, July 1–Sept. 11 (brochure with checklist).

313. S.R.G.M., *Recent Gifts and Purchases*, Sept. 16–Oct. 16.

314. S.R.G.M., *David Hare*, Sept. 30–Oct. 30 (brochure with checklist).

315. S.R.G.M., *From the American Collection*, Sept. 30–Dec. 5.

316. S.R.G.M., *Lucio Fontana, 1899–1968: A Retrospective*, Oct. 21–Dec. 8 (catalogue and newsletter).

317. S.R.G.M., *A Year with Children*, Nov. 18–Dec. 4.

318. S.R.G.M., *From the American Collection: New Additions*, Nov. 22, 1977–Jan. 8, 1978.

319. S.R.G.M., *Forty Modern Masters: An Anniversary Show*, Dec. 16, 1977–Feb. 1, 1978 (brochure and checklist).

1978

320. S.R.G.M., *Jiří Kolář at the Guggenheim Museum*, Jan. 19–March 26 (brochure with checklist).

321. S.R.G.M., *Collection: American Sculpture*, Jan. 24–April 16.

322. S.R.G.M., *Willem de Kooning in East Hampton*, Feb. 10–April 23 (catalogue and brochure).

323. S.R.G.M., *The Evelyn Sharp Collection*, April 1–Oct. 1 (catalogue and brochure).

324. S.R.G.M., *Salvador Dalí–Special Viewing*, April 25–30.

325. S.R.G.M., *Young American Artists: 1978 Exxon National Exhibition*, May 5–June 11 (catalogue and brochure).

326. Washington, D.C., National Collection of Fine Arts, Smithsonian Institution, *Attilio*

Salemme: Inhabitant of a Dream, March 3–May 7; traveled to S.R.G.M., May 19–July 4 (catalogue).

327. Los Angeles, Calif., Frederick S. Wight Art Gallery, University of California, *Alberto Burri: A Retrospective View 1948–1977*, Sept. 25–Dec. 4, 1977; traveled to San Antonio, Tex., Marion Koogler McNay Art Institute, Jan. 8–Feb. 19; Milwaukee, Wis., Milwaukee Art Center, March 30–May 21; S.R.G.M., June 20–Aug. 27 (catalogue and brochure).

328. S.R.G.M., *School of Paris: The Solomon R. Guggenheim Museum Collection*, July 7–Oct. 1.

329. Amsterdam, Stedelijk Museum, *Hendrik Nicolaas Werkman 1882–1945: "Druksel" Prints and General Printed Matter*, Sept. 16–Nov. 6, 1977; traveled to S.R.G.M., Aug. 18–Sept. 15; Pittsburgh, Pa., Museum of Art, Carnegie Institute, Oct. 5–Nov. 19; Los Angeles, Calif., Los Angeles County Museum of Art, Feb.–March 1979; La Jolla, Calif., La Jolla Museum of Contemporary Art, April–May 1979 (catalogue).

330. Paris, Musée National d'Art Moderne, Centre Georges Pompidou, *Henri Michaux*, March 15–June 14; traveled to S.R.G.M., Sept. 8–Oct. 15; Montreal, Musée d'Art Contemporain, Nov. 2–Dec. 10 (catalogue and brochure).

331. S.R.G.M., *Selected Acquisitions*, Sept. 8–Oct. 15 (brochure and checklist).

332-T. Midland, Mich., Midland Art Center, *Prints from the Guggenheim Museum Collection*, Sept. 17–Oct. 22; Brookings, S.Dak., South Dakota Memorial Art Center, Nov. 19–Dec. 24; Tucson, Ariz., University of Arizona Museum of Art, Jan. 21–Feb. 25, 1979; Tampa, Fla., Tampa Bay Art Center, March 25–April 29, 1979; Mansfield, Ohio, The Mansfield Art Center, July 29–Sept. 2, 1979; Anchorage, Alaska, Anchorage Historical and Fine Arts Center, Sept. 30–Nov. 4, 1979; Shreveport, La., Shreveport Art Guild, Dec. 2, 1979–Jan. 6, 1980; Ames, Iowa, Brunnier Gallery, Iowa State Center, Feb. 3–March 9, 1980; Tyler, Tex., Tyler Museum of Art, March 29–May 11, 1980; Minneapolis, Minn., University Gallery, University of Minnesota, June 8–July 13; Little Rock, Ark., Arkansas Art Center, Aug. 10–Sept. 15, 1980. Traveled under the auspices of the American Federation of Arts (catalogue).

333. S.R.G.M., *Mark Rothko, 1903–1970: A Retrospective*, Oct. 27, 1978–Jan. 14, 1979; traveled to Houston, Tex., The Museum of Fine Arts, Houston, Feb. 8–April 1, 1979; Minneapolis, Minn., Walker Art Center, April 21–June 10, 1979; Los Angeles, Calif., Los Angeles County Museum of Art, July 3–Sept. 26, 1979 (catalogue and brochure).

334. S.R.G.M., *OMA: The Sparkling Metropolis*, Nov. 16–Dec. 17 (brochure).

335. S.R.G.M., *The Justin K. Thannhauser Collection* (permanent installation), opened Dec. 14 (collection catalogue).

336. S.R.G.M., *A Year with Children*, Dec. 22, 1978–Jan. 7, 1979.

1979

337. S.R.G.M., *Collection: Art in America after World War II*, Jan. 18–Feb. 25.

338. S.R.G.M., *Piet Mondrian at the Guggenheim*, Jan. 18–May 6.

339. S.R.G.M., *Modern Masters in France*, March 1–Aug. 12 (brochure).

340. S.R.G.M., *The Planar Dimension: Europe, 1912–1932*, March 9–May 6 (catalogue and brochure with checklist).

341. S.R.G.M., *Rufino Tamayo: Myth and Magic*, May 18–Aug. 12 (catalogue and brochure).

342. S.R.G.M., *Master Drawings and Watercolors of the Nineteenth and Twentieth Centuries, the Baltimore Museum of Art*, Aug. 24–Oct. 14. Organized by the American Federation of Arts (catalogue).

343. S.R.G.M., *Matisse in the Collection of the Baltimore Museum of Art*, Aug. 24–Oct. 14.

344. S.R.G.M., *George Rickey*, Sept. 7–Oct. 14 (brochure with checklist).

345-T. Tokyo, Daimaru Museum, *Modigliani*, Sept. 13–Oct. 16; Osaka, Daimaru Museum, Oct. 25–Nov. 6. Organized by the Solomon R. Guggenheim Museum in cooperation with the Mainichi Newspapers (catalogue).

346. S.R.G.M., *Joseph Beuys*, Nov. 2, 1979–Jan. 2, 1980 (catalogue and brochure).

347. S.R.G.M., *Paul Klee 1879–1979: Anniversary Selection*, Dec. 1, 1979–March 27, 1980.

348. S.R.G.M., *A Year with Children*, Nov. 15–Dec. 5 (brochure).

1980

349. S.R.G.M., *Ad Reinhardt and Color*, Jan. 11–March 9 (catalogue).

350. S.R.G.M., *British Art Now: An American Perspective, 1980 Exxon International Exhibition*, Jan. 11–March 9; traveled under the auspices of the American Federation of Arts to San Diego, Calif., San Diego Museum of Art, March 28–April 25; Savannah, Ga., Telfair Academy of Arts and Sciences, May 14–June 11; Austin, Tex., University Art Museum,

University of Texas, July 6–Aug. 17; traveled under the auspices of the British Council to London, Royal Academy of Arts, Oct. 18–Dec. 14 (catalogue).

351. S.R.G.M., *Selected Acquisitions*, Feb. 5–March 16.

352. Pittsburgh, Pa., Museum of Art, Carnegie Institute, *Eduardo Chillida: The Graphic Works*, Oct. 26, 1979–Jan. 6, 1980; traveled in part to S.R.G.M., March 21–May 11 (catalogue and brochure with checklist).

353. S.R.G.M., *New Images from Spain*, March 21–May 11; traveled to San Antonio, Tex., Marion Koogler McNay Art Institute, July 20–Aug. 31; San Francisco, Calif., San Francisco Museum of Modern Art, Oct. 5–Nov. 30; Tucson, Ariz., Tucson Museum of Art, Jan. 17–March 8, 1981; Colorado Springs, Colo., Colorado Springs Fine Arts Center, April 25–June 15, 1981; Albuquerque, N.M., Museum of Albuquerque, Sept. 20–Nov. 29, 1981 (catalogue).

354. S.R.G.M., *Kinetics around a Fountain: Pol Bury*, May 17–June 22 (brochure).

355. S.R.G.M., *1900–1980 from the Guggenheim Museum Collection*, May 23–Nov. 2 (collection catalogue: *Handbook: The Guggenheim Museum Collection, 1900–1980*).

356. S.R.G.M., *Some Recent Acquisitions*, June 24–Aug. 10.

357. S.R.G.M., *The Evelyn Sharp Collection*, June 24–Aug. 20, portions on view throughout 1980 (catalogue).

358. S.R.G.M., *Some Recent Acquisitions*, Aug. 12–Sept. 8.

359. S.R.G.M., *Agam: Beyond the Visible*, Sept. 25–Nov. 2 (brochure).

360. S.R.G.M., *Paul Klee: Works from the Collection*, opened Oct. 18.

361. S.R.G.M., *Expressionism: A German Intuition, 1905–1920*, Nov. 14, 1980–Jan. 18, 1981; traveled to San Francisco, Calif., San Francisco Museum of Modern Art, Feb. 19–April 26, 1981 (catalogue and brochure).

362. S.R.G.M., *A Year with Children*, Dec. 18, 1980–Jan. 8, 1981.

1981
363-T. Baltimore, Md., The Baltimore Museum of Art, *Kandinsky Watercolors: A Selection from the Solomon R. Guggenheim Museum and the Hilla von Rebay Foundation*, Jan. 6–March 1; Atlanta, Ga., The High Museum of Art, March 28–May 31; Cleveland, Ohio, Cleveland Museum of Art, July 21–Sept. 27; Chicago, Ill., David and

Alfred Smart Gallery, University of Chicago, Oct. 15–Nov. 29; San Diego, Calif., San Diego Museum of Art, Dec. 18, 1981–Jan. 31, 1982; Honolulu, Hawaii, Honolulu Academy of Arts, April 9–May 16, 1982; Portland, Oreg., Portland Art Museum, June 15–Aug. 15, 1982; Chapel Hill, N.C., The William Hayes Ackland Art Museum, University of North Carolina, Sept. 6–Oct. 17, 1982; Gainesville, Fla., University Gallery, University of Florida, Oct. 31–Dec. 12, 1982 (catalogue).

365. S.R.G.M., *Contemporary Americans: Museum Collection and Recent Acquisitions*, Jan. 29–April 12.

366. S.R.G.M., *Nineteen Artists—Emergent Americans: 1981 Exxon National Exhibition*, Jan. 30–April 5 (catalogue and brochure).

367. S.R.G.M., *Richard Navin: The Mycenae Circle*, Feb. 13–March 8 (catalogue).

368. S.R.G.M., *Arshile Gorky, 1904–1948: A Retrospective*, April 24–July 19; traveled to Dallas, Tex., Dallas Museum of Fine Arts, Sept. 11–Nov. 6; Los Angeles, Calif., Los Angeles County Museum of Art, Dec. 3, 1981–Feb. 28, 1982 (catalogue and brochure).

369. S.R.G.M., *Selections from the Guggenheim Museum Collection: Precursors of Arshile Gorky*, April 24–July 19.

370. S.R.G.M., *The Sibyl H. Edwards Bequest*, May 20–Sept. 27 (brochure with checklist).

371-T. Toyama, Japan, The Museum of Modern Art, *Toyama Now '81* (U.S. section, "Photorealism," organized by the Solomon R. Guggenheim Museum), July 5–Sept. 23 (catalogue).

372. S.R.G.M., *Jean Dubuffet: A Retrospective Glance at Eighty*, July 31–Sept. 27 (catalogue).

373. S.R.G.M., *Abstract Expressions, 1930–1950: Works from the Collection*, July 31–Sept. 27.

374. S.R.G.M., *Postwar American Painting from the Permanent Collection*, Oct. 6–Nov. 8.

375. S.R.G.M., *Recent Acquisitions, 1979–1981*, Oct. 6–Nov. 8.

376. S.R.G.M., *Seven Photorealists from New York Collections*, Oct. 6–Nov. 8 (brochure with checklist).

377. S.R.G.M., *Art of the Avant-Garde in Russia: Selections from the George Costakis Collection*, Oct. 16, 1981–Jan. 3, 1982; traveled to Houston, Tex., The Museum of Fine Arts, Houston, March 11–May 9, 1982; Ottawa, The National Gallery of Canada, July 8–Sept. 6, 1982; Indianapolis, Ind., Indianapolis Museum of Art, Oct. 17–Dec. 2, 1982; Chicago, Ill., Museum of

Contemporary Art, Jan. 14–March 13, 1983; Stockholm, Moderna Museet, April 23–Aug. 7, 1983; London, Royal Academy of Arts, Sept. 17–Nov. 13, 1983; Munich, Städtische Galerie im Lenbachhaus, Jan. 18–March 11, 1984; Hannover, Kestner-Gesellschaft, March 23–May 13, 1984; Helsinki, Helsingin Kaupungin Taidemuseo, June 15–Oct. 28, 1984 (catalogue and brochure).

378. San Francisco, Calif., San Francisco Museum of Modern Art, *Giorgio Morandi*, Sept. 24–Nov. 1; S.R.G.M., Nov. 20, 1981–Jan. 17, 1982; Des Moines, Iowa, Des Moines Art Center, Feb. 1–March 14, 1982. Organized by the Des Moines Art Center (catalogue).

379. S.R.G.M., *A Year with Children*, Dec. 17, 1981–Jan. 10, 1982.

1982
380. S.R.G.M., *Kandinsky in Munich: 1896–1914*, Jan. 22–March 21; traveled to San Francisco, Calif., San Francisco Museum of Modern Art, April 22–June 20; Munich, Städtische Galerie im Lenbachhaus, Aug. 17–Oct. 17 (catalogue and brochure).

364-T. Rome, Pinacoteca Capitolina, *Guggenheim, Venezia–New York: Sessanta opere, 1900–1950*, Jan. 23–March 28. Organized by the Peggy Guggenheim Collection, with the Solomon R. Guggenheim Museum (catalogue).

381. S.R.G.M., *Dan Flavin*, Jan. 29–March 14.

382. S.R.G.M., *Recent Acquisitions, 1981*, Feb. 4–July 1.

383. S.R.G.M., *Italian Art Now: An American Perspective, 1982 Exxon International Exhibition*, April 2–June 20 (catalogue).

384. S.R.G.M., *Jack Tworkov: Fifteen Years of Painting*, April 6–June 20 (catalogue).

385-T. Sydney, Art Gallery of New South Wales, *Kandinsky: Selected Works from the Solomon R. Guggenheim Museum and the Hilla von Rebay Foundation*, May 13–June 13; Brisbane, Queensland Art Gallery, June 21–Aug. 8; Adelaide, Art Gallery of South Australia, Aug. 26–Sept. 26; Perth, Art Gallery of Western Australia, Oct. 8–Nov. 7; Melbourne, National Gallery of Victoria, Nov. 12–Dec. 12 (catalogue).

386. S.R.G.M., *The New York School: Four Decades, Guggenheim Museum Collection and Major Loans*, July 1–Aug. 29 (brochure).

387. S.R.G.M., *Recent Acquisitions, 1981–1982*, July 1–Sept. 6.

388. S.R.G.M., *Asger Jorn*, Sept. 14–Nov. 7; traveled to London, Barbican Art Gallery, Feb. 15–April 10, 1983; Silkeborg, Denmark,

Silkeborg Kunstmuseum, May 7–June 5, 1983 (catalogue).

389. S.R.G.M., *Öyvind Fahlström*, Sept. 14–Nov. 7; traveled to Minneapolis, Minn., Walker Art Center, Feb. 6–March 27, 1983 (catalogue).

390. S.R.G.M., *Sleeping Beauty–Art Now*, Sept. 14–Nov. 7; traveled to Philadelphia, Pa., Port of History Museum, Dec. 17, 1982–Jan. 30, 1983; Los Angeles, Calif., Los Angeles Municipal Art Center Gallery, March 5–April 17, 1983 (catalogue).

391. S.R.G.M., *Jan Matulka: Recent Acquisitions*, Sept. 21–Nov. 7.

392. S.R.G.M., *Sixty Works: The Peggy Guggenheim Collection*, Nov. 18, 1982–March 13, 1983 (catalogue).

393. Houston, Tex., Institute for the Arts, Rice University, *Yves Klein (1928–1962): A Retrospective*, Feb. 5–May 2; traveled to Chicago, Ill., Museum of Contemporary Art, June 18–Aug. 29; S.R.G.M., Nov. 19, 1982–Jan. 9, 1983; Paris, Musée National d'Art Moderne, Centre Georges Pompidou, Feb. 17–May 23, 1983 (catalogue and brochure).

394-T. New York, N.Y., Hastings Gallery, The Spanish Institute, *Spanish Drawings and Graphics from the Guggenheim Museum*, Nov. 12–Dec. 17; Framingham, Mass., Danforth Museum of Art, Dec. 27, 1982–Feb. 27, 1983.

395. S.R.G.M., *American Sculpture from the Permanent Collection*, Nov. 23, 1982–March 13, 1983.

396. S.R.G.M., *A Year with Children*, Dec. 11, 1982–Jan. 17, 1983.

1983
397. Paris, Musée National d'Art Moderne, Centre Georges Pompidou, *Yves Tanguy: A Retrospective*, June 17–Sept. 27, 1982; traveled to Baden-Baden, Staatliche Kunsthalle Baden-Baden, Oct. 17, 1982–Jan. 2, 1983; S.R.G.M., Jan. 21–Feb. 27 (catalogue and brochure with checklist).

398. S.R.G.M., *An Homage to Joan Miró at Ninety*, Jan. 21–Feb. 27 (brochure with checklist).

399. S.R.G.M., *Dan Flavin*, Jan. 21–Feb. 27.

400. S.R.G.M., *Jean Dubuffet*, Jan. 21–March 13.

401. S.R.G.M., *Pol Bury Fountain*, Jan. 21–Sept. 5.

402. S.R.G.M., *Julio González: A Retrospective*, March 11–May 8; traveled to Frankfurt, Städelsches Kunstinstitut und Städtische Galerie, June 16–Aug. 14; Berlin, Akademie der Künste, Sept. 4–Oct. 23 (catalogue and brochure).

403. S.R.G.M., *Recent Acquisitions: Works on Paper*, March 17–May 15.

404. S.R.G.M., *Aspects of British Art from the Solomon R. Guggenheim Museum Collection*, March 25–May 8 (brochure).

405. S.R.G.M., *Jean Ipoustéguy: Sculpture and Ten Works on Paper*, May 20–July 17 (brochure with checklist).

406. S.R.G.M., *Recent European Painting*, May 20–Sept. 4.

407. S.R.G.M., *Acquisition Priorities: Aspects of Postwar Painting in Europe*, May 20–Sept. 11 (catalogue with checklist).

408. S.R.G.M., *Summer Sculpture Show*, May 23–Sept. 4.

409. S.R.G.M., *Jean Dubuffet, Les Phénomènes: August 1958–April 1962*, May 24–Sept. 11.

410. S.R.G.M., *Recent Acquisitions, 1983*, July 22–Sept. 25.

411-T. Lawrence, Kans., Helen Foresman Spencer Museum of Art, University of Kansas, *Early Modern Art from the Guggenheim Museum*, Aug. 15, 1983–June 15, 1984 (brochure).

412. Chicago, Ill., Museum of Contemporary Art, *Charles Simonds*, Nov. 7, 1981–Jan. 3, 1982; traveled to Los Angeles, Calif., Los Angeles County Museum of Art, Jan. 28–March 21, 1982; Fort Worth, Tex., Fort Worth Art Museum, April 13–May 30, 1982; Houston, Tex., Contemporary Arts Museum, June 21–Aug. 15, 1982; Omaha, Nebr., Joslyn Art Museum, Jan. 15–March 6; S.R.G.M., Sept. 23–Oct. 30 (special installation of *Age* at Guggenheim; catalogue and brochure).

413. S.R.G.M., *New Perspectives in American Art: 1983 Exxon National Exhibition*, Sept. 30–Nov. 27 (catalogue).

414. S.R.G.M., *Twentieth-Century Sculpture: A Selection from the Permanent Collection*, Sept. 30–Dec. 11.

415-T. Tokyo, Tokyo Metropolitan Teien Art Museum, *Modern Art in the West*, Oct. 1–Dec. 25 (catalogue).

416-T. Birmingham, Ala., Birmingham Museum of Art, *American Art: Post World War II Painting and Sculpture*, Oct. 13, 1983–April 1, 1985 (brochure).

417. S.R.G.M., *Trends in Postwar American and European Art*, Nov. 8–27, 1983.

418. S.R.G.M., *Kandinsky: Russian and Bauhaus Years, 1915–1933*, Dec. 9, 1983–Feb. 12, 1984; traveled to Atlanta, Ga., The High Museum of Art, March 15–April 29, 1984; Zurich, Kunsthaus Zürich, May 30–July 15, 1984; Berlin, Bauhaus-Archiv, Aug. 9–Sept. 23, 1984 (catalogue and brochure).

419-T. San Antonio, Tex., San Antonio Museum of Art, *Myth and Reality: The Art of Modern Latin America*, Dec. 11, 1983–Sept. 9, 1984.

420. S.R.G.M., *Homage to Lisbeth Bissier*, Dec. 12, 1983–Feb. 12, 1984 (brochure with checklist).

421. S.R.G.M., *Japanese Art in the Guggenheim Museum Collection*, Dec. 16, 1983–Feb. 19, 1984.

1984
Venice, Gallerie dell'Accademia, *Jackson Pollock 1942–1947*, Jan. 19–March 31. Organized by the Peggy Guggenheim Collection (catalogue).

422-T. Sydney, Art Gallery of New South Wales, *The Moderns*, Feb. 7–March 25 (catalogue).

423. S.R.G.M., *Postwar American Art from the Collection*, Feb. 17–March 18.

424. S.R.G.M., *Walter Stein*, Feb. 17–March 25 (brochure with checklist).

425. S.R.G.M., *Picasso: The Last Years, 1963–1973*, March 2–May 13. Organized by Gert Schiff for the Grey Art Gallery and Study Center, New York University, and shown at the Guggenheim (catalogue).

426. S.R.G.M., *A Year with Children*, March 30–April 29.

427. S.R.G.M., *Eduardo Arroyo*, March 30–June 3.

428. S.R.G.M., *Michael Singer*, March 30–July 8 (catalogue).

429-T. Allentown, Pa., Allentown Art Museum, *Modern Sculpture from the Guggenheim*, April 15, 1984–Jan. 27, 1985 (brochure).

430. Washington, D.C., National Gallery of Art, *Juan Gris*, Oct. 16–Dec. 31, 1983; Berkeley, Calif., University Art Museum, University of California, Feb. 1–April 8; S.R.G.M., May 18–July 8. Organized by the University Art Museum (catalogue).

431. S.R.G.M., *Painting in Paris, 1909–1927: A Selection from the Permanent Collection*, May 25–Sept. 16.

432. S.R.G.M., *Recent Acquisitions*, June 8–Aug. 5.

433. S.R.G.M., *From Degas to Calder: Major Sculpture and Works on Paper from the Guggenheim Museum Collection*, July 20–Sept. 9 (brochure and checklist).

434. S.R.G.M., *Expressionist Watercolors and Drawings*, Aug. 10–Oct. 14.

435-T. Worcester, Mass., Worcester Art Museum, *Paul Klee from the Guggenheim: The Bauhaus Years*, Sept. 11, 1984–Feb. 28, 1985 (catalogue).

436. S.R.G.M., *Will Insley: The Opaque Civilization*, Sept. 21–Nov. 25 (catalogue).

437. S.R.G.M., *Australian Visions: 1984 Exxon International Exhibition*, Sept. 25–Nov. 25; traveled to Brisbane, Queensland Art Gallery, Jan. 10–Feb. 10, 1985; Sydney, Art Gallery of New South Wales, Feb. 26–April 7, 1985; Perth, Art Gallery of Western Australia, May 2–June 2, 1985 (catalogue).

438-T. Ann Arbor, Mich., The University of Michigan Museum of Art, *The Wild Eye: The Influence of Surrealism on American Art*, Sept. 28, 1984–June 16, 1985 (catalogue).

439. S.R.G.M., *Horst Antes: Votives*, Oct. 12, 1984–Feb. 3, 1985 (brochure with checklist).

440. S.R.G.M., *Norris Embry*, Oct. 12–Dec. 16.

441. Buffalo, N.Y., Albright-Knox Art Gallery, *Robert Motherwell*, Oct. 1–Nov. 27, 1983; traveled to Los Angeles, Calif., Los Angeles County Museum of Art, Jan. 5–March 4; San Francisco, Calif., San Francisco Museum of Modern Art, April 12–June 3; Seattle Art Museum, June 21–Aug. 5; Washington, D.C., The Corcoran Gallery of Art, Sept. 15–Nov. 4; S.R.G.M., Dec. 7, 1984–Feb. 3, 1985 (catalogue, brochure, and checklist).

442. S.R.G.M., *Henri Michaux, 1899–1984: In Memoriam*, Dec. 21, 1984–Feb. 3, 1985.

1985

443. S.R.G.M., *Ree Morton: Manipulations of the Organic*, Feb. 8–March 24.

Venice, Gallerie dell'Accademia, *Nove artisti della "Scuola di New York,"* Feb. 8–April 8. Organized by the Peggy Guggenheim Collection (catalogue).

444. S.R.G.M., *Kandinsky in Paris: 1934–1944*, Feb. 15–April 14; traveled to Houston, Tex., The Museum of Fine Arts, Houston, June 8–Aug. 11; Milan, Palazzo Reale, Sept. 19–Nov. 10; Vienna, Museum des 20. Jahrhunderts, Dec. 5, 1985–Jan. 26, 1986 (catalogue and brochure).

445. S.R.G.M., *Frankenthaler: Works on Paper 1949–1984*, Feb. 22–April 21; Edmonton, The Edmonton Art Gallery, May 11–July 7;

Cambridge, Mass., Harvard University Art Museums, Oct. 5–Nov. 24; Baltimore, Md., The Baltimore Museum of Art, Dec. 15, 1985–Feb. 16, 1986; San Francisco, Calif., San Francisco Museum of Modern Art, March 6–April 27, 1986; Houston, Tex., The Museum of Fine Arts, Houston, June 14–July 27, 1986. Organized by the International Exhibitions Foundation (catalogue).

446-T. P.G.C., *Six Modern Masters from the Guggenheim Museum, New York*, March 10–April 8; Nov. 1–Dec. 30 (catalogues in English and Italian); Milan, Padiglione d'Arte Contemporanea, *I Maestri del Guggenheim*, May 5–July 26 (catalogue).

P.G.C., *Tauromaquia: Goya–Picasso*, March 3–April 8; Nov. 1–Dec. 30; Milan, Padiglione d'Arte Contemporanea, May 12–July 26; Bari, Castello Svevo, April 5–May 31, 1986; London, Warwick Arts Trust, Sept. 24–Oct. 26, 1986; Antibes, France, Musée Picasso, Dec. 10, 1986–Feb. 8, 1987; Madrid, Cason del Buen Retiro, April 30–June 6, 1987; Barcelona, Palau de la Virreina, June 30–Aug. 25, 1987; New Brunswick, Canada, Beaverbrook Art Gallery, May 15–Aug. 29, 1993 (several editions of catalogue).

447. S.R.G.M., *A Year with Children*, March 29–April 28.

448. S.R.G.M., *Eduardo Chillida*, March 29–May 12 (catalogue).

449. Baltimore, Md., The Baltimore Museum of Art, *Gilbert and George*, Feb. 19–April 15, 1984; traveled to Houston, Tex., Contemporary Arts Museum, June 23–Aug. 19, 1984; West Palm Beach, Florida, The Norton Gallery and School of Art, Sept. 29–Nov. 25, 1984; Milwaukee, Wis., Milwaukee Art Museum, Jan. 11–March 17; S.R.G.M., April 26–June 16 (catalogue).

450. Washington, D.C., National Gallery of Art, *Mark Rothko: Works on Paper*, May 6–Aug. 5, 1984; Pittsburgh, Pa., Museum of Art, Carnegie Institute, Nov. 3, 1984–Jan. 6, 1985; Houston, Tex., The Menil Foundation, Jan. 27–March 3; S.R.G.M., May 3–June 16; Milwaukee, Wis., Milwaukee Art Museum, Nov. 17, 1985–Jan. 2, 1986; Portland, Oreg., Portland Art Museum, Feb. 9–April 6, 1986; San Francisco, Calif., San Francisco Museum of Modern Art, May 4–June 29, 1986; St. Louis, Mo., The St. Louis Art Museum, July 18–Sept. 1, 1986. Organized by the Mark Rothko Foundation, Inc., and the American Federation of Arts (catalogue).

451. S.R.G.M., *Giulio Paolini*, May 17–July 7.

452. S.R.G.M., *Painterly Visions, 1940–1984: The Guggenheim Museum Collection and Major Loans*, June 28–Sept. 2 (brochure and checklist).

453. S.R.G.M., *Recent Acquisitions*, July 12–Sept. 15.

454. S.R.G.M., *Alfred Jensen: Paintings and Works on Paper*, Sept. 10–Nov. 3 (catalogue).

455. S.R.G.M., *New Horizons in American Art: 1985 Exxon National Exhibition*, Sept. 12–Nov. 3 (catalogue).

456. S.R.G.M., *Pablo Serrano: The Guitar and Cubism*, Sept. 20–Nov. 10 (catalogue).

457-T. Berkeley, Calif., University Art Museum, University of California, *Early Modern Art*, Oct. 7, 1985–Jan. 11, 1987.

458. S.R.G.M., *Jiří Kolář: Chiasmages*, Nov. 15, 1985–Jan. 5, 1986 (brochure).

459. S.R.G.M., *Transformations in Sculpture: Four Decades of American and European Art*, Nov. 22, 1985–Feb. 16, 1986 (catalogue).

1986

460. S.R.G.M., *Recent Acquisitions*, Jan. 10–March 9.

461. S.R.G.M., *By the Muse Inspired*, Feb. 12, 1986–Jan. 5, 1987.

P.G.C., *Homage to Jean Hélion: Recent Works*, March 6–April 14 (catalogue).

462-T/484-T. Hamilton, N.Y., The Picker Art Gallery, Colgate University, *Abstraction, Non-Objectivity, and Realism: Twentieth-Century Painting from the Solomon R. Guggenheim Museum*, March 9, 1986–May 31, 1987.

463. S.R.G.M., *Jack Youngerman*, Feb. 28–April 27 (catalogue).

464. Dallas, Tex., Dallas Museum of Art, *Naum Gabo: Sixty Years of Constructivism*, Sept. 29–Nov. 17, 1985; Toronto, Art Gallery of Ontario, Dec. 13, 1985–Feb. 9, 1986; S.R.G.M., March 7–April 27; Berlin, Akademie der Künste, Sept. 7–Oct. 19; Düsseldorf, Kunstsammlung Nordrhein-Westfalen, Nov. 20, 1986–Jan. 11, 1987; London, Tate Gallery, Feb. 11–April 20, 1987. Organized by the Dallas Museum of Art and the Kunstsammlung Nordrhein-Westfalen (catalogue).

465-T. P.G.C., *A Half-Century of European Painting, 1910–1960, from the Guggenheim Museum, New York*, March 6–April 14; Frankfurt, Schirn Kunsthalle Frankfurt, June 22–Aug. 24 (catalogue).

466. S.R.G.M., *A Year with Children*, March 14–April 13.

467. S.R.G.M., *Charles Seliger*, March 14–May 18 (brochure with checklist).

468-T. Madrid, Biblioteca Nacional, *Contrastes de forma: Abstracción geométrica, 1910–1980, de las colecciones del Solomon R. Guggenheim Museum y The Museum of Modern Art, New York*, April 17–June 8; Buenos Aires, Museo Nacional de Bellas Artes, July 15–Aug. 25; São Paolo, Museu de Arte de São Paulo/Assis Chateaubriand, Sept. 18–Oct. 19; Caracas, Museo de Arte Contemporáneo de Caracas, Nov. 11, 1986–Jan. 4, 1987. Organized by the Solomon R. Guggenheim Museum and the International Council of the Museum of Modern Art (catalogue).

469. S.R.G.M., *Enzo Cucchi*, May 6–July 6 (catalogue).

470. S.R.G.M., *German Realist Drawings of the 1920s*, May 16–July 6; Cambridge, Mass., Busch-Reisinger Museum, Harvard University Art Museums, July 26–Sept. 28; Stuttgart, Staatsgalerie Stuttgart, Oct. 25–Dec. 28. Organized by the Harvard University Art Museums (catalogue).

471. S.R.G.M., *Proposal for a Guggenheim Museum Addition–Showcase for Hidden Treasures*, May 20–Sept. 21 (installed in part through Nov. 9).

472. S.R.G.M., *Jan Groth*, July 18–Sept. 1 (catalogue).

473. S.R.G.M., *The Expressive Figure from Rousseau to Bacon: European Art in the Guggenheim Museum Collection*, July 18–Sept. 21 (catalogue and checklist).

474. S.R.G.M., *Homage to Louise Nevelson: Selection of Works from the Permanent Collection*, July 24–Sept. 1 (brochure with checklist).

475. S.R.G.M., *Richard Long*, Sept. 12–Nov. 30 (catalogue).

476. S.R.G.M., *Angles of Vision: French Art Today, 1986 Exxon International Exhibition*, Oct. 3–Nov. 30 (catalogue).

P.G.C., *Jean Dubuffet and Art Brut*, Nov. 16, 1986–March 16, 1987 (catalogue).

477. London, Tate Gallery, *Oskar Kokoschka, 1886–1980*, June 11–Aug. 10; traveled to Zurich, Kunsthaus Zürich, Sept. 4–Nov. 9; S.R.G.M., Dec. 9, 1986–Feb. 16, 1987 (exhibition altered for Guggenheim presentation; catalogue and brochure).

478. S.R.G.M., *The Knife Ship from "Il Corso del Coltello,"* Dec. 16, 1986–Feb. 16, 1987 (previously shown in Venice, Campo dell'Arsenale, Sept. 6–8, 1985; catalogue).

1987
479. S.R.G.M., *Recent Acquisitions*, Feb. 20–March 22.

480. S.R.G.M., *Pierre Alechinsky: Margin and Center*, Feb. 27–May 3; traveled to Des Moines, Iowa, Des Moines Art Center, Oct. 2–Dec. 6; Hannover, Kunstverein Hannover, Feb. 28–April 17, 1988; Brussels, Musées Royaux des Beaux-Arts de Belgique, Musée d'Art Moderne, May 5–June 26, 1988 (catalogue).

481-T. Iowa City, Iowa, University of Iowa Museum of Art, *Two Collections, Two Views: Selections from the Solomon R. Guggenheim Museum and the University of Iowa Museum of Art*, Feb. 7–Aug. 16, 1987.

482. S.R.G.M., *Revised Proposal for a New Addition*, Feb. 24–early Sept. (brochure).

483. S.R.G.M., *Peggy Guggenheim's Other Legacy*, March 6–May 3; P.G.C., *La eredità sconosciute di Peggy Guggenheim*, Oct. 31, 1987–Jan. 10, 1988. Organized by the Solomon R. Guggenheim Museum and the Peggy Guggenheim Collection (catalogues in English and Italian).

485. S.R.G.M., *Contemporary American and European Drawings: Recent Gifts of Norman Dubrow*, March 27–May 12.

486. Zurich, Kunsthaus Zürich, *Joan Miró, A Retrospective*, Nov. 21, 1986–Feb. 1, 1987; Düsseldorf, Städtische Kunsthalle Düsseldorf, Feb. 14–April 20; S.R.G.M., May 15–Aug. 23. Organized by the Kunsthaus Zürich and Städtische Kunsthalle Düsseldorf; altered for Guggenheim presentation (catalogue and brochure).

487. S.R.G.M., *A Year with Children*, May 29–July 5.

488. S.R.G.M., *Emerging Artists: 1978–1986: Selections from the Exxon Series*, Sept. 3–Nov. 1 (catalogue).

489. S.R.G.M., *Jan Dibbets*, Sept. 11–Nov. 1; Minneapolis, Minn., Walker Art Center, Jan. 17–March 27, 1988; Detroit, Mich., The Detroit Institute of Arts, April 29–June 19, 1988; West Palm Beach, Fla., The Norton Gallery and School of Art, July 30–Oct. 2, 1988; Eindhoven, Stedelijk Van Abbemuseum, Nov. 6, 1988–Jan. 1, 1989. Organized by the Walker Art Center (catalogue).

490-T. Columbia, S.C., Columbia Museum of Art, *A Quiet Revolution: American Abstract Art from the Solomon R. Guggenheim Museum*, Oct. 1, 1987–Aug. 28, 1988 (catalogue).

491. S.R.G.M., *Fifty Years of Collecting: An Anniversary Selection, Painting by Modern Masters*, Nov. 13, 1987–March 13, 1988 (catalogue).

492. S.R.G.M., *Fifty Years of Collecting: An Anniversary Selection, Sculpture of the Modern Era*, Nov. 13, 1987–March 13, 1988 (catalogue).

493. S.R.G.M., *Fifty Years of Collecting: An Anniversary Selection, Painting since World War II in Europe*, Nov. 13–Dec. 20 (one catalogue for nos. 493–95).

494. S.R.G.M., *Fifty Years of Collecting: An Anniversary Selection, Painting since World War II in Latin America*, Dec. 23, 1987–Jan. 31, 1988 (one catalogue for nos. 493–95).

1988
495. S.R.G.M., *Fifty Years of Collecting: An Anniversary Selection, Painting since World War II in North America*, Feb. 4–March 13 (one catalogue for nos. 493–95).

P.G.C., *Tre artisti italo-americani: Giorgio Cavallon–Costantino Nivola–Italo Scanga*, March 2–April 4; traveled to Cagliari, Cittadella dei Musei, July 27–Aug. 28; Bari, Castello Svevo, Sept. 10–Oct. 12 (catalogue).

496. S.R.G.M., *Josef Albers: A Retrospective*, March 24–May 29; traveled to Baden-Baden, Staatliche Kunsthalle Baden-Baden, June 12–July 24; Berlin, Bauhaus-Archiv, Aug. 10–Oct. 4; Pori, Finland, Pori Art Museum, Oct. 19–Dec. 3 (catalogue and brochure).

497. S.R.G.M., *Aspects of Collage, Assemblage and the Found Object in Twentieth-Century Art*, March 29–May 22 (brochure).

498. S.R.G.M., *Hans Reichel*, May 6–June 19 (brochure with checklist).

499. S.R.G.M., *Modern Treasures from the National Gallery in Prague*, June 3–Sept. 18; Quebec, Musée du Québec, Sept. 30–Nov. 20. Organized by the Solomon R. Guggenheim Museum and the Národní Galerie (catalogue).

Mantua, Palazzo Ducale, *Arte italiana del dopoguerra dai musei Guggenheim*, June 18–Sept. 30. Organized by the Peggy Guggenheim Collection (catalogue).

500-T. Katonah, N.Y., Katonah Gallery of Art, *Jiří Kolář, Chiasmage, Selections from the Solomon R. Guggenheim Museum*, Aug. 8–Sept. 25 (brochure).

501. Munich, Kunsthalle der Hypo-Kulturstiftung, *Georges Braque*, March 4–May 15; S.R.G.M., June 10–Sept. 11. Organized by the Solomon R. Guggenheim Museum and the Kunsthalle der Hypo-Kulturstiftung (catalogue).

502. S.R.G.M., *Recent Acquisitions*, June 24–Sept. 4.

503. S.R.G.M., *Hans Hinterreiter*, Sept. 9–Oct. 23.

504. S.R.G.M., *A Year with Children*, Sept. 23–
Nov. 5.

505. S.R.G.M., *Return to the Object: American and
European Art of the 1950s and 1960s from the
Guggenheim Museum Collection*, Sept. 23–Nov. 27.

506. S.R.G.M., *Andy Warhol, Cars*, Sept. 30–
Nov. 27; Tokyo, Shinjuku Isetan Museum,
April 27–May 23, 1989; Kyoto, Kyoto Daimaru
Museum, May 25–June 5, 1989; Shibukawa,
Hara Museum ARC, June 11–Aug. 5, 1989;
Sapporo, Hokkaido Museum of Modern Art,
Aug. 26–Sept. 24, 1989; Fukuoka, Fukuoka
Prefectural Museum of Art; Oct. 3–29, 1989;
Takamatsu, Kagawa Prefectural Cultural
Center, Nov. 3–26, 1989. Organized by the
Kunsthalle Tübingen and Werner Spies
(catalogue).

507. S.R.G.M., *Landmarks of New York*, Oct. 10–
Oct. 31.

508. S.R.G.M., *Douglas Davis*, Oct. 28–Nov. 27
(brochure with checklist).

509-T. Prague, Národní Galerie, *Modern
Treasures from the Solomon R. Guggenheim
Foundation*, Nov. 1, 1988–Jan. 1, 1989; Berlin,
Nationalgalerie, Jan. 19–March 19, 1989
(catalogue).

P.G.C., *Omaggio a Lucio Fontana*, Nov. 4,
1988–March 5, 1989; traveled to New York,
N.Y., Murray and Isabella Rayburn Foundation,
Homage to Lucio Fontana, April 12–June 16, 1989
(catalogue).

510. S.R.G.M., *The Early Years: Non-Objective
Paintings from the Permanent Collection*,
Nov. 11–Dec. 4 (brochure with checklist).

511. S.R.G.M., *Gifts of Mr. and Mrs. Alexander
Liberman*, Dec. 2, 1988–Jan. 29, 1989.

512. S.R.G.M., *Viewpoints: Postwar Painting and
Sculpture from the Guggenheim Museum Collection
and Major Loans*, Dec. 9, 1988–Jan. 22, 1989
(brochure).

1989
513. Toledo, Ohio, The Toledo Museum
of Art, *Refigured Painting: The German
Image 1960–88*, Oct. 30, 1988–Jan. 8, 1989;
S.R.G.M., Feb. 10–April 23; Düsseldorf,
Kunstmuseum Düsseldorf, May 20–July 30;
Frankfurt, Schirn Kunsthalle Frankfurt,
Sept. 12–Nov. 12. A selection shown
concurrently at Williamstown, Mass.,
Williams College Museum of Art,
Feb. 10–March 26. Organized by the Solomon
R. Guggenheim Museum and the Williams
College Museum of Art (catalogue, brochure,
and checklist).

514. S.R.G.M., *Arnulf Rainer*, May 13–July 9;
Chicago, Museum of Contemporary Art,

July 29–Oct. 15; Vienna, Historisches Museum
der Stadt Wien, Nov. 15, 1989–Jan. 30, 1990;
The Hague, Haags Gemeentemuseum, Jan.–
Feb. 1990. Organized by the Haags
Gemeentemuseum in collaboration with the
Solomon R. Guggenheim Museum (catalogue).

515. S.R.G.M., *A Year with Children*, May 19–
June 11 (brochure).

516. S.R.G.M., *Hannelore Baron*, May 19–July 23
(brochure with checklist).

517. S.R.G.M., *Selections from the Permanent
Collection*, May 26–Sept. 3.

518. S.R.G.M., *Mario Merz*, Sept. 28–Nov. 26
(catalogue and checklist).

519-T. *Kandinsky: Works from the Hilla von Rebay
Foundation*, Westport, Conn., Westport Arts
Center, Oct. 1–15.

520. S.R.G.M., *Jenny Holzer*, Dec. 12, 1989–
Feb. 25, 1990 (catalogue and brochure).

521. S.R.G.M., *Geometric Abstraction and
Minimalism in America*, Dec. 15, 1989–Feb. 28,
1990 (checklist).

522. S.R.G.M., *Piet Mondrian and the
Non-Objective*, Dec. 15, 1989–Feb. 18, 1990
(checklist).

1990
523. S.R.G.M., *Masterpieces from the Collection*,
varied installation on view Feb. 21–April 29.

524-T. Venice, Fondazione Giorgio Cini,
*Mondrian and De Stijl and Masters of the Modern
Ideal*, May 19–Sept. 2 (catalogue).

P.G.C., *La France à Venise* (part of 44th Venice
Biennale), May 23–Sept. 30 (catalogue).

P.G.C., *The Guggenheim Museum Salzburg: A
Project by Hans Hollein*, May 25–Sept. 1; traveled
to Salzburg, Residenzgalerie, July 1–Sept. 1
(catalogue).

525-T. Salzburg, Residenzgalerie, *Masterpieces
from the Guggenheim Museum*, July 25–Sept. 1
(catalogue and brochure).

P.G.C., *Contemporary Art in a Modern Context*,
Sept. 9, 1990–Sept. 9, 1991 (brochure).

526-T. Venice, Palazzo Grassi, *From van
Gogh to Picasso, from Kandinsky to Pollock:
Masterpieces of Modern Art*, Sept. 9–Dec. 9;
Madrid, Museo Nacional Centro de Arte Reina
Sofía, *Obras maestras de la colección Guggenheim:
De Picasso a Pollock*, Jan. 17–May 13, 1991;
Tokyo, Sezon Museum of Art, *Masterpieces
from the Guggenheim Collection: From Picasso to
Pollock*, June 20–Sept. 1, 1991; Sydney, Art
Gallery of New South Wales, *Masterpieces*

from the Guggenheim, Sept. 22, 1991–Jan. 12,
1992; Montreal, The Montreal Museum of Fine
Arts, *Masterpieces from the Guggenheim*, Feb. 4–
April 26, 1992 (exhibition modified for each
venue; separate catalogue for each venue).

527-T. St. Petersburg, Fla., Museum of Fine
Arts, *Twentieth-Century European Paintings from
the Guggenheim Museum* (Collection-Sharing
Program), Sept. 23, 1990–Aug. 31, 1991
(catalogue and checklist).

528-T. Coral Gables, Fla., The Lowe Art
Museum, University of Miami, *A Claim to
Primacy*, Oct. 11–Dec. 9 (catalogue and
checklist).

1991
529-T. Youngstown, Ohio, The Butler
Institute of American Art, *Postwar America:
Works from the Collection of the Guggenheim
Museum*, Jan. 20–Nov. 30 (checklist).

530-T. Indianapolis, Ind., Indianapolis Museum
of Art, works lent through the Guggenheim
Museum's Collection-Sharing Program for the
Indianapolis Museum of Art's reinstallation,
March 22–Nov. 30.

531-T. Madrid, Banco Bilbao Vizcaya Corporate
Headquarters, *Kandinsky acuarelas: Colección
del Museo Solomon R. Guggenheim y de la
Fundación Hilla von Rebay*, April 9–June 1;
Rome, Palazzo delle Esposizioni, *Kandinsky:
Acquerelli dal Museo Guggenheim*, June 7–Aug. 4;
Vienna, Historisches Museum der Stadt Wien,
*Kandinsky Aquarelle aus dem Guggenheim
Museum*, Oct. 3–Dec. 1 (separate catalogue for
each venue).

532-T. Santander, Spain, Museo Municipal
de Bellas Artes de Santander, *Museo Guggenheim:
Las últimas vanguardias 1940–1991*, July 29–
Sept. 8. Organized by the Solomon R.
Guggenheim Museum; Universidad
Internacional Menéndez y Pelayo; Junta del
Puerto de Santander; Museo Municipal de Bellas
Artes de Santander; and Dirección General de
Bellas Artes, Archivos y Museos del Ministerio
de Cultura (catalogue and checklist).

533-T. Cedar Rapids, Iowa, Cedar Rapids
Museum of Art, *A Selection of Works from the
American Abstract Art Section*, Oct. 26, 1991–
May 31, 1992 (brochure).

1992
P.G.C., *Homage to Gastone Novelli*, Jan. 24–
April 7 (catalogue).

P.G.C., *Arshile Gorky: Works on Paper*,
April 15–June 28; traveled to Rome, Palazzo
delle Esposizioni, Oct. 14–Nov. 30; Lisbon,
Museu Calouste Gulbenkian, July 21–Aug. 27,
1993 (catalogue).

534. S.R.G.M. and G.M.S., *The Guggenheim*

Museum and the Art of This Century, three-part exhibition. S.R.G.M.: "Masterpieces from the Permanent Collection," June 22–Sept. 7 (staggered de-installation), and "Dan Flavin," June 22–Aug. 27; G.M.S.: "From Brancusi to Bourgeois: Aspects of the Guggenheim Collection," June 28–Sept. 6 (second floor installed through Sept. 27; commemorative magazine).

535. G.M.S., *Marc Chagall and the Jewish Theater*, Sept. 23, 1992–Jan. 17, 1993; traveled to Chicago, Ill., The Art Institute of Chicago, Jan. 30–May 7, 1993 (catalogue).

536. Frankfurt, Schirn Kunsthalle Frankfurt, *Die grosse Utopie: Die russiche Avantgarde 1915–1932*, March 1–May 10; Amsterdam, Stedelijk Museum, *De Grote Utopie: De Russiche Avant-garde 1915–1932*, June 5–Aug. 23; S.R.G.M., *The Great Utopia: The Russian and Soviet Avant-Garde, 1915–1932*, Sept. 25, 1992–Jan. 3, 1993; Moscow, State Tretiakov Gallery, April 28–Aug. 1, 1993. Organized by the Solomon R. Guggenheim Museum, State Tretiakov Gallery, State Russian Museum, and Schirn Kunsthalle Frankfurt (catalogues in German, Dutch, English, and Russian).

537. Washington, D.C., The Corcoran Gallery of Art, *Robert Rauschenberg: The Early 1950s*, June 15–Aug. 11, 1991; Houston, Tex., The Menil Collection, Sept. 27, 1991–Jan. 5, 1992; Chicago, Ill., Museum of Contemporary Art, Feb. 8–April 19, 1992; San Francisco, Calif., San Francisco Museum of Modern Art, May 14–Aug. 2, 1992; G.M.S., Oct. 23, 1992–Jan. 25, 1993. Organized by the Menil Collection (catalogue).

538. G.M.S., *New York 1947–1958: Selections from the Guggenheim Museum*, Oct. 23, 1992–Jan. 25, 1993.

539. S.R.G.M., Thannhauser Gallery 2, permanent-collection reinstallation, Dec.

P.G.C., *Giuseppe Santomaso: Lettere a Palladio*, Dec. 1, 1992–April 2, 1993 (catalogue in Italian and English).

1993

540. S.R.G.M., *Lothar Baumgarten: America Invention*, Jan. 28–March 7 (catalogue and handout).

541. S.R.G.M., *Richard Serra*, Jan. 8–May 19.

542. Minneapolis, Minn., Walker Art Center, *Photography in Contemporary German Art: 1960 to the Present*, Feb. 9–May 31, 1992; traveled to Dallas, Tex., Dallas Museum of Art, and Fort Worth, Tex., Modern Art Museum of Fort Worth, Aug. 16–Oct. 11, 1992; St. Louis, Mo., The St. Louis Art Museum and Forum for Contemporary Art, Nov. 19, 1992–Jan. 3, 1993; G.M.S., Feb. 10–May 9; Los Angeles, Calif.,

Lannan Foundation, May 22–Aug. 22; Cologne, Museum Ludwig, Sept. 10–Nov. 17; Basel, Museum für Gegenwartskunst, Feb. 12–April 17, 1994; Humlebaek, Denmark, Louisiana Museum for Modern Art, Aug. 12–Oct. 20, 1994 (catalogue in English).

543. S.R.G.M., *Osmosis: Ettore Spalletti and Haim Steinbach*, March 18–June 13 (catalogue).

544. G.M.S., *"Four Rooms" and a "House Ball": Pop and the Everyday Object*, Jan. 27–April 25.

545. S.R.G.M., *Picasso and the Age of Iron*, March 19–June 13; Fort Worth, Tex., Modern Art Museum of Fort Worth, Aug. 1–Oct. 17 (catalogue and handout).

546. G.M.S., *Paul Klee at the Guggenheim Museum*, May 7–Nov. 5; traveled to Madrid, Banco Bilbao Vizcaya Corporate Headquarters, *Paul Klee. Colección del Guggenheim Museum*, Nov. 15, 1993–Jan. 29, 1994; Bilbao, Rekalde Ikustaretoa (Sala de Exposiciones Rekalde), *Paul Klee, Guggenheim Museoaren Bilduma/ Paul Klee. Colección del Guggenheim Museum*, Feb. 9–March 18, 1994 (catalogues in English and Spanish).

547. G.M.S., *Singular Dimensions in Painting*, May 26, 1993–Jan. 4, 1994 (brochure).

P.G.C., *Drawing the Line Against AIDS*, June 8–13; G.M.S., Oct. 6–19 (553). Organized in conjunction with Art Against AIDS Venezia under the aegis of the 45th Venice Biennale (catalogue in English).

P.G.C., *Il suone rapido delle cose: John Cage* (part of 45th Venice Biennale), June 13–Oct. 10.

548. G.M.S., *A Year with Children*, June 9–19.

549. S.R.G.M., *House Beautiful*, June 24–July 1.

550. S.R.G.M., *Modern Masterpieces from the Permanent Collection*, June 25–Oct. 1.

551. S.R.G.M., *Rebecca Horn: The Inferno-Paradiso Switch*, June 25–Oct. 1. Included site-specific installations at G.M.S., June 27, 1993–Jan. 11, 1994, and at P.G.C., June 9–Oct. 18. Traveling to Eindhoven, Stedelijk Van Abbemuseum, *Rebecca Horn*, Nov. 20, 1993–Jan. 30, 1994; Berlin, Nationalgalerie, Staatliche Museen zu Berlin–Preußischer Kulturbesitz, March 4–May 1, 1994; Vienna, Kunsthalle Wien, May 27–Aug. 7, 1994; London, Tate Gallery and Serpentine Gallery, Sept. 27, 1994–Jan. 8, 1995; Musée de Grenoble, March 4–May 28, 1995 (catalogues in English and German).

552. G.M.S., *Mario Merz*, July 2–Sept. 20.

P.G.C., *Immagini Italiane*, Aug. 31–Nov. 1; traveled to Naples, Villa Pignatelli, Nov. 20,

1993–Jan. 6, 1994; New York, N.Y., The Murray and Isabella Rayburn Foundation, Jan. 28–March 5, 1994. Organized by the Aperture Foundation (related issue of *Aperture*, also published in Italian).

553. G.M.S., *Drawing the Line Against AIDS*, Oct. 6–19 (catalogue).

554. S.R.G.M., *Roy Lichtenstein*, Oct. 7, 1993–Jan. 16, 1994 (brochure and checklist); traveling to Los Angeles, The Museum of Contemporary Art, Jan. 26–April 3, 1994; Montreal, The Montreal Museum of Fine Arts, May 26–Sept. 5, 1994; Munich, Haus der Kunst, Oct. 13, 1994–Jan. 9, 1995; Hamburg, Deichtorhallen Hamburg, Feb. 8–April 30, 1995; Brussels, Les Expositions du Palais des Beaux-Arts, June 2–Sept. 3, 1995; Columbus, Ohio, Wexner Center for the Arts, September 21, 1995–Jan. 7, 1996 (catalogues in English and German).

555. G.M.S., *Virtual Reality: An Emerging Medium*, Oct. 23–Nov. 1, 1993.

556. G.M.S., *Industrial Elegance*, Nov. 7, 1993–March 27, 1994. Organized and tour arranged by Steelcase Design Partnership (catalogue).

557. S.R.G.M., *Robert Mapplethorpe: Self Portraits*, Nov. 9, 1993–Feb. 23, 1994.

558. G.M.S., *Watercolors by Kandinsky at the Guggenheim Museum*, Nov. 12, 1993–Aug. 28, 1994 (catalogue).

559-T. Bilbao, Rekalde Ikustaretoa (Sala de Exposiciones Rekalde), *Guggenheim Bildumaren Maisu-Lan Modernoak/Obras maestras modernas de la colección Guggenheim*, Dec. 1, 1993–Feb. 10, 1994; Vienna, Kunstforum Bank Austria, *Meisterwerke aus dem Guggenheim*, March 3–June 12, 1994; Hamburg, Hamburger Kunsthalle, *Meisterwerke aus dem Guggenheim Museum*, June 30–Sept. 25, 1994; Helsinki, Ateneum, *Mestariteoksia Guggenheim Museosta/Mästerwerk från Guggenheim Museet*, Oct. 14, 1994–Jan. 15, 1995 (catalogues in Euskera/Spanish, German, and Finnish/ Swedish).

1994

560. S.R.G.M., *Robert Morris: The Mind/Body Problem*, Feb. 3–May 1, and Guggenheim Museum SoHo, Jan. 15–April 4 (catalogue and handout); traveling to Hamburg, Deichtorhallen Hamburg, March 10–May 7, 1995; Paris, Musée National d'Art Moderne, Centre Georges Pompidou, May 27–Aug. 1995.

561. S.R.G.M., *A Temple of Spirit: Frank Lloyd Wright's Designs for the Guggenheim Museum*, March 4–Sept. 8.

562. Malibu, The J. Paul Getty Museum, *Women on the Edge: Twenty Photographers in Europe, 1919–1939*, Aug. 24–Nov. 28, 1993; traveled to

S.R.G.M., March 11–May 31 (catalogue and brochure).

P.G.C., *I libri d'artista italiani del Novecento*, March 23–May 22. Organized by the Peggy Guggenheim Collection and Ralph Jentsch (related books in Italian and English).

P.G.C., *Josef Albers: Vetro, colore e luce*, March 30–July 10; traveling to Rome, Palazzo delle Esposizioni, July 21–Oct. 3; Valencia, Spain, IVAM Centre Julio González, *Josef Albers: Vidrio, color y luz*, Nov. 3, 1994–Jan. 8, 1995; Bottrop, Germany, Josef Albers Museum, winter 1995; S.R.G.M., *Josef Albers: Glass, Color, and Light*, June 7–Sept. 17, 1995; Smith College Museum of Art, Northampton, Massachusetts, fall 1995. Organized by the Peggy Guggenheim Collection and the Josef Albers Foundation (catalogues in English, Italian, and Spanish).

563. Los Angeles, The Museum of Contemporary Art, *Rolywholyover   A Circus*, Sept. 12–Nov. 28, 1993; traveling to Houston, The Menil Collection, Jan. 14–April 2; G.M.S., April 23–Aug. 7; Mito, Japan, Art Tower Mito Contemporary Art Center, Nov. 3, 1994–Feb. 26, 1995; Philadelphia, Philadelphia Museum of Art, April 2–June 11, 1995 (catalogue in English).

564. S.R.G.M., *The Tradition of the New: Postwar Masterpieces from the Guggenheim Collection*, May 20–Sept. 11 (brochure).

565. G.M.S., *A Year with Children*, June 9–23.

566. Vienna, Graphische Sammlung Albertina, *Oskar Kokoschka, Das Frühwerk, Zeichnungen und Aquarelle, 1897–1917*, March 2–May 23; S.R.G.M., *Oskar Kokoschka, Works on Paper: The Early Years, 1897–1917*, June 10–Aug. 24. New York venue organized by the Solomon R. Guggenheim Museum and the Graphische Sammlung Albertina, Vienna (catalogues in German and English).

567. Yokohama Museum of Art, *Japanese Art After 1945: Scream Against the Sky*, Feb. 5–March 30; G.M.S., Sept. 14, 1994–Jan. 8, 1995; San Francisco, San Francisco Museum of Modern Art and the Center for the Arts at Yerba Buena Gardens, May 31–Aug. 27, 1995. U.S. tour organized by the Japan Foundation, the Guggenheim Museum, and the San Francisco Museum of Modern Art in association with InterCultura (catalogues in Japanese/English and English).

568. S.R.G.M., *The Italian Metamorphosis, 1943–1968*, Oct. 6, 1994–Jan. 22, 1995 (catalogue, CD-ROM, and brochure); travels to Germany, Wolfsburg, Kunstmuseum Wolfsburg, 1995.

Publications

The following bibliography is a complete listing of books and catalogues produced by the Solomon R. Guggenheim Foundation. All books were published in New York by the Solomon R. Guggenheim Foundation, Museum of Non-Objective Painting, Solomon R. Guggenheim Museum, or Guggenheim Museum, or in Venice by the Peggy Guggenheim Collection, unless otherwise noted. Publications produced by the Peggy Guggenheim Collection prior to 1979 (the year that the Solomon R. Guggenheim Foundation assumed full responsibility for its operation) are not included, nor are exhibition catalogues produced by other publishers.

The abbreviation exh. cat. denotes exhibition catalogue. Exhibition and publication titles are the same unless otherwise noted. For full exhibition information, see the exhibition history on pp. 314–29. Exhibition numbers listed in the exhibition history appear here in parentheses.

1937

Solomon R. Guggenheim Collection of Non-Objective Paintings: Second Enlarged Catalogue. Exh. cat., accompanied *Solomon R. Guggenheim Collection of Non-Objective Paintings* (3-T). Foreword by Yarnell Abbott, essay by Hilla Rebay. 88 pages. (The first collection catalogue accompanied *Solomon R. Guggenheim Collection of Non-Objective Paintings* [1-T] and was published in 1936 by the Carolina Art Association, Charleston, South Carolina.)

1938

Solomon R. Guggenheim Collection of Non-Objective Paintings: Third Enlarged Catalogue. Exh. cat., accompanied *Solomon R. Guggenheim Collection of Non-Objective Paintings* (4-T). Essay by Hilla Rebay. 122 pages.

1939

Art of Tomorrow: Fifth Catalogue of the Solomon R. Guggenheim Collection of Non-Objective Paintings. Exh. cat., accompanied *Art of Tomorrow* (unnumbered exhibition). Essay by Hilla Rebay. 184 pages.

Solomon R. Guggenheim Collection of Non-Objective Paintings: Fourth Catalogue. Exh. cat., accompanied *Solomon R. Guggenheim Collection of Non-Objective Paintings* (5-T). Essay by Hilla Rebay. 44 pages.

1945

Kandinsky. Exh. cat., accompanied *In Memory of Wassily Kandinsky* (43). Ed. by Hilla Rebay. Text by Wassily [Vasily] Kandinsky. 48 pages.

Wassily Kandinsky Memorial. Exh. cat., accompanied *In Memory of Wassily Kandinsky* (43). Text by Wassily [Vasily] Kandinsky, essay by V. Agrarych. 124 pages.

1946

Kandinsky, Wassily [Vasily]. *On the Spiritual in Art.* Ed. by Hilla Rebay. 154 pages.

Memorial Exhibition: Wassily Kandinsky (1866–1944). Exh. cat., accompanied *Memorial Exhibition of Paintings by Wassily Kandinsky (1866–1944)* (53-T). Introduction by Hilla Rebay. 24 pages.

1947

Kandinsky, Wassily [Vasily]. *Point and Line to Plane.* Ed. by Hilla Rebay. Preface by Hilla Rebay, foreword and introduction by Wassily [Vasily] Kandinsky. Trans. from the German by Howard Dearstyne and Hilla Rebay. 206 pages.

Laszlo Moholy-Nagy Memorial. Exh. cat., accompanied *In Memoriam Laszlo Moholy-Nagy* (57). Essay by Hilla Rebay, text by Laszlo [László] Moholy-Nagy. 40 pages.

1948

Hilla Rebay. Exh. cat. (61). Introduction by Elise Ruffini. 24 pages.

1953

Sixty Years of Living Architecture: The Work of Frank Lloyd Wright. Exh. cat. (80). Text by Frank Lloyd Wright. 36 pages.

Younger European Painters: A Selection. Exh. cat. (82). Introduction by James Johnson Sweeney. 60 pages.

1954

Solomon R. Guggenheim Collection. Exh. cat., accompanied *The Solomon R. Guggenheim Museum: A Selection from the Museum Collection* (88-T). Introduction by Doris Shadbolt. 48 pages.

Younger American Painters: A Selection. Exh. cat. (86). Introduction by James Johnson Sweeney. 80 pages.

1955

A Selection from the Solomon R. Guggenheim Museum, New York. Exh. cat. (93-T). Foreword by Arthur Lismer. 24 pages.

1957

Jacques Villon, Raymond Duchamp-Villon, Marcel Duchamp. Exh. cat. (101). Foreword by James Johnson Sweeney, texts by André Breton, Marcel Duchamp, Raymond Duchamp-Villon, Walter Pach, Réne-Jean, and Jacques Villon. 88 pages.

Piet Mondrian: The Earlier Years. Exh. cat. (108). Letter from Piet Mondrian to James Johnson Sweeney. 16 pages.

1958

Guggenheim International Award, 1958. Exh. cat. (114). Foreword by James Johnson Sweeney. 30 pages.

1959

A Handbook to the Solomon R. Guggenheim Museum

Collection. Introduction by James Johnson Sweeney. 272 pages.

Twenty Contemporary Painters from the Philippe Dotremont Collection, Brussels. Exh. cat. (115). Foreword by James Johnson Sweeney, introduction by Paul Fierens. 20 pages.

1960

Before Picasso; After Miró. Exh. cat. (123). Introduction by James Johnson Sweeney. 24 pages.

Guggenheim International Award, 1960. Exh. cat. (124). 36 pages.

1961

Abstract Expressionists Imagists. Exh. cat., accompanied *American Abstract Expressionists and Imagists* (133). Introduction by H. H. Arnason. 136 pages.

Elements of Modern Painting. Exh. cat., accompanied *Elements of Modern Art* (132). Rev. ed., 1962, published as *Modern Art: An Introductory Commentary.* Exh. cat., accompanied *Elements of Modern Art* (143-T). Text by Thomas M. Messer. 40 pages.

Modern Masters from the Collection of the Solomon R. Guggenheim Museum. Exh. cat. (129). Preface by Thomas M. Messer. 28 pages.

One Hundred Paintings from the G. David Thompson Collection. Exh. cat. (128). Introduction by G. David Thompson. 60 pages.

Paintings from the Arensberg and Gallatin Collections of the Philadelphia Museum of Art. Exh. cat. (125). Introduction by Henry Clifford. 40 pages.

1962

Antoni Tàpies. Exh. cat. (140). Foreword by Lawrence Alloway. 32 pages.

Fernand Léger: Five Themes and Variations. Exh. cat. (139). Introduction by Thomas M. Messer. 116 pages.

Jan Müller, 1922–1958. Exh. cat. (138). Essays by Thomas M. Messer and Dody Müller. 32 pages.

Modern Sculpture from the Joseph H. Hirshhorn Collection. Exh. cat. (145). Preface by Thomas M. Messer, foreword by Abram Lerner, text by H. H. Arnason. 252 pages.

Philip Guston. Exh. cat. (142). Essay by H. H. Arnason. 128 pages.

Vasily Kandinsky 1866–1944: A Retrospective Exhibition. Exh. cat. First edition (146-T), 108 pages. Second edition (147), 128 pages. Introduction by Thomas M. Messer, essays by Jean Cassou, Kenneth C. Lindsay, and H. K. Röthel. (Special supplement, *Special Loan*

of Paintings from the U.S.S.R. [1963], with introduction by Thomas M. Messer, essays by Nina Kandinsky and Will Grohmann, 20 pages, accompanied the catalogue for exhibition no. 147 at the Solomon R. Guggenheim Museum.)

1963

Cézanne and Structure in Modern Painting. Exh. cat. (153). Essay by Daniel Robbins. 36 pages.

Francis Bacon. Exh. cat. (155). Preface by Thomas M. Messer, introduction by Lawrence Alloway. 80 pages.

Six Painters and the Object. Exh. cat. (149). Essay by Lawrence Alloway. 28 pages.

1964

Albert Gleizes, 1881–1953: A Retrospective Exhibition. Exh. cat. (163, 164-T). Essay by Daniel Robbins. 136 pages.

Alexander Calder: A Retrospective Exhibition. Exh. cat. (166). Introduction by Thomas M. Messer. 92 pages.

American Drawings. Exh. cat. (165). Foreword by Thomas M. Messer, introduction by Lawrence Alloway. 68 pages.

Frederick Kiesler: Environmental Sculpture. Exh. cat. (161). Foreword by Thomas M. Messer, text by Frederick Kiesler. 44 pages.

Guggenheim International Award, 1964. Exh. cat. (157). Introduction by Lawrence Alloway. 128 pages.

Van Gogh and Expressionism. Exh. cat. (162). Text by Maurice Tuchman. 44 pages.

1965

Edvard Munch. Exh. cat. (180). Essays by Johan H. Langaard and Sigurd Willoch. 110 pages.

Gustav Klimt and Egon Schiele. Exh. cat. (170). Introduction by Thomas M. Messer, essays by Alessandra Comini, James T. Demetrion, and Johannes Dobai. 124 pages.

Jean Xceron. Exh. cat. (178). Essay by Daniel Robbins. 64 pages.

Masterpieces of Modern Art. Exh. cat., accompanied *Masterpieces of Modern Art, by Courtesy of the Thannhauser Foundation* (174). Foreword by Harry F. Guggenheim. 80 pages.

Paintings from the Collection of the Solomon R. Guggenheim Museum. Exh. cat. (173). Foreword by Thomas M. Messer. 88 pages.

William Baziotes: A Memorial Exhibition. Exh. cat. (171). Introduction by Lawrence Alloway, statements by William Baziotes. 58 pages.

1966

Barnett Newman: The Stations of the Cross: lema sabachthani. Exh. cat. (185). Statement by Barnett Newman, essay by Lawrence Alloway. 44 pages.

The Emergent Decade: Latin American Painters and Painting in the 1960's. Publication related to exhibition no. 179. Introduction by Thomas M. Messer, texts by Cornell Capa. Published by Cornell University, Ithaca, N.Y., and the Solomon R. Guggenheim Museum. 192 pages.

European Drawings. Exh. cat. (183). Introduction by Lawrence Alloway. 82 pages.

Gauguin and the Decorative Style. Exh. cat. (187). Introduction by Lawrence Alloway, text by Marilyn Hunt. 48 pages.

Jean Dubuffet 1962–66. Exh. cat. (190). Introduction by Lawrence Alloway, text by Jean Dubuffet. 78 pages.

Systemic Painting. Exh. cat. (189). Introduction by Lawrence Alloway. 68 pages.

Vasily Kandinsky: Painting on Glass (Hinterglasmalerei), Anniversary Exhibition. Exh. cat. (191). Introduction by Hans Konrad Röthel. 54 pages.

1967

Guggenheim International Exhibition, 1967: Sculpture from Twenty Nations. Exh. cat. (197). Preface by Thomas M. Messer, introduction by Edward F. Fry. 154 pages.

Joseph Cornell. Exh. cat. (194). Essay by Diane Waldman. 60 pages.

Paul Klee, 1879–1940: A Retrospective Exhibition. Exh. cat. First edition (192), 148 pages (revised and reprinted in 1967). Second edition (193-T), 128 pages. Text by Felix Klee, introduction by Will Grohmann.

1968

Acquisitions of the 1930's and 1940's: A Selection of Paintings, Watercolors and Drawings in Tribute to Baroness Hilla von Rebay, 1890–1967. Exh. cat. (202). Introduction by Thomas M. Messer. 136 pages.

Mastercraftsmen of Ancient Peru. Exh. cat. (209). Introduction and text by Alan R. Sawyer. 112 pages.

Neo-Impressionism. Exh. cat. (199). Introduction by Thomas M. Messer, essay and text by Robert L. Herbert. 264 pages.

Paul Feeley (1910–1966): A Memorial Exhibition. Exh. cat. (201). Introduction by Gene Baro. 76 pages.

Paul Klee Exhibition at the Guggenheim Museum:

A Post Scriptum. Publication related to exhibition no. 192. Essay by Thomas M. Messer. 40 pages.

Rousseau, Redon, and Fantasy. Exh. cat. (205). Introduction and text by Louise Averill Svendsen. 56 pages.

1969

Constantin Brancusi, 1876–1957: A Retrospective Exhibition. Exh. cat. (224). Introduction by Thomas M. Messer, essay by Sidney Geist. 164 pages.

David Smith. Exh. cat. (215). Introduction and text by Edward F. Fry. 188 pages.

Nine Young Artists, Theodoron Awards. Exh. cat. (217). Texts by Edward F. Fry and Diane Waldman. 28 pages.

Roy Lichtenstein. Exh. cat. (223). Essay by Diane Waldman. 114 pages.

Selected Sculpture and Works on Paper. Exh. cat. (220). 160 pages.

Works from the Peggy Guggenheim Foundation. Exh. cat. (211). Introduction by Peggy Guggenheim. 184 pages.

1970

Carl Andre. Exh. cat. (234). Essay by Diane Waldman. 84 pages.

Contemporary Japanese Art: Fifth Japan Art Festival Exhibition. Exh. cat. (237). Introduction by Edward F. Fry. 84 pages.

Fangor. Exh. cat. (238). Introduction by Margit Rowell. 36 pages.

Francis Picabia. Exh. cat., accompanied *Francis Picabia: A Retrospective Exhibition* (233). Essay by William A. Camfield. 168 pages.

On the Future of Art. Introduction by Edward F. Fry, essays by J. W. Burnham, Louis I. Kahn, Herbert Marcuse, Annette Michelson, James Seawright, B. F. Skinner, and Arnold J. Toynbee. Published by Viking Press, New York, sponsored by the Solomon R. Guggenheim Foundation. 144 pages.

Selections from the Guggenheim Museum Collection, 1900–1970. Exh. cat. (232). Introduction by Louise Averill Svendsen. 440 pages.

1971

Guggenheim International Exhibition, 1971. Exh. cat. (239). Essays by Edward F. Fry and Diane Waldman. 44 pages, with 21 artists' booklets.

John Chamberlain: A Retrospective Exhibition. Exh. cat. (247). Essay by Diane Waldman. 104 pages.

Piet Mondrian, 1872–1944: Centennial Exhibition. Exh. cat. (244). Introduction by L. J. F. Wijsenbeek, essays by Max Bill, Joop Joosten, Nelly van Doesburg, and R. P. Welsh. 224 pages.

Robert Mangold. Exh. cat. (245). Essay by Diane Waldman. 44 pages.

Ten Young Artists: Theodoron Awards. Exh. cat. (243). 24 pages.

1972

Amsterdam Paris Düsseldorf. Exh. cat. (256). Preface by Thomas M. Messer, introductory essays by Cor Blok, Blaise Gautier, and Jürgen Harten. 88 pages.

Eva Hesse: A Memorial Exhibition. Exh. cat. (261). Essays by Robert Pincus-Witten and Linda Shearer. 114 pages.

Jean Dubuffet: A Retrospective. Exh. cat. (265). Introduction by Thomas M. Messer, essay by Margit Rowell. 306 pages.

Joan Miró: Magnetic Fields. Exh. cat. (257). Essays by Rosalind Krauss and Margit Rowell. 160 pages.

Kandinsky at the Guggenheim Museum. Exh. cat. (252). Introduction by Thomas M. Messer. 156 pages.

Masterpieces of Modern Art: A Picture Book of Nineteenth and Twentieth Century Masterpieces from the Thannhauser Foundation. Introduction by Thomas M. Messer. 88 pages.

Robert Ryman. Exh. cat. (250). Introduction by Diane Waldman. 52 pages.

Ten Independents: An Artist-Initiated Exhibition. Exh. cat. (249). Introduction by Dore Ashton. 20 pages.

1973

Futurism: A Modern Focus: The Lydia and Harry Lewis Winston Collection, Dr. and Mrs. Barnett Malbin. Exh. cat. (271). Essays by Marianne W. Martin and Linda Shearer. 252 pages.

Richard Hamilton. Exh. cat. (268). Introduction by John Russell, commentary by Richard Hamilton. 104 pages.

1974

Alberto Giacometti: A Retrospective Exhibition. Exh. cat. (275). First edition accompanied exhibition at the Solomon R. Guggenheim Museum. Essay by Reinhold Hohl. 204 pages. Second edition accompanied exhibition at traveling venues. 132 pages.

Ilya Bolotowsky. Exh. cat. (277). Introduction by Adelyn D. Breeskin, interview with Ilya Bolotowsky by Louise Averill Svendsen and Mimi Poser. 136 pages.

Soto: A Retrospective Exhibition. Exh. cat. (279). Interview with Soto by Claude-Louis Renard (in English, French, and Spanish). 136 pages.

1975

Aristide Maillol: 1861–1944. Exh. cat. (291). Essay by John Rewald. 140 pages.

Brice Marden. Exh. cat. (283). Essay by Linda Shearer, statement by Brice Marden. 68 pages.

František Kupka, 1871–1957: A Retrospective. Exh. cat. (289). Essays by Meda Mladek and Margit Rowell. 328 pages.

Jiří Kolář. Exh. cat. (288). Texts by Jindrich Chalupecky, Jiří Kolář, Thomas M. Messer, Raoul-Jean Moulin, and Wieland Schmied. 140 pages.

Max Ernst: A Retrospective. Exh. cat., accompanied *Max Ernst: A Retrospective Exhibition* (282). Essay by Diane Waldman. 272 pages.

The Solomon R. Guggenheim Museum: Frank Lloyd Wright. Essay by Louise Averill Svendsen. 48 pages.

1976

Acquisition Priorities: Aspects of Postwar Painting in America. Exh. cat. (302). Foreword by Thomas M. Messer. 120 pages.

The Guggenheim Museum Collection: Paintings 1880–1945. 2 vols. Texts by Angelica Zander Rudenstine. 762 pages.

Horia Damian: The Hill. Exh. cat. (300). Essay by Radu Varia. 64 pages.

Twentieth-Century American Drawing: Three Avant-Garde Generations. Exh. cat. (293). Essay by Diane Waldman. 128 pages.

1977

Ensor. Exh. cat., accompanied *James Ensor: A Retrospective* (306). Essay by John David Farmer. Published by George Braziller, New York, for the Solomon R. Guggenheim Foundation and the Art Institute of Chicago. 128 pages.

Kenneth Noland: A Retrospective. Exh. cat. (309). Essay by Diane Waldman. Published by the Solomon R. Guggenheim Foundation in collaboration with Harry N. Abrams, New York. 162 pages.

Lucio Fontana, 1899–1968: A Retrospective. Exh. cat. (316). Essay by Erika Billeter. 112 pages.

Nine Artists: Theodoron Awards. Exh. cat. (308). Introduction by Linda Shearer. 36 pages.

Paul Klee, 1879–1940, in the Collection of the

Solomon R. Guggenheim Museum, New York.
Exh. cat., accompanied *Klee at the Guggenheim Museum* (310). Essay by Louise Averill Svendsen. 84 pages.

1978
The Evelyn Sharp Collection. Exh. cat. (323). 96 pages.

The Guggenheim Museum: Justin K. Thannhauser Collection. Introduction and text by Vivian Endicott Barnett. 216 pages.

Mark Rothko, 1903–1970: A Retrospective. Exh. cat. (333). Text by Bernard Malamud, essay by Diane Waldman. Published by Harry N. Abrams, New York, in collaboration with the Solomon R. Guggenheim Foundation. 296 pages.

Prints from the Guggenheim Museum Collection. Exh. cat. (332-T). Introduction by Linda Konheim. 72 pages.

Willem de Kooning in East Hampton. Exh. cat. (322). Essay by Diane Waldman. 152 pages.

Young American Artists: 1978 Exxon National Exhibition. Exh. cat. (325). Introduction by Linda Shearer. 72 pages.

1979
British Art Now: An American Perspective, 1980 Exxon International Exhibition. Exh. cat. (350). Introduction and text by Diane Waldman. 156 pages.

Joseph Beuys. Exh. cat. (346). Introductions by Joseph Beuys and Caroline Tisdall, essay by Caroline Tisdall. 288 pages.

The Planar Dimension: Europe, 1912–1932. Exh. cat. (340). Essay by Margit Rowell. 160 pages.

Rufino Tamayo: Myth and Magic. Exh. cat. (341). Essay by Octavio Paz (in English and Spanish). 248 pages.

1980
Ad Reinhardt and Color. Exh. cat. (349). Essay by Margit Rowell. Published by Thames and Hudson, London, and the Solomon R. Guggenheim Foundation. 72 pages.

Expressionism: A German Intuition, 1905–1920. Exh. cat. (361). Introduction by Paul Vogt, essays by Wolf-Dieter Dube, Horst Keller, Eberhard Roters, Martin Urban, and Paul Vogt. 336 pages.

Handbook: The Guggenheim Museum Collection 1900–1980. Collection catalogue related to the exhibition *1900–1980 from the Guggenheim Museum Collection* (355). Rev. ed., 1984. Introduction and texts by Vivian Endicott Barnett. 528 pages.

Kandinsky Watercolors: A Selection from the Solomon R. Guggenheim Museum and the Hilla von Rebay Foundation. Exh. cat. (363-T). Essays by Vivian Endicott Barnett and Louise Averill Svendsen. 76 pages.

New Images from Spain. Exh. cat. (353). Essay by Margit Rowell. 144 pages.

1981
Arshile Gorky, 1904–1948: A Retrospective. Exh. cat. (368). Essay by Diane Waldman. Published by Harry N. Abrams, New York, in collaboration with the Solomon R. Guggenheim Foundation. 286 pages.

Art of the Avant-Garde in Russia: Selections from the George Costakis Collection. Exh. cat. (377). Essays by Margit Rowell and Angelica Zander Rudenstine. 320 pages.

Jean Dubuffet: A Retrospective Glance at Eighty. Exh. cat. (372). Texts by Jean Dubuffet, Morton L. Janklow, and Thomas M. Messer. 32 pages.

Nineteen Artists–Emergent Americans: 1981 Exxon National Exhibition. Exh. cat. (366). Introduction by Peter Frank. 92 pages.

Richard Navin: The Mycenae Circle. Exh. cat. (367). Introduction by Thomas M. Messer, text by Richard Navin. 20 pages.

1982
Asger Jorn. Exh. cat. (388). Essay by Troels Andersen. 100 pages.

Italian Art Now: An American Perspective, 1982 Exxon International Exhibition. Exh. cat. (383). Essay by Diane Waldman. 144 pages.

Jack Tworkov: Fifteen Years of Painting. Exh. cat. (384). Essay by Andrew Forge. 64 pages.

Kandinsky in Munich: 1896–1914. Exh. cat. (380). Foreword by Carl E. Schorske, essays by Peter Jelavich and Peg Weiss. 312 pages.

One Hundred Works: The Peggy Guggenheim Collection/Cento Opere: La Collezione Peggy Guggenheim. Foreword by Thomas Messer (in English and Italian). 128 pages.

Öyvind Fahlström. Exh. cat. (389). Texts by Erró, Öyvind Fahlström, Olle Granath, Pontus Hultén, Billy Klüver, Matta, Claes Oldenburg, Robert Rauschenberg, and Carl Frederik Reuterswärd. 120 pages.

Sixty Works: The Peggy Guggenheim Collection. Exh. cat. (392). Foreword by Thomas M. Messer. 68 pages.

Sleeping Beauty–Art Now: Scandinavia Today. Exh. cat., accompanied *Sleeping Beauty–Art Now* (390). Essays by Øystein Hjort and Pontus Hultén. 136 pages.

1983
Acquisition Priorities: Aspects of Postwar Painting in Europe. Exh. cat. (407). Foreword by Thomas M. Messer. 104 pages.

Handbook: The Peggy Guggenheim Collection. Published in Italian as *Guida: La Collezione Peggy Guggenheim*. Introduction by Thomas M. Messer, texts by Lucy Flint. Published by the Solomon R. Guggenheim Foundation and Harry N. Abrams, New York. 224 pages. Rev. eds., 1986, *Handbook: The Peggy Guggenheim Collection* and *Guida: Collezione Peggy Guggenheim*. Additional texts by Elizabeth C. Childs. Published by the Solomon R. Guggenheim Foundation. 336 pages.

Julio González: A Retrospective. Exh. cat. (402). Essay by Margit Rowell. 216 pages.

Kandinsky at the Guggenheim. Introduction by Thomas M. Messer, essay and texts by Vivian Endicott Barnett. Published by the Solomon R. Guggenheim Museum and Abbeville Press, New York. 312 pages.

Kandinsky: Russian and Bauhaus Years, 1915–1933. Exh. cat. (418). Essay by Clark V. Poling. 360 pages.

New Perspectives in American Art: 1983 Exxon National Exhibition. Exh. cat. (413). Essay by Diane Waldman. 160 pages.

Yves Tanguy: A Retrospective. Exh. cat. (397). Essay by Roland Penrose. 24 pages.

1984
Australian Visions: 1984 Exxon International Exhibition. Exh. cat. (437). Essays by Memory Holloway and Diane Waldman. 100 pages.

From Degas to Calder: Major Sculpture and Works on Paper from the Guggenheim Museum Collection. Exh. cat. (433). Introduction by Thomas M. Messer. 28 pages.

Michael Singer. Exh. cat. (428). Essay by Diane Waldman. 84 pages.

Will Insley: The Opaque Civilization. Exh. cat. (436). Text by Will Insley, interview with Will Insley by Linda Shearer. 88 pages.

1985
Alfred Jensen: Paintings and Works on Paper. Exh. cat. (454). Essays by Maria Reidelbach and Peter Schjeldahl. 80 pages.

Kandinsky in Paris: 1934–1944. Exh. cat. (444). Essays by Vivian Endicott Barnett and Christian Derouet. 268 pages.

New Horizons in American Art: 1985 Exxon National Exhibition. Exh. cat. (455). Essay by Lisa Dennison. 120 pages.

Peggy Guggenheim Collection, Venice: The Solomon R. Guggenheim Foundation. Introduction and texts by Angelica Zander Rudenstine. Published by Harry N. Abrams, New York, and the Solomon R. Guggenheim Foundation. 844 pages.

Transformations in Sculpture: Four Decades of American and European Art. Exh. cat. (459). Essay by Diane Waldman. 272 pages.

1986
Angles of Vision: French Art Today, 1986 Exxon International Exhibition. Exh. cat. (476). Essays by Lisa Dennison. 156 pages.

Enzo Cucchi. Exh. cat. (469). Essay by Diane Waldman. 194 pages.

The Expressive Figure from Rousseau to Bacon: European Art in the Guggenheim Museum Collection. Exh. cat. (473). Text by Susan B. Hirschfeld. 16 pages.

Jack Youngerman. Exh. cat. (463). Essay by Diane Waldman. 104 pages.

Jan Groth. Exh. cat. (472). Essay by Carter Ratcliff. 76 pages.

Oskar Kokoschka 1886–1980. Exh. cat. (477). Essay by Richard Calvocoressi. 248 pages.

Richard Long. Exh. cat. (475). Essay by R. H. Fuchs. Published by Thames and Hudson, London, and the Solomon R. Guggenheim Foundation. 240 pages.

1987
Emerging Artists, 1978–1986: Selections from the Exxon Series. Exh. cat. (488). Essay by Diane Waldman. 144 pages.

Fifty Years of Collecting: An Anniversary Selection, Painting by Modern Masters. Exh. cat. (491). Introduction by Thomas M. Messer. 152 pages.

Fifty Years of Collecting: An Anniversary Selection, Painting since World War II: Europe, Latin America, North America. Exh. cat., accompanied *Fifty Years of Collecting: An Anniversary Selection, Painting since World War II in Europe* (493); *Fifty Years of Collecting: An Anniversary Selection, Painting since World War II in Latin America* (494); and *Fifty Years of Collecting: An Anniversary Selection, Painting since World War II in North America* (495). Introduction by Thomas M. Messer. 148 pages.

Fifty Years of Collecting: An Anniversary Selection, Sculpture of the Modern Era. Exh. cat. (492). Introduction by Thomas M. Messer. 148 pages.

Joan Miró: A Retrospective. Exh. cat. (486). Essays by Jacques Dupin, Robert S. Lubar, Thomas M. Messer, Joan Miró, and Werner Schmalenbach. Published by the Solomon R. Guggenheim

Foundation in collaboration with Yale University Press, New Haven. 270 pages.

Peggy Guggenheim's Other Legacy. Published in Italian as *Le eredità sconosciute di Peggy Guggenheim.* Exh. cat. (483). Essays by Melvin P. Lader and Fred Licht. Published by the Solomon R. Guggenheim Foundation and Arnaldo Mondadori, Milan. 88 pages.

Pierre Alechinsky: Margin and Center. Exh. cat. (480). Text by Octavio Paz, interview with Pierre Alechinsky by Michael Gibson. 176 pages.

1988
Josef Albers: A Retrospective. Exh. cat. (496). Essays by Mary Emma Harris, Charles E. Rickart, and Nicholas Fox Weber. 304 pages.

1989
Jenny Holzer. Exh. cat. (520). Essay by Diane Waldman and interview with Jenny Holzer by Diane Waldman. Published by the Solomon R. Guggenheim Foundation and Harry N. Abrams, New York. 116 pages.

Mario Merz. Exh. cat. (518). Essay by Germano Celant and interview with Mario Merz by Germano Celant. Published by the Solomon R. Guggenheim Museum and Electa, Milan. 300 pages.

Refigured Painting: The German Image, 1960–88. Exh. cat. (513). Ed. by Michael Govan, Thomas Krens, and Joseph Thompson. Essays by Michael Govan, Heinrich Klotz, Thomas Krens, Hans Albert Peters, Jürgen Schilling, and Joseph Thompson. Published by the Solomon R. Guggenheim Foundation and Prestel-Verlag, Munich. 292 pages.

1990
From van Gogh to Picasso, from Kandinsky to Pollock: Masterpieces of Modern Art. Exh. cat. (526-T). Ed. by Germano Celant, Lisa Dennison, and Thomas Krens. Essays by Vivian Endicott Barnett, Maurizio Calvesi, Umberto Eco, Thomas Krens, and Fred Licht. Published by the Solomon R. Guggenheim Foundation and Bompiani, Milan. 392 pages.

1991
Kandinsky: Acquerelli dal Museo Guggenheim. Exh. cat. (531-T). Essay by Susan B. Hirschfeld (in Italian). Published by the Guggenheim Museum and Edizione Carte Segrete, Rome. 192 pages.

Kandinsky acuarelas: Colección del Museo Solomon R. Guggenheim y de la Fundación Hilla von Rebay. Exh. cat. (531-T). Essays by Vivian Endicott Barnett, Fernando Huici, and Fred Licht (in Spanish). 196 pages.

Kandinsky Aquarelle aus dem Guggenheim Museum. Exh. cat. (531-T). Essay by Susan B. Hirschfeld (in German). 192 pages.

Masterpieces from the Guggenheim. Exh. cat. (526-T). Essays by Umberto Eco, Thomas Krens, and Fred Licht. 320 pages.

Masterpieces from the Guggenheim Collection: From Picasso to Pollock. Exh. cat. (526-T). Essays by Umberto Eco, Thomas Krens, and Fred Licht (in Japanese). 348 pages.

Museo Guggenheim: Las últimas vanguardias 1940–1991. Exh. cat. (532-T). Introduction by Carmen Giménez, essays by Jean-Christophe Ammann, Francisco Calvo Serraller, Thomas Krens, Nancy Spector, and Diane Waldman (in Spanish). 136 pages.

Obras maestras de la colección Guggenheim: De Picasso a Pollock. Exh. cat. (526-T). Essays by Francisco Calvo Serraller, Umberto Eco, Thomas Krens, and Fred Licht (in Spanish). 368 pages.

Watercolors by Kandinsky at the Guggenheim Museum: A Selection from the Solomon R. Guggenheim Museum and the Hilla von Rebay Foundation. Second ed., 1993. Exh. cat. (558). Essay by Susan B. Hirschfeld. 188 pages.

1992
Giuseppe Santomaso: Lettere a Palladio. Exh. cat. (Peggy Guggenheim Collection). Essay by Fred Licht (in Italian and English). 48 pages.

The Great Utopia: The Russian and Soviet Avant-Garde, 1915–1932. Exh. cat. (537). Essays by Natalia Adaskina, Vivian Endicott Barnett, Susan Compton, Catherine Cooke, Charlotte Douglas, Svetlana Dzhafarova, Hubertus Gassner, Evgenii Kovtun, Aleksandr Lavrentev, Irina Levedeva, Nina Lobanov-Rostovsky, Christina Lodder, Elena Rakitin, Vasilii Rakitin, Jane A. Sharp, Aleksandra Shatskikh, Anatolii Strifalev, Margarita Tupitsyn, and Paul Wood. 748 pages.

Guggenheim Commemorative Magazine. Published on the occasion of the reopening of the Solomon R. Guggenheim Museum and the opening of the Guggenheim Museum SoHo (534). 80 pages.

Guggenheim Magazine 2 (fall 1992). 64 pages.

Guggenheim Museum: A to Z. Ed. by Nancy Spector. Texts by Jan Avgikos, Jennifer Blessing, Cornelia Lauf, Nancy Spector, et al. 298 pages.

Guggenheim Museum: Thannhauser Collection. Essays by Vivian Endicott Barnett, Fred Licht, and Paul Tucker, catalogue by Vivian Endicott Barnett. 192 pages.

Homage to Gastone Novelli. Exh. cat. (Peggy Guggenheim Collection). Essay by Annarita Fuso (in English and Italian). 34 pages.

Marc Chagall and the Jewish Theater. Exh. cat. (535). Introduction by Jennifer

Blessing, essays by Susan Compton and Benjamin Harshav. 224 pages.

Masterpieces from the Guggenheim. Also published in French as *Chefs-d'oeuvre du Musée Guggenheim.* Exh. cat. (526-T). Essays by Umberto Eco and Thomas Krens. 256 pages.

1993

Art of This Century: The Guggenheim Museum and Its Collection. Essays by Clare Bell, Jennifer Blessing, Lisa Dennison, Andrea Feeser, Michael Govan, Thomas Krens, Bruce Brooks Pfeiffer, Nancy Spector, and Diane Waldman. 340 pages.

Guggenheim Bildumaren Maisu-Lan Modernoak/ Obras maestras modernas de la colección Guggenheim Exh. cat. (559-T). Essay by Thomas Krens. 224 pages (in Euskera and Spanish).

Guggenheim Magazine 3 (summer 1993). 80 pages.

Guggenheim Magazine 4 (fall 1993). 72 pages.

Lothar Baumgarten: America Invention. Exh. cat. (540). Artist's project by Lothar Baumgarten, introduction by Michael Govan, essays by Vincent Crapanzano, Hal Foster, Michael Govan, Robert S. Grumet, N. Scott Momaday, and Craig Owens. 112 pages.

Masterpieces from the Peggy Guggenheim Collection. Essay by Philip Rylands. 264 pages.

Osmosis: Ettore Spalletti and Haim Steinbach. Exh. cat. (543). Essays by Germano Celant and Nancy Spector, artists' project by Ettore Spalletti and Haim Steinbach, interview with Ettore Spalletti and Haim Steinbach by Germano Celant. 112 pages.

Paul Klee at the Guggenheim Museum. Exh. cat. (546). Introduction by Lisa Dennison, essay by Andrew Kagan. 208 pages.

Paul Klee. Colección del Guggenheim Museum. Exh. cat. (546). Preface by Carmen Giménez, introduction by Lisa Dennison, essay by Andrew Kagan (in Spanish). 184 pages.

Picasso and the Age of Iron. Exh. cat. (545). Introduction by Carmen Giménez, essays by Dore Ashton and Francisco Calvo Serraller. 336 pages.

Rebecca Horn. Exh. cat., accompanied *Rebecca Horn: The Inferno-Paradiso Switch* (551). Interviews with Rebecca Horn by Germano Celant and Stuart Morgan, essays by Giuliana Bruno, Germano Celant, Katharina Schmidt, and Nancy Spector. 348 pages.

Roy Lichtenstein. Exh. cat. (554). Text by Diane Waldman, chronology by Clare Bell. 408 pages.

1994

Capolavori della Collezione Peggy Guggenheim. Essay by Philip Rylands. 240 pages (in Italian).

Guggenheim Magazine 5 (spring/summer 1994). 80 pages.

Guggenheim Magazine 6 (winter 1994–95). 72 pages.

The Italian Metamorphosis, 1943–1968. Exh. cat. (568). Introductions by Germano Celant and Umberto Eco; essays by Jennifer Blessing, Andrea Branzi, Gian Piero Brunetta, Germano Celant, Anna Costantini, Teresa de Lauretis, Dennis Doordan, Maurizio Fagiolo dell'Arco, Giorgio Galli, Vittorio Gregotti, Micaela Martegani Luini, Luigi Settembrini, Penny Sparke, Valerie Steele, Pandora Tabatabai Asbaghi, Marcia E. Vetrocq, and Italo Zannier; chronology by Lisa Panzera. 740 pages.

The Italian Metamorphosis, 1943–1968. Exh. CD-ROM (568). Published by ENEL and the Solomon R. Guggenheim Museum.

Josef Albers: Glass, Color, and Light. Second ed., 1994. Exh. cat. (Peggy Guggenheim Collection). Essays by Fred Licht and Nicholas Fox Weber, catalogue by Brenda Danilowitz. 152 pages.

Josef Albers: Vetro, colore e luce. Exh. cat. (Peggy Guggenheim Collection). Essays by Fred Licht and Nicholas Fox Weber, catalogue by Brenda Danilowitz. 152 pages (in Italian).

Josef Albers: Vidrio, color y luz. Exh. cat. (Peggy Guggenheim Collection). Essays by Fred Licht and Nicholas Fox Weber, catalogue by Brenda Danilowitz. 152 pages (in Spanish).

Mark Rothko in New York. Text by Diane Waldman. 144 pages.

Meisterwerke aus dem Guggenheim. Exh. cat. (559-T, Vienna). Essays by Ingried Brugger, Lisa Dennison, Peter Gorsen, Michael Govan, Thomas Krens, and Klaus Albrecht Schröder. 246 pages (in German).

Meisterwerke aus dem Guggenheim Museum. Exh. cat. (559-T, Hamburg). Essay by Thomas Krens. 176 pages (in German).

Mestariteoksia Guggenheim Museosta/Mästerwerk från Guggenheim Museet. Exh. cat. (559-T). Essays by Thomas Krens, Soili Sinisalo, and Markku Valkonen. 224 pages (in Finnish and Swedish).

Oskar Kokoschka, Works on Paper: The Early Years, 1897–1917. Exh. cat. (566). Essay by Alice Strobl and Alfred Weidinger. 192 pages.

Rebecca Horn. Exh. cat. (551). Introduction by Wulf Herzogenrath and Toni Stooss, interviews with Rebecca Horn by Germano Celant and Stuart Morgan, essays by Giuliana Bruno,

Germano Celant, Katharina Schmidt, and Nancy Spector (in German). 360 pages.

Robert Morris: The Mind/Body Problem. Exh. cat. (560). Essays by David Antin, Maurice Berger, Jean-Pierre Criqui, Rosalind Krauss, Annette Michelson, and W. J. T. Mitchell, catalogue by Kimberly Paice. 328 pages.

Roy Lichtenstein. Exh. cat. (554). Text by Diane Waldman, chronology by Clare Bell. 394 pages (in German).

The Solomon R. Guggenheim Museum. Text by Bruce Brooks Pfeiffer. 90 pages.

Index of Reproductions

Works of art are listed by artist, and then by date. Photographs depicting artists are listed before their works of art.

Alloway, Lawrence, 1966. Fig. 105.

Apollinaire, Guillaume. Fig. 82.

————, frontispiece of *Calligrammes: Poèmes de la paix et de la guerre (1913–1916)*, 1917. Fig. 84.

Archipenko, Alexander, *Carrousel Pierrot*, 1913. Plate 44.

————, *Médrano II*, 1913–14? Plate 43.

Arp, Jean, *Head and Shell*, ca. 1933. Plate 86.

————, *Crown of Buds I*, 1936. Plate 88.

Art of This Century. Figs. 92, 93, 100.

Balla, Giacomo, *Abstract Speed + Sound*, 1913–14. Plate 39.

Barr, Alfred H., Jr., illustration for *Cubism and Abstract Art*, 1936. Fig. 96.

Bauer, Rudolf, *Invention (Composition 31)*, 1933. Plate 49.

Besant, Annie, and Charles W. Leadbeater, illustration for *Thought-Forms*, 1901. Fig. 89.

Beuys, Joseph. Fig. 115.

————, *The Pack*, 1969. Fig. 114.

Blavatsky, Helena Petrovna. Fig. 88.

Brancusi, Constantin, works by, installed in the Solomon R. Guggenheim Museum, 1993. Fig. 10.

————, *Bird in Space*, 1932–40. Plate 87.

Braque, Georges. Fig. 79.

————, *The Clarinet*, 1912. Plate 26.

————, *Fruit Dish and Glass*, 1912. Fig. 80.

Buren, Daniel, *Inside (Center of Guggenheim)*, 1971. Fig. 103.

Cézanne, Paul, *Man with Crossed Arms*, ca. 1899. Plate 3.

Chagall, Marc, *The Soldier Drinks*, 1911–12. Plate 28.

————, *Paris through the Window*, 1913. Plate 27.

Chamberlain, John, *Dolores James*, 1962. Plate 115.

Cornell, Joseph, *Swiss Shoot-the-Chutes*, 1941. Plate 85.

————, *Untitled (Grand Hôtel de l'Observatoire)*, 1954. Plate 93.

Dalí, Salvador, *Untitled*, 1931. Plate 79.

————, *Birth of Liquid Desires*, 1931–32. Plate 76.

Degas, Edgar, *Dancers in Green and Yellow*, ca. 1903. Plate 10.

de Kooning, Willem, *Composition*, 1955. Plate 108.

————, *. . . Whose Name Was Writ in Water*, 1975. Plate 109.

Delaunay, Robert, *Eiffel Tower with Trees*, summer 1910. Plate 31.

————, *The City*, 1911. Plate 30.

————, *Eiffel Tower*, 1911. Plate 32.

————, *Red Eiffel Tower*, 1911–12. Plate 33.

————, *Window on the City No. 3*, 1911–12. Plate 29.

————, *Simultaneous Windows (2nd Motif, 1st Part)*, 1912. Plate 34.

————, *Windows Open Simultaneously (1st Part, 3rd Motif)*, 1912. Plate 35.

Delaunay, Sonia Terk, design for Blaise Cendrars's *La Prose du Transsibérien et de la Petite Jehanne de France*, 1913. Fig. 83.

Delvaux, Paul, *The Break of Day*, July 1937. Plate 81.

De Maria, Walter, *Cross*, 1965–66. Plate 128.

————, *Museum Piece*, 1966. Plate 129.

————, *Star*, 1972. Plate 130.

Dibbets, Jan, instructions for *The Shortest Day of 1970*. Fig. 110.

Duchamp, Marcel, *Nude (Study), Sad Young Man on a Train*, 1911–12. Plate 38.

Eiffel Tower, 1889. Fig. 75.

Ernst, Max, and Peggy Guggenheim. Fig. 94.

Ernst, Max, *Little Machine Constructed by Minimax Dadamax in Person*, 1919–20. Plate 77.

————, *The Postman Cheval*, 1932. Plate 84.

————, *The Antipope*, December 1941– March 1942. Plate 75.

Fini, Léonor, *The Shepherdess of the Sphinxes*, 1941. Plate 92.

Flavin, Dan, *Untitled (to Tracy, to celebrate the love of a lifetime)*, 1992. Fig. 121.

Gabo, Naum, *Column*, ca. 1923. Plate 74.

Gauguin, Paul, *Haere Mai*, 1891. Plate 18.

————, *In the Vanilla Grove, Man and Horse*, 1891. Plate 17.

Giacometti, Alberto, studio of. Fig. 91.

————, *Model for a Square*, 1931–32. Plate 89.

————, *Woman with Her Throat Cut*, 1932 (cast 1940). Plate 90.

Gorky, Arshile, *Untitled*, summer 1944. Plate 96.

Gottlieb, Adolph, *W*, 1954. Plate 104.

————, *Mist*, 1961. Plate 105.

Grand Canal in Venice, Italy. Fig. 15.

Guggenheim, Peggy. Figs. 90, 95, 98.

————, and Max Ernst. Fig. 94.

————, and Jackson Pollock, 1943. Fig. 101.

Peggy Guggenheim Collection. Fig. 99.

Guggenheim, Solomon R. Fig. 3.

————, Plaza Hotel suite of. Figs. 7, 8.

Solomon R. Guggenheim Museum. Figs. 1, 2, 67–71.

————, construction photos by William H. Short, 1956–59. Figs. 59–64.

Guggenheim Museum Bilbao, Frank O. Gehry and Associates' model for. Fig. 16.

Guggenheim Museum Salzburg, Hans Hollein's model for. Fig. 17.

Guggenheim Museum SoHo. Fig. 14.

Hesse, Eva, *Expanded Expansion*, 1969. Plate 125.

Hofmann, Hans, *The Gate*, 1959–60. Plate 112.

Holzer, Jenny, Selections from *The Survival Series* and *The Living Series*, 1989. Fig. 120.

————, Selections from *Truisms, Inflammatory Essays, The Living Series, The Survival Series, Under a Rock, Laments*, and new writing, 1989. Fig. 119.

Horn, Rebecca, *Paradiso*, 1993. Fig. 122.

In Memory of Vasily Kandinsky, installation view, 1945. Fig. 6.

Judd, Donald. Fig. 109.

Kandinsky, Vasily, *Blue Mountain*, 1908–09. Plate 1.

————, cover for *The Blue Rider Almanac*, 1912. Fig. 81.

Kandinsky, Vasily (cont.), *Improvisation 28 (second version)*, 1912. Plate 22.

————, *Black Lines*, 1913. Plate 48.

————, *Painting with White Border*, 1913. Plate 50.

————, *Composition 8*, 1923. Plate 2.

————, illustration for *Point and Line to Plane*, 1926. Fig. 86.

————, *Several Circles*, 1926. Plate 52.

————, *Dominant Curve*, 1936. Plate 51.

Kelly, Ellsworth, *Blue, Green, Yellow, Orange, Red*, 1966. Plate 121.

Klee, Paul, *Flower Bed*, 1913. Plate 24.

————, *In the Current Six Thresholds*, 1929. Plate 53.

————, *New Harmony*, 1936. Plate 56.

Kline, Franz, *Painting No. 7*, 1952. Plate 110.

Kosuth, Joseph, *'Titled (Art as Idea as Idea)' {Water}*, 1966. Plate 127.

Larionov, Mikhail, *Glass*, 1912. Plate 41.

Léger, Fernand, *The Smokers*, 1911–12. Plate 36.

————, *Nude Model in the Studio*, 1912–13. Plate 37.

————, *The Great Parade* (definitive state), 1954. Plate 5.

LeWitt, Sol, instructions for *Five Wall Drawings*, 1971. Fig. 111.

Lichtenstein, Roy, *Preparedness*, 1968. Plate 118.

Lissitzky, El, *Untitled*, ca. 1919–20. Plate 68.

Long, Richard, *Chalk Circle*, 1986. Fig. 116.

————, *River Avon Mud Circle*, 1986. Fig. 116.

Louis, Morris, *Saraband*, 1959. Plate 113.

Magritte, René, *Empire of Light*, 1953–54. Plate 7.

Malevich, Kazimir, *Morning in the Village after Snowstorm*, 1912. Plate 42.

————, *Untitled*, ca. 1916. Plate 67.

Manet, Edouard, *Before the Mirror*, 1876. Plate 9.

————, *Woman in Evening Dress*, 1877–80. Plate 12.

Mangold, Robert, *Circle In and Out of a Polygon 2*, 1973. Plate 122.

Man Ray, *Untitled*, 1923. Plate 54.

————, *Untitled*, 1927.

Mapplethorpe, Robert, *Self-Portrait*, 1988. Fig. 18.

Marc, Franz, *Stables*, 1913. Plate 23.

Marini, Marino, *The Angel of the City*, 1948 (cast 1950?). Plate 91.

Martin, Agnes, *White Stone*, 1965. Plate 123.

Matter, Herbert, cover for *Six Painters and the Object*, 1963. Fig. 106.

————, cover for *Systemic Painting*, 1966. Fig. 107.

Merz, Mario, *Niger Crocodile*, 1972 (1989 reconstruction, detail). Fig. 113.

————, *Unreal City, Nineteen Hundred Eighty-Nine*, 1989. Fig. 118.

Messer, Thomas M. Fig. 104.

Miró, Joan, *The Tilled Field*, 1923–24. Plate 4.

————, *Seated Woman II*, February 27, 1939. Plate 83.

Moholy-Nagy, László, *T1*, 1926. Plate 69.

————, *AXL II*, 1927. Plate 70.

————, *B-10 Space Modulator*, 1942. Plate 71.

————, *Dual Form with Chromium Rods*, 1946. Plate 72.

Mondrian, Piet. Fig. 87.

———, *Still Life with Ginger Pot I*, 1911–12. Plates 45, 59.

———, *Still Life with Ginger Pot II*, 1911–12. Plates 46, 60.

———, pages from *Sketchbook I*, 1912–14. Plates 57, 58.

———, *Composition VII*, 1913. Plate 61.

———, *Composition No. 8*, 1914. Plate 62.

———, *The Sea*, 1914. Plate 47.

———, *Composition 1916*, 1916. Plate 63.

———, *Composition 2*, 1922. Plate 64.

———, *Composition 1A*, 1930. Plate 65.

Montmartre, Paris. Fig. 76.

Morris, Robert, *Untitled*, 1970. Plate 126.

———, instructions for *Instruction-Learning-Memory*, 1971. Fig. 112.

Motherwell, Robert, *Personage (Autoportrait)*, 1943. Plate 94.

———, *Elegy to the Spanish Republic No. 110*, 1971. Plate 111.

Museum of Non-Objective Painting. Fig. 5.

Nauman, Bruce, *Green Light Corridor*, 1970–71. Plate 8.

"New Art Museum Will Be New York's Strangest Building," *Life*, October 8, 1945. Fig. 9.

Noguchi, Isamu, *Lunar*, 1959–60. Plate 116.

O'Keeffe, Georgia, *Pelvis with Shadows and the Moon*, 1943. Fig. 40.

Oldenburg, Claes, Coosje van Bruggen, and Frank O. Gehry, *The Knife Ship*, 1986. Fig. 117.

Parthenon, detail of West Frieze. Fig. 74.

Pevsner, Antoine, *Anchored Cross*, 1933. Plate 73.

Picabia, Francis, *The Child Carburetor*, 1919. Plate 78.

Picasso, Pablo. Fig. 77.

———, *Le Moulin de la Galette*, 1900. Plate 19.

———, *Woman Ironing*, 1904. Plate 21.

———, *Young Acrobat and Child*, 1905. Plate 20.

———, *The Poet*, 1911. Plate 25.

———, *Still Life with Chair Caning*, 1912. Fig. 78.

———, *Woman with Yellow Hair*, 1931. Plate 6.

———, *On the Beach*, 1937. Plate 82.

Pollock, Jackson, and Peggy Guggenheim, 1943. Fig. 101.

Pollock, Jackson, *Croaking Movement*, 1946. Plate 100.

———, *Eyes in the Heat*, 1946. Plate 99.

———, *Alchemy*, 1947. Plate 103.

———, *Enchanted Forest*, 1947. Plate 101.

———, *Ocean Greyness*, 1953. Plate 102.

Rauschenberg, Robert, *Untitled*, 1963. Plate 117.

Read, Herbert. Fig. 102.

Rebay, Hilla. Figs. 4, 85.

Reinhardt, Ad, "How to Look at Modern Art in America," *P.M.*, June 2, 1946. Fig. 97.

Renoir, Pierre Auguste, *Woman with Parrot*, 1871. Plate 11.

Rothko, Mark, *Sacrifice*, 1946. Plate 95.

———, *Untitled (#18)*, 1963. Plate 106.

———, *Untitled (Black on Grey)*, 1970. Plate 107.

Ryman, Robert, *Classico 4*, 1968. Plate 120.

Serra, Richard, and Diane Waldman, 1971. Fig. 108.

Serra, Richard, *Strike (to Roberta and Rudy)*, 1969–71. Plate 124.

Seurat, Georges, *Farm Women at Work*, 1882–83. Plate 14.

———, *A Sunday on La Grande Jatte—1884*, 1884–86. Fig. 72.

———, *Three Models*, 1886–88. Fig. 73.

Severini, Gino, *Sea = Dancer*, January 1914. Plate 40.

Smith, David, *Cubi XXVII*, March 1965. Plate 114.

Still, Clyfford, *Jamais*, May 1944. Plate 97.

Taliesin, Spring Green, Wisconsin. Figs. 21, 22.

Tanguy, Yves, *The Sun in Its Jewel Case*, 1937. Plate 80.

Toulouse-Lautrec, Henri de, *Au salon*, 1893. Plate 13.

van Doesburg, Theo, *Counter-Composition XIII*, 1925–26. Plate 66.

van Gogh, Vincent, *Head of a Girl*, 1888. Plate 16.

———, *Letter to John Peter Russell*, late June 1888. Plate 15.

Waldman, Diane, and Richard Serra, 1971. Fig. 108.

Warhol, Andy, *Orange Disaster*, 1963. Plate 119.

Wright, Frank Lloyd. Figs. 20, 65, 66.

———, architectural drawings for the Solomon R. Guggenheim Museum, 1943–58. Figs. 11–13, 19, 23–39, 46–55.

———, models for the Solomon R. Guggenheim Museum, 1945–47. Figs. 41–45.

———, pavilion for *Sixty Years of Living Architecture*, 1953. Figs. 56–57.

———, Plaza Hotel suite of. Fig. 58.

Exhibition/Technical Services

Pamela Myers, *Administrator for Exhibitions and Programming*
David Heald, *Photographer*
Samar Qandil, *Photography and Permissions Associate*
Cara Galowitz, *Manager of Graphic Design Services*
Michelle Martino, *Project Graphic Designer*
Adrienne Shulman, *Lighting Technician*
Wendy Cooney, *Lighting Technician*
Scott Wixon, *Manager of Installation Services*
Anibal Gonzalez-Rivera, *Manager of Collection Services*
Joseph Adams, *Senior Museum Technician*
Peter Costa, *Senior Museum Technician*
David Veater, *Senior Museum Technician*
Lisette Baron-Adams, *Museum Technician*
James Cullinane, *Museum Technician*
Jocelyn Groom, *Museum Technician*
Bryn Jayes, *Museum Technician*
William Smith, *Museum Technician*
Dennis Vermeulen, *Museum Technician*
Guy Walker, *Museum Technician*
Peter Read, Jr., *Manager of Fabrication Services*
Jon Brayshaw, *Museum Technician/Carpenter*
David Johnson, *Museum Technician/Carpenter*

Facilities

Mark DeMairo, *Facilities Manager*
John Carey, *Assistant Facilities Manager*
Peter McGrath, *Assistant Facilities Manager*
Walter Christie, *Electrician*
Michael Lavin, *Senior Electronic Technician*
William Graves, *Chief Engineer*
Alfred Bracci, *Watch Engineer*
Abraham Edwards, *Watch Engineer*
Lawrence Goonan, *Watch Engineer*
Zenon Cegielko, *Assistant Watch Engineer*
Karl Garland, *Assistant Watch Engineer*
Neukyn Goumelle, *Assistant Watch Engineer*
Francisco Lugo, *Assistant Watch Engineer*
Gary Karjala, *Maintenance Foreman*
Raymond Taylor, Sr., *Maintenance Foreman*
Armando Helliger, *Maintenance Mechanic*
Fred Taylor, *Maintenance Mechanic*
Clotilde Donato, *Administrative Assistant*

Finance and Administration

Gail Harrity, *Deputy Director for Finance and Administration*
Lorraine Cheng, *Administrative Coordinator*
Amy Husten, *Manager of Budget and Planning*
Ronald Casa, *Budget and Planning Analyst*
Paul Pincus, *Senior Accounting Finance Analyst*
Jin Hong, *Assistant Controller*
Mary Seto, *Payroll Manager*
Daniel Flamholtz, *Accounting Analyst*
Natalie Siegel, *Accounting Assistant*
Maureen Ahearn, *Accounts Payable Analyst*
Jess Montojo, *Accounts Payable Analyst*

Information Systems

Richard Roller, *Director of Information Systems*
David Goodman, *Network Systems Manager*
John Stachyra, *Network Specialist*
Steven Birnbaum, *Information Systems Specialist*
Robert Bowen, *PC Support Specialist*

Learning Through Art

Esther Kaufman, *Development Director*
Kim Rozzi, *Education Director*
Nancy Easton, *Education Associate*
Alice Keim, *Assistant to the Executive Director*
Shana Dambrot, *Development Assistant*
Luigi Gasparinetti, *Program Development*
Maria Chua, *Bookkeeper*
Anne Rhodes, *Education Assistant*

Legal

Judith Cox, *General Counsel*
Nicole Pasquini, *Legal Assistant*

Membership

Susan Madden, *Membership Program Manager*
Lucy Mannix, *Membership Marketing Manager*
Stefan Keneas, *Membership Data Assistant*
Robin Weiswasser, *Membership Programs Assistant*

Office Services

John Woytowicz, *Office Services Manager*
Ronald Peaslee, *Office Services Assistant*
Irene Mulligan, *Receptionist*
Marie Pierre-Antoine, *Receptionist*
Alin Paul, *Mailroom Coordinator*
Kay Frank Bonsu, *Mailroom Assistant*

Personnel

Nina Chacko, *Personnel Director*
David Duncan, *Benefits Coordinator*
Diane Maas, *Volunteer Coordinator*
Laurie Price, *Employment Coordinator*
Patricia Quintyn, *Personnel Assistant*

Public Affairs

Catherine Vare, *Director of Communications*
Christine Ferrara, *Public Affairs Coordinator*
Donna Vetrano, *Public Affairs Coordinator*
Luisa Guglielmotti, *Public Affairs Assistant*

Publications

Anthony Calnek, *Director of Publications*
Elizabeth Levy, *Production Editor*
Laura L. Morris, *Associate Editor*
Edward Weisberger, *Assistant Managing Editor*
Jennifer Knox, *Assistant Editor*

Registrar

Linda Thacher, *Exhibitions Registrar*
Lynne Addison, *Associate Registrar, Exhibitions*
Laura Latman, *Associate Registrar, Collections*
MaryLouise Napier, *Assistant to the Registrar, Exhibitions*
Aileen Silverman, *Assistant to the Registrar*
Hubbard Toombs, *Assistant to the Registrar, Inventory and Traffic*

Retail Operations

Stuart Gerstein, *Director of Wholesale and Retail Operations*
Steven Buettner, *Operations Manager*
Lacey High, *Manager of External Sales*
Alain Frank, *Production Assistant*
Edward Fuqua, *Book Buyer*
Thomas Dalby, *Customer Service Representative*

Olga Poupkova, *Customer Service Representative*
Robin Seaman, *Assistant Controller for Retail Operations*
Marilyn Perez, *Retail Analyst*
Lawrence Weisberg, *Accounting Assistant*
Wayne McKenzie, *Warehouse Manager*
Lenburg Fogle, *Assistant Warehouse Manager*
Gerardo Gonzalez, *Assistant Warehouse Manager*
Christopher Garraway, *Receiving Clerk*
Desmond Anderson, *Shipping Clerk*
Lawrence Kendle, Jr., *Shipping Clerk*
Carl Gouveia, *Stock Clerk*
Dorrell Stewart, *Stock Clerk*
Sylvan Walsh, *Stock Clerk*

Retail Operations, Store Staff

Douglas Denicola, *Store Manager*
Laura French, *Store Manager*
Nabeal Ayari, *Assistant Store Manager*
Gary Bartlett, *Assistant Store Manager*
Janis Burns, *Assistant Store Manager*
Suzette Culliton, *Assistant Store Manager*
Lisanne Paulin, *Assistant Store Manager*
Kimberly Becoat, *Sales Associate*
Roberto Belem, *Sales Associate*
Michael Deardorff, *Sales Associate*
Michael Muccio, *Sales Associate*
Jonathan Raney, *Sales Associate*
Kevin Searcy, *Sales Associate*
Angela Smith, *Sales Associate*
Anna Verbin, *Sales Associate*
Faune Yerby, *Sales Associate*

Security

Thomas Foley, *Security Manager*
Marie Bradley, *Assistant Security Manager for Administration*
Robert Fahey, *Security Supervisor*
Daniel Dixon, *Security Trainer*
Salvatore Bessetti, *Assistant Security Supervisor*
James Bessetti, *Assistant Security Supervisor*
José Fussa, *Assistant Security Supervisor*
Robert Keay, *Assistant Security Supervisor*
Scott Lewis, *Assistant Security Supervisor*
Kevin McGinley, *Assistant Security Supervisor*
Todd Murphy, *Assistant Security Supervisor*
Raymond Taylor, Jr., *Assistant Security Supervisor*
Carol Warner, *Assistant Security Supervisor*
Gregory Weinstein, *Assistant Security Supervisor*
James McCutcheon, *Fire Safety Director*
Enell Agyeman, *Gallery Guard*
Dwayne Anderson, *Gallery Guard*
Akim Aznaurov, *Gallery Guard*
Frank Balsamo, *Gallery Guard*
Haim Ben-Zwi, *Gallery Guard*
Donna Blackburn, *Gallery Guard*
Jefferson Cherubin, *Gallery Guard*
Patrick Chery, *Gallery Guard*
Richard Christie, *Gallery Guard*
Garrett Comba, *Gallery Guard*
Colleen Corbett, *Gallery Guard*
Gustavo Cortez, *Gallery Guard*
Edwin Cruz, *Gallery Guard*
Alec Cushman III, *Gallery Guard*
Bimal Das, *Gallery Guard*
Anthony Delvino, *Gallery Guard*
Steven DeRiseis, *Gallery Guard*

Donna Diemer, *Gallery Guard*
John DiMarco, *Gallery Guard*
Daniel Dorce, *Gallery Guard*
Kevin Dresser, *Gallery Guard*
Martin Dusan, *Gallery Guard*
Chandra Eaton, *Gallery Guard*
Michael Evans, *Gallery Guard*
Akin Fafowora, *Gallery Guard*
Michael Faherty, *Gallery Guard*
Adina Ferber, *Gallery Guard*
Kwesi Gyenfi, *Gallery Guard*
Linda Hardman, *Gallery Guard*
Michael Heffernan, *Gallery Guard*
Harry Hesselbach, *Gallery Guard*
Dean Jackson, *Gallery Guard*
Lejeune Jean Baptist, *Gallery Guard*
Brett Jenkins, *Gallery Guard*
Lawrence Jenzen, *Gallery Guard*
David John, *Gallery Guard*
Natalie Johnson, *Gallery Guard*
Patricia Keating, *Gallery Guard*
Michael Kimmel, *Gallery Guard*
Walter King, *Gallery Guard*
Tzemovir Kirov, *Gallery Guard*
Gary Lindgren, *Gallery Guard*
Henry Mack, *Gallery Guard*
Devon Madison, *Gallery Guard*
Mario Martini, *Gallery Guard*
Lorenzo McBean, *Gallery Guard*
John McCree, *Gallery Guard*
Luke McCullough, *Gallery Guard*
Susan McGuire, *Gallery Guard*
Junior McKenzie, *Gallery Guard*
Lenroy Mills, *Gallery Guard*
David Moran, *Gallery Guard*
Genoveva Munoz, *Gallery Guard*
Jennifer Noonan, *Gallery Guard*
Juan Ortega, *Gallery Guard*
Charles Orth-Pallavicini, *Gallery Guard*
Felix Padilla, *Gallery Guard*
Joel Paul, *Gallery Guard*
Jeffrey Pavone, *Gallery Guard*
Kevin Pemberton, *Gallery Guard*
Lyonel Pierre-Antoine, *Gallery Guard*
Winston Pusey, *Gallery Guard*
Franc Ranzinger, *Gallery Guard*
Michael Rechner, *Gallery Guard*
Scott Redden, *Gallery Guard*
Albert Rivera, *Gallery Guard*
Sandro Rodorigo, *Gallery Guard*
Hiram Rodriguez-Mora, *Gallery Guard*
Robert Rominiecki, *Gallery Guard*
Carlos Rosado, *Gallery Guard*
John Saxe, *Gallery Guard*
Green Seymour, *Gallery Guard*
Eric Simpson, *Gallery Guard*
Barbara Smith, *Gallery Guard*
Jonathan Smith, *Gallery Guard*
Christopher Spinelli, *Gallery Guard*
Martin Tischler, *Gallery Guard*
Freddy Velastegui, *Gallery Guard*
Andre Violenus, *Gallery Guard*
James Wallerstein, *Gallery Guard*
Roger Walton, *Gallery Guard*
Ken Weathersby, *Gallery Guard*
Eddie Wiesel, *Gallery Guard*
Leonard Wilson, *Gallery Guard*

Andrew Wint, *Gallery Guard*
Tyrone Wyllie, *Gallery Guard*

Visitor Services

Suzette Sherman, *Director of Visitor Services*
Elizabeth Weinberg, *Manager of Visitor Services*
Barbara Morehouse, *Tour and Group Assistant*
Esther Wahl, *Marketing Communications Coordinator*
Wesley Jessup, *Visitor Services Assistant*
Elyse Cogan, *Visitor Services Desk Supervisor*
Charles Emmer III, *Visitor Services Desk Supervisor*
Robin Reid, *Visitor Services Desk Supervisor*
John Angeline, *Visitor Assistant*
Peyton Jefferson, *Visitor Assistant*
Valerie Kennedy, *Visitor Assistant*
Shelley Miller, *Visitor Assistant*
John Mix, *Visitor Assistant*
Steven Potter, *Visitor Assistant*
Tod Roulette, *Visitor Assistant*
Pamela Tanowitz, *Visitor Assistant*

Peggy Guggenheim Collection

Philip Rylands, *Deputy Director*
Fred Licht, *Curator*
Paul Schwartzbaum, *Conservator*
Renata Rossani, *Administrator*
Claudia Rech, *Development and Public Affairs Officer*
Michela Bondardo, *Consultant for Corporate Communications*
Annarita Fuso, *Public Affairs Assistant*
Laura Micolucci, *Accountant*
Gabriella Andreatta, *Accounting Assistant*
Fabio Bobatz, *Sales Associate*
Roberta Chiarotto, *Sales Associate*
Elena Reggiani, *Sales Associate*
Chiara Barbieri, *Deputy Director's Assistant*
Alessandro Claut, *Security*
Franco Pugnalin, *Security*
Daniele Regolini, *Security*
Emilio Trevisan, *Security*
Siro De Boni, *Maintenance*